They Must Be Represented

Reproduced

The Politics of Documentary

PAULA RABINOWITZ

VERSO

London · New York

First published by Verso 1994

Verso
UK: 6 Meard Street, London W1V 3HR
USA: 29 West 35th Street, New York, NY 10001-2291

Verso is the imprint of New Left Books

Illustrations
Figure 1 Arthur Munby Collection, Trinity College, Cambridge. *Figure 2* Library of Congress LC–USF342–8134A. *Figure 3* Library of Congress LC–USF342–8135A. *Figure 4* From *Karl Marx 'Capital' in Lithographs* (New York: Ray Long and Richard Smith 1934), following p.11. *Figure 5* From *Karl Marx 'Capital' in Lithographs* (New York: Ray Long and Richard Smith 1934), following p.22. *Figures 6–7* Museum of Modern Art Film Stills Archive. *Figure 8* Library of Congress LC–USF34–19360–E. *Figure 9* Library of Congress LC–USF34–18401–E. *Figure 10* Library of Congress LC–USF34–21053–C. *Figures 11–15* Museum of Modern Art Film Stills Archive. *Figure 16* Chick Strand. *Figure 17* Women Make Movies, Inc. *Figure 18* Chick Strand. *Figures 19–20* Zeitgeist Films. *Figure 21* Women Make Movies, Inc. *Figure 22* Author's Collection.

ISBN: 978-1-85984-025-2

British Library Cataloguing in Publication Data
A catalogue record for this book is available from the British Library

Library of Congress Cataloging-in-Publication Data
A catalogue record for this book is available from the Library of Congress

Typeset by Yorkhouse Typographic Ltd, London W13 8NT
Printed and bound in Great Britain by Biddles Ltd, Guildford and King's Lynn

For David, from beginning to end

Contents

Preface and Acknowledgements

'We lived in an age of documentation,' asserts Fialka Jourová, the young narrator of Iva Pekárková's novel *Truck Stop Rainbows*, her past tense a hopeful gesture toward a future markedly different after the Velvet Revolution swept Stalinists from power in Prague and made keeping clandestine documents unnecessary. Possessing an East German-made camera, Fialka appoints herself the job of photographing plant mutations caused by the sulphurous smoke spewing out of state-owned factories and the toxic pesticides coating the fields of collective farms. In pursuit of her documents, she hitchhikes rides from truck drivers throughout the Socialist Republic of Czechoslovakia, shooting diseased flowers – seven-leaved clovers, two-headed dandelions, tulips with eight petals – hiding her 'files' in plain sight, these 'botanical monstrosities' stored among the many nature shots she takes professionally for magazines.

The age of documentation corresponds to the age of mechanical reproduction, as Walter Benjamin called it: sound and image recorded on tape and film to resemble the natural world heard and seen by the human senses. This age is largely past, in the West as well as in Eastern Europe, not because the need to document disappeared with a freer political system, as Fialka hopes – in the 'free world' we too must document the natural and social mutations wrought by capitalism – but because the age of mechanical reproduction, the age of realisms as diverse as Balzac and Brecht, has largely given way to the age of electronic simulation and virtual reality. Digitalized images and sound can literally remake history, seating Hillary Rodham Clinton on the White House lawn for tea with Eleanor Roosevelt as *Mother Jones* did a few years ago, sampling James Brown with J.S. Bach. Even though this book discusses documentary images made within the last few years, it is, too, a testament to an era already past, one that depended on the mechanics of sight and sound codified and manufactured under monopoly capitalism. Our present moment of post-industrial, late capitalism perhaps requires another mode of postmodern representation. Luddite that I am, as my sons endlessly remind me, I cannot imagine what form it might take. Thus I am telling the story of the politics and rhetoric of documentary as it has been practiced in the United States during the past half-century or so – our age of documentation.

Many people and institutions have helped to make possible this study, which I began working on over a decade ago just a few blocks from where I completed it. Michael Sprinker has been a kind, attentive, and argumentative editor, giving me the help I required during a time when he had other, more pressing concerns on his mind. Carol Mason, my research assistant, tirelessly tracked down bibliographic and filmographic sources for me; her wry humor and common sense cut through a lot of hazy ideas to focus on the crucial issues. Careful readings of key chapters by T.V. Reed, Nancy Armstrong, Carolyn Porter, George Lipsitz, Ann-Lou Shapiro, Sherry Linkon, and Bill Mullen were invaluable in clarifying my project. Many conversations with Charlotte Nekola, Alice Echols, Rey Chow, Con Samaras, and Ruth Bradley sent my phone bill soaring, but as ever ensured that I had the best in feminist insights about film, writing, photography, culture, politics, America, and how these things go together – telephone theory. Their words form the subterranean voices murmuring within my prose. Maria Damon, Marty Roth, Rita Copeland, John Mowitt, David Wallace, Alan Wald, Noël Sturgeon, Sally Stein, and Laura Wexler, among many others, offered pointed comments at exactly the right moments.

I could not have written this without the financial support of a number of institutions: Wesleyan University Center for the Humanities offered me a year-long residency and a Mellon Postdoctoral Fellowship to begin writing the book; a McKnight Summer Fellowship and Single Quarter leave from the University of Minnesota's College of Liberal Arts gave me large chunks of time away from teaching to research and write portions of the book; the Graduate School of the University of Minnesota provided a research assistant; the Program in American Culture of the University of Michigan invited me to be a Visiting Scholar to complete the manuscript. Special thanks go to Richard Ohmann who, as director of the Center for the Humanities, hosted the ideal working space for scholars; Pat Camden and Jackie Rich gave endlessly of their time and vast skills. The other fellows at the Center created an intellectual environment one only dreams of and rarely finds possible in the Academy: Ann DuCille, Gary Spears, Indira Karamcheti, Betsy Traube, and Steve Vogel among them spent many hours listening to me as I worked out ideas over coffee and drinks. More recently, Linda Eggert, June Howard, and Margarita de la Vega-Hurtado welcomed me back to the University of Michigan's Program in American Culture.

I was able to get valuable comments on sections of the book after presenting them at George Mason University, University of Minnesota, University of Michigan, Wayne State University, Bard College, Kenyon College, Wesleyan University, UC Irvine, UCSD, American Studies Association, Modern Language Association, Semiotic Society, and the Teoría Fílmica/Teoría Feminista conference in Valencia. I owe much to my students in various seminars on documentary, feminist theory, and the 1930s at Wesleyan and Minnesota. It is in the classroom that one's claims truly get the grilling they deserve.

Chapter 1 first appeared in a slightly different form in *History and Theory*; a version of chapter 2 appeared in *Cultural Critique*; some portions of chapter 3 first appeared in 'Commodity Fetishism: Women in *Gold Diggers of 1933*,' in *Film Reader*. Permission to use images was given to me by Zeitgeist Films, Chick Strand, Women Make Movies, Inc., Library of Congress, Museum of Modern Art, and the Master and Fellows of Trinity College, Cambridge. I thank Mary Corliss at MOMA Film Still Archives, Adrian at Zeitgeist Films, Cathy Garrett at Pacific Film Archives, Peter Filardo, archivist at the Tamiment Library at New York University, for helping me locate stills and permissions. Thanks to Adrienne Rich for inspiration and permission to quote from *An Atlas of the Difficult World*. Tim Burnett, reference librarian of the Harlan Hatcher Graduate Library at the University of Michigan, helped track down obscure citations.

Finally, love and thanks to my two sons, Jacob and Raphael, who waited almost patiently for me to finish this project. The book is dedicated to David Bernstein who for nearly two decades has been object, agent, and representative of my love and work. As I was putting the finishing touches on this manuscript, the people of South Africa were casting ballots in the first all-race election in that nation's history. That the most vicious regime on the planet during my lifetime could transform itself into a multi-racial democratic state through the tenacity of the people's political will and hope gives me a sense of wonder at the promise of the future. I dedicate this book to all who have struggled to end apartheid there; may we be as successful here too.

Ann Arbor–Minneapolis–Middletown–Minneapolis–Ann Arbor, 1982–94

They cannot represent themselves; they must be represented.

KARL MARX

There is no document of civilization which is not at the same time a document of barbarism. And just as such a document is not free of barbarism, barbarism taints also the manner in which it was transmitted from one owner to another.

WALTER BENJAMIN

I promised to show you a map you say but this is a mural
then yes let it be   these are small distinctions
Where do we see it from is the question.

ADRIENNE RICH

INTRODUCTION

The Work of Intellectuals in the Age of

Post/Modern Representation

While I was completing the final revisions of this manuscript, Marlon Riggs, director of *Tongues Untied* and other films, died of AIDS. The bizarre saga of his moving portrait of African-American gay men serves as a telling instance of the multiple and contradictory ways in which documentary representations are put to use by their audiences. Commissioned originally for the Public Broadcasting Service (PBS) showcase of independent documentaries, *Point of View*, and partially funded by a grant from the National Endowment for the Arts (NEA), *Tongues Untied* was withdrawn from most television stations after organized protests by the self-appointed censors, Donald Wildmon, head of the American Family Association, and North Carolina Senator Jesse Helms. But such is the strange history of images that the film did appear on local television after all, or rather, a brief thirty-second segment of two, leather-clad black men kissing appeared, as part of an advertisement for Patrick Buchanan's presidential campaign during the Georgia Republican primary race. Buchanan was chastising then-President George Bush for allowing the National Endowment for the Arts (NEA) to sponsor this 'pornography' under his watch. As a result, Riggs's film attained unprecedented notoriety for a documentary, a fact made especially perverse because practically no one had seen it. His story of giving voice to marginalized people only to have those in power fight over who was going to suppress those voices and, in so doing, ensuring the voices would be heard because of their notoriety, details the ways in which documentary forms, despite the intentions of directors and producers, on the one hand, censors, on the other, take on a life of their own. Audiences of all stripes do what they will with images, no matter how instrumental their makers. In this case, Riggs's film ultimately was influential – the controversy alerted audiences to

1

demand that it be shown across the country, with video providing a large part of the orders.

For a parallel case of audience agency superseding filmic intention, consider the Canadian Film Board's production of Bonny Klein's *Not a Love Story*, which is designed to persuade its viewers of the dangers and degradations pornography poses for women. It features Linda Lovelace, recently converted from porn star to demure and outraged feminist, taking viewers on a tour of the explicit sex industry. As she and others mourn for themselves and the women still working, they make sure we understand how debasing the work is by including extended clips of hard-core porn films and magazines. *Not a Love Story* is one of the most popular and highest grossing documentaries ever produced by the Canadian Film Board; however, audiences in a nation with restrictions on the public display of pornography are not necessarily seeing a tale of mourning and outrage; many are watching for the crotch shots which are meant to horrify, not titillate.

Tongues Untied and *Not a Love Story*, both made during the Reagan–Bush–Mulrooney–Thatcher era by members of newly outspoken movements for gay and women's liberation, are part of a puzzling contradiction: in a period of political repression by the New Right – launching a backlash against gains in civil rights for minorities, women, and gays, defunding the arts, and curtailing fringe economies supporting artists and activists – documentary films were exhibiting a renaissance. Their audiences grew and their effectivity was enormous: Erroll Morris's *Thin Blue Line* helped rectify a criminal injustice and free an innocent man; Michael Moore's *Roger and Me* became a smash hit as it revealed the corporate strategy of 'downsizing' to be a vicious attack on the lives of working people; Barbara Kopple's *American Dream* won her a second Academy Award by delving into the complexities of contemporary unionism. While this moment of documentary may itself be a last instance of the power of mechanical reproduction in an age of electronic simulation, the films point to the varied ways in which cultural representations can have political agency.

An introduction is designed to give readers a preview of the coming pages, but because it is written toward the end of a work, it holds an air of finality as well. Walter Benjamin, whose words I play on and with here and whose presence I feel as a ghost walking through my writings and dreams, suggested that the work itself is the death mask of the idea – inspiration being endlessly more alluring than reification – the dream more compelling than the deal, as Jerre Mangione would remind us. As I have worked on this project – and its genesis I can recall quite accurately; the idea coming to me as I crossed over the newly completed underground postmodernist law library through the mock-medieval cloisters of the University of Michigan Law School on my way to work – I have found that despite there always being one more thing to say, it may never get said. This book is a far cry from my original conception. Then, I was thinking about why, despite being raised by an abstract expressionist painter, I love realism so much; why documentaries in film, photography, and print excite me. And why, despite being didactic, dogmatic, predictable, and thoroughly un(post)modern, they appeal to so many others as well. At that time, docudramas were becoming a weekly television event, the networks casting about for a way to maintain audiences and finding it in the headlines. Yet the first docudramas – *Roots* and *Holocaust* – found their sources in the archives. Really, I concluded, it was history that held imaginative power over me and so many others; during the amnesiac years of Reaganism, remembering the stories of yesterday seemed politically important. But what could one make of the falsification of history at the core of the docudrama, which owed more to the afternoon soap operas than to historical evidence? One couldn't expect commercial television to provide an antidote to the erasure of memory which was threatening political culture in America. Besides, docudrama was not documentary.

At the same time, radical film critics centered around the British journal *Screen* were launching a trenchant attack on realist conventions. Citing Brecht's critiques of Lukács's celebration of nineteenth-century realist novels and following Godard's pointed manipulations of filmic narrative, these theorists, influenced by Althusser's theories of subjectivity and ideology, were challenging my desire. What I liked was theoretically suspect. Their righteousness mirrored the heightened rhetoric surrounding abortion and pornography of American feminists as we hunkered down to thwart the perceived French invasion and the actual right-wing backlash. Poststructuralist critiques of the subject were throwing the whole project of feminism – even its name – into question. At the same time, the Christian Right was mounting a campaign to reverse whatever gains we had made in the 1970s. The reactions, though varied, boiled down to a retreat from the broad critiques of gender and militant calls for separatist spaces, into a narrow debate about correct and incorrect sex. Again, I felt under attack; I liked being fucked by men, and I was a mother (of a son) to boot. What I was became politically suspect, too.

This project then, like most work, has its origins in autobiography – in my need to come to some understanding of my pleasure. But it also has much to do with my work on the 1930s. Anyone with even a

3

passing interest in the decade (and who among us has not been formed by it?) references it through the images of hungry migrants caught by the Farm Security Administration (FSA) photographers. These faces of privation and want haunt those of us born into the middle class of mid-century America. They are our others, ourselves, just as the street urchins crowding New York's Lower East Side a decade before them wore the faces of my parents. The images of poverty are a staple of liberal society's guilt; I, a child of the 1950s urban America. By the time Lyndon Johnson had declared the War on Poverty after Bobby Kennedy had toured tenant farms in the South and Edward R. Murrow had revealed the *Harvest of Shame*, my family was comfortably ensconced in the suburbs. Johnson's rhetoric of shame – how could the wealthiest nation allow such privation? – was a personal indictment. I could not help but notice the disparity between my grandmother's closed and smelly Brooklyn apartment and my clean and new split-level.

In the 1930s, the government had sent photographers into the Hoovervilles, shanty towns, migrant camps and slums of America, revealing to the small-town middle class 'how the other half lived' or, less anachronistically, 'one third of a nation – ill-housed, ill-clothed, ill-fed.' I had already seen their faces – or at least some of them – and I suppose these memories clouding the discrepancies behind my parents' speedy rise from New York's Jewish ghetto fueled my lust for looking at the documents of the 1930s – as did my training as a 1950s television viewer. Those black-and-white images which entered our life daily held the aura of truth. The old 1930s and 1940s movies let me know something about the silent realm of my parents' past. (I knew they didn't live like Miriam Hopkins in *Design for Living*, but they had watched her and the others every Saturday afternoon of their childhood in Williamsburg.) Because most movies were in Technicolor by the 1950s, it was TV with its corny confessional shows like *Queen for a Day* and *Dragnet* and the nightly ritual of news that bred my taste for the Real. Even the cartoons spoke historical truths as the Warner Brothers rodents, who lived inside modest homes in the Haxwell Mouse coffee cans they scavenged from the trash, experienced meatless Tuesdays along with everyone else during the war. My history lessons came from mice. (Perhaps in part explaining the extraordinary impact of *Maus*, Art Spiegelman's dark cat-and-mouse comic books, recounting his father's story of surviving the holocaust.) Like the FSA photographs, 1950s TV presented a remote black-and-white world of real suffering, one to contrast with the two-toned Chevy in our driveway and the lavender walls of my suburban bedroom. History, truth, and reality were recorded without living color.

4

When I discovered William Stott's book *Documentary Expression and Thirties America*, it was as though I had found the Holy Grail. Here was an account of America's secrets and my own desire. Stott chronicled how documentary forms conveyed meaning and why they became the predominant form of liberal and radical culture in the 1930s. Documentary is a modern term, coined in 1926 by the filmmaker, John Grierson, to describe the 'value' of Robert Flaherty's visual account of the daily life of Polynesian islanders, *Moana*. However, documentary images, caught by still and moving cameras, precede this moment. Benjamin speaks of Atget's streets as the scenes of a crime, and police photography represents one of the first documentary uses of the camera. Jacob Riis took his mercury flashes and camera into the Eastside tenements because showing 'How the Other Half Lives' might effect social reforms which had not been achieved by the mere telling. As early as 1893 the Lumières' cinematograph recorded and displayed daily street scenes around the world. What was the impulse to reveal the truth through images; why assume that once poverty was seen it could be eliminated? The visual experience might force a response where words would not. Why? As Abigail Solomon-Godeau points out, only half a century earlier, when Engels detailed *The Conditions of the Working Class in England*, it never occurred to social reformers to include visual images. Words were enough. Henry Mayhew's *London Labour and London Poor*, a massive testament to the ravages of industrial capitalism, relies on description and occasional interviews to document poverty in 1854. Yet by the 1892 English edition, Engels's work included maps and diagrams. It would have been unthinkable to present a documentary about working-class privation without visual aids. What had happened in those intervening fifty years? Why does it take another quarter-century before a name can be given to this procedure of visualization?

A technological change – the mercury flash – had enabled Jacob Riis to see the dark and squalid interiors of tenements; but the change was ideological as well, transforming ways of seeing into supervision which, according to Foucault, begins in the eighteenth century and culminates in the dual technologies of cinema and psychoanalysis at the end of the nineteenth. Visualizing the poor presented glimpses into dark recesses akin to the symptoms of the unconscious structuring dreams and hysteria. If the middle class possessed depth, the poor dwelled there. It was an/other place; and more than simply talk about it, it could be seen.

The report that seeks to account for – but, more importantly, to change – reality owes much to the rise of what Denise Riley and others have called 'the social' in the mid-nineteenth century. The social, understood as the growing public-sphere activities which are akin to politics, but not quite political, akin to economics, but not quite, can be thought of as the irruption of the household into public view. With the social, which demands a range of new knowledges to manage, middle-class women enter the public arena, and new technologies – photography and reportage among them – become crucial to determining the domain of social science, the survey of one segment of the population by another. To get a clear sense of the social, writers needed to develop mimetic effects which were adequate to the task of translating areas previously outside the view of observers. Of course, the photograph seemed to do just this without mediation.

This 'publicity of the private,' as Roland Barthes called it, is connected to the modern state, welfare, surveillance, and revolution. Dziga Vertov believed a new kind of seeing – Kino-Eye – could be induced by the movie camera. Like the storming of the Winter Palace, it would change the world by bringing to light that which had never been seen, much less imagined, before. Documentary circulates between the public and private, personal and political spheres by becoming simultaneously an aesthetic and archival object – part-fiction, part-truth; or if you will, at once base and superstructure, economic practice and cultural form. This boundary-crossing is why I insist that gender is a central category within documentary rhetoric, though one often ignored, suppressed, or resisted, because it is not always clear who occupies what position when. For instance, during the 1930s, a small army of female photographers became makers of documentary images which have become icons, objectifying poverty and reifying its machinery. They confounded the simplistic notion that women are objectified through visual representations. Which women? one must ask. Besides, what is so bad about objectification? Objects can speak also – listen to the commodities in *Capital* – and what they say perhaps undoes the subject itself. The social *uses* of documentary – their 'value' to Leftists, radicals, reformers, and so forth, but also to governments and corporations – develop from their simultaneous and dual place between object and subject. Is this the source of the appeal of documentary for those on the Left, particularly socially conscious intellectuals and artists, for whom the aesthetics of realism may be suspect? Does the invocation of reality destabilize realism, or more firmly install it? Why pick up a tool used as much for social control as for radical change?

One goes somewhere as a documentarian – Polynesia, Alabama, Poland, downtown; the documentarian is drawn elsewhere by an other. Documentary is based on exchange. Carolyn Steedman describes how the watercress girl interviewed by Mayhew got something as well as gave something from her story. In their discussion of an early report on female blacksmiths, Nancy Armstrong and Leonard Tennenhouse argue that the intended audience of documentary, like the listener of the joke, participates in the degradation of the third, the object of scrutiny, the butt of the joke. However, the documentarian is also subject to mockery as an outsider. And this is crucial to documentary rhetoric. The joke is on everyone; it's a knowing outrage. Dorothea Lange described the remarkable circumstances of her picture now known as Migrant Mother as an exchange; she later recalled: 'She seemed to know I might do something for her and that she might do something for me.' This is the economy – even when ridicule is the point – in which documentary works. Claude Lanzmann gains entry into a former Nazi commander's house to get him to detail the murders at Treblinka on a hidden camera by lying. We are complicit in the theft of truth, truth gained as the film-maker deceives his lying informant.

These exchanges and boundary crossings are crucial to the political projects of radical documentaries. What is at stake, I believe, is the status, meaning, interpretation, and perhaps even control of history and its narratives. Documentaries, whether prose reports, moving or still images, demand narratives. The viewing subject, the talking head, the edited sequence, and the caption all tell stories. Photography may be dumb, as Martha Rosler asserts; but as she also points out, documentary speaks volubly. Its purpose is to speak and confer value on the objects it speaks about. What it says, to whom, about whom, and for whom – and *how* it says it – is what my book is about.

Documents may appear to be neutral sources of historical truth, but documentaries have and present values; they are persuasive, not simply artifactual. A document purports to tell the truth, but it is always suspect because the truth-claim depends on differentiating itself from fiction, naming itself as non-fiction.[1] Documentary forms often claim to occupy the neutral position of the document. However, the rhetoric of political documentary – from the reportage of the 1930s to the feminist counter-cinema of the 1980s – foregrounds sexual, class, racial, and gender differences within its address. These differences construct a spectator whose position is located within history, essentially remaking the relationship of truth to ideology by insisting on advocacy rather than objectivity.

My book analyzes the long-standing link between political subcultures and documentary practices in the United States. By historicizing the rhetorical strategies employed by political documentaries, I consider the various ways in which documentary films call up an audience (usually of the already converted), outline a 'liberated zone' within production and distribution networks, and effect change, not only within the sphere of the 'political' but also within that of the 'cultural' and 'theoretical.' These processes are historically specific to their periods of production and to their associated political struggles. Each chapter raises questions about a series of interlocking topics. What are the relations of power embedded in the particular form of documentary discussed? How were these understood/ignored at the time of their production? What impact did these documentary styles have on the Left and on popular culture? How might we theorize the interconnections among leftist politics, documentary rhetoric, and theories of subjectivity and agency? Where do we go from here?

I found myself describing this book as a quirky history of political documentaries in twentieth-century America. What I meant by this was simply that I was not writing a comprehensive chronicle of documentary forms and practices. Instead, I had focused on a selection of distinctive instances over half a century in which the genre took profound turns in direction and scope. These shifts followed the major political issues galvanizing radical critiques during the twentieth century – the Depression, the Vietnam War, civil rights and decolonization, women's and gay and lesbian liberation. But I am not arguing for a one-to-one correspondence between political movements (and their constituencies) and documentary rhetoric. Rather, I want to trace a series of problematics – in Althusser's sense – moments of heightened contradiction which pinpoint some of the theoretical issues I feel the works raise.

As I have said, I like the work I am studying; morbid and sometimes dull as it is, I find it deeply compelling – the appeal to emotion that is at the heart of the genre and its rhetoric ensures that this will always be so, especially if the audience conforms to the terms established by the piece. This audience I conceive of as a different form of spectatorship from that understood by contemporary cinesemiotics and psychoanalytical film theory. I insist on the word 'audience,' with its corporeality implicitly featured. The subject produced and provoked by documentary, I maintain throughout the book, is a subject of (potential) agency, an actor in history. And the performance of the documentary is precisely to remand, if not actively remake, the subject into a historical agent. Oddly, then, documentary rhetoric – despite being overlaid with a gloss of objectivity gleaned from its assignation as nonfiction, hence historical, factual, and thus presumably objective – also derives from agitprop. Its function is to induce feeling, thought, and action.

8

As such, it seems to me that documentary presents itself as much more performative than even fictional forms. Precisely because fictional performances (at least those coded within realistic conventions) efface their constructions through naturalizing gestures, the response within the audience is contained; but in shifting the site of documentary from the object of vision to the subject of action by insisting on the dynamic relationship of viewer to view, documentary forms invoke performance within their audiences as much as within their objects. If performance and action are at the center of documentary rhetoric, then it seems that what is being produced is less a psychoanalytical and more an ethnographic scene; an encounter in which observation slides into participation which somehow exceeds transference and identification. I am in effect both discussing documentary ethnography and pursuing an ethnography of documentary.

To do this, I have decided that a chronicle of twentieth-century American documentary would be less useful than a series of case studies addressing various problematics. Central to the book is a discussion of the place of radicals and intellectuals (and radical intellectuals) in American political life.[2] Documentary performance and address is always about crossing boundaries – racial, sexual, class, gender, regional, temporal – as outsiders to a subculture enter into it, or as insiders from a subculture project it outward; and the intellectual – whether in Gramsci's terms traditional or organic, universal or specific in Foucault's typology – acts as the coyote smuggling across borders.

Case study, as Carolyn Steedman shows in her theoretical microhistory, *Landscape for a Good Woman*, provides an antidote to the perpetual blind-spots in traditional historiography and autobiography precisely because it calls attention to gaps and contradictions, the discrepancies in narrative. Case study provides an alternative history to that of either annal or chronicle by emphasizing the subjectivity of the historian. Much is revealed about the obsessions of the narrator by looking at which cases are studied. Moreover, while to a certain extent the case study seems to lift an object out of its context, in other ways, by juxtaposing one with another, new contexts are forged. Because the history of the Left in twentieth-century America is itself so ruptured – primarily because of Cold War hysteria, but also because of Stalinism, racism, sexism, and the peculiar insulation of the United States from much of the world's devastation during this century – no wars actually fought on US soil – it is difficult to write a narrative history anyway. The history of radical movements has been charted as a series of 'waves,' and while this model has many faults (I myself have been quite critical of the class-biased way in which feminist discourse was seen to disappear after 1920 precisely when it emerges within working-class movements), it is partly true that activism has been episodic in this country. The case study seems to allow for an analysis of the episodic nature of both documentary practices and left movements.

Finally, this book is about the ways in which subcultures – especially radical intellectuals who see themselves more or less representative of marginalized groups in the American political landscape – represent themselves, and are in turn re-presented within dominant culture. Marx's famous chide to the French peasantry – 'they cannot represent themselves; they must be represented' – seen as a paradigmatic colonizing gesture (to be balanced perhaps when he enables commodities to speak for themselves) provides an early example of documentary reportage and the title of this book. In fact, *The Eighteenth Brumaire of Louis Bonaparte* is a model of engaged reportage. As political theory, biting satire, detailed description, and thrilling plot, it perhaps begins the genre. Marx's serialized account of Louis Bonaparte's disastrous reign prefigures the standard documentary report in which weekly or monthly instalments shock readers about strikes, wars, and mass movements. But who is being represented? Clearly, Marx peeped behind the curtain of French political economics to unveil the sinister class alignments forming in post-revolutionary Paris. But he also provided his readers with a solid look at his own methods of analysis, his own idiosyncratic ways of seeing. Dziga Vertov's 1929 manifesto defined 'Kino-Eye' as a 'new emphasis of the "unplayed" film over the played film,' so that documentary not only recorded history, but intervened in its (cinematic) construction, baring the devices of framing and editing. His desire to make 'the invisible visible, the obscure clear, the hidden obvious, the disguised exposed' was tied to an explicitly political project of reinventing reality in post-revolutionary Russia.[3] It presented a cinematic update to Marx's textual methodology. New technologies, new political revolutions, new media, but the form and rhetoric remain remarkably consistent.

In the same way that Janet Malcolm's recent dissection of the problematics of biography, *The Silent Woman*, revealed as much about her own dilemmas as a journalist as it did those of Plath's biographers (and of Plath, her mother, husband, children, in-laws and friends), Marx's method is both objective and subjective at the same time. Of course, the pre-eminent advocate and practitioner of the case study – Sigmund Freud – used his own dreams to develop his theories of both their interpretation and his method of analysis. What is the subject and what is the object of *The Interpretation of Dreams*? In his 'Fragment of an Analysis,' Freud is forced to admit, finally, that Dora had something to teach him. Again, who is the subject and who the object of this study?

FIGURE 1   Robert Little, 'Ellen Grounds, aged 22, a broo wench at Pearson and Knowles's Pit, Wigan, taken 11 September 1873.'

FIGURE 2   Walker Evans, 'Floyd Burroughs' Bedroom, Hale
County, Alabama, Summer 1936.'

FIGURE 3   Walker Evans, 'Fireplace and Objects
in a Bedroom of Floyd Burroughs' Home, Hale
County, Alabama, Summer 1936.'

FIGURE 4   Hugo Gellert, 'Primary Accumulation,' from
Karl Marx 'Capital' in Lithographs.

FIGURE 5   Hugo Gellert, 'Commodities,' from
Karl Marx 'Capital' in Lithographs.

FIGURE 6   'Forgotten Man,' *Gold Diggers of 1933*.

FIGURE 7   Veronica Lake and Joel McCrea share a free donut in *Sullivan's Travels*.

FIGURE 8   Dorothea Lange, 'February 1939. Migrant family outfit on US 99 between Bakersfield, California and [Tehachapi] Ridge en route to San Diego.'

FIGURE 9　Dorothea Lange, 'January 1939. Gas station, Kern County, California.'

FIGURE 10　Dorothea Lange, 'November 1938. Camped in the rain behind billboard, three families, fourteen children. On US 99 near Famoso, Kern County, California.'

FIGURE 11   Ditch-digging scene from *Our Daily Bread*.

FIGURE 12   *The Plow That Broke the Plains.*

FIGURES 13–14 *The River.*

The case study format, then, is central to the exchange in documentary address. And this exchange I see as primarily rhetorical.

Terry Eagleton has been perhaps the foremost advocate of adapting the practices of rhetoric to contemporary polemics of literary history, theory, and criticism. Rhetoric also suggests the ways in which documentary method, its mode of investigation, is linked to issues of gender, sexual, racial, and class differences. Recent theorists of documentary, such as Thomas Guynn and Bill Nichols, have argued that the documentary film is primarily discursive: it seeks overtly to persuade its viewers by taking a side and arguing it. Rhetoric, according to Eagleton, does just that. It is fundamentally performative, interested in examining the ways discourses are constructed in order to achieve their desired effects. Interested and activist, rhetoric stakes a position from which to make its case.

The original subtitle of my book – which I sometimes wrote as History and the Rhetoric of Gender, and sometimes as Gender and the Rhetoric of History in American Political Documentaries, I could never remember which – called attention to the very ways in which both terms, gender and history, are rhetorical. Each constructs performances: on the one hand, of individual bodies in space; on the other, of social groups over time. The form of documentary itself relies on these performances which narrate differences among social actors and practices. Judith Butler has argued persuasively for understanding gender as fundamentally performative, a fixed inscription across a range of bodies which serves political as well as sexual desires. Walter Benjamin's theses on history present a rhetorical picture of the practice of history – the Angel of History functions as the performance artist of historical time clocking the rubbish of the past as it fills the dustbins of the present. For both these theorists bodies and boundaries are fixed and then transgressed in an effort to shore up and subvert social order. Documentary practice exists in precisely this kind of discursive space. Inside and outside, it is representative: it represents and is a representative of cultural formations comprised of bodies and theses – gendered histories.

Representation and realism – these are the effects of documentary advocacy. Clearly, political documentary has seen its mission to point out 'problems' within the social fabric of a nation with the aim of changing them; sometimes the work of documentary has been to gather support for a particular 'solution' to a crisis, but increasingly political documentaries serve another representative function – that of self-definition. Radical reportage and documentary films often provide the Left, or its various subcultures, with a self-understanding. It represents itself to itself – an act of identity – as it represents its

FIGURE 15   Publicity photograph for *An American Family*.

FIGURE 16 *Mosori Monika.*

FIGURE 17 Senegalese women's faces in publicity still for *Reassemblage*.

FIGURE 18 *Soft Fiction.*

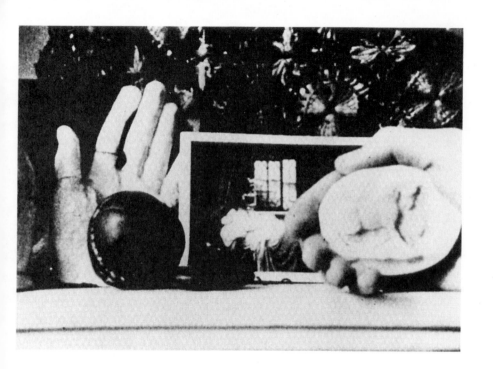

FIGURES 19–20 *Journeys from Berlin/1971.*

FIGURE 21 *Far from Poland*. 'On location in Princeton, New Jersey, with Honora Fergusson as the Polish journalist Barbara Lopienska, and William Raymond as "K-62."'

FIGURE 22 East Cambridge, Massachusetts, 1974.

positions to a wider community – an act of recruitment. Moreover, radical documentary constructs objects of radical desire; it depicts the subject and object of revolution to itself and through itself, producing an identity that both includes yet differs from its audience. This is a highly personal form which takes as its subject public affairs; but it is also a political practice which comes from private vision.

Documentaries construct not only a vision of truth and identity but an appropriate way of seeing that vision. The sequence of images and words lays out a narrative that produces meanings already understood within conventionalized forms and genres. For example, the ethnographic film depends on the construction of an exotic whose culture is open to inspection by the invisible camera and its scientist/operator. The truths displayed produce an order, a history, and thus a narrative about the relationship of the 'primitive' to 'progress,' self to other.[4] Documentaries that repress the presence of the documentarian's voice or body posit a natural truth captured at random in words or images and seemingly open to direct consumption by the audience. Alternatively, films that invoke the authenticity of experience through the first person – the talking head – turn the lens slightly, and divert the spectator from the object of documentary toward the subject of narrative – a subject with whom the spectator can identify as the source of truth, as the authority, as the author. The documentary text, then, is deeply invested in narrative forms of difference. Who looks at whom? This question is at the heart of image, word, and sound within documentary rhetoric.

What can one make of a genre so indebted to realism in an age of anti-realist effects? T.V. Reed argues for considering the work of many twentieth-century writers and activists as postmodern realism, a revision of the standard markings of the realist text in light of the self-consciousness of its conceits as an effect. As dramatists of the Real, documentarians know that they are constructing reality out of the materials at hand. Increasingly the efforts of the documentarian have been aimed at displaying this constructedness in more and more overt ways. When Paul Rotha (and many others) faulted Pare Lorentz for the 'over-complex editing' and 'mannered quality,' he was objecting to the way that *The Plow That Broke the Plains* called attention to itself as 'propaganda' rather than successfully integrating its message within its story.[5] Lorentz's highly controlled pictures were later rejected by film-makers seeking in living cinema – documentaries without narration, musical scores, re-enactments – films that presented a direct rendering of sight and sound. Yet the highly constructed editing of Frederick Wiseman's *Titicut Follies*, for instance, and its occasional reminders of the film-maker's presence, invited the viewer to consider again the construction of documentary meaning, even if the message was implied. More recently, film-makers have included their bodies, and with them their voices, in the documentary film. Michael Moore and Jill Godmilow are integral to the portraits of workers struggling in one case to deal with loss of jobs in Flint auto plants, in the other with the emergence of democratic movements in Poland. The film-maker and the documentary process itself are subject to reflection as much as the issues under scrutiny. The reality effect becomes more and more self-reflexive, but its presence remains. In the various guises and strategies documentary film-makers have used one finds precisely the conditions of a modernist, even postmodernist realism first called for by Bertolt Brecht in his famous argument with Georg Lukács over the meanings and purposes of realism for political artists and critics.

They Must Be Represented is divided into three parts, more or less conforming to three moments of heightened political crisis in the United States – the 1930s, the 1960s (which as we all know slide into the 1970s), and the 1980s to the present – each moment corresponds roughly to the emergence into cultural and political visibility and mobilization a previously hidden, subaltern population – the poor and working class, Third World peoples in and outside the belly of the beast, women's and gay liberation struggles, respectively. Thus each section analyzes various ways in which new 'subjects of agency' were represented, chose to represent themselves, and etched out an audience who could respond as political actors to the issues raised by the massive social, economic, and political changes inaugurated by the Depression and decolonization both in the United States and else-where, and experienced in family structure and sexuality after women's re-entry into the labor force, birth control, and AIDS. In addition to this Introduction, I include a chapter that theorizes the complex relationships between history, documentary, and memory. It serves as an overview of critical discussions of documentary cinema and sets out the key terms that are important to me – representation and agency.

Part I focuses on the 1930s. However, unlike my previous work, it is not concerned with the artists and writers who identified with left-wing movements during that decade. Instead, the three chapters look at various independent radicals, liberals, and even a self-serving careerist whose documentary works so powerfully invoked images and tropes first circulated within the Left that their very distance from left-wing politics confirms its centrality during the Depression years. Here

documentary films, reportage, and photographs sketched a new public culture which combined popular culture and people's culture – one
element being the province of commercial interests, the other of their
radical critics. The burgeoning mass media of radio, movies, and
picture magazines caused new constituents of the American public to
surface – in this case, poor, rural, Southern tenants struggling to eke
out an existence on the depleted land or forced off it by the drought
and dust storms to join the great migrations westward to California
from Oklahoma, Arkansas, and the rest of the Plains.

My attention to the liberals' use of documentary forms to effect
change suggests the power of the radical critiques and its genres,
which had tried to refashion socialist realism in America, on those
outside the influence of Party rhetoric and organization. It also points
to the connections among various media in forging public knowledge
and attitudes about social problems. The newly visible poor could
hardly enter the public culture through documentaries about them.
These genres were clearly intended for a middle-class audience of
voters, who would be swayed by the scenes of privation to support New
Deal policies. Yet visualization is often a precursor to mobilization;
seeing oneself as an object being the first step toward political subjectivity. The photographs, writings, and films I discuss reveal the complex
processes of cross-class alliances when those connections are first
forged through relations of looking. These contradictions mark the
limits of 1930s documentary address.

Part II considers race and ethnicity and the implantation of domestic culture into the public sphere following the social upheavals of the
1960s. In the late 1960s, Americans began traveling to North Vietnam
as anti-war activists; women's writings about the Vietnam War –
oppositional work produced by established and little-known writers –
looked at the place of female intellectuals in this war, which was itself
an intellectuals' war. Their race and gender confounded the questions
about the place of intellectuals in Cold War America once the 1960s
social movements – student activism for civil rights and against the
Vietnam War, women's liberation, Stonewall – opened new ways of
doing politics. 'History in Your Own Home' explores the rise of
identity politics in mass-mediated forms – public television and
network docudrama. The popularized *cinéma vérité* of Craig Gilbert's
PBS series *An American Family* gave upper-middle-class suburban
whites an identity and presence as a distinct cultural group. Documentary ethnography need not necessarily travel to exotic and other
locales; one could look into the many rooms of this Santa Barbara
family to discover strange rituals of all sorts. *Roots* was among the first

and most controversial yet successful docudramas; it brought African-Americans into focus as history's sufferers and survivors.

These serialized TV shows used the formula of the 'American family' and focused on the internal dynamics of the home to outline generations of conflicts among races, classes, and religions. This family saga motif sets the stage for and is the direct outcome of middle-class women's emergence into the public sphere in large numbers in the workforce, in educational institutions, through radicalizing struggles for sexual freedom and abortion rights, as well as affirmative action. The cultural politics of identity and ethnicity begin within the self, constructed in the maze of family networks; history's impact is filtered through family conflicts and the emotional organization of psyches formed in the two-parent home of TV fantasy left over from 1950s sitcoms.

Part III begins by looking at 'ethnographies of women,' as avant-garde documentary film-maker Chick Strand calls her film *Soft Fiction*, to discuss alternative views of spectatorship among women to those proposed by psychoanalytical semiotics dominating feminist film theory. I look at how theories of spectatorship can censor work as surely as theories of pornography do. From there I turn to a discussion of 'national bodies' in the experimental films of three contemporary women directors: Jill Godmilow's *Far From Poland*, Yvonne Rainier's *Journeys from Berlin/1971*, and Trinh T. Minh-ha's *Surname Viet, Given Name Nam*. I consider the ways in which racial, ethnic, sexual, and gender differences recast socialist struggles to create new political analyses and alternative visions within cinematic representations. These formal innovations, radical though they might be within documentary practice, may be as compromised as the movements they dissect.

Finally, the book closes with a cautionary tale as I dissect the use of George Holliday's tape of Rodney King's beating at the hands of Los Angeles police officers in March 1991. This chapter explores the complex nature of unmediated raw documentary image and the way in which linguistic captions rewrite visual language. The beating, trial, and uprising highlight the gruesome persistence of racism plaguing the United States at the end of a century of unmitigated horrors. The work of documentary in this age has been to show this horror unflinchingly, but one wonders, after the acquittal of the four police officers by a California jury, whether that is enough. Perhaps we are simply saturated with documentary images. Lanzmann's refusal to include footage from the extermination camps in *Shoah* points to another path for documentary – the imaginative recuperation of memory through the spoken word. After more than a century of looking, what more is there to see? The question still remains: What is to be done?

1

Wreckage upon Wreckage: History,

Documentary, and the Ruins of Memory

His eyes are staring, his mouth is open, his wings are spread. This is how one pictures the angel of history. His face is turned toward the past. Where we perceive a chain of events, he sees one single catastrophe which keeps piling wreckage upon wreckage and hurls it in front of his feet. The angel would like to stay, awaken the dead, and make whole what has been smashed. But a storm is blowing from Paradise; it has got caught in his wings with such violence that the angel can no longer close them. This storm irresistibly propels him into the future to which his back is turned, while the pile of debris before him grows skyward.[1]

I

Walter Benjamin, chronicler of modernity, called for a history that could redeem the past by catapulting it into the present. His figure of the Angel of History whose face turns toward the past as he is blown into the wreckage of the future might also represent the documentary film-maker, who can only make a film within the historical present, even as it evokes the historical past. Documentary is usually a recon-struction – a re-enactment of another time or place for a different audience, a graphing of history in and through the cinematic image and taped sound onto the present.

In 1945, as the Allied troops entered the concentration camps of Bergen-Belsen and Dachau, cameramen were filming the eerie land-scape. Some of the footage was eventually put together by the British Ministry of Information into the shocking film *Memory of the Camps*, or in its longer, 69-minute version, *A Painful Reminder*. Never released because of the stark images of the camps, the film was originally intended for viewing by the German people as part of the deNazification program. Because of its disturbing images of mass graves being excavated and filled with emaciated corpses by captured SS guards, the film was considered so inflammatory to the newly forged post-war alliances that the British government suppressed it. It languished in the archives of the Imperial War Museum until the mid-1980s, when it was recovered by another generation of film-makers and was finally screened as part of another documentary on the making of the film and on its history for *Frontline*, narrated by Trevor Howard.[2]

Intended to be shown to the German people who were steadfastly refusing to 'know anything,' the footage was meant to elicit remorse in the general population. The images are so horrific, as tractors maul the fragile skeletons, that they become strangely haunting, almost elegiac. Sidney Bernstein, Minister of Information, at a loss as to how to turn this material into a film – documentary footage is not the same as documentary cinema – recruited Alfred Hitchcock, master of narrative, suspense and horror, to offer advice on how to construct the film. The resulting establishing shot: blond children play before a bucolic Bavarian cottage nestling within a forest; the camera pans through the trees to reveal barbed wire and piles of flesh and bones. This Hitchcockian touch may have invoked the official censorship of the film; it was the narrative established by the pan – the heart of darkness beating within the German people – more than the footage of the camps alone, which was potentially damaging to the post-war alliance.

At the heart of this documentary project was a cinema of memory. The mission of the cameramen was to record a historical aberration. Filming an essentially ephemeral event, a vanishing custom, a disappearing species, a transitory occurrence is the motivation behind most documentary images. Documentary films provide a stability to an ever-changing reality, freezing the images within their frames for later instructional use. *A Painful Reminder* and its history encapsulate virtually all the issues circulating around the three terms important to this chapter: history, documentary, cinema. It suggests that images themselves, as Martha Rosler says of photographs, 'are dumb'; their meaning is constructed in the web of interpretations we give them through technology – for example, sound, montage – to convey context, narrative, and subjectivity.[3] The edited montage of the cottage and the camp, one image following another, served as 'captions,' to use Walter Benjamin's word for each image.[4]

As I lay out the terms of this chapter – documentary, history, memory – I realize that there are numerous possible permutations in thinking about this intersection: the history of documentary cinema;

the uses of history in documentary; the uses of document(arie)s by historians; the encoding of history in documents; the uses of cinema as documents; the place of memory in historical and documentary accounts; the incursion of cinema into memory; and so forth. According to the *OED*, history has long been defined as a narrative, while documentary (a relatively modern word, coined by Jeremy Bentham in the first decade of the nineteenth century) concerns evidence. History tracks the 'whole train of events connected with a country, society, person, thing, etc . . .' But a document, whose obsolete definition encompasses 'teaching, instruction, warning,' is lodged in an object which 'furnishes evidence or information.' The relationship is clear – history relies on documents to support its narrative. But where does documentary fit in? Its (not very useful) definition 'of the nature of or consisting in documents' is matched with its two rare usages: 'affording evidence'; 'relating to teaching.' The documentary, then, is meant to instruct through evidence; it poses truth as a moral imperative.

John Grierson's 1926 review of Robert Flaherty's *Moana* is generally considered the first use of the term documentary to distinguish non-fiction film. According to Grierson, Flaherty's re-creations of the daily life of a young Polynesian boy had 'documentary value.'[5] The film held a moral as well as an aesthetic currency for its audience by presenting itself as truthful. Known as the father of documentary, Flaherty nevertheless relied on re-enactment and restaging to achieve his moral and narrative coherence. Not unlike Sergei Eisenstein who used amateurs as actors to restage the powerful events of the Soviet revolution, Flaherty manipulated reality to give a picture of reality. But the ideas and theories involved in documentary as a category of cinema opposed to fiction film were most fully articulated in Dziga Vertov's 1929 Kino-Eye manifestos. In contrast to Eisenstein's re-creations, however, Vertov's film-making technique was closer to newsreel as he took his camera onto the streets of Russia and filmed the events of daily life. His decisive break with newsreel, however, came in his overt depiction of the film-making process – shooting, cutting, editing – as a part of the record.

Because Flaherty relied on both acting (on replaying daily life) and a story based on the chronology of a day's activity, his films presented the history of a subject indebted to nineteenth-century narrative forms. Vertov, on the other hand, sought to create a 'new emphasis of the "unplayed" film over the played film, [to] substitute the documentary for *mise en scène* to break out of the proscenium of the theater and to enter the arena of life itself.' Tied to the post-revolutionary project of remaking social relations, cinema, in Vertov's view, needed to break from its connections to the theatrical and make 'visible the invisible, the obscure clear, the hidden obvious, the disguised exposed' by filming the mechanics of production and revolution, including the mechanics of cinema – stockpiling 'the factory of facts.'[6]

Actually, Vertov's championing of Kino-Eye – the discovery of truth through the cinematic apparatus achieved through its 'conquest of space, the visual linkage of people throughout the entire world . . . [and] conquest of time' – had it origins in the earliest public uses of cinema. 'The movie camera,' he notes, 'was invented in order to penetrate deeper into the visible world, to explore and record visual phenomena, so that we do not forget what happens and what the future must take into account.'[7] His belief that the Kino-Eye was a scientific improvement over the human eye echoed the first claims for cinema as an apparatus for 'the recording . . . and reproduction' of movement.[8]

In the 1890s, the Lumière brothers sent teams of camera operators along with film processors and projectors across the continents to document and display their inventions by filming the daily lives and environments of ordinary people. One of the money-making schemes the Lumières devised was a quasi-simultaneous filming and projecting tour of the big cities of the Americas, Europe, and Africa. The Lumière cameramen would place their fixed cameras at a busy down-town intersection and capture the passers-by on foot, horse and buggy, or trolley, then inform whoever stopped to watch them that they could see themselves that evening at the cinema. These images were juxta-posed with those from other parts of the world so that Egyptian pyramids rose up on Broadway; the exotic and the mundane becom-ing interchangeable. Credited as the fathers of newsreel and docu-mentary cinema, the Lumières also pioneered interactive viewing, a kind of direct cinema years ahead of its institutional practice.[9] The Lumières' cinematograph represented an important moment in achieving the simultaneity of image and experience. If history repre-sents a retrospective narrative, the document or newsreel appeals to a self-identical presence as truth. The sense of immediacy-as-truth/ truth-as-immediacy was central to the earliest scientific and modernist uses of the cinema.[10] This 'incredible science,' as Prince Vlod calls the cinematograph in Francis Ford Coppola's 1992 film *Bram Stoker's Dracula*, suggests that the amusement of early cinema was not neces-sarily its resemblance to the theatrical experience; rather, it was understood as an exhibit,[11] designed both to document the world for itself and instruct an audience in film reception.[12]

As the example of the British footage of the concentration camps indicates, the relation of documentary to history is more than a tracing of the ways documentary emerges over time. Documentary films have made important gestures and interventions into both public and private history as well. Documentary, then, is always historical film-making; but it is also ethnographic. Since 1922, when Robert Flaherty restaged *Nanook of the North*'s walrus kill, the form has been linked to anthropological fieldwork in a number of ways. Standard texts on ethnographic film call for an unobtrusive camera, which attempts to position itself like the fly on the wall and invisibly observe the activities taking place before it.[13] But Flaherty had radically intervened into Eskimo culture to achieve a dramatic effect; his film, made with funding from a French fur company, recreated actual events through staged performances with tools and techniques never used by Nanook. The effect produced a spectacle of otherness wholly conforming to Western, indeed Hollywood, patterns of vision and narrative. Clearly, the premisses of the ethnographic film – that the medium is itself transparent and thus will give us direct insight into the 'mind' of the Other – presents a special, racialized ideology about the logic of the apparatus as a construction of knowledge.[14]

These trends, inherited from the earliest moments of cinema through its flowering in the silent era, were drastically modified with the advent of sound. Once a narrator could oversee the visual information through voice – either with a voice-over or through direct speech – documentary visuals often served as illustrations for the soundtrack. However, since the 1960s, when documentarians began to experiment with living cinema, *cinéma vérité*, direct cinema,[15] documentaries again attempted to capture a pure cinematic truth. As in the earlier period, debates about how this could be achieved followed the divergent paths outlined by the Lumières, Flaherty, and Vertov. Did one simply set up a camera and shoot life as it happened? Or was the presence of the camera and crew bound to impinge on reality? Was the point of documentary merely to record, or instead to recast, the visible and audible world through the cinematic apparatus?

Direct cinema, the formally radical mode of documentary film-making prevailing from the mid-1950s through the mid-1970s, sought to express the most intimate details of day-to-day experience – whether those events dramatized national conflicts (as in the Drew Associates film, *Crisis: Behind a Presidential Decision*), bureaucratic violence (as in Frederick Wiseman's adumbration of the dehumanizing penal institutions for the mentally ill, *Titicut Follies*),[16] or private life (as in Craig Gilbert's *An American Family*, the twelve-part series made for PBS in 1971 about the Louds, an upper-middle-class family from Santa Barbara, whose divorce unfolded before the camera).[17] The idea of being unobtrusive was, as everyone realized, a fantasy – if nothing else, wires, microphones, camera, and lights were continually present – not to mention their operators. However, Drew insisted that by choosing wisely an event could be so engrossing for its participants that the film crew's presence had little impact on the happenings; after all, egocentric politicians or wealthy hermits were simply too self-absorbed to pay much attention to it.[18] Still, the control of the film-making process lay with the director as he (and most direct cinema was practiced by male directors) edited the footage into its final form. 'It's in *cinéma vérité*,' explains Ellen Hovde, co-editor of *Grey Gardens*, 'that the editing takes on the same importance as the camerawork – and camerawork and editing combined *are* directing, in *cinéma vérité*.'[19]

One of the critiques fired at the direct cinema movement was its lack of social context – its naturalizing of the viewing process or, in Benjamin's words, its lack of a 'caption.'[20] 'The body represented by documentary film,' claims Bill Nichols, 'must be understood in relation to a historical context which is a referent, not an ontological ground. History is where pain and death occur but it is in representation that the facts and events gain meaning.'[21] As 'star' of the documentary, the presence of the body, especially the body in pain, signifies truth and realness which seem to defy contextualization. Without the film-maker present on screen, however, the camera's view is disembodied and so dehistoricized, while the filmed bodies are simultaneously overinvested with meaning yet deprived of agency. Thus, by repressing the sight of the film-maker's body, the implicitly middle-class and masculinist and white perspective of the film-makers was eclipsed.

Cinéma vérité came in for various critiques by film-makers who stressed the need for overt political commitment in their work. Without the social criticism embedded in the caption (which in cinema comes in the forms of voice-overs, inter-titles, interviews, archival footage, montage, and so forth), direct cinema can espouse that which it seeks to expose. The failure to challenge problematic self-representations was at the heart of the controversies over *California Reich* (1975) and *Blood in the Face* (1991), two *cinéma vérité* exposés of neo-Nazism. Both came under attack by the Left for their failure to criticize their subjects. In fact, in *Blood in the Face*, the subjects are delighted that the film is being made by James Ridgeway, a respected left-wing journalist, because they know it will get wide distribution, unlike the film being made by a crew of insiders. The premiss of *California Reich* is that the neo-Nazis will repel their audience – who are invited into their living room to watch a domestic scene where small children speak about growing up to kill 'niggers and kikes' – by exposing their racism and anti-Semitism as the rantings of mad men and women. But the film-makers' intentions to ridicule their subjects through exposure are taken over by the subjects themselves, who use this scene to spread the message that they are like anyone else – doting parents showing off their precocious children. Simply displaying horror – skeletal remains

21

of the Nazi holocaust or latter-day reincarnations of Nazi racism – without comment, as Sidney Bernstein had realized, is not enough: raw footage needs editing; bodies need historicizing.

This dilemma at the heart of *cinéma vérité* was what political documentarians sought to undo. For instance, ethnographers shifted toward a more interactive approach, including filming themselves filming, and portraying informants as canny actors, or actually handing over equipment to the ethnographic objects to make their own (subjective) work.[22] This level of self-reflexivity and self-consciousness about the cinematic apparatus was meant to alter the relationship of the subject and object of documentary address. The move toward cinematic self-determination by those denoted in the ethnographic film as 'other,' or abused in classic Hollywood's racist depictions of peoples of color, or excluded from 'the news,' grew out of the political struggles for self-determination by colonized peoples which inspired the Newsreel collectives in the late 1960s. These film-makers responded from within the belly of the beast to the calls for a 'third cinema' emanating from Latin America.

In many ways, the relationship of documentary and history which animated Vertov's work was rearticulated in the words and films produced after the 1968 publication of the manifesto by the filmmakers Fernando Solanas and Octavia Getino, 'Towards a Third Cinema.'[23] Their 1967 film *Las Horas de las Hornas* presented a powerful resurrection of the interventionist documentary form by actively engaging it in the struggle for decolonization in Latin America. Their film employed many techniques gleaned from Brechtian theatrical forms of the epic (as well as from Vertov's Kino-Pravda) to tell the story of (Argentinian) national self-determination through cinematic self-reflexivity. Its impact on the emerging cinemas of the Third World was profound, offering as it did a 'third' way out of the commercial studio productions of Hollywood and the auteurist cinema of Europe toward a communal and populist use of the medium.[24]

Unlike direct cinema which had dominated American documentary film-making since the Drew Associates followed Kennedy and Humphrey as each toured Wisconsin's small towns in pursuit of the presidential nomination in *Primary* (1960), Solanas and Getino advocated a cinema which intervened in history. These two poles – activist/interventionist cinema and a cinema of detached observation – appear miles apart, but the subject chosen for observation can elicit intervention while activist film-makers might find themselves observers of history. Critic Ana M. Lopez argues that what *Las Horas* unleashed was a kind of self-reflexive and analytical cinema, which culminated in the Patricio Guzman and Equipo Tercer Ano film made during the 1973 *coup* against President

22

Allende, *The Battle of Chile*. In an infamous sequence ending the first section, Argentinian cameraman Leonardo Henricksen films his own death after he refuses to heed the commands of an army officer to cease filming. In this terrible moment, repeated during the second part from the point of view of an Equipo cinematographer, the distinction between history and its representation in the documentary dissolves. The spectator becomes aware of the immediacy of the film through its star, the mortal body. However, Ana Lopez adds, unlike living cinema, *Battle of Chile* was a scripted documentary. Its film-makers, possessing limited film stock and aware of the pressures and limitations imposed by the instability of the pre-*coup* months, decided to plot out the film carefully, thus enabling them to 'produce what they termed an *analytical* documentary, more like an essay than agitprop.'[25] In preparing extensively for the film before shooting, the film-makers undercut the apparent transparency of documentary cinema: they first made a political analysis of the situation in Chile which in turn structured their film-making decisions. Thus a film that appears to record events as they unfold before the camera – history in the making – actually followed a theoretical outline as it tracked the 'fifteen or twenty battlegrounds within the larger conflict'[26] – historiography in the scripting, if you will.[27]

II

History, according to Bill Nichols, represents the excess of documentary rhetoric. It is that to which all documentaries refer and that which can never be wholly contained by the documentary: 'Always referred to but never captured,' he writes, 'history, as excess, rebukes those laws set to contain it; it contests, qualifies, resists, and refuses them.'[28] This concept of history as documentary's excess implies an analogy between documentary and history and historiography and history: history, according to Fredric Jameson's reading of Louis Althusser, stands as the 'absent cause, it is inaccessible to us except in textual form.'[29] Documentary films, like the criticism of them, speak about themselves as contradictory texts. Full of self-doubts about their status as organs of truth and reality, the films and their criticism unravel like so much celluloid on the cutting-room floor, revealing both productive and problematic sites for historical inquiry. Film's relationship to historical meaning and history's dependence upon, yet refusal of, film's form leave a space for active viewing. Both construct political subjects, whose self-consciousness about their positions lends itself to an analysis of the past and of the present. These subjects of agency have a responsibility to the future.

If classical narrative cinema constructs a subject of desire through mechanisms akin to the psychoanalytical processes of identification and refusal in its spectator,[30] the historical documentary – the documentary that seeks to intervene in history – mobilizes a subject of agency. This subject clearly desires too, but the desire is directed toward the social and political arenas of everyday experiences as well as world-historical events shaping those lives and away from the purely psychosexual manifestations of lack and plenitude, differentiation and identification, which characterize the fetishistic forms of narrative desire. Of course, there is no clear-cut distinction between inner and outer forms of desire; I want to suggest, however, that each has acquired different traits – narrative and documentary – to represent the Real.

In its supposedly purest form, *cinéma vérité*, documentary sought to re-present reality – including the inner reality of the subject – through the precise selection of objects surveyed by the camera and sounds recorded by the microphone: objectivity produced subjective truths. What the film-maker saw and heard of any event was what the film viewer would ultimately see. The visible and audible renderings of real life hold a powerful claim to truth in contrast to the scripted, performed, staged, costumed, key-lit, fictionalized, in short, artificial, images of classic narrative cinema. Yet narrative also makes a claim to reality – or rather, in the case of classic narrative, to verisimilitude and realism – to reveal something truthful about the workings of human emotion. Thus the close-up heightens emotional intensity, the 180-degree rule sutures the viewer into the scenic space, a match-on-action maintains temporal flow, and so forth.

These two modes of presenting the Real – the survey of objects and the disclosure of subjectivity – are often seen as incompatible modes of filmic address. Yet they share a number of similar features and premises and thus often coexist in the same film. Ultimately, both confirm cinema's privileged access to the Real: one by exactly indexing the profilmic scene, the other by eclipsing the distance between screen and spectator. Each poses the cinematic project as a revelation of reality, acknowledging the documentary aspects of fiction films – their investment in 'the redemption of physical reality' as Siegfried Kracauer claimed, or in 'an aesthetic of reality' to use André Bazin's phrase – as much as the fictionality of documentary.

For example, Spike Lee begins his historical drama *Malcolm X* (1992) with a stunning credit sequence intercutting George Holliday's 81-second videotape of Rodney King's beating at the hands of four police officers with a screen-filling American flag over which is heard Malcolm's inflammatory rhetoric denouncing white America. Lee's interpolation of documentary footage into a classic narrative film has many antecedents – *Reds, Zelig, Medium Cool* – dating back at least to Busby Berkeley's recreations of urban street life and Depression breadlines in his otherwise zany musical comedy, *Gold Diggers of 1933*.

In *Malcolm X*, Rodney King's beating brings the words uttered thirty years earlier into the present. Each image – the flag and the beating – and the oratory are so ideologically charged that the message is delivered like a sledgehammer. The 'video *vérité*' tape of police brutality which figured so centrally in the racial politics of 1992 is bookended with the documentary footage of Malcolm bleeding into the images of young children demonstrating in Soweto, and of Nelson Mandela speaking to a schoolroom full of children. These irruptions of the Real – which recur in the film in documentary footage of Martin Luther King in Selma and Birmingham, Alabama – seem wildly at odds with the film's epic sweep, which places the actor Denzel Washington in a series of carefully wrought period-pieces as it tracks the transformation of a nation and its hero. The film literalizes these transformations: Malcolm changes his hair each time he changes his head. His attempts to transform his life will not succeed until he frees himself from the prison of his mind, and conversely, every major change *in* Malcolm's head is accompanied by a change *on* his head. He conks his hair three times to straighten it – once to begin a career as a hustler, once as he begins his years in jail, once before beginning his study of Islam – he buzzcuts his hair after his conversion in prison; and after his journey to Mecca, he returns bearded to proclaim his rejection of the teachings of Elijah Muhammed. Surface and depth merge as the 'reality' of the documentary footage confirms the realism and historical truth of Lee's vision of Alex Haley's version of Malcolm's life.

Another example from popular culture, but one that inverts this logic of inner truth, outer sign is *Madonna: Truth or Dare* (1991). Here, the queen of artifice, whose career has been marked by makeovers and whose performances appropriate those of other stars – from Marilyn Monroe to the voguing legends who shade Marilyn in the numbers from the Blonde Ambition tour which the film tracks – is supposedly displayed for us 'as she really is.' The film relies on the conventions of *cinéma vérité* rather than those of classic narrative to tell its Truth. But, as Warren Beatty cynically (or so he thinks) remarks, 'Everything she does is for the camera.' Madonna's *vérité* documentary, shot by Richard Leacock, turns the 'truth' of her desire into a staged dare. One premiss of direct cinema is that, eventually, even the most polished public figures will unmask themselves in private and, like Humphrey and Kennedy during the grueling hours of the Wisconsin primary, give us a glimpse of their doubts, exhaustion, or temper. But Madonna never relaxes her guard. When the camera rolls, she acts. Always performing, always changing hair color, costume, make-up, her body also produces visual evidence of change. But what inner transformations follow her chameleon-like maneuvers? The same manipulations of cinematic language that reconciled inside and outside for Spike Lee's Malcolm are undercut by Madonna's savvy manipulations of the medium and its genres. Her documentary truth is as constructed as Spike Lee's fictional history *Malcolm X*. Both these films (and their makers) are highly conscious of their place in the cinematic, political, racial, and sexual histories of twentieth-century America, and they play to our knowledge about these histories, but they can do so because the two modes of address – *cinéma vérité* and narrative – rely on similar logics and conventions to tell their truths.

But what does this long digression say about the subject of agency, who I claim as the spectator of the historical or more typically the political documentary? What kind of film creates the conditions for his/her possibility? By the subject of agency, on the most simplistic level, I mean that a film produces more than the 'desire to desire,' as Mary Ann Doane suggests is typical of melodrama; it calls its audience to action. This reaction was precisely what Bertolt Brecht claimed for his epic theater. His form called for rejecting the Aristotelian imperatives for catharsis and closure by pushing the audience through discontinuous and disjointed effects to discomfort, and eventually thought and action. Agitprop relies on agitation *and* propaganda – first stir people up, make them jittery, and then give them a message. This pattern was beautifully employed in Pare Lorentz's two great films from the 1930s, *The Plow That Broke the Plains* (1936) and *The River* (1937), both financed by Federal money and intended to inspire widespread public support for rural electrification and the Tennessee Valley Authority, respectively, and the New Deal in general.[31] Yet like their more recent heirs, these documentaries inspire emotional responses akin to classic melodrama. 'A film like *Union Maids*,' says Ruth McCormick, 'very likely owes its popularity to the fact that it appeals to the heart more than the head.'[32]

The historical documentary not only tells us about the past, but asks us to do something about it as well – to act as the Angel of History and redeem the present through the past. This seems clear when the film also has an explicitly political agenda, like Barry Brown and Glenn Silber's 1980 film, *The War at Home*, which was made to release the four men accused of bombing the Army Math Building at University of Wisconsin from jail. However, even Ken Burns's seemingly balanced PBS film, *The Civil War* (1990), which presents the words and images of other times, other places, to show the horrors of war, wants us to remember (and remember in a certain, nostalgic way), which as Benjamin insists, is also a political act. The spectator of documentary, this subject of agency, also desires, but desires to remember and remake history. But how is this spectator hailed by the documentary if the psychosexual processes of identification and disavowal central to classical narrative address are routed away from interiority and located in evidence? Primarily through an appeal to feeling.

To mark the twentieth anniversary of 'America's leading magazine on the art and politics of the cinema,' film-maker and *Cineaste* editor Dan Georgakas cites a number of unsettling trends in contemporary radical documentaries that have corrupted through cliché the efficacy of political film-making. Despite the rich revival of the American political documentary between the 1960s (starting with Emile de Antonio's *Point of Order* (1964) on the Army–McCarthy hearings) and the late 1980s, Georgakas believes that radical films have 'indulged intellectual shortcuts or persisted in techniques blunted by overuse.'[33] Often, he charges, what begins as a stylistic innovation quickly hardens into convention and cliché as film after film juxtaposes talking heads with archival footage to show up the naiveté of the past, or compiles out-of-context footage in quick montages without acknowledging the complexities undergirding the original sources. Georgakas's complaints about the content of political documentaries were echoed by critics centered on the British film journal *Screen*, influenced by Brecht and Althusser, who challenged film's formal complicity with bourgeois ideologies lodged in realism.[34]

For instance, Georgakas is particularly critical of Connie Fields' film *The Life and Times of Rosie the Riveter* (1980) for its failure to address a number of crucial issues: that in the 1940s many women believed they were entering the workforce temporarily; that the majority of 'Rosies' were white ethnics from northern cities or southern white Protestants; that at least two of the women featured were members of the Communist Party of the United States of America. Fields interviewed over seven hundred women before she settled on the five who comprise her portrait of Rosie. These women – Jewish, black, Asian-American – were hardly typical; but more importantly, their presentation of the struggles they led within unions and against management gives the impression that they were simply strong, independent women. While this is an appealing impression to impart to young women who are the audience for the film (it is a staple of women's studies courses), it also diminishes the significance of political organizations in conducting campaigns on behalf of workers, women, and minorities.

Julia Reichert and Jim Klein's film *Seeing Red*, like many American films about explicitly radical movements in America – *The Wobblies*, *The Good Fight*, *Union Maids* – plays down the conflicts and contradictions experienced by the participants within these movements. Instead, we hear the stories of a group of elderly men and women who are presented as appealing old people giving a sanitized version of radicalism in general, and the CPUSA in particular.[35] All these films rely on a form of oral history to propel their narratives. The talking head holds a tremendous authority on screen, especially when she counters traditional mystifications about past history.[36] Yet talking heads, despite signifying truthfulness, can only tell a partial truth. 'From a historian's point of view,' writes Sonya Michel,

> these privileged subjects can become problematic if a film limits its perspective by relying on them as sole or even primary informants. While oral history subjects are frequently both engaging and uniquely informative, their accounts of historical events or periods can be partial, fragmentary, idiosyncratic and sometimes – deliberately or unintentionally – misleading.[37]

Testimony is always a partial truth, so when film-makers authorize their subjects to speak and thus provoke their audiences to act, it can only be a supplementary gesture toward truth. Yet the 'political' documentary often fails to register this, presenting, like the ethnographer, the appearance of 'wholeness.' And so its call to a subject of agency depends on the psychosexual cinematic conventions of narrative desire.

III

Claude Lanzmann's 1985 9 hour 23 minute epic documentary of remembrance, *Shoah*, traces the annihilation of Europe's Jews without recourse to the visual artifacts of the holocaust. In this, both the form and content of historical documentary are challenged. In fact, Lanzmann rejects the designation of documentary film altogether. *Shoah*, he insists, is 'art' because only art can ask the questions of history and memory his film attempts to answer. What is the place of visual and audio records in an event whose purpose was to erase all evidence of its occurrence? For Lanzmann, the fundamental problem is constructing evidence where no documents exist.

    Shoah reimagines the relationship of viewer to film, and of history to documentary, by producing a historical document without references. Lanzmann makes visible the unseen, the witnessing of an event without witness, through speech: the purpose of the extermination camp was not only to annihilate a people, but to erase the evidence of its existence, to deny the power of looking and of telling. Lanzmann lets us look at the grass-covered remains of the crematoria and the faces of those once there; he prods his subjects to tell what their eyes looked on forty years before: sights no one should ever have seen, sights never meant to be seen or spoken of, because the observers were meant to die. Lanzmann's film asks much of its audience but far less than he demands of his subjects, who reluctantly bare themselves before his camera because they understand their words are themselves documents, or as he calls them, incarnations. In *Shoah*, the weight of evidence lies in the spoken word and its ability to evoke visual memory as the foundations of historical justice. It is the differing testimonies of the three 'actors' of his film (and of the holocaust) – its victims, the surviving Jews; its perpetrators, the Nazis; and its bystanders, the Poles – about what they did and did not *see* which forms the document itself and implicates the viewer in historical remembrance.[38] In his insistence on the primacy of the voice, Lanzmann pushes the historical documentary beyond the limits of visualization; it is not necessary actually to look at the footage of the extermination camps, it is enough, he says, to look at those who have looked and to hear their emotional testimony.[39]

Partly because of its recognition of the fragmentary quality of truth, a recognition inscribed in its address rather than orchestrated through its form, *Shoah* interrogates the documentary project. At one point in Lanzmann's saga, Raul Hilberg, the renowned historian of the holocaust, reads a document, the *Fahrplananordnung 587* for a railway transport to Treblinka from various ghettos in Poland. This 'document' is the trace of ten thousand dead Jews. Framed against a lovely, snow-covered scene outside his Vermont window, Hilberg gives a lesson in reading, in the semiotics of historical analysis, and so guides us in the practice of Lanzmann's film. Reading for absences as much as presences, Hilberg discerns that this piece of paper represents all that is left of more than ten thousand men, women, and children whose lives were lost and whose accumulated wealth, seized by the Nazis, paid for their final journey to death. Reading absences, traces, and supplements, the historian and documentarian become deconstructors, who take apart the lack of the historical record and in the process refashion new historical narratives.

Lanzmann provides lessons about the meaning of documents for history. By pushing the various speakers to disclose memories never before revealed, Lanzmann demonstrates that documents themselves must be constructed. Lanzmann badgers his witnesses into disclosing that which they would prefer to forget; perhaps the most painful scene occurs when the barber Abraham Bomba, whose job at Treblinka was to cut women's hair in preparation for the gas chamber, breaks down in tears and asks Lanzmann to stop filming. Lanzmann has come to hear Bomba's tale in the Israeli barber shop where he still cuts hair, the camera zooms in close on Bomba's face as he tries to evade the lens; Lanzmann softly prods him to continue against his will.[40] In so doing, he implicates himself and his audience in the retrieval of forgotten knowledge; we are collaborators in its loss if we let these painful memories remain secret, but we are guilty of invasions of privacy if we insist on knowing. What are the limits of privacy when one's life experience contributed to the making of world-historical events and one's recollections their only substantial evidence? Hilberg's Vermont study provides a respite from the horrible memories of the survivors, the perverse denials of the Poles, the lies of the Nazis, the incessant chugging of train wheels. The horrible ordinariness of this railway order becomes a record of erasure; its normality exceeds and unlocks the event for the careful reader, the attentive listener. Lanzmann is fascinated by Hilberg's accounting:

> '*But why is this document so fascinating, as a matter of fact? Because I was in Treblinka, and to have the two things together . . .*
>
> 'Well, you see, when I hold a document in my hand, particularly if it's an original document, then I hold something which is actually something that the original bureaucrat held in his hand. It's an artifact. It's a leftover. It's the only leftover there is. The dead are not around . . .'[41]

Hilberg's lesson comes late in the film. For much of the first few hours, like the Jews during the first years of the Final Solution, the audience remains confused. What happened in Chelmno? Who can be trusted? As the circle tightens around Auschwitz and the other extermination camps, truth is inescapable: death everywhere; survival becomes evidence. So when Filip Muller's Czech compatriots from Theresienstadt are finally pushed into the gas chambers, singing the Czech national anthem and the *Hatikvah*, he chooses to join them. But a woman who recognizes him tells him to leave: 'You must get out of here alive. You must bear witness to our suffering . . .' (p. 165). In the final sequence, Simha Rotten, known as 'Kajik,' recalls his return to Warsaw the day after the uprising: 'I was alone throughout my tour of the ghetto. I didn't meet a living soul. At one point I recall feeling a kind of peace, of serenity. I said to myself: "I'm the last Jew. I'll wait for morning and for the Germans" '(p. 200).

'Made against its own possibility,' because the holocaust was 'not only the destruction of a people, but a destruction of the destruction,' *Shoah* itself becomes a historical document. The 'Jews in the film don't talk for themselves; they are spokespeople for the dead.' The survivors never describe how they survived, rarely use the pronoun 'I'; they speak as 'we,' speak not for themselves but for the dead whose voices rise up from the landscape. This is the importance of the multiple languages and levels of interpretation and translation that are woven through the film: 'A film without a mother tongue; a film with broken language,' a film refusing totality and visuality. The film records 'the look of those who have seen' but not what they have seen. It is an artifact against the erasure of history, of the 'artifacts,' as Raul Hilberg calls them, the traces of an event whose purpose was to erase its own record. Lanzmann calls the film 'an incarnation . . . an experience,' refusing to see it as archival – for him it is a highly *constructed*, physical act, a movement over time and space which will make us 'the contemporaries of *their* deaths,' forcing us to endure, something denied those killed in the death camps.[42]

Lanzmann's role as interrogator, as witness, as translator, as occasion for the deciphering of the traces of a history under erasure, is also an occasion for the examination of the place of the historian and film-maker in history and documentary. Lanzmann's refusal to use the by now clichéd images of the camps recorded by the SS themselves or by the Allies after liberation gestures to their lack. These images of genocide cannot begin to reveal the stories of death and survival locked in the survivors' memories. The filmed images from the camps have become cultural icons, their very familiarity a memento of their emptiness. Rather, it is the word 'Treblinka' naming a railway depot that holds the powers of horror, to use Kristeva's phrase. At this place of death the train still stops.

The station placard, like Lanzmann's film, demands that we rethink the use and meaning of voices and images. His travels through the landscapes of Europe to see again the movement of those who looked before cautions us about our use of the images we receive from the past. As Hilberg says, they are leftovers, still nourishing, but hardly fresh. *Shoah* asks that we deconstruct the documentary images left us from the holocaust and instead hear the voices of the survivors who implore us to become the contemporaries of the dead and so give them their history.

Jill Godmilow, director of *Far From Poland* (1984), calls for 'deconstructing the documentary . . . to reformulate language – not just verbal language but visual language as well. To poke holes in the existing language, to make spaces, so that there is a possibility for imagination and action to work through it.'[43] Her experience of making *Far From Poland*, a staged documentary about Solidarity made wholly in the United States, forced her to rethink the codes of documentary address – codes which naturalize the world, make sense of it, and reinforce its social relations by smoothing out contradictions. The desire to make 'something that satisfies as *film experience* – in terms of length, interest, rhythm, moral dilemma, characterizations of good and bad, etc.' she says, 'can't dream. It can't provoke imagination.'[44]

This desire to dream, to provoke imagination, seems to lead the documentary away from the realm of history and truth and into the realm of art and artifice. How are we to judge historical documentaries if they call themselves dreams? In documentary, the viewer is asked to participate in a series of contracts – between film and its object, between film-maker and audience, between reality and representation. In the traditional documentary, the response to the film is usually confined to whether the viewer agrees or disagrees with the content. On rare occasions the 'protagonist' of the film succeeds in convincing the viewer to follow its position – save the dolphins by boycotting tuna, for example – but the construction of the cinematic argument is left unexamined. In deconstructionist documentaries such as *Shoah* and *Far From Poland*, the object of the film is to produce a new and disturbing knowledge of history and of its rhetoric – of both its content and its form. Like the Angel of History, we are asked to become complicit in the process of making meaning, of making history. We are made uncomfortable, not by images of appealing dolphins bleeding on the deck of the tuna boat or by the emaciated limbs and swollen bellies of hungry children in Somalia, but by the codes which give those images the power to make us say 'Oh, how awful,' and go on about our lives.

Godmilow says that before working on *Far From Poland* she could not imagine how a documentary could escape the limits of *vérité*, archival footage, and testimony. In *Far From Poland*, she recreates and fictionalizes Solidarity and her and others' reactions to it, and in so doing calls up a myriad of responses to the movement, depending on one's relationship to its image, its ideas, and their re-enactment; it's a playful manipulation of the medium and the message.

Lanzmann pushes the limits of committed documentary with a brutality that forces us not only to listen to the evasions of the Poles who saw, the denials of the Nazis who acted, and the memories of the Jews who survived, but to his stake in divulging the truth. When he chastises his Polish translator for blunting the edge of his questions, we sense a curious reconfiguring of moral value; his pursuit of the truth of history becomes a personal attack on her decency. He forces us to witness the extremes of documentary probing; after seeing this film it is impossible naively to accept documentary truths as innocent disclosures – we know that they are pried from reluctant sources. Still, Walter Benjamin would remind us that 'every image of the past that is not recognized by the present as one of its concerns threatens to disappear irretrievably.'[45] *Shoah* instructs its audience about the workings of the Final Solution from the perspective of its victims, an impossible task because they cannot testify. The men and few women who speak can only tell what *they* saw – a broken picture told in a broken language.[46] The film forces its viewers to consider our desire for historical truths, our complicity in constructing historical narratives, our investment in the historical present; as such it calls forth our subjectivities as historical agents: looking and listening are also historical acts.

PART I

Pictures of Poverty

2

Voyeurism and Class Consciousness:

James Agee and Walker Evans Praise

Famous Men

. . . the age of Photography corresponds precisely to the explosion of the private into the public, or rather into the creation of a new social value, which is the publicity of the private: the private is consumed as such, publicly . . .

(Roland Barthes, *Camera Lucida*)

Photography is dumb.

(Martha Rosler, *Three Works*)

If one takes Barthes at his word, then all the comfortable categories by which we have theorized gender, history, and representation – such as the capitalist separation of the spheres of production and reproduction, the public and private, political and domestic, masculine and feminine – disappear at the very moment of their inception. By bringing the images of daily life and ordinary people into public view, photography remakes vision and in so doing produces (or reproduces) new forms of (class) consciousness.

I am fascinated by the photographic image, by what I can see of the world, its people, and their objects, but also by what those images let me see of myself. Looking at photographs is both a transgressive and comfortable act – difference is domesticated, brought home for inspection, open to critique, but the everyday is also glaringly made strange, remarking on one's own position even as another's life is revealed. This chapter explores the interrelationship between looking and power, or more technically, between voyeurism and class consciousness, and the implications this link has for radical intellectuals like myself who inhabit yet challenge bourgeois culture. I believe the history of photography, which argues about the photograph's impre-cise status between art and document, mirrors the troubling relation-ship of the leftist intellectual and her objects of knowledge – often cultures and classes different from her own. Because it distinguishes observer from observed, yet brings the two into intimate contact, the photograph embodies this contradiction but seems unable to enter the realm of political effectivity. Is this also true of the radical intellectual?

As histories of bourgeois subjectivity, both photographic documents and personal narratives are intimately linked, each indicating middle-class normality through absence. The photograph, revealing the lack of material objects in the lives of the poor, affirms by contrast the abundance of its viewer; the case study, revealing the lack of coherence in the neurotic's story, affirms by contrast the health of the well-plotted life.[1] Composed of photographs and narrative, *Let Us Now Praise Famous Men*, James Agee's and Walker Evans's Depression era repor-tage of 'the daily living' of three Southern tenant families, transforms their documentary project 'to recognize the stature of a portion of unimagined existence' into an uncanny history of middle-class percep-tion and its relationship to the powers and pleasures of looking at others. The complicity between readers and authors in the con-struction of a social order that can find no place for 'an appallingly damaged group of people,' except 'a soft place in their hearts,' pro-duces a text that challenges us to refuse its authority and break our expectations;[2] yet its post-1960s emergence as a 'genuine American classic' according to the cover blurb demands that we reread it to discover what else we observe of ourselves and others in it.

Agee's 'printed words' and Evans's 'motionless camera' produce the power of the gaze as a sexual and class practice. *Let Us Now Praise Famous Men* links the construction of the gaze – as a relationship of bourgeois subject to its object – and the mobilization of class conscious-ness – as the resistance of that reified object to its history. In so doing, James Agee and Walker Evans express and critique their uneasy relationship to each other and to their objects of knowledge, shedding light on the connections between the psychosexual desires and political effectiveness of people like myself.

In order to make my argument, an argument that crosses a number of boundaries – between print and photography, reportage and theory – that the scene of class domination is the same as the scene of voyeur-ism, both depending on an (unspoken) desire of the object of the bourgeois subject's knowledge repossessing her power in difference, I bring together a curious array of characters. They inhabit the nine-teenth and twentieth centuries, British and American cultures, Marxist and Freudian theories, and literary and art histories. I set up an imaginary conversation between Walter Benjamin, Georg Lukács, and Sigmund Freud on classed vision. Arthur Munby, James Agee, and Louise Gudger talk about the female subject, further marginalized by childhood and poverty. In much the same way that Carolyn Steedman juxtaposes Dora's case history with the story of the watercress girl in *Landscape for a Good Woman*, by defying geographical, temporal, and class boundaries, these 'conversations' enable each voice to speak over and against those already speaking for and about the others. Trinh T. Minh-ha suggests that the 'conversation of man with man' is always a 'conversation of "us" with "us" about "them".'[3] Agee's and Evans's text bears this out, but it also indicates the moments of resistance when their objects defy them, challenge them, and reverse the gaze to produce another form of consciousness.

Lukács's theory of class consciousness contains, especially in his outline of bourgeois perception, an analysis of documentary photography that parallels that of Walter Benjamin, while Freud's discussions of scopophilia reveal class(ed) consciousness. In nineteenth-century Britain, Arthur Munby kept diaries and photographs to remember his encounters with poor and working-class women and girls. These records historicize the tensions Agee and Evans express as committed artists in twentieth-century America. Munby's comments about Ellen Grounds's large 'size' and Rat Man's 'curiosity' about his governess's undergarments tell us much about why Louise Gudger's 'paralyzing eyes' so disturb Agee. A reading of Agee's and Evans's text, which stands as a paradigmatic instance of the problems intellectuals face when they search out and describe their social others, tells much about the limits and possibilities of the documentary project.

I

Both the subject and object of its proper knowledge . . .
(Lukács, *History and Class Consciousness*)

That the invention of photography coincides with the rise of commodity culture and serves as evidence of it, Walter Benjamin, the most astute theorist of photography, has made clear. Like the commodity itself, and the woman within commodity culture, photography's contribution to fabricating a society of the spectacle is dual – photographs are themselves objects of the gaze as well as purveyors of images. The relations of looking and being looked at while deeply implicated in the construction of sexual and gender positions always reveal class markers on bodies; moreover, the visual manifestations of class position also depict bourgeois constructions of sexuality. The photographic image reinforces bourgeois culture even when it seeks to expose its damaging effects as in the case of documentary photographs that reveal 'How the Other Half Lives.' Yet these objects – the classed, sexed, and gendered bodies of visual imagery – have the power to hold the gaze of their viewers; they are produced by *and* produce the 'political unconscious' of middle-class culture.

Drawing connections between visual culture and bourgeois subjectivity, Georg Lukács's 1921 adumbration of Marx's theories of commodity fetishism, 'Reification and the Consciousness of the Proletariat' published in *History and Class Consciousness*, whose title furnishes the basis for this chapter, articulates the processes of class differentiation. For Lukács, class consciousness within the proletariat is dependent on the working class's ability to *see* itself as object and subject simultaneously. Reification produces a 'doubling of personality . . . splitting up of men into an element of the movement of commodities and an (objective and impotent) *observer* of that movement.'[4] Bourgeois culture is fundamentally a specular culture – a culture of 'the [passive] observer of society' whose 'contemplative' stance is incapable of overcoming the 'antinomies' of reification through the 'practical.'[5]

For Lukács, the only resource the proletariat has in the face of bourgeois hegemony of 'knowledge, culture and routine' is its 'ability to *see* the social totality . . . to *see* the reified forms as processes between men; to *see* the immanent meaning of history . . . raise it to consciousness and put it into practice.'[6] The proletariat must 'adopt its own point of view' based on its 'place in society' vis-à-vis the 'perceiving subject' of bourgeois culture.[7] As a class that embodies the subject and object simultaneously, its coming into consciousness marks a potential break with the culture of spectatorship, producing revolutionary praxis, according to Lukács's hopeful predictions. But Lukács's attention to the culture of the specular reveals the limits of class-conscious vision as outlined in Marxist theory. What we come to understand as class consciousness from Lukács is not how it develops, but rather how it is expressed within commodity culture.[8] Like the failure of the camera to produce a social critique because 'it can only re-present the visible . . . it cannot show, but only refer to, social forces,' the commodity cannot disclose its own emergence.[9] The learning process of class consciousness comes from the proletariat's own understanding of itself as a commodity and producer of commodities simultaneously. But where does that leave those outside the process of commodity production – women, children, or the tenant farmers Agee and Evans document?

Without a theory of the transmission of class consciousness from one generation to the next, from one gender to the other, Lukács's visualized proletariat enters fully formed into the structures of social processes as adult and male through commodity production. But there is more to the working class than that. For instance, vision as a psychosocial process also structures both sexual and gender relations, and it does so within the child so that the awareness of difference is first mapped through an awareness of generational difference. The consciousness of the proletariat, then, is little more than the rearticulation of bourgeois culture, the first instance of which already takes place as every (middle-class) child passes through early childhood.

Thus at this point we might turn to Freud to understand how Lukács's theory of class consciousness entangles seeing and knowing in ways similar to those suggested by Freud's linkage of scopophilia to epistemophilia, and as such participates in the consolidation of bourgeois ideologies of class. Freud argued that the constituent ego instincts – scopophilia, the pleasure in looking; and epistemophilia, the pleasure in knowing – were linked to the 'cruelty instinct' which is expressed actively as sadism – the desire to master. Scopophilia, epistemophilia, and the desire to master as ego instincts depend on social relations – I look *at* some object or that object looks *at* me – and produce narratives – my looking, knowing, and mastering suggest a development of my ego.

Freud's discussions of voyeurism, the 'perverse' form of scopophilia, are most fully elaborated in his case study of an obsessional neurosis, otherwise known as the Rat Man case. The Rat Man's story begins as he recounts his earliest 'sexual life' characterized as a 'scene' in which he '[crept] under [the] skirt' of his governess and fingered her genitals. 'After this,' he says, 'I was left with a burning and tormenting curiosity to see the female body.' Each time his governess took him and his sisters to the baths, he would await the moment when she undressed to 'appease my curiosity.'[10] In his discussion of the analysis of the Rat Man, Freud observes that 'the histories of obsessional patients almost invariably reveal an early development and premature repression of the sexual instinct of looking and knowing . . .'[11] While Freud fails to register the significance of just what the Rat Man is looking at – his servant's body – he does link the Rat Man's obsessive behavior after his father's death to his ambivalence about his father's wealth and his premarital sexual interest in a woman of 'humble means,' as well as his own sexual desire for his father. In addition to the homoerotic component of looking, Freud intuited the class-based significance of the scopophilic instinct and its perverse manifestation, voyeurism, late in his writings. He cryptically notes that it is not only 'in proletarian

39

families that it is perfectly possible for a child . . . to be a witness of the sexual act between his parents.'[12] But, he stresses, usually among his middle-class patients the memory of parental intercourse is coded in such a way as to reveal its origin in fantasy and in the passive form of scopophilia: the desire to be looked at. The presumption here seems to indicate that among the poor and working classes, it is quite common for the child to see sexual intercourse because children sleep in the same room, even the same bed, as their parents.

I think this single sentence opens up Freud's theories about voyeurism to a class analysis. For the Rat Man, whose 'curiosity' begins as he looks under his governess's skirts, sexuality depends as much on class as on anatomical differences. Perhaps, then, economic circumstances produce a different experience of seeing and knowing (for) the child of poverty. This difference becomes crucial to James Agee as he documents the lives of the three tenant families.

Active and passive looking implicitly reveal masculine and feminine subject positions in Freud's analysis. Yet they also suggest other differential relations, particularly those coded as class differences, as, I believe Freud's gesture toward class awareness indicates.[13] In other words, Freud's theories of sexuality, because they represent a classed sexuality, are also a theory of class. Lukács's depiction of proletarian consciousness as one that 'serves and observes' commodities (including itself as a commodity) connects the simultaneity of the subject/object position to that of the photographic image and so to scopophilia, linking it to a theory of ego development and sexual differentiation.[14] As such, it also undermines its own intuition about the potential for working-class revolution.

Admittedly, I am making much of the fragmentary inferences in Freud's nod to a class-based sexuality and Lukács's glimpse of a specularly based class consciousness. But these nods and glimpses provide the background for my look at voyeurism through James Agee's prose and Evans's photographs in *Let Us Now Praise Famous Men*. Their text, which celebrates, exposes, perpetuates, and challenges the gendered, classed, (and at points) racial disparities organizing not only vision and narrative, but political and economic relations in Depression America, attempts to circumvent generic boundaries separating text from image, fiction from documentary, 'the people' from the self. Their attempts to write other stories, encode other images, than those of either sadism or revolution indicate their discomfort (and mine) with their subjectivity as they try to open up a space in which the objects of their political desire resist their imaging and inscription.[15] Like me, Agee constructs his position as a voyeur – a 'spy,' a 'bodyless eye,' an 'alien' – yet those he looks at look back at him. The voyeur, like the radical intellectual, needs its objects *and* their resistance, and it is in this double knowledge, as Lukács noted, that the other holds the potential to revise the terms of power.

But before I turn to *Let Us Now Praise Famous Men*, I want to begin, as all discussions of middle-class consciousness must, in nineteenth-century Britain with the diary and photograph collection of Arthur J. Munby. Munby's catalog of the clothing and work habits, speech patterns and countenances of the working women he spied crossing London Bridge or walking the lanes of Wigan are tinged with nostalgia, desire, and transference. His position as a middle-class man afforded him access to approach and inspect these women. His 'curiosity' is driven by sexual and class differences – seeing them he must know them, knowing them he must own them, in the form of their images and stories, which he keeps in his collection and diary. Following the conventions of nineteenth-century domesticity, Munby's desires are kept secret; they represent a private arrangement he strikes with members of the working class. His diary and collection speak to and serve personal desire even as they endorse and encode political and economic power. The writings and images from the 1930s, however, moved personal literary and visual expressions into the public realm as they attempted to document, record, and ultimately, change the world.

Munby's private observations of working women in London, Wigan, and throughout continental Europe nevertheless served as documentary evidence for labor reformers eager to restrict women's work. His search for young working women, as well as his curious relationship with Hannah Cullwick – his servant and wife – who often posed for photographers dressed in the garb of a variety of working men and women, however, served his own desire to seek a 'completeness of relief . . . after London life' in a 'new world chatting with rough hearty men, rough hearty wenches; treated by all as an equal, hearing their broad salient speech and speaking it too as far as I can do so . . .'[16]

Social reformers like Henry Mayhew in Britain or Lewis Hine in the United States explored the dark caverns of working-class quarters ostensibly to expose and better their conditions. However Munby's work, like Agee's after him, comes out of a personal connection with his subjects. He went to Wigan to live among the 'pit broo wenches,' he posed with them and posed them for his collection of photographs and *cartes de visite* picked up in his travels across Britain. On 10 September 1873 he writes:

> I reached Wigan . . . and walked up Scholes, the main street of the colliers' quarter of Wigan, to call on Ellen Grounds, the nearest of my friends, and

learn from her the news of the pits . . . . Then we talked about being 'drawed aht.' Ellen said she had been 'drawed aht' twice 'i' my pit claes', and has seen her own picture hanging up for sale. It is not good however . . . . So Ellen promised to come tomorrow in her pit clothes to Wigan market-place . . . . The only question was, whether she should come with a black face or a clean one. She observed that one often looks just as well with a black face and I left the point to her discretion; but asked to see her working dress . . . . Ellen went upstairs and came down again with her trousers over her arm . . . a pair of trousers made up of various colors, but toned down by coaldust to blackish brown. They were warmly lined and wadded, especially at the knees, to protect them when kneeling among coals or crawling up the shoot; a garment well fitted to keep warm the legs of a woman doing outside work. And (which spoke well for the fair wearer) the *inside* of the trousers was clean . . . .'[17]

Munby's interest in Ellen's clothes may have a more prurient sound to it than Agee's near-religious ecstasy at the Cézanne blues of the overalls worn by the tenant farmers (or Evans's art historical quotation of Van Gogh's *Les Soulières*), but at least Munby asked to inspect the articles. Agee's surreptitious inspection of the Gudgers' possessions, which he likens to masturbating in his grandfather's house, leaves him unable to look them in the eye. But Munby proudly poses with Ellen he says, to 'show how nearly she approached me in size' (Figure 1).

In conventional left-wing iconography – for instance, John Sloan's *Masses* prints – it is the bourgeois woman who controls the bodies of working-class women through her gaze. The bourgeoisie as 'passive observer' is represented as female, whose position of moral superiority is bought with her access to social and economic power, while the proletariat by virtue of this logic is of necessity male. The structural position of the worker within commodity culture is feminized; but the Left's metaphors of gender insist on his virility. This masculinized worker can overcome the 'antinomies' of reification. In this configuration, however, the working-class woman can appear only as a prostitute (as sex worker) and the bourgeois male drops from sight. Innocent of the violence of the gaze, his eyes are elsewhere.

Thus Munby's collection of *cartes de visite* presents a catalog of the curious – the phenomenon of the working woman in an era when bourgeois femininity demanded that women shrink from performing heavy labor. What makes these working women so interesting to Munby, aside from their masculine dress, is their obvious pleasure in their strength, in their bodies, in their occupations. He records a conversation with a 'trotter scraper,' and marvels that mucking around in offal has not affected her desirability. Munby's phantasma of virile femininity and his ability to control its depiction surely represent one of the most extreme examples of the collusion between the visual dimension of class difference and voyeurism as its sexualized expression. What I want to argue, and why I have enlisted Munby in my argument, is that this slippage between class power and sexual knowledge operates again and again in the documentaries using image and text to reveal 'the other half.'

II

Participation and observation are socially inevitable lines of conduct . . .
(Lukács, 'Idea and Form in Literature')

According to Lionel Trilling, 1930s cultural expressions in the United States were marked by a 'social consciousness' that often was 'without fiber and contradiction,' because it drew its energy 'too much from the drawing room' and its sentiment from 'a pity which wonderfully served the needs of the pitier.'[18] In his 1942 review of *Let Us Now Praise Famous Men*, Trilling was distinguishing the recently published 'photo-textual documentary book,' as John Puckett calls it, from most of the reportage of the 1930s.[19] However, by 1941, the year it and Richard Wright's *12 Million Black Voices* was published (and the United States entered the Second World War), this form, and more importantly the concerns it embraced, no longer held the liberal imagination. Both the form and its concerns depended on the extraordinary achievements of Roy Stryker's Historical Section of the Farm Security Administration (FSA). This agency sent photographers across America (but primarily to the South and Midwest) to document the devastation wreaked on rural America by the economic and climatological disasters of the 1930s in order to persuade Congress to implement many of the New Deal's agricultural programs. However, in 1930s America, documentary photography, which was institutionalized by the Federal government, effaced its politics. At most, Roy Stryker's 'shooting scripts' asked Dorothea Lange in 1936 for 'some good slum pictures in the San Francisco area . . . . Do not forget that we need some of the rural slum type of thing, as well as the urban'; and by 1940 demanded of Jack Delano 'autumn pictures . . . cornfields, pumpkins . . . . Emphasize the idea of abundance – the "horn of plenty" – and pour maple syrup over it – you know mix well with white clouds and put on a sky-blue platter.'[20]

Despite or because of this, Evans insisted that his work could build a 'record' but with 'NO POLITICS whatever.'[21] Evans seems to be resisting the bureaucratic maneuverings of New Dealism, but also safekeeping his status as artist. Nevertheless, the project to record initiated by the FSA *was* political and instrumental; it sought social change. Stryker's team needed to provide evidence of the brutalizing conditions of rural poverty to ensure that the programs instituted by the New Deal would continue; but they also needed to create arresting images, icons that could enter and alter cultural memory.[22] Of course, the history of photography is fraught with disagreements about its status – tensions between photography as art and as record, between posed versus candid images, over public versus private ownership – precisely because the photograph represents a commodified and reproducible form.[23]

These tensions represent some of the same ones animating leftist discussions of the newly emerging genre of reportage. As a form that sought to overcome the divisions between literature and history, private thought and public action, subjectivity and objectivity, reportage appeared to overcome the contradictions literary radicals felt between their position as intellectuals and their allegiance to the working class. American Marxist criticism of the 1930s unproblematically celebrated reportage as *the* genre best suited to reproduce the proletarian realism first advocated by Michael Gold.[24] Reportage seemed to provide the seamless melding of culture and politics, intellectual and proletarian, observer and participant, art and ideology, called for in much of the criticism.[25] Through its first-person narrative the reader was placed in the middle of unfolding events, seeing them through the eyes of the narrator as directly as possible.

Typically, reportage foregrounds a rather ecstatic voice of an 'I' who proclaims a presence, a self, an identity, that is directly connected to 'the people.' This 'I' generally gives way, toward the end of the piece, to the more utopian and less conventional pronoun 'we,' drawing the reader into direct contact through the narrator with the masses. Richard Wright's *12 Million Black Voices*, however, employs the 'we' throughout. The story of black migration North is of course also his story, one that becomes subsumed within that of the masses. But in a more typical piece, journalist and revolutionary, Agnes Smedley, begins 'The People of China,' simply: 'I rode from the village and town through Fan Chang district.' First, Smedley conveys her authenticity as an observer through statements such as 'I saw many thousands of children growing into manhood and womanhood during the war in mental darkness.' She saw; but moreover, she interpreted what she saw. Then she recounts her increasing participation in the struggle through her own suffering as she lives under constant artillery fire and contracts malaria. Finally, the eye of the journalist and the I of the revolutionary merge with her subject so that Smedley becomes part of the masses when 'we ate bitterness.'[26] This movement from eye/I to we coded quite neatly the ideal transition from middle-class intellectual to class-conscious historical actor needed to create the revolution in writing and in practice. Presumably, if one read enough of these accounts, one would be moved off the couch and into the street as well. However, as Trilling noted in his review of *Let Us Now Praise Famous Men*, guilt, pity, and sentimentality were more often the result.

In 1932, Georg Lukács had condemned proletarian literature in general because the mechanical fetishization of the fact served as a petit-bourgeois compensatory gesture toward objectivity but was really just another form of the overly subjective psychological novel.[27] Lukács's analysis might have formed the core of Trilling's review ten years later. For both critics what seems most appalling about the literature of social consciousness was its embarrassingly self-serving disclosures, its desire to appease the guilt of the left-wing intellectual in the face of depression, fascism, and working-class militancy. For Lukács, genuine reportage never 'simply depicts' the facts, but 'always presents a connection, discloses causes and proposes consequences.' Reportage caught a moment, fixed a particular case, and drew from its typicality an analysis of the larger social relations containing it. The realist novel, by contrast, 'portrayed' totality in its sweeping dialectical movement between subject and object, form and content. Lukács opposed a mechanically objective fiction, what he called 'the reportage novel,' because of its 'fetishistic dismemberment of reality . . . [its] inability to see relations between people (class relations) in the "things" of social life,' i.e. its complicity with commodity culture.[28]

Walter Benjamin also denounced the work produced by the New Objectivity writers and photographers for their 'New Matter of Fact-ness.' According to Benjamin's reading, this genre commodified class struggle and so 'has made the struggle against poverty an object of consumption' for its mostly bourgeois audience. For all these critics, reportage could never overcome its conditions of production because even when it was conscious of its class alignment, it still 'fail[ed] to alienate the productive apparatus from the ruling class.'[29] Eventually, Robert Warshow would complain that reportage, in fact virtually the entire culture of the Left in the 1930s, tended 'to distort and eventually destroy the emotional and moral content of experience, putting in its place a system of conventionalized "responses".'[30] Anti-Stalinist critic of popular culture Warshow glimpses a horror not so much at the contamination of genres (as did Lukács) nor at the contamination of intellectuals (as did Benjamin), but at the debasement and contamination of authentic 'experience' itself (as if, paradoxically, 1930s literary radicalism was in fact the first instance of the postmodern condition).[31]

III

> an appallingly damaged group of people . . .
> (James Agee, *Let Us Now Praise Famous Men*)

In many ways, James Agee and Walker Evans's *Let Us Now Praise Famous Men* strives to produce that 'authenticity' so lacking in reportage.[32] Appearing as a quintessentially postmodern text – mixing genres, forms, and discourses, circling back obsessively on its grammar, empowering yet resisting language and image[33] – this 'classic of the thirties' documentary genre . . . epitomizes the rhetoric in which it was made, and explodes it, surpasses it, shows it up,' according to the book's most enthusiastic critic, William Stott.[34] Agee continually reminds us of his position as outsider. Listing himself and Evans as 'spy' and 'counter-spy' respectively in 'Persons and Places,' he wonders what his intrusive presence looks like to the people whose 'living' he has come 'to reproduce and communicate as nearly exactly as possible' (p.232). His attempts to see himself through their eyes even as he scrutinizes them means 'the centers of my subject are shifty' (p.10). Yet his narrative remains intact, drawing on the powerful generic conventions, not only of the documentary or its hybrid reportage, but of the spiritual autobiography – the conversion narrative that looks for signs amidst the ordinary for proof of one's righteousness.[35]

For Agee, the signs are best discovered through photography: 'the camera seems to me, next to unassisted and weaponless consciousness, the central instrument of our time' (p. 11). Words cannot embody; their meanings are arbitrary; but the camera can 'perceive simply the cruel radiance of what is' (p. 11). In addition to being many other things, the entire book is a paean to the power of vision. Most important, of course, are Walker Evans's photographs, which constitute the prelude to Agee's prose and establish looking as a prevailing practice. Even in a passage not concerned with recording images, toward the end of the book when Agee recounts his first night spent with the Gudgers without Evans, he uses cinematic and photographic metaphors:

> But from where I say, 'The shutters are opened,' I must give this up, and must speak in some other way, for I am no longer able to speak as I was doing, or rather no longer able to bear to. Things which were then at least

immediate in my senses, I now know only as at some great and untouchable distance; distinctly, yet coldly as through reversed field-glasses, and with no warmth or traction or faith in words: so that at best I can hope only to 'describe' what I would like to 'describe,' as at a second remove, and even that poorly. (p. 403)

As a 'bodyless eye,' Agee hopes to look as deeply as a camera: 'one reason I so deeply care for the camera is just this: so far as it goes . . . and handled cleanly and literally in its own terms, as an ice-cold, some ways limited, some ways more capable, eye, it is . . . incapable of recording anything but absolute, dry truth' (p. 234).

However, Agee's medium is 'not a still or moving camera, but is words' (p. 235) and it is the insufficiencies of language that propel his narrative on and on. The stubborn linearity of print and its tendency to metaphorize makes language suspicious. ' "Description," ' writes Agee echoing Lukács, 'is a word to suspect' because 'words cannot embody, they can only describe' (p.238). But the eye can locate sounds in space, grasp simultaneity and depth, enact the 'globular' through its compression of space (p.111). The endlessly meandering prose, circling back on itself, repeating incantationally the names of objects hidden in drawers, displayed on walls, is an attempt to encode this globular vision of the camera and eye and to proclaim his authority through spectatorship. He declares imperially, 'If I were not here; and I am alien; a bodyless eye; this would never have existence in human perception' (p.187); but his musings are interrupted by a 'violin wasp' who 'is not unwelcome here: he is a builder; a tenant. He does not notice; he is no reader of signs' (p.188).

The three vignettes that begin the text, 'Late Sunday Morning,' 'At the Forks,' and 'Near a Church,' highlight, through intensely visual interactions between Agee and others – black tenants singing for their white landlord, starving and almost demented white croppers, and a young black couple – the discordant relations among black and white, and rich and poor in rural Alabama. They display the twisted pose Agee and Evans must assume within the cotton culture when they set out to produce 'this record and analysis [as] exhaustive, with no detail, however trivial it may seem, left untouched, no relevancy avoided' (pp. xiv–xv). In each case, Agee tries to dislodge the meaning and effects of his class and race and gender, desperately trying to communicate through looks and slight gestures that he is not like the white Southerner male landowners who represent power and authority for the poor white and black tenants; however, he shows these attempts at camaraderie as futile, and even destructive and dangerous for each group of people. He *must* act the part assigned him by the landlords and ask the men to sing another song, then another, and then flick them fifty cents. He *must* offend the porch sitters by attempting to speak to them at all, by seeing their failure. He *must* frighten the young black couple as he runs after them, leaving the woman trembling with fear for herself and her husband at his approach. Because of his position, he cannot help himself and his awkward moves toward reciprocity will always backfire, further alienating and embarrassing those he seeks to comfort. And when Agee rails against his complacent readers and strikes a pose of humility before the tenants (but arrogance before his audience), he implicates us in his predicament as well.

The ability to see, to read signs, is power; and this is nowhere more clear than in the passages about Louise Gudger during which she and Agee are locked in an intensely symbiotic gaze. He stares at her as she poses for her family portrait the first day he and Evans meet the three families:

> and it is while I am watching you here, Louise, that suddenly yet very quietly I realize a little more clearly that I am probably going to be in love with you: while I am watching you in this precious imposture of a dress, standing up the strength of your father and looking so soberly and so straight into the plexus of the lens through those paralyzing eyes of yours . . . (p. 369)

In this scene ten-year-old Louise's paralyzing eyes seem to hold the same power over him as the camera holds. He appears subject to her visual control; yet she is the spectacle trapped by the power of the camera to capture her as her father wants her to look.

Later, when he returns without Evans to the Gudgers' house, she fixes her gaze on his plexus, becoming in a sense the camera that had earlier fixed her. This interchange of looks between Louise, Agee, and the imaginary camera is charged with sexual energy put into play through the gaze:

> something very important to me is happening, and this is between me and Louise. She sits squarely and upright in her chair . . . watching me, without smiling, whether in her mouth or her eyes: and I come soon to realize that she has not taken her eyes off me since we entered the room: so that my own are drawn back more and more uncontrollably toward them and into them. From the first they have run chills through me, a sort of beating and ticklish vacuum at the solar plexus, and though I already have frequently met them I cannot look into them long at a time . . . (p. 400)

Again, Agee empowers the ten-year-old girl because her gaze functions as the camera's – implacable, central, invariable – and able to (trans)fix him with its power. This girl looks differently.

The photo session which inaugurates the relationship between the families and Agee and Evans has revealed a number of differences among and within the families. Agee describes the painful embarrassment of Sadie Ricketts before the camera as she attempts to resist her husband's insistence that her family be photographed. Her dishevelled children are brought into stark contrast when George Gudger arrives with his family in their Sunday clothes, which Agee discerns to be the cheapest imitation of middle-class attire. Minute class distinctions among the tenants point up the larger class differences dividing the families from Agee and Evans, and the gender hierarchy prevailing means Sadie is subject to the desires of both her husband and the strange men. Agee is not unaware of the visual exchanges that pass between the members of the families – in fact, he enters into them with Sadie and Louise – yet he insists that he is powerless to overcome their shame before the lens and once again speaks silently by looking into 'the unforgiving face, the eyes, of Mrs Ricketts' and then telling us of his pain at causing her pain: 'I know I have lost whatever shameful little I had gained for her, and it is now hard for me to meet her eyes at all, the whole thing has become so complicated and so shameful. (It occurs to me now as I write that I was as helpless as she; but I must confess I don't want to make anything of it)' (p. 370).

Agee's dilemma about his relationship to his subjects becomes an anxiety about the form of the book – its lack of a center – and incidentally resembles Lukács's distress over the blurred generic boundaries of the reportage novel. The decision to narrate or describe which differentiates realist from naturalist fiction for Lukács is connected to the distinction between knowing and seeing which marks bourgeois culture. The naturalistic writer, like the journalist whom Agee deplores, can only see details packed up tightly, but the realist novelist can reveal totality, can know the social relations embedded within the objects of the world.

Agee's denunciations of journalism declare his separation from the reified vision of the bourgeoisie. The globular vision he desires could begin to 'embody' totality in a form that differs from realist fiction; yet it too begins with the details of a man's life and expands to include family, work, environment, and on and on. But like peeling back layers of onion skin to reveal some essence only to be foiled in one's pursuit, the 'center' shifts. This shifting becomes the structuring device for Agee's twin perspectives – documentary and autobiography, description and narration. Reportage sought to realign this tension by incorporating the eye/I and its other to produce the we, but Agee knows he cannot bridge this gap. Yet he searches endlessly for a way, and in one of several endings, seems to locate it in the bodies of two children.

Declaring that 'the last words of this book have been spoken,' he leaves us with 'descriptions of two images' (p. 441). The first is of Squinchy Gudger relaxing into sleep while being nursed, whose face is 'beatific' against his mother's breast and who is 'the Madonna's son, human divinity sunken from the cross at rest against his mother, and more beside, for at the heart and leverage of that young body, gently, taken in all the pulse of his being, the penis is partly erect' (p. 442). Once again, Agee has re-presented the scene for us through references to high bourgeois culture – a classic image from Renaissance painting in this case. Then he discovers an even more 'universal' figure:

> And Ellen where she rests, in the gigantic light: she, too, is completely at peace . . . her knees are flexed upward a little and fallen apart, the soles of the feet facing: her blown belly swimming its navel, white as flour; and blown full broad with slumbering blood into a circle: so white all the outward flesh, it glows of blue; so dark, the deep hole, a dark red shadow of life blood: the center and source, for which we have never contrived any worthy name, is as if it were breathing, flowering, soundlessly, a snoring silence of flame; it is as if flame were breathed forth from it and subtly played about it: and here in this breathing and play of flame, a thing so strong, so valiant, so unvanquishable, it is without effort, without emotion, it shall at length outshine the sun. (p. 442)

Agee's text refuses a 'center'; yet it obsessively seeks one in all the usual places – here we are strangely back to the Rat Man whose 'desire to see the female body' initiated his obsessive 'curiosity' to peer beneath surfaces. This ecstatic vision of the 'center and source,' twenty-month-old Ellen's flaming navel, returns to another conventional image of 'uncanny' power. Unlike the Rat Man, whose illicit peerings up his governess's skirts sparked his 'curiosity,' Agee is an active inscriber of anatomical difference. Its representation here recenters *his* 'curious' text by reinstating sexual difference as an 'ordering.'[36] If the objects Agee has presented to us throughout the book resist 'ordering' within the norms of bourgeois culture – although he has certainly sought to establish them there by likening them to icons familiar from art, music, and literary histories – his 'images' of sexual difference reposition these things within the seemingly stable representations of sexual difference that orders bourgeois culture.[37] The sight of these children asleep and open to inspection, described with these words which are 'not words,' concludes the record of tenant farmers' lives. Their 'unimagined existence' has been reordered into a more legible story and image, as class difference becomes 'embodied' by sexual difference – erect penis, bloody hole.

When Agee finally concludes the book with the third 'On the Porch' section, the movement from the documentary image of the tenants to the narrative of his own subjectivity is complete, and with it, the movement from visual to descriptive, from the people to the self. So the final mood of the book is the quiet eroticism of Evans and Agee listening to the foxes baying while the two men curl up for the night on the porch, talking and finally falling to sleep. Ultimately, the narrative closure of the two asleep repeats the closure of the documentary vision Agee presented with the two sleeping children. Just as the Rat Man's curiosity betrayed his desire for his father, the desire to see and to know the tenants that has propelled the two men leads them to each other.[38]

Voyeurism and its attendant sadism is at the heart of the documentary narrative, which depends on the power of the gaze to construct meanings for the writer and the reader of 'the people.' Furthermore, the two terms – documentary, narrative – remain at odds with each other. Insisting on a particularity of vision and a polemic, yet requiring the conventions of plot and structure, reportage is a 'bastard' genre.[39] Agee constantly reminds us of the painful embarrassment his position as a Harvard-educated, white, male writer creates for all his subjects, himself among them. Agee may read himself into the tenants' lives with, according to Paul Goodman, 'insufferable arrogance,'[40] but, 'as readers of this book,' writes Ruth Lechlitner, 'we have moved in on Mr. Agee (even as he moved in on the cotton tenant families) and we learn possibly as much about him (and the things about ourselves which he represents) as we do about the sharecroppers. Perhaps this . . . is the book's chief social documentary value.'[41] No matter what its political intentions, the documentary narrative invariably returns to the middle class, enlisting the reader in a process of self-recognition. We read ourselves into the people. What the middle-class man sees of the tenants in Alabama can only be read back through his vision as (uncanny) images. The 'eye' and the 'I' have become interchangeable for narrator and reader, and the 'subject' of the work shifts from an examination of the families to a disclosure of the self.

This seems less clear when we look at Evans's photographs. They resist narrative in so far as they remain uncaptioned. They present an anachronism, a throwback to a 'generation that was not obsessed with going down to posterity in photographs, rather shyly drawing back into their private space in the face of such proceedings . . . for that very reason allowed that space, the space where they lived, to get onto the plate with them.'[42] Evans's photographs of the three families, their homes and environs, invite us to contemplate this lost era by refusing to name his subjects. But perhaps in so doing, or in ceding the work of captioning to Agee's prose, he suggests just how much the 'caption become[s] the most important part of the photograph.'[43] When Walker Evans refuses captions and lets the images speak, he resists the movement 'whereby photography turns all life's relationships into literature'; yet the sequencing of the photographs tells its own kind of story, and their silence still foregrounds another's vision especially after Agee's words reinvest the images with new narrative capital.[44] Agee's pose of self-indulgent sexual obsessive works, because Evans's photographs seem to withhold all sentimentality through their insistence that the object of the photograph directly address him, the subject, and then us, the subject at a remove.[45] They proclaim, in the process, 'This is Art!' despite Agee's plea 'Above all else: in God's name don't think of it as Art' (p. 15); they also, through Agee's text, become political, despite Evans's demand for 'NO POLITICS, whatever!' Walker Evans's photographs as much as possible resist sensationalism. Still, his photographs of bodies and beds and kitchens and stores, the images that frame Agee's text, participate in the same work that Munby's collection of working women in England did (Figure 2). Their collection reveals the ways differences can be organized and contained.

IV

How is it we got caught?

(Agee, as Annie Mae)

In the by now mythical tale, James Agee and Walker Evans set out in summer 1936 on assignment for *Fortune* magazine to document the lives of white tenant farmers in Alabama's cotton belt. Evans was on loan from Roy Stryker's Historical Section of the Farm Security Administration because Stryker wanted as broad an exposure of the plight of rural poverty as possible, and the slick mass circulation magazines gave him easy access to a large audience. As the story goes, the 20,000 words, already far too long for the magazine, became 40,000, then more and more as Agee continued to write and revise. It was not until 1941 that Houghton Mifflin published a small edition of *Let Us Now Praise Famous Men* which, despite many fine reviews (here the myth veers from reality), sold poorly and languished unread, until its reissue in 1960 helped renew interest in Depression-era literature, photography, and politics. In the ensuing decades Agee's and Evans's work has assumed the status of a 'masterpiece' of modernist or postmodernist realism.[46]

By the 1980s, *Let Us Now Praise Famous Men* had spawned an eerie industry of rephotographic projects, as journalists, film-makers, and photographers tracked down the Tingles, Fields and Burroughs to rephotograph them and to elicit their impressions of the 'famous' book.[47] In these works, Agee and Evans often have come under indictment as invaders, intellectuals who pried into the lives of innocent folk and revealed all the dirty secrets of poverty in America. According to these stories, some family members are still angry and bitter about the way they were portrayed, and talk of lawsuits and reparations to get some of the money Evans and Agee ostensibly made from their images. But others assure us that Agee's words and Evans's photographs were 'true.' In any case, a whole new generation of middle-class spectators is encouraged simultaneously to inspect the faces and stories of the Southern rural poor – now living in trailers rather than pine shacks – as well as to castigate the two men who originally brought these faces and stories to us.

However, we are not asked to think of ourselves as co-conspirators – as spy and counter-spy, as Agee identified himself and Evans – but as moral guardians of propriety who need to question the voyeuristic exposé attendant on the first inspection – but never that of the second revisit. *And Their Children After Them* attempts to historicize the families by describing the demise of cotton tenancy. This 'sequel' to *Let Us Now Praise Famous Men* reproduces its format, beginning with uncaptioned photographs and continuing with details of the families and their descendants. Yet it is prefaced by the sensational account of Maggie Louise Gudger's suicide by rat poison.[48] Ironically, Sherrie Levine's appropriations of Evans's images seem somehow purer in their very effort to demonstrate the impurity of photography. Coming 'After Walker Evans,' she at least refuses to invade the subjects of Evans's images' lives, and instead takes over only the images themselves. Just as *Fortune* was a specious location from which to launch a critique of capitalism, so too *The New York Times* or PBS or *American Photographer* seem unlikely sites in which a critique of liberalism can occur.[49]

The critique of capitalism implicitly and explicitly argued in these texts reveals yet another trope for the elaboration of a gendered bourgeois subjectivity. The power of narrative and image ensures that 'the people' are recontained within the frame of 'the self.' They remain unremarkable; nothing can be said, after all, of those who can best be seen as 'photographs,' 'fragments,' 'bits,' 'lumps,' and 'pieces' (p. 13), whose difference emanates from the 'leverage' and 'source' of anatomy (p. 442) (Figure 3).

The histories of bourgeois subjectivity, photography, and psychoanalysis are intimately linked: Freud understood sexuality as a series of questions involving visual representations; subjectivity developed through a series of impartially understood scenes, and psychoanalysis re-presented those scenes through the talking cure. A visual culture knows itself through words. Benjamin, in 'The Author as Producer,' says that writers must become photographers and photographers must write the meanings of their images in the caption. Agee and Evans working (as collaborators) together apart recontextualize each other's texts, as images and words penetrate, contradict, and illuminate each other. Agee's 'honesty' (Stott), his 'authenticity' (Orvell), his 'guilt' (Trilling) about his position as 'spy' contaminate Evans's 'tact and respect' (Hersey) for his subjects' lives and the objects in their possession, while Evans's bestowal of 'timeless dignity, beauty and pain of wounded lives' redeems Agee's self-indulgence.[50] Still, in all Agee's 471 pages of 'caption' (though he rejects that name), we are riveted by the camera, by the importance of looking into the eyes of an 'appallingly damaged group of human beings,' and of having them see him and us in turn. This is the meaning of 'At the Forks,' 'Late Sunday Morning,' and 'Near a Church.' This is the meaning of Louise's, Ivy's, and Sadie's eyes; a meaning that is quite different from Ellen Woods' flaming center: the unknowable, but fully visible hole which marks her difference, and her invisibility.

Agee's honesty masks his complicity in erasing the different gazes of the tenants. He rails against the false merger with the working class which so infuriated Benjamin about most intellectuals' posturings. But Agee cannot escape the confessional narrative of bourgeois selfhood: the story that encodes the middle class as the subject and object of its own narcissistic and self-loathing gaze. The story that seeks to 'know' through what it can 'see' of the other finds, not the other but itself. Still, despite all his looking around, Agee opens himself, like a woman in the text, to 'the wide open eyes' of Louise and the other women; thus it is Evans's masculine pose, as detached observer of surfaces, that overcomes the gender and genre confusions of the book, returning it to the visual and narrative conventions of bourgeois culture.

Because genre depends on the representations of repressive 'orderings' like sexual difference, its power to recontain any transgressions, to re-establish conventions, is also that which produces gender, sexual, class, and racial hierarchies in bourgeois culture. Looking across classes at the underclass requires looking underneath their skirts, inspecting their pants, because the middle class knows itself as a spy whose desire is somehow 'curious.' Louise's 'stolid' stare feels to Agee like another kind of looking, even another kind of knowing, but it in the end tells a familiar story: her resistance as a girl who openly looks is supplanted by Ellen's 'to-be-looked-at-ness.' Without a radical break from the regimes of vision and narrative we will only see and write with the eyes and hands of those who have already looked us over and described what they've seen (of) themselves.

3

Margaret Bourke-White's Red Coat;

or, Slumming in the Thirties

I

A popular Irving Berlin song from 1933 invited its financially strapped middle- and working-class listeners to 'go slumming on Park Avenue.' Written in the midst of the worst year of the Depression, when unemployment soared between 25 and 33 per cent, the song sarcastically played upon the (downward) class mobility caused by the 1929 Crash. This turning of the class tables was a common theme in Hollywood as well, where spunky golddiggers displayed their goods ('We're in the Money') to entice wealthy men who visited the seedy nightclubs in which they performed before they retreated to the safety of their men's clubs.

During the 1920s, 'when Harlem was in vogue,' wealthy whites had traveled uptown, to take in the atmosphere of jazz and high living offered in Harlem's famous night spots. A decade before, tour buses passed through the ghettoes of the Lower East Side and were assaulted with missiles of paving stones and garbage according to Mike Gold's autobiographical novel *Jews Without Money*. The class and ethnic boundaries superintending America's cities were rigid; yet popular culture encouraged their permeability: for the wealthy WASP elite, black and Jewish ghettoes provided a voyeuristic thrill. But after the stock market crashed, popular culture unleashed a new pastime – working stiffs gleefully surveying the lives of the tragically rich whose means left them incapable of adapting to straitened times.

If we take Irving Berlin seriously, then we can begin to understand class as *both* a social practice and a representation, precisely in the ways that Joan Scott and Teresa de Lauretis argue gender operates in culture.[1] In his famous sentence describing the peasants and small

56

landowners of post-revolutionary France, Marx asserted, 'They cannot represent themselves; they must be represented.'[2] His doubled sense of representation is a political practice; someone must speak for, stand in for, perform as, the inchoate and unformed group – not yet a class because it cannot represent itself, yet surely a class because it can be represented – to and for itself and others. If representation is crucial to class formation and expression, then class, like gender, is performative, divined in the exchanges among representatives of and for classes. These exchanges were themselves the subject of intense representation and theorizing during the 1930s, a decade when class, racial, and gender divisions were both more pronounced than today and more thoroughly contested.

My project of revisioning 1930s documentary is necessarily about revising myself as well. Each individual, as Antonio Gramsci reminds us, 'is the synthesis not only of existing relations but of the history of these relations. [S]he is a précis of the past.'[3] Those of us drawn to pursue our scholarship in and among the remnants of leftist culture of the 1930s do so in part as a search for ourselves: we look carefully for evidence of a past moment when radical intellectuals felt they warranted a place in history. My discovery of radical women writers and artists of the 1930s coincided with my own recognition of myself as a radical woman writer in my thirties. Only after completing two books on women's literary radicalism did I understand that I was searching for a model that could tell me that it was possible to be all those things – radical, woman, intellectual, activist, mother – I felt I was (or wanted to be). Those women stepped out of the confines of their class and gender to join striking truckers in struggle as Meridel LeSueur's narrator does when she claims 'I Was Marching.' Those who could forthrightly assert *I Change Worlds* with Anna Louise Strong who fought in the trenches of Spain and China during that decade clearly presented a model sorely lacking in my own experience. They were fearless, ecstatically declaring 'I Went to the Soviet Arctic,' as Ruth Gruber did, to 'find women.' They had a sense of solidarity and community as Ella Ford did when she announced in the *New Masses*: 'We Are Mill People'; and they challenged us to take a political position, demanding to know 'Which Side Are You On?' These women, whose biographies belie their declarations of authority – revealing how difficult it was to be the Amazons of their and my imagination – had something to say to another generation of women freed by feminist agitation and other social movements for political change.

In writing about their struggles, I now see I was desperately seeking our own. Perhaps all scholarship is primarily autobiographical, perhaps it is simply that the dilemmas they faced as women and radicals and intellectuals have not been solved, because the terms through which we know the women and their struggles are already embedded in cultural assumptions about gender and politics which have made the 1930s so troubling for Americans. The middle-class women who went slumming in the 1930s present me with a complicating image of myself as I, too, slum in the 1930s seeking pleasures, thrills, and answers of my own. Perhaps my story will enable another one to surface: that of the middle-class women intellectuals of the 1930s whose situation gives a unique view of the quandary middle-class intellectuals in America find themselves in today.

To analyze how class represents, I want to explore the politics and meaning of boundary crossings – of slumming, so to speak. These crossings occur tellingly at moments of *visual* encounters between those whose lives were privileged to observe and regulate and detail the behaviors of others – journalists, novelists, photographers, and social workers – and their subjects, usually, because this is the Depression decade, the poor. As vehicles of regulation, exposé, and reification, photography and fiction become central mechanisms of class representation. This chapter looks at the complicated relations of cross-class looking encoded in the lives, novels, and images of working-class and middle-class women during the 1930s. It seeks out the tensions at the borders of class and racial boundaries when women cross them. Fiction and reportage by radical women – both middle-class and working-class – describe one horn of the dilemma I am tracing. Margaret Bourke-White, one of the highest paid women of the 1930s whose photographs helped propel *Life* magazine's spectacular success, embodies another. When a middle-class woman looks across her class privilege at another woman, what does she see? And because she herself is always also an object under investigation, how is she seen in turn? Can a working-class woman see herself? And because she is already under surveillance, might she refuse to look at others?[4]

The history of middle-class inspection of the poor begins long before 1920s slumming, and its purpose was more likely the regulation of (working people's) desires than the expression of (middle-class) pleasures. Nancy Armstrong has detailed the ways in which the rise of the domestic woman figured in eighteenth-century British novels placed middle-class women in a position to regulate their own lives and the lives of their children. According to Denise Riley and Linda Gordon, the consolidation of feminism and social reform movements in nineteenth-century Britain and America ensured that middle-class women would also regulate and superintend the lives of poorer females who failed to live up to proper standards of housekeeping and femininity. Oversight would keep all deviations firmly in view in order to ameliorate them.[5] Moreover, with the invention of the mercury flash in the 1890s one could not only see into the dark spaces of poverty but, like Jacob Riis, photograph the tenements of New York's Lower East Side. The projects of state and capitalist regulation, reportage and fiction, documentary photography and feminism are thus curiously interwoven; each mode overseeing itself, its objects, and its others. But in the 1930s, a radical critique of capitalism turned the lens through which middle-class women looked over (and after) their poorer sisters.[6]

In 1928, Virginia Woolf powerfully etched the intimate links between feminism and writing. She produced a new understanding of British literary history by acknowledging the history of women's oppression and of their achievements as writers. Her formula – that to be a writer a woman needed 'five hundred pounds a year and a room of one's own' – signaled that literature was the province of the middle class who could afford time and space to meditate and study and write: 'the poor poet has not in these days, nor has had for two hundred years, a dog's chance.'[7] In her perambulations traced in the lecture/ essay, the narrator periodically finds herself alone in a room looking from her window at the absurd but everyday bustle below.

This image of the writer separated from the streets, surveyor and overseer of the lives of her subjects, links the project of literary production to those of bourgeois domestic maintenance. There, too, as Nancy Armstrong has demonstrated, the middle-class woman learned to display her skills by self-inspection and projection onto the objects surrounding her. She assumed authority as the supervisor of her domestic surroundings, her qualities of perception indicating her intrinsic value. Like the early bourgeois 'domestic woman' Armstrong analyzes, Woolf's writer is set apart in her own room because of class difference. Rebecca Harding Davis had portrayed this in her 1861 novella 'Life in the Iron Mills' which begins as another unnamed middle-class female narrator stands at her window watching the mill workers trudge along the path before her as they return from work. Like Davis, Woolf notes that it is unlikely that we will find many working-class artists – male or female. Nevertheless, in the pages of contemporaneous socialist journals, writers were calling for a new 'proletarian' poetics to replace that of a defeated high modernism. Woolf herself wrote an introductory essay for a book of working-class women's tales collected by the Cooperative Working Women's Guild a few years later, entitled *Life as We Have Known It*.

The idea that literary production resulted from the observations of life, rather than from what one has known of it, simply reinforced the sense that writing and looking were the privileges of the middle class. Michael Gold's novel *Jews Without Money*, an enactment of his calls for proletarian art – a writing which would dramatize the lives of those in the tenements – brought the narrator downstairs. Smashing the pane of glass separating writer from the street-life below, he insisted that stories and their telling were also activities of the poor and working class.

Usually, the poor represent an absence in literary discourse – the *non-dit*, in Pierre Macherey's term – of the worlds and works of both high realism and high modernism. But, with Gold's call for proletarian literature, a new arena opened up for middle-class writers as well. Still, their desire to know and transmit (if not transform) the lives of poor and working-class subjects maintained the conventional boundaries separating art from life, seeing from knowing. The form of reportage was, in some measure, an attempt to refigure these relations; yet, when these boundaries were violated, they confounded generic (and gender) conventions. For example, when journalist Martha Gellhorn traveled America to record *The Trouble I've Seen* and found 'Ruby,' the eponymous girl of the first part of her book, she was at a loss to account for Ruby's behavior. No convenient story emerged to trace either Ruby's defiant pride (as well as her outlandish clothes) prostitution offered her, nor her shame at her mother's ineffectual morality which consigned them to poverty. But Gellhorn was also ambivalent about the social worker who saved Ruby from her unfit mother and lodged her safely with a middle-class family. It is not clear just what is the 'trouble' here – poverty, childhood prostitution, inappropriate mothering, or straitlaced social workers – nor what the 'I' who has seen it has learned or intends to do about it. As a reporter, Gellhorn is troubled by what she has seen, but she maintains her 'traditional' distance.[8] Is she slumming, even if her travels across class boundaries never yield a thrill?

Writings by and about radical women intellectuals, whose metaphoric annihilation as actors in the historical movement of the proletariat was doubled through their class *and* gender differences, stressed that they were always 'foreigners' among the American people and within the American Left.[9] 'Ruby' presented a typical feature of much radical women's writing of the 1930s: the inevitable scene in which the white middle-class social worker – proper representative of the state – enters the home of the working-class mother to supervise her failed attempts at homemaking. The occasion for the state's interest in the home of the poor was usually the arrest of a wayward daughter for prostitution. The blame for her transgressive sexuality – the money from which did not always see its way back into the home, but was used selfishly to buy pretty things for the young girl – was securely lodged on the inept mother. As the social worker surveys the filthy apartment cluttered with laundry and rancid food, howling babies underfoot, she registers the distance between her classed understandings of proper femininity and maternity and offers a view into the slovenly house-keeping of the poor. However, despite being ground down, the mothers fight back, if only to comment on the impossibility of living up to the standards of bourgeois housekeeping on a few dollars a week from relief.[10] Their anguish – the pain registered on the face of Dorothea Lange's Migrant Mother or the blank stare of a sharecrop-per's wife caught by Margaret Bourke-White – was a shameful admis-sion that middle-class culture had failed to make over the face of America in its own image.

Even when the heroine of a feminist proletarian novel like Fielding Burke's *Call Home the Heart* was an 'organic intellectual' like Ishma, the mountain-woman-turned-mill-worker and union activist rather than a well-to-do newspaper woman, the motives of the female intellectual were suspicious. In the penultimate scene of the novel, Ishma single-handedly saves a black union organizer, Butch Wells, from a lynching at the hands of her former husband and his friends. Shaming them with the threat that she will kill herself and leave them with the reputation of having attempted to rape her, Ishma uses her whiteness and femininity to save a fellow worker. Burke restages the highly charged gender, racial, class, and sexual dynamics of lynching and rape through a subversion of stereotypes. Inverting the historical myth that the rape of a white woman by a black man causes his lynching at the hands of white men, Ishma, the working-class white woman, prevents Butch being lynched by charging the white men with rape. Later, at Butch's home, she is confronted with her own racism, marring the heroism of her act when his wife, Gaffie, seizes Ishma in an embrace and kisses her:

> Her lips were heavy, and her teeth so large that one needed the sure avouch of eyes to believe in them. It was impossible to associate her with woe, though tears were racing down her cheeks. As her fat body moved she shook off an odor that an unwashed collie would have disowned. 'Bressed angel, bressed angel ob do Lawd,' she kept repeating, and with a great sweep enveloped Ishma, her fat arms encircling the white neck, her thick lips mumbling at the quivering white throat . . . .The fleshy embrace, the murky little room, the smoking ashes, the warm stench, the too eager faces shining greasily at the top of big, black bodies, filled Ishma with uncontrol-lable revulsion.[11]

This heady hint of interracial lesbianism so disturbs Ishma that she reinstates racial stereotypes of black womanhood – as an animal, a mammy, a sexual predator. Disgraced in the eyes of the community, especially Derry Unthank, a white doctor and party member who has overseen Ishma's political education, she flees back to the mountains and her first husband. As protagonist of the novel, Ishma holds center-stage in the drama unfolding around her during the mill workers' strike. Her sexuality, limited by lack of contraception to a series of heterosexual 'marriages' (she never actually marries anyone), sparks her political commitments. Her pursuit of sexual freedom *and* economic equality set her apart from the proper, white, middle-class women of the mill town and from the less assertive women of her class. She is exceptional, but she can never fully become a radical because of her racism. Here, the white female (organic) intellectual again is separated from other women, whose bodily excess – too much money, too many children, too much flesh, whatever – threatens her political identity.

In both cases, the authors, themselves middle-class women, could not overcome through their prose the racial or class differences dividing women. The ideal of fraternity, often figured in the image of the maternal collective engulfing disparate workers within its embrace, escaped their women characters, as if class and racial divisions, marked by tasteless clothing and expressive sexuality, on one hand, a well-cut suit and heroic behavior, on the other, were more extreme among women.[12] Writing produced by working-class authors during the 1930s also dramatized class and racial divisions through the awkward distances produced when one's body is on display; but they challenged the stances of either passive observation or flight from confrontation. 1930s women's radical fiction reversed a classic image from Dickens's novels through *Stella Dallas*: the poor waif (or elderly mother) looking in longingly at the opulent dining rooms of the wealthy. It often placed poor and working women inside and subject to the view of those passing by.

For instance, in Ramona Lowe's painful story, 'The Woman in the Window,' a wry revision of Fannie Hurst's 1933 melodramatic novel *Imitation of Life*, Mrs Jackson answers a help wanted advertisement for a cook, only to discover she must dress the part of Aunt Jemima and fry chicken in the window of Mammy's restaurant. Her children, shamed by the taunts of white children who see her, challenge her to quit her demeaning job. But she explains that her job is cooking and it puts food on their table and shoes on their feet and that *'when a body say nigger, You turn roun' 'n' give'm such a thrashin' they woan never forget.'*[13] Her self-possession, in spite of her public humiliation, her demand that her employers address her as Mrs Jackson and raise her pay, her insistence to her children that some work is dignified and some not 'but it all got t' be done,' inverts Woolf's use of the window. Here the window is for display not for observation. It provides a glimpse of the object at work, not a view for the writing subject. Mrs Jackson may be the spectacle, but she is also the theorist of her position; an object who speaks back by simply asserting the need that drives her to claim her objectification. 'She leaned against the table and looked out, and the world looked in curiously at the embodiment of a fiction it had created' (p.82). This woman in the window challenges Woolf's to cross through the glass, like Alice, and enter another world, to think another set of relations than observer/observed, subject/object, inside/outside.

But that project is terribly difficult, and the awkward and often tragic attempts to cross class divides highlight social exclusions among women. These divisions – marking those who belong from those outside – are central to social privileges learned and experienced in childhood. Two books from the mid-1980s, *Landscape for a Good Woman* and *The House on Mango Street*, begin their explorations of 1950s girlhoods lived without resources with an image remarkably resonant with those I have been tracking in 1930s texts. Carolyn Steedman remembers seeing her mother cry only once:

> We both watched the dumpy retreating figure of the health visitor through the curtainless windows. The woman had said: 'This house isn't fit for a baby.' And then she stopped crying, my mother, got by, the phrase that picks up after all difficulty (it says: it's like this; it shouldn't be like this; it's unfair; I'll manage): 'Hard lines, eh Kay?' . . . And I? I will do everything and anything until the end of my days to stop anyone ever talking to me like that woman talked to my mother. It is in this place, this bare, curtainless bedroom that lies my secret and shameful defiance. I read a woman's book, meet such a woman at a party (a woman now, like me) and think quite deliberately as we talk: we are divided: a hundred years ago I'd have been cleaning your shoes. I know this and you don't.[14]

Steedman's tale of women's differences in post-war London turns on the view offered into her deprivation by an official, a representative of the state, whose comments confirm Steedman's (and her mother's and sister's) illegitimacy. The three of them can only watch impassively from their bare, exposed window, shamed, yet knowing.

In a similar vein, Sandra Cisneros begins her novel with the story of a nun passing Esperanza, her young narrator, playing on the street:

> Where do you live? she asked
> There, I said pointing up to the third floor.
> You live *there*?
> *There.* I had to look to where she pointed – the third floor, the paint peeling, wooden bars Papa had nailed on the windows so we wouldn't fall

out. You live *there*? The way she said it made me feel like nothing. *There*. I
lived *there*. I nodded.

I knew then I had to have a house. A real house. One I could point to.[15]

Again, an official woman, representative of the church this time,
instills shame in a young girl by marking the distance between herself
and the windows from which Esperanza's family looks out. Neither the
health visitor nor the nun inhabits the seats of power; they are
representatives sent to supervise the lives of those outside the view of
power, yet subject to it. They remain guardians of the street and the
home, of decency, patrolling the lives of these young girls, reminding
them of the things they lack, of their terrible needs which can barely be
spoken, much less met. Both stories condemn the female representative's insensitivity; blind to the hurt produced by their distance from
the lives of those they visit and instruct, they offer no hope of ever
learning about them – or themselves.

However, in her epic 1934 short story 'I Was Marching,' Meridel
LeSueur traced the clumsy awakening of a middle-class woman to the
experiences of working-class solidarity. Written in part to assuage the
condemnation she had suffered at the hands of *New Masses* editor
Whittaker Chambers for her earlier piece of reportage, 'Women on
the Breadlines,' the first-person narrator is wary: a woman, a middle-
class woman, a middle-class woman writer, who watches herself as
much as she watches others and for whom language, the representation of an event, is more profound than its experience. 'For two
days,' she writes,

> I heard of the strike. I went by their headquarters, I walked by on the
> opposite side of the street and saw the dark old building that had been a
> garage and lean, dark young faces leaning from the upstairs windows. I had
> to go down there often. I looked in . . . I stayed close to the door, watching.
> I was afraid they would put me out. After all, I could remain a spectator. A
> man wearing a polo hat kept going around with a large camera taking
> pictures.[16]

This introduction establishes the narrator as an outsider, the
middle-class onlooker who, as Georg Lukács theorized in *History and
Class Consciousness*, perceives social relations as a 'passive observer,'
much as one might view a theatrical performance. But LeSueur's
narrator is drawn into the union hall, the masses of bodies working
together and suffering in unison claim her and after days on the picket

line and pouring coffee she finds herself an insider. 'I was marching,' she declares finally,

> with a million hands, movements, faces, and my own movement was repeating again and again, making a new movement from these many gestures, the walking, falling back, the open mouth crying, the nostrils stretched apart, the raised hand, the blow falling, and the outstretched hand drawing me in. I felt my legs straighten, I felt my feet join in that strange shuffle of thousands of bodies moving with direction, of thousands of feet, and my own breath with the gigantic breath. As if an electric charge had passed through me, my hair stood on end, I was marching. (p.171)

Where the narrator began her tale by emphasizing sight, her looking in and looking on, the concluding ecstatic push of humanity incorporates feet, hands, nostrils, mouths, hair, but refuses to name the eyes.

LeSueur clearly wants to ease the separation which vision, the observation of the working-class other, produces by erasing the presence of the eye. Her final cry, 'I was marching,' despite its individualism, subsumes her body into the masses, the 'we' which has begun its funeral march. In a gesture repeated endlessly in proletarian fiction, the collective engulfs its characters and reforms them into an earth-shuddering force. Still, the narrator reasserts her presence here, I believe, because it is so important to LeSueur that she indicate that the relationship between middle-class woman and worker could be other than one of merely onlooker. She needs to return to her embodied presence to alert us to the fact that she does not merely see, she also moves. She is not slumming; she has crossed the threshold.

As in Lowe's story, the workers are inside, their heads glimpsed from the street below on which collect 'artists, writers, professionals, even businessmen and women' who watch with 'longing' and 'fear' the dark and solemn faces within. Those on the street (and notice how women are joined with the representative types of the middle class) remain unnoticed and uncomprehending. Despite gathering before the union hall, they appear as fully cut off from history as Woolf's narrator or Steedman's woman author. They need to enter the space behind the workers' doors and windows to enter history. And they need to do so with their marching feet, not their watching eyes. It was by passing through the door that LeSueur's narrator could overcome her distance from the working class – a distance, she noted in 'The Fetish of Being Outside,' that was fundamental to bourgeois, particularly romantic, notions about artists and writers – and to transform fiction from a tool of (self-)exploration into a space where boundaries between self and other blurred. And so 'change worlds,' as Anna Louise Strong emphatically proclaimed.

II

If looking at the bodies of working-class women marks a separation between professionals and the poor, then surely photographers, particularly female photographers, presented the most troubling figure of reform during the 1930s. The Depression spawned the careers of some of America's most prominent women photographers: Dorothea Lange and Marion Post Wolcott who both worked for the FSA; Berenice Abbott who worked for the WPA; and Margaret Bourke-White who was the only *Life* photographer with photo credits. These women negotiated precarious positions for themselves as artists, documentarians, and commercial photographers by using the signs of middle-class femininity – their supervising eyes – to track the impact of the Depression and the New Deal on the lives and landscapes of America's poor.

Paradoxically, the Depression provided middle-class women with opportunities to move out of the previously restricted roles open to them. They could travel the world as journalists, photographers, organizers, and teachers. In their desire to make this opportunity meaningful, to 'change worlds,' they found their poorer sisters a moving target for their work. Certainly, these women made their mark on the backs of the poor women who filled their accounts and peopled their photographs, but without the middle-class incursion into the private lives of the poor their stories and faces would barely be heard and seen at all. Moreover, the mobility open to middle-class women meant that poor and working women could get a close look at their more comfortable sisters. As Muriel Rukeyser noted in a poem, what they saw – 'more of a corpse than a woman' – was not always desirable. This doubled and contradictory interaction is mirrored in the curious status of the 1930s as a period in American literary and cultural history.

Nancy Armstrong argues that the modern bourgeois individual is most fully embodied in the woman, because she is the repository of feelings not information, the center of desire rather than wealth. But what are the consequences of recognizing the female worker whose body traverses the spaces of the domestic and the economic? If we agree that the engendering of knowledge is an attribute of bourgeois society, we might fruitfully describe one project of the radicals writing novels or taking pictures during the 1930s as discovering a working-class form of knowledge. But proletarian theorists described class divisions through gender differences: the effeminate bourgeoisie was bound to be replaced by the virile working class. Knowledge was still deeply gendered, and this formula excluded women as agents of history. A working-class woman could have no place, no knowledge, because in this configuration she is insufficiently gendered and inappropriately classed. Not fully feminine because she works, neither is she a worker, because she does women's work. Her body is a site of the dual labor of productivity and reproduction and so appears outside the divisions constituting knowledge. Understanding this reconfiguration of gender, class and knowledge might provide one means of revisioning the 1930s.

What fiction and photography from the 1930s establish is the contradictory relationship of the state, capitalism, the family, art, and sexuality within the bodies positioned in and among those institutions. 1930s literary and photographic works by committed intellectuals – male and female – attempted to refashion the domestic narratives of nineteenth-century realism by foregrounding the objects of labor – workers' bodies, spaces, and tools. This reconstruction of the bourgeois relations embodied in the fiction of domesticity deforms conventions separating words, pictures, classes, and genders by making connections between political action and aesthetic representation, interpellating (male, worker's) history in (female, bourgeois) fiction.[17]

For example, the final volume of Josephine Herbst's trilogy *Rope of Gold*, which brings the story of the Trexler family into the 1930s, cleverly refashions one plot of nineteenth-century domestic fiction – the family saga – through the interpolation of documentary intertexts. Herbst uses excerpts from some of her own reportage, blurring the line between fact and fiction. The novel further blurs the gender and class divisions separating intellectual and manual labor, the home and the workplace. The domestic space is brought into the workplace as the Flint auto workers set up house during the sit-down strike; political strategizing in Realengo 18, the Cuban sugar soviet, goes on over dinner and cards. Victoria Chance, the radical journalist, writes herself out of the narrative as she travels by bus north to participate in a strike; Steve Carson, the militant striker, begins to write his narrative on the shop floor.

Documentary reportage and photography embraced these confusions bringing the observing, (usually) bourgeois individual writer or photographer into the participating (usually) proletarian mass to show the horrors of capitalism at home or fascism abroad. However, the presumptions of political efficacy lodged in the documentary project are based in the same ideal of depth modeled by bourgeois forms of knowledge: the psychological reading of the image. The documentary desire to 'expose' the crimes of bourgeois culture constructs an other class known not through the penetration of the subject but through the display of objects. Paradoxically, that objectified class then assumes the function of the psychological subject; its surface masks another layer of meaning to be penetrated. In this sense, the Left's use of the documentary image to reveal classed relations of power is an attempt to let the objects speak – in much the same way that Marx allowed commodities a voice in *Capital* to speak of their lack of value – and so challenges the construction of bourgeois subjectivity. Yet this challenge to the workings of subjective realism with a contesting realism of the object falters at the precise moment that the image is read by its audience. To whom do the objects speak? Those bourgeois subjects slumming among them?

In the appendix to *Let Us Now Praise Famous Men*, James Agee includes a *New York Post* clipping about Margaret Bourke-White. Quoted in its entirety it stands as the only place where middle-class women enter the text. May Cameron's breezy article describes Bourke-White's presence as flamboyant and flashy; her entrance signaled by the 'reddest coat in the world' she sports. After the thousands of words Agee has used to detail the meager wardrobe hanging on the nails of the Gudgers' bedroom walls and his meditation on the impossibility of fulfilling desire when space is so cramped and the body so exhausted by daily chores, this flagrant display of wealth and female sexual allure is intended to stun and more to discredit the most popular and widely known female photographer of the decade. Bourke-White's career as a Luce photographer, for *Fortune* and for *Life*, parallels Agee's own history of employment for the Time/Life empire; but she was among the highest paid women in America while he eked out a meager salary there. It is perhaps his queasiness about this fact that gives his citation an extra bite. The column stands unremarked – it needs no comment – save a footnote indicating its source as 'a liberal newspaper.'[18] But why do we feel Bourke-White to be so brazen in her red coat? Clearly, it has something to do with the image of the coat juxtaposed with the threadbare denim and calico of the tenant farmers she photographed for the book, *You Have Seen Their Faces*, produced with her second husband, Erskine Caldwell.

Bourke-White's signature style, 'the caterpillar view,' which she achieved by 'literally crawl[ing] between the legs of my competitors and pop[ping] my head and camera up for part of a second,' was unseemly.[19] It displayed her arrogance toward her subject as she purposely imaged black preachers and white tenant farmers from unflattering low angles. Moreover, these images are captioned with quotations gleaned from the conversations Caldwell had as Bourke-White shot: 'The legends under the pictures are intended to express the authors' own conceptions of the sentiments of the individuals portrayed, they do not pretend to reproduce the actual sentiments of these persons.'[20] Agee himself had ventured into the minds of Emma and Annie Mae Gudger, inventing soliloquies for them, but the layout of *You Have Seen Their Faces* juxtaposed captions and image. Evans's photos in *Praise* stand as testaments on their own.[21]

Even more than FSA photographers, Bourke-White made her living as a voyeur, as a middle-class tourist among the neediest people, sending dispatches back to the comfortable living rooms of *Life* magazine's readers. Her first assignment for *Life*, which coincided with its inaugural issues for which she provided the cover story, traced the new boom-towns of the West growing up around the multi-million dollar water projects of the Columbia River Basin. Her assignment to send back pictures from the town of New Deal, Montana disarmed her editors, who expected the architectural shots characteristic of Bourke-White's early career. Instead, what they received, 'everything from fancy ladies to babies on the bar,' she wired the New York office, 'surprised' her editors.[22] They expected 'construction pictures as only Bourke-White can take them. What the Editors got was a human document of American frontier life, which to them at least, was a revelation.'[23]

Bourke-White's revelation about New Deal was that not only were there women living amidst the trailers and cement block cabins, but these fancy women might be mothers carting children along with them. This slice of life, the basic theme of all *Life* magazine articles, opened the lives of the poor and working class to public scrutiny. Bourke-White's invasion of the homes of the impoverished meant she was a

> foreigner who acted like one. I remember one occasion when we went into a cabin to photograph a Negro woman who lived there. She had thick, glossy hair, and I had decided to take her picture as she combed it. She had a bureau made of a wooden box with a curtain tacked to it and lots of little homemade things. I rearranged everything. After we left, Erskine spoke to me about it. How neat her bureau had been. How she must have valued all her little possessions and how she had them tidily arranged *her* way, which was not my way. This was a new point of view to me. I felt I had done violence.[24]

We wonder at Bourke-White's naiveté and at her arrogance.

Touching and rearranging objects had been something that Agee and Evans agonized over as they perused the shacks of the three tenant families who became the subject of *Praise*. Bourke-White's breezy entrance into a poor black woman's private space clearly marked off class and racial positions: one was the photographer from the North; the other the sharecropper of the South. Letting '*you*,' her middle-class audience, 'see *their* faces,' preserved the distance between her self and audience and the photographic objects contained in the book.[25] Despite recounting this incident retrospectively, Bourke-White seems to have learned nothing. We still know nothing of the woman – not her name, her town, her occupation: she is a negro woman with thick, glossy hair. I, for one, feel ashamed for her and for Bourke-White and ultimately for myself. The 'violence' that Bourke-White performed is rather akin to slumming. Still, something instructive is going on in this encounter about disjunctures between women and the attempts to overcome them. Their failures need recognition; they are crucial to revisioning the 1930s as a lived moment in our histories.

Looking across classes, like all transgressive looking, makes public the spectacle of private desire. Because the poor live outside the realm of bourgeois privacy, their lives are open to the inspection and regulation or amelioration of both the state and its radical opponents. The New Deal projects to document both the effects of the Depression and the benefits of government intervention helped erase the divide between public and private. The photographs to come out of the New Deal (including those of New Deal) melded the two spheres by bringing 'their' faces to 'you.' However, no matter how 'surprised' the editors of *Life* magazine were at Bourke-White's photographs of New Deal, Montana, the folks there end up revealing a familiar story: the story of *Life*.

The abuse poured on Bourke-White by Agee was picked up by critic William Stott, who condemns Bourke-White's photographs as 'maudlin' and 'sensationalistic,' with their faked quotations for captions and their excessive craft.[26] His most telling condemnation comes because *You Have Seen Their Faces* was so successful; it made Bourke-White a great deal of money. This 'double outrage: propaganda for one thing and profit-making out of both propaganda and the plight of the tenant farmers . . . was morally shocking to Agee and me,' says Walker Evans,

> [p]articularly so since it was publicly received as the *nice* thing to do, the *right* thing to do. Whereas we thought it was an evil and immoral thing to do. Not only to cheapen them, but to profit by them, to exploit them – who had already been so exploited. Not only that but to exploit them without even *knowing* that was what you were doing.[27]

Evans calls Agee's attack 'vicious,' but justified, and goes on to repeat it for another generation.

Their 'vicious' critiques of Bourke-White *were* fully justified. But there is more to it. And to my mind that has to do with the gendered terms by which 1930s radical intellectuals described themselves and their work. In an effort to divorce themselves from the doubly feminized realms of popular and bourgeois culture, radical intellectuals were fervently committed to a 'virile' poetics which would give voice to the new worker and ultimately a new world. Hugo Gellert's illustrated edition of *Capital*, published in 1934, presents the picture of a masculine proletariat – man, woman, and child – with muscles bulging and ready to walk triumphantly into the future once the shackles of wage slavery are overthrown (Figures 4–5). That Bourke-White imaged a defeated peasantry pandered to middle-class sympathy for this vanishing breed – the tenant farmer. Yet it also resisted the vision of the powerful masculine worker who fired the imagination of male intellectuals. In so doing, she clearly asserted her privileged position both as observer of the poor and as disseminator of their images, without even gesturing toward guilt, much less solidarity. She kept wearing her red coat despite the threadbare muslin rags shrouding the slender bodies of those she photographed. Surely this was part of her crime – she flaunted her difference.[28]

In *Sensational Designs*, Jane Tompkins discusses the vilification Harriet Beecher Stowe received for writing (and making money from) *Uncle Tom's Cabin*. Contemporary criticism, fearing the feminization of American culture, railed against the dangerous sentiment oozing from Stowe's book. In condemning the popularity of this work by aligning popularity with femininity, thus marking off the serious work of men as unsentimental, unpopular, and artful, the cultural work of middleclass women is rendered suspect. Their political interventions, if they rely on popular sentiments, and the gender divisions privileging certain kinds of cultural practices over others, ensures that their cultural work will go unrecognized. *You Have Seen Their Faces* is a direct heir to *Uncle Tom's Cabin*, complete with the same equation of blacks, the poor, and women with suffering.[29] So Margaret Bourke-White's 'superior red coat . . . and such fun' made for her by Dietrich's designer Howard Greer, presumably paid for from the profits from her book (which she worked on by taking unpaid leave from her *Life* job), makes Agee's and Evans's project all the more morally superior. Evans eschewed sentimentality in the pictures; he claimed to have 'brought photographic style back around to the plain relentless snapshot,'[30] 'against the gigantism and bathos of Margaret Bourke-White, against the lurid excitements of *Life*.'[31] Agee catalogued simple objects in his prose; he remarked obsessively on their roles as 'spy and counter-spy.' And they never made a dime from their book. Thus *Let Us Now Praise Famous Men* is a 'classic,' and we are left feeling embarrassed by Bourke-White's efforts.

Bourke-White's acknowledged 'violence' was represented in countless incidents recorded in radical women's writings of the 1930s. Their
dilemma about giving voice to working-class women was foregrounded when the 'foreigners,' representatives of the state or the
public realm – writers, organizers, social workers, photographers –
encountered poor women walking picket lines, hustling drinks, fixing
stews, or retreating into silence. Recognizing the uneasy differences
between women was crucial to women's revisioning of class relations in
1930s America. For some, this led to radical action, to an attempt to
cross the threshold separating women, through identification, even
glorification; for others, it remained a kind of socially responsive
slumming, moving through the lives of the poor not for pleasure or
thrills, but out of a sense of largesse, which left both working-class and
middle-class women trapped in their conditions, though perhaps
offering a glimpse, for each, of the restraints limiting their lives and
the possibilities of changing them.

The working-class female body was a vivid text in 1930s America,
from Mae West strutting before Cary Grant or W.C. Fields, to Ruby
Keeler dancing her heart out on top of a taxi, to Ginger Rogers
hawking her goods in Pig Latin, Hollywood presented 'working girls'
whose bodies were traded as showgirls or as prostitutes to keep off the
dole. Their energy and voluptuousness contrasted with the image of
the hollowed out, empty men on the breadlines. These Hollywood
dream girls were a far cry from the Migrant Mother's gaunt cheek-
bones and sad eyes, from the tough, grim faces of the women in New
Deal who were barely getting by and hanging on. Yet these contrasting
images, coupled with the vital 'revolutionary girl' celebrated in poetry
by Maxwell Bodenheim and sketched in cartoon by Hugo Gellert, the
women who 'sure [we]re scrappers,'[32] as they fought police and scabs
on picket, all indicate the varied space that a working woman could
occupy in 1930s American culture. There was a gap between what a
working-class woman could look like – and by extension accomplish –
and what her middle-class sister could only imitate, imagine, or
observe.

Looking at the bodies of working-class females was certainly not a
new activity in the 1930s. When Henry Mayhew walked the streets of
London in the 1840s and found 'the little watercress girl . . . although
only eight years of age had already lost all childish ways, was indeed, in
thoughts and manner, a woman,' the curiosity she represented for him
lay in her failure to express proper femininity.[33] But the 1930s in
America opened up a particular kind of visualization of the working-
class female body, one which was founded on a transaction between

middle-class women's opportunities to write, to photograph, to organize, and to reform, and which faltered on the very inequities which
made poorer women their objects of narrative, image, and action. For
rarely could either escape their lot.

The 1930s provided an opening for middle-class women to enter the
public sphere, often through the inspection of the private lives of
women poorer and darker and less powerful than themselves. As
ethnographic imperialists, as tourists amidst the other half, their
motives were sometimes suspect, their projects often corrupted. Lacking a place within dominant or radical cultures, these women looked
to the objects traditionally left to their care – poor women – for
inspiration, guidance, knowledge, and use. Yet even in their most
arrogant and sentimental appropriations, the silenced and invisible
objects of capitalist and patriarchal oppression could be heard, their
faces could be seen. Without Fielding Burke's attempt to unpack
Southern racism and its corrosive effects on working-class solidarity,
without Meridel LeSueur's push through the doorway of the
union hall, without even Margaret Bourke-White's invasion of the
homes and churches of black and white tenants, working-class and
poor women's determination, struggles, and failures might remain
unremarked and unremarkable. In this transaction, I am suggesting,
we find an earlier incarnation of the 'politics of disparity' and 'entrustment' theorized by contemporary Italian feminists – a politics that
acknowledges women's class and generational differences as 'an
exchange between these to moments of female humanity, between the
woman who wants and the woman who knows.' A politics based on
recognition of a 'regime of exchange' that insists that 'women owe
women.'[34]

The stories and images we do have are not simply transparent views
of social reality. The working-class woman resists theorizing in the
usual terms, but that does not mean we must assume that she is any less
of a subject. To do so is surely to reproduce the terms which margina-
lize or romanticize the working class and women. Failed resistance is
not the same thing as no resistance.[35] Still, we too need to be aware of
our position as we revision the 1930s. Are we a new generation of
committed female intellectuals overseeing and regulating the stories
and pictures of that other time? What is it we expect to know about
them? How is our gaze shaping the 1930s into something other than
what they were for the women who lived through them? What do we
want from the archives when we go slumming in the 1930s? These are
open-ended questions meant to draw attention to our complicity in the
representations of class, racial, and gender differences operating in

our work, even when our work is committed to exposing and eradicating the inequities caused by those differences. An earlier generation of women was moved to represent those who 'must be represented.' Their attempts often resembled slumming, especially when they sported 'superior red coats' as they worked; still they left us with an array of images which speak to us across time about deprivation and struggle – and the importance of women's urge to step out of bounds.

4

People's Culture, Popular Culture, Public

Culture: Hollywood, Newsreels, and

FSA Films and Photographs

In the middle of *Let Us Now Praise Famous Men*, James Agee includes his responses to a 1939 *Partisan Review* survey asking authors to comment on the politics of writing because *Partisan Review* had refused to print them. He is typically caustic, venting his fury over how 'betraying' they are in their elision of the popular with the people.[1] Bruce Robbins points out in his reading of this incident in *Secular Vocations* that Agee betrays his own ambivalence, one I have explored at length, about his role as an intellectual documenter of the people in the guise of a *Fortune* reporter. Robbins notes a discomfort with the people, the popular, and the public within Agee: 'The "people," written about, cannot ever be the "public," written to or for. Thus he declares that he doesn't want his book to be "popular" while asking his publishers to print it . . . on cheap newsprint.'[2] Agee's balancing act as a public intellectual, between people's self-effacing spokesmen, lone visionary truth-teller, and writer for the popular Luce empire, notes Robbins, are paradigms for the dilemmas of professionalism facing committed writers. Robbins's commentary concludes a chapter in which he has looked at Raymond Williams's spy novel *Loyalties*, arguing that as an emblem for the ambiguities of professionalism, the spy neatly contains contradictions. Like Williams, Agee knew this – he spies continually through the belongings of the Gudgers, invading their minds to produce their thoughts, gleefully using the resources of Luce for other purposes.[3] The spy appears as a (wo)man of leisure, whose work is always disguised as something else, crossing borders between legitimacy and illegitimate behavior. If the spy is the fitting emblem for the intellectual and most spectacularly for the documentarian, it is because s/he calls forth suspicions that what you see is not what you get.

Seeing what is there for the taking is, of course, what documentary reports are supposed to be all about; so the bargain the documentarian strikes with her audience is always contradictory: 'Believe what I show you because I am a spy – because I have gotten this information in a less than candid manner. Believe the legitimacy of what you are to see despite its being gotten illegitimately.' Watching this provides a double thrill; we know Claude Lanzmann is secretly filming the Nazi commandant from Treblinka in *Shoah* and lying to his face, denying he will ever repeat what he has heard. Walker Evans often carried his 35 mm camera under his jacket to snap photos on the streets and subways of New York; Dorothea Lange let her husband Paul Taylor chat with her subjects while she stood apart, unobtrusively shooting. Barbara Kopple was able to get footage of the Hormel meatpacking plant for her film about the P-9 strike in Austin, Minnesota by posing as a New York City high school student interested in meatpacking. She hid her camera in her coat to film the assembly-line process for *American Dream*. In these cases, secrets and lies, those most private acts of betrayal, conspire to inform public knowledge and reveal truths.

This chapter explores the curious configuration of liberal public culture forged in the 1930s by the differing, though often connected, constructs of 'the people' and 'the popular.' My contention is that the supposedly separate spheres of documentary, particularly political documentary, and fiction, especially Hollywood's dream-machine, commingled during the 1930s to create the makings of a mass-cultural public sphere in which certain icons of the nation – usually of the nation in crisis – converged and took on meanings that still resonate for us today. These liberal responses by corporate and government agencies were directly connected to the general cultural strategies of the Communist Party's Popular Front, ironically making later House of Un-American Activities Committee assertions that the Federal government and Hollywood were infiltrated by Communists partially correct. The political ideas and cultural activities developed to encompass the widely diverse political perspectives gathered within the Popular Front downplayed revolutionary critiques of capitalism and stressed the unity of democratic peoples and institutions fighting a common enemy – fascism. By incorporating more radical responses to the crises of Depression and war, the Popular Front in effect provided a model both in form and content for creating a national public culture; both the strengths and the weaknesses of this consolidation need to be taken into account in any discussion of 1930s public culture.[4]

The central focus of the chapter are the two government-sponsored documentary films by Pare Lorentz – *The Plow That Broke the Plains* and *The River*. Much has been written about these films, but, as I hope to show, they need to be understood as participating in a much larger series of changes in visual culture – the production of the first truly national popular visual culture – which include Hollywood musicals, Movietone Newsreels, independently produced features, and competing definitions of that illusive object of both corporate and radical desire, the American public or people. As such, this chapter argues implicitly for seeing documentary rhetoric as central, not marginal, to popular forms of twentieth-century American culture. As subsequent chapters will show, it becomes increasingly difficult to distinguish documentary from fictional modes of address.[5] If documentary rhetoric begins to merge with its other, and because documentary has held a special appeal for radical artists and intellectuals in the twentieth century, can we continue to view radical culture as a subculture, an alternative culture, or must we begin to see it as contributing to a national public culture of images? None of the works surveyed in this chapter can be seen as radical, each work emerged out of large corporate or governmental bureaucracies and their makers were staunch liberals; yet such was the power of a left-wing critique of capitalism during the Depression, that even the most commercial and/or official representations of culture engaged with the issues foregrounded by radicals.

Rita Felski has argued that a feminist counter-public sphere has emerged in post-Women's Liberation Movement America. It can be found not in the usual sites of political discourse, precisely because feminist rhetoric proclaimed that the 'personal is the political' and so circulates elsewhere. Until the 1992 election and the aftermath of the shoddy treatment of Anita Hill's allegations of sexual harassment, which surfaced before the Senate Judicial Committee's confirmation hearings for Supreme Court nominee, Clarence Thomas, women's organizing did not feed into electoral politics as much as convene around counter-institutions such as battered women's shelters, rape crisis and abortion counseling and most spectacularly – this year when Toni Morrison won the Nobel Prize for Literature – in fiction, poetry, film, and theory nurtured by women's studies programs, women's bookstores, and film festivals. Consequently, Felski argues, traditional notions about the public sphere need to be rethought in light of the differing politics of the women's movement. Nancy Fraser has explained how the terms of the discussion of the public sphere borrowed from Jürgen Habermas are unsuitable to understanding women's 'unruly practices' as cultural outlaws – outsiders to the discourses of law and power which usually circumscribe the public sphere and are often situated instead within and through popular culture.[6] We need to rethink how subaltern groups create counter-public cultures and how their alternatives effect the dominant public spaces organizing the political and cultural life of a nation.[7]

Of course, Gramsci's discussions of the war of position – the term itself indicating the importance of situating bodies in space – comes to mind, as does Benjamin's discussion of the Paris arcades as sites of the new consumer culture of capitalism which featured individual taste and social mobility as hallmarks of social intercourse. The *flâneur* who took his turtle for a stroll in order to interrupt the frenetic pace of commercial capitalism flowing through the arcades was creating a counter-public culture of leisure and dandyism, which could disrupt the shock of modernity, even as he represented a figure of modernist protest. His point about Baudelaire's poetics of the crowd is precisely that cultural forms produce different kinds of political responses. Masses and elites bumped into each other parading through the arcades, and this new configuration of the urban space fashioned public culture into a political force – classes intermingled in unprecedented ways in the arcade. Shopping meant more than purchasing commodities, something that required money; windows opened the commodities to the inspection of everyone producing new desires, but also leveling a social order because to window-shop was just as powerful as ownership (a point Dreiser makes clear in *Sister Carrie*). Benjamin's insistence that cultural practices seemingly far removed from traditional politics – shopping arcades, modernist poetry – could acquire the import of politics suggests that in theorizing the place of the popular and of the people in public culture one needs to look beyond traditional politics to the organization of culture.

The standard take on popular culture is that it functions like a sponge soaking up immediately whatever subcultural trends lurk among America's outsiders – African-Americans, workers, Jews, hillbillies – cleans it up for widespread popular (read white, middle-class and middle-brow) consumption. But that view approaches culture as a one-way street wherein 'authentic' irruptions of difference and defiance are recuperated and eviscerated by mass culture. Perhaps the exchange is just that, an exchange – a complex roadway with overpasses, underpasses, entrances, and exits crisscrossing in many directions. Maybe popular culture invented documentary expression as much as it appropriated it. If history is also collective memory, then it is impossible to imagine a history of twentieth-century America that does not include the work of Hollywood on the fantasy life and thus actual development of its citizens.[8] Pare Lorentz's *Plow That Broke the Plains* and *The River* were heirs to the documentary impulse found in the great Soviet films of the 1920s, forged in Murnau's *Tabu* made with

Robert Flaherty, expanded by Grierson in *The Drifters*, but also inflecting such widely diverse films as *Gold Diggers of 1933* and *Our Daily Bread*. By the time Lorentz was fashioning the rhetoric of US documentary film – a rhetoric that held sway until *cinéma vérité*, television news, and deconstructive techniques opened up other forms, but which certainly continues in the many educational films shown in high schools or on nature programs – his images were already at play within popular culture. Pare Lorentz wrote admiring reviews of both Dorothea Lange's photography and King Vidor's films before and after embarking on his film-making career. Lange viewed the surrounding Hoovervilles, relief agencies, and strikes and found a photographic subject among the 'forgotten men' standing idly by the docks and on the breadlines near her studio. 'White Angel Breadline' was made during the winter of 1932–33, shortly before Roosevelt's 4 March inaugural address. Had he seen the picture when it was published in *Camera World*? Surely Busby Berkeley too was moved to portray these same defeated men; *Gold Diggers of 1933* opened in June 1933. These diverse images addressed the Depression through the figure of the forgotten man associated with Roosevelt's first New Deal speech, but hadn't he appropriated the image from the torch song by E.Y. (Yip) Harburg, 'Brother, Can You Spare a Dime?' a 1932 hit recorded by Bing Crosby?

The works I look at here – Lange's photographs, especially those in her book with Paul Schuster Taylor *American Exodus*, King Vidor's *Our Daily Bread*, Preston Sturges's *Sullivan's Travels*, both Lorentz films and the Warner Bros musical directed by Mervyn LeRoy, *Gold Diggers of 1933* – move between popular culture and people's culture to fashion 1930s public culture. Roosevelt's use of the radio broadcast fireside chats and Hollywood's control of the many movie theaters spread across the nation established a national public culture in the United States. Prior to these widespread popular media, local newspapers and politics served to demark more regional cultures within the nation; but radio and movies knit together diverse populations and the uses of the mass media for political purposes in the United States and Germany in particular signaled a new configuration of state organization.[9] This 'culture industry,' as two of its most vehement critics, Theodor Adorno and Max Horkheimer, called it, threatened to coalesce a mass culture so completely that fascism was inevitable. Their grim picture of popular culture accorded with their first-hand observations in Germany, and were hardly assuaged after they emigrated to the United States, where they surveyed Hollywood with horror.[10]

Recently, Andrew Ross has explored the vexed relationship between intellectuals and popular culture; much anxiety is currently being expressed over the demise of the intellectual and dangers of television violence, etc. Generally, these bouts of hysteria rephrase previous moral panics as new media and new segments of the population emerge into political visibility. Bruce Robbins argues that the so-called decline of the intellectual from *Luftmensch* to professional is fraught with ambivalent meanings about the place of work, pleasure, ideas, and action in American life of the late twentieth century. This nexus, centering on the role of the committed intellectual in the popular life of the nation, has antecedents in 1930s trafficking between documentary forms and popular culture.

We're in the Money

Even though LeRoy claimed that with *Gold Diggers of 1933* he was moving away from the realistic quasi-documentary form he had employed in the first gangster film of the decade, *Little Caesar*, his 'grander, gayer, splashier, more lavish' musical still evoked Depression images already familiar to middle-class radio listeners of Bing Crosby and FDR and readers of *Camera World*, and lived out daily by rural and urban working and poor people.[11] The narrative is a typical backstage musical; it follows the careers of three chorines, Carol (Joan Blondell), Polly Parker (Ruby Keeler), and Trixie Lorraine (Aline McMahon), who simultaneously desire leading roles in their shows and marriage to wealthy men. Both ends are strategies to avoid the poverty awaiting them as young, single women struggling through the Depression. The story begins with their unemployment as theater after theater is forced to close by the banks. However, they discover that their former director, Barney Hopkins (Ned Sparks), plans to mount another production if he can raise $15,000. This impossible sum fortuitously appears when Brad (Dick Powell), the song-writing nextdoor neighbor and boyfriend of Polly, volunteers to provide the cash if his music and his neighbors are featured. The show goes into rehearsal, but problems begin when Brad's older brother (Warren William) and family lawyer (Guy Kibbee) appear from Boston to prevent Brad's involvement with a 'show girl.' It becomes apparent that Brad is a Boston Brahmin, not a big-time hood. His family does not go into show business, nor marry down. This insult inspires the three women to 'gold dig' these stodgy gentlemen; the men fall in love with them; the show goes on and is a hit, and the women are thus assured financial security one way or another.

Despite the conventional plot, *Gold Diggers of 1933* is rare in one respect: it offers one of the few instances when the effects of the

Depression are registered through the lives of single women.[12] Early in the film, we see the three roommates fixing breakfast by ingeniously stealing milk and eggs from a neighbor's windowsill while Carol, the torch singer, says dreamily:

> I can remember not too long ago, a penthouse on Park Avenue, with a real tree, and flowers, and a fountain, and a French maid, and a warm bath perfumed with salts from Yardley, and a dress, a little model of Schiaparelli's and downstairs a snappy roadster, and a drive through the park – and now – stealing milk!

Her fantasy foreshadows her class pretensions, which will again surface as she proceeds with her gold digging; moreover, the fantasy neatly avoids pointing out where the money for this privileged life came from. Trixie, the comic relief, provides a lesson in capitalist economics, and with it a grimmer if equally opulent picture of the source of female pleasure and wealth:

> That's all right, the dairy company stole it from a cow . . . . Just a year ago I was on my way to Havana – and birds were singing – and the skies were blue – and I said to the big mug in the next pew – 'I need a couple of hundred dollars, Big Boy' – and he said, 'In my pants pocket' – and I just reached over and took five hundred dollars out of his pants pocket – just like that – And now I have to go out and kidnap a bottle of milk![13]

For both these women an eerie equivalence is established between their previous wealth and their petty theft today. This scene immediately follows the opening sequences revealing the harsh effects of the Depression on the theater business. The film begins with Fay Fortune (Ginger Rogers) gaily singing the oxymoronic 'We're in the Money' as she and a chorus of blondes are costumed in giant Liberty-head dimes, only to have their performance broken up by the cops who confiscate props, dragging them offstage and ripping costumes off the women as payoff for debts. Being in and out of money was a fairly random or at least fairly frequent, situation for these women. Having a part or a sugardaddy ensured temporary opulence; without work – either legitimate on stage or illicit in bed – these women become scavengers – stealing milk from the neighbors, dodging the landlady, borrowing clothes to put together one respectable outfit when the possibility of work arises.

While LeRoy asserted that by spring 1933 with Roosevelt in office the nation was coming out of the Depression, the facts belie his optimistic view. Thirty-three per cent of the nation was unemployed, and virtually no programs were in place to deal with the threats of hunger and violence. Moreover, his own rosy assessment of the times is belied by the words of his surrogate in the film, Barney Hopkins, who describes his vision of the revue after hearing Brad Roberts's moving musical response to the men he passed standing on the breadlines in Times Square:

> That's just what this show's about – the Depression – men marching – marching in the rain – marching – marching – doughnuts and crullers – jobs – jobs – marching – marching – marching – in the rain – and in the background will be Carol – spirit of the Depression – a blue song – no – not a song – but a wailing – a wailing – and this woman – this gorgeous woman – singing this number that tears your heart out – the big parade – the big parade of tears. (p.72) (Figure 6)

Barney's picture of hollowed-out men, wailing, tearful women, hunger, and unemployment fit the standard trope the Left used to figure post-First World War masculinity.[14] His call for the big parade – men marching, marching – even anticipates the title of the 1934 winner of the best proletarian novel by Clara Weatherwax, but with a comic twist. He assures Trixie a part: 'The gay side, the hard-boiled side, the cynical and funny side of the Depression . . . I'll make 'em laugh at you starving to death!' (p.74).

The hard-boiled side of the Depression is usually associated with the gangster and crime genres in film and literature – Chandler's and Hammett's hard-boiled detectives, Cagney and Robinson as gang leaders – which exaggerate realism into a provocative view of capitalist exploitation. The criminal organization becomes the only unregulated laissez-faire capitalist business in America after prohibition outlaws liquor sales; the lone detective emerges as the last unfettered, enterprising individual within corporate bureaucracy. Each offers a critique of the economic and social crisis engulfing America. But the comic genres of screwball and musical were able to speak outright about what was allegorized by the harsher, darker genres.[15] *Gold Diggers of 1933*, this 'gayer and splashier' film, could actually utter the word 'Depression,' could explicitly link unemployment to petty crime – theft, prostitution, etc. – and it did so through a show of solidarity among women who normally competed for the favors of wealthy men for their livelihoods.

If the image of the hungry man and unemployed veteran shuffling along the breadline came to signal the emptiness of American masculinity during the Depression, the image of the woman of the streets clearly is fraught with another sort of (sexualized) ambivalence. Again, *Gold Diggers of 1933* quite explicitly yokes women's bodies and money in an economy of pleasure and plenty, temporarily disrupted by hard times. When the show is threatened after the 'juvenile' suffers a bout of lumbago, the producers turn to Brad to step in. However, Brad refuses to go on stage because his stentorian brother is in the audience. Trixie confronts him:

> Do you know what this means – if the show doesn't go on? It means that all those girls in this show – all those poor kids who threw up jobs – and who'll never get other jobs in these times – all those kids been living on nothing – starving themselves these five weeks we've been rehearsing – hoping for this show to go on – and be a success – They're depending on you! . . . God knows what will happen to those girls – They'll have to do things I wouldn't want on *my* conscience. And it'll be on *yours* . . . (p. 95)

Here the motif of the backstage drama, which depends on the random hazards of performing to give the chorus girl her big break, are turned slightly by gender and class differences. Brad resists his big break; he fears his brother, who can cut off his trust fund, a resource chorus girls lack. Trixie spells out how interdependent the girls in the show are on work and on working together. Like 'perfectly matched pearls' and the petals and cogs in the floral and mechanical arrangements Busby Berkeley choreographs them in, these girls need everything in place – much as capitalism does – to work.[16] Without the collective work afforded by the show, each woman will be forced to use her individual body to survive. When she goes out on the street there are no breadlines to feed her: as Carol sings in the 'Forgotten Man' number, 'Every woman's got to have a man.' And that is not only for love; as Meridel Le Sueur pointed out the year before, 'Women on the Bread-lines' were viewed with suspicion; a woman standing on the street waiting was there for only one reason – and it wasn't soup.[17]

Again, the sexual dimensions of woman's position in the economy are revealed by Peabody in his reminiscences:

> I remember, in my youth, I trod the primrose path on the Great White Way. There I learned the bitter truth that all women of the theater are chiselers, parasites, or – as we called them then – gold diggers. I remember well one experience I had with a woman of the theater. It was after the big Harvard game, we came down, a stout company of young blades, out to learn about life. I met this girl at the stage door . . . (p. 109)

Peabody's tale, replete with the stilted diction of another era and another class than that of the up-to-date but down-and-out show people, produces another set of hardy young men – not the sons of the working class who were shipped off to war and death in the trenches, but the scions of wealth for whom the battle lines are drawn along the Great White Way. Danger is in the form of greedy women, 'chiselers, parasites, gold diggers,' who sap one's money as surely as the war sapped the manhood of the lost generation. His warning about the consequences of women's performances of desire ultimately goes unheeded; he's the worst patsy of the three, falling for Trixie who finds him 'the kind of man I've been looking for. Lots of money and no resistance' (p. 134). She shamelessly approves the class distinctions within prostitution: selling oneself is no sin; the crime is being forced to do it unprotected on the street.

In one of Willard Van Dyke's letters to his wife, written while filming *The River*, he describes visiting a whorehouse in Huntsville, Alabama with John Bridgeman, the government agent dispensing funds. One of the girls invites Van Dyke into her room even though he does not want sex. There he finds a neat room with a framed picture of William Powell (the actor who portrayed debonair Nick Charles in the *Thin Man* series), another of Shirley Temple, and a few copies of *True Romance*. He receives a lesson in the political economy of prostitution when she informs him that 'a girl couldn't make any money if she only took on three men a night.'[18] Movie stars and *True Romance* are certainly the stuff of popular fantasies of escape; however, at least one Communist woman writer, Hope Hale Davis, has described how she earned her living (and provided subversive stories for working-class readers) writing for *Love Stories* and *True Romance*.[19] Like the descriptions Agee and Bourke-White detail of the interiors of the Southern tenant farmers' homes they enter, the picture Van Dyke paints is of a carefully arranged private space full of the icons of popular culture, but one that was also for 'her work' turning it into a public space.

The linkage of the chorus line to the breadline suggests still further ambivalence about the state of America's economy (and morality) during the Depression. Despite the effort that goes into chorus line work, as Richard Dyer has astutely noted, it is the fantasy of abundance, energy, pleasure, and effortless movement that gives the musical its (ideological) appeal.[20] This work looks fun, lining up for hours on end suggests a disturbing idleness even if the women are in constant motion. Moreover, unlike the women on chorus lines, men on breadlines, on line for handouts or nonexistent jobs, clearly were not productive at all. Berkeley makes this point doubly clear by placing these 'forgotten men' who are in Barney's words 'marching, marching' on a conveyor belt their endless steps leading them nowhere, the machinery of production/war/consumption becoming an endless loop leading from nowhere to nowhere, leaving Carol to beg for a handout from those who 'put a rifle in his hand' while walking the streets. They are the ultimate detritus of war and overproduction. Berkeley's method of working links the breadlines and the chorus lines – men shuffling nowhere while women 'Shuffle off to Buffalo.' He had studio technicians design complex machinery for his numbers which ate up most of the films' budgets.[21] The very vitality of the chorines in marked contrast to the haggard, depleted army invokes longstanding anxieties about the meaning of work for Americans, about gender relations, and about the kinds of 'opportunity' available to 'the people.' Douglas McArthur and Dwight Eisenhower had just led troops in an assault on the Bonus Army marchers camped across the Potomac from the White House. The image of Washington burning and troops deployed to combat veterans became an emblem of the class divisions plaguing the nation, while within the Left at least, the chorus girl was one of the few female workers who could be represented. Few as they are, one does find among the pages of the *New Masses*, *Daily Worker*, and *New Theater* testimonials and exposés of the backbreaking work, long hours, sexual and physical dangers, of chorus line work. Its organization resembles a sexualized and feminized form of assembly-line production within heavy industry. Each individual dancer subsumed by the whole; yet the whole remaining utterly dependent on the simultaneous efforts of individual workers.[22] In short, *Gold Diggers of 1933* both mocks and sympathizes with the plight of working-class men and women – those forgotten on the lines of capitalism.

We'll be in California Yet[23]

This whole complex scenario – of sex, work, money, relief – is replayed at the end of the decade in Preston Sturges's spoof of LeRoy's spoof, *Sullivan's Travels*. John Sullivan, director of such smash hits as 'Ants in Your Plants of 1939,' declares he wants to make a picture about the struggle between labor and capital, about social problems, only to discover that on his salary, he hasn't a clue about poverty and need. His producer humors him and says, sure, 'but with a little sex,' and sends Sullivan on a cross-country vagabond (Figure 7). Sullivan's travels lead him back inevitably to Hollywood – the dreamland where he relies on the costume department for his rags, and the publicity department follows him with a chef and doctor as he wanders the land with Veronica Lake, a down-and-out actress returning to Chicago after refusing a few casting couches. Eventually, Sullivan succeeds in slipping out of Hollywood's reach and lands on a chain gang as a vagrant. When he realizes that there is no justice for the poor and homeless and that he will spend his life draining swamps, he announces that he is film director John Sullivan's murderer in order to get his picture in the newspaper. As a media specialist he knows how to manipulate publicity and free himself, but not before he learns his lesson – that laughter, the humor provided by cartoons, brightens the lives of those less fortunate than he – white convicts and the black congregation that invites them to church for a night's entertainment. By the 1940s, with the economy heating up and war imminent, Depression kitsch could be unabashedly satirized. Hollywood was vindicated; it had made a film of John Steinbeck's *The Grapes of Wrath*, and besides 'the people' liked popular culture. Sturges's darkly funny reverse send-up of Steinbeck's book owed much to Dorothea Lange's and Paul Taylor's phototextual book of 1939, *American Exodus*, in which they document the economic and natural disaster of the Dust Bowl by chronicling the end of a way of life. The Southern tenant farmers they find will soon be arriving at the borders of California, even entering Hollywood and winning an Oscar in the process the same year that Sullivan rides the rails (Figure 8).

It was amidst the ruins of rural America that the most poignant images of the Depression were found. The gold diggers and forgotten men of musical comedy wailed and marched in an urban landscape still gleaming with the skyscrapers erected during the Jazz Age. But the land, on which a whole way of life had survived, was 'just fit fer to hold the world together,' according to one young sharecropper (p. 21). The 'Record of Human Erosion' that Lange and Taylor together set out to document linked human and natural disasters in much the same way as Lorentz had; however, as portrait photographer and social scientist, each found the effects on populations through the telling details found on individual faces and in personal testimonies. Explicitly rejecting the bathos of *You Have Seen Their Faces*, *An American Exodus* presents itself as 'adher[ing] to the standards of documentary photography . . . . Quotations which accompany photographs report what the persons photographed said, not what we think might be their unspoken thoughts' (p. 15). The images chronicle the displacement of bodies from land as it is rearranged from part of a human community into an abstract commodity, often with a keen sense of irony. Not only does Taylor's commentary act as captions for the images, but Lange herself often captioned through the image (Figure 9). Lange collected some of the remarks made to her while she photographed: 'Burned out, blowed out, eat out, tractored out.' The speakers unknowingly repeat lines from *Plow* as they connect the drought with larger economic and political transformations; 'the tractor's as strong against us as the drought,' they tell her. 'Every time you kill a mule you kill a black man.' Then remark, 'a picture of me cain't do no harm' (pp. 41, 135). In her attention to the individual face, Lange presents the connections between 'human' and 'erosion' in a way that Lorentz does

86

not. Here the plow breaks up more than the plains – the land – it destroys a community, a way of life, families and individual bodies and finally alters the nation as a whole. From *Sullivan's Travels* to *American Exodus* popular and documentary forms tracked the movement of people across the continent, refiguring relationships to land, self, nation, and culture.

Roland Barthes observed that the era of photography ushered in a new form of social experience – 'the publicity of the private' – by which I take him to mean a collapse of the gendered and spatial conventions of bourgeois culture dividing domestic from political instituted in the late seventeenth century. These separate spheres most rigidly enforced during the mid-nineteenth century had already eroded at this very moment, and it was photography, among other technologies, that had contributed to the blurring of borders. The peculiar status and appeal of the photograph – as sentimental and personal *memento mori*, and as public, official record of crime, disaster, ceremony – calls up simultaneously distinct associations from both personal and political sources. A mugshot is also a portrait; a snapshot a record of an event. An erotic photograph mass-marketed began in the privacy of a bedroom, and so forth. The meanings and practices of the photograph – its ability both to capture a particular moment and utterly transcend it, surviving long after its subject (and its maker) have passed on – serve to undo neat chronological history. Photographs are always doubled (at least) events – records of the camera's presence at the moment they were taken, and representations of that moment for another set of eyes. Here history and image rearrange themselves as the image produces historical meaning as much as history makes sense of the image.[24]

I do not need to remind my readers of the power of images – a power that includes their ability to exceed the original impulse of their creation. For instance, the troubling story of Lange's 'Migrant Mother,' told and retold, offers with acute poignancy an example of discourse as repository of meaning – the photograph as much as its checkered history includes a woman and her children, a photographer, a government bureau, popular magazines, museums, scholars, and a changing public – an image and tale composed, revised, circulated, and reissued in various venues until whatever reality its subject first possessed has been drained away and the image become icon.[25] Other images by Lange, of course, work this way as well, recasting history through their iconicity. We might consider 'White Angel Breadline' another case in which image and history begin to collapse and realign. What caused her, like so many artists in the 1930s, to leave her studio and walk the streets, wander the highways, to seek out those who would never set foot in her workplace? Her road shots often included billboards whose slogans provided satirical commentary on the 'American Exodus,' which she and her husband Paul Schuster Taylor were documenting (Figure 10).[26] On occasion she dissembled, as Maren Stange has shown of her excerpting from the bureaucratic response to a woman's request for burial funds by putting those words, essentially reported speech, into the mouth of her forlorn, high plains woman. At other times she merely recorded facts as in the captions for her FSA photos or for those done in the 1940s of the Japanese Relocation Camp photographs, with equally powerful effects. She knew how to manipulate poses and arrange figures; James Curtis has argued convincingly that she used all her resources as a portrait photographer to pose the Migrant Mother for maximum empathetic effect.[27] Sally Stein and Sandra Phillips demonstrate how Lange used symbol and gesture to convey excess meanings, involving ideas about land, family, community, and body, through composition, angle, lighting, and so forth.[28] She captioned visually as well as with words, producing startling interventions into portraiture, into official record-keeping, into privacy.[29]

Lange not only figured the publicity of the private, but in her discovery of the intimate moments of individuals standing apart from a social apparatus and coiled within their own bodies according to Sally Stein's complex reading of the meanings of bodily harm and pain in both the national and Lange's imagination, Lange found a visual language for conveying physical pain and exhaustion. In a nation focused on FDR's crippled body as a metaphor for the economic paralysis facing the nation, Stein argues, Lange, as a crippled woman, foregrounded isolated bodies leaning on feeble supports to suggest the ruinous effects of social forces on individuals. Phillips argues, using a quotation from Lange's son, that the 'family was an act of imagination' for Lange, and that this imagined act became the sustaining metaphor for her documentary efforts to account for changes in the social, economic, and political relations in the United States from the 1930s through the 1960s. Lange also figured the privacy of the public. Lange's work as iconic 1930s documentary images had enormous impact on the documentary film-makers of the 1930s, who in turn influenced Hollywood's directors to 'sing a song of social significance.' But it was also Hollywood and the popular films flooding the nation's cheap movie theaters from Warner Brothers and RKO studios especially that helped shape and disseminate the conventions of documentary pose, subject, and impact as much as Hollywood picked up on documentary expression.

Perhaps the most interesting example of the slippage among popular culture, people's culture, and public cultures had been King Vidor's independently produced 1934 film, *Our Daily Bread*. Vidor claims he got the idea for the film from a newspaper account of a collectively run farm established by the unemployed which relied on the barter system to eke out a subsistence during the Depression; its credits declare the film was 'inspired by the headlines of today.' He wanted to use the power of film to disseminate this idea to a wider audience. With a script by Joseph Mankiewicz, the film moves in and out of B-movie conventions with its Mary Astor-like good girl heroine, its John Garfield-like working stiff, its Jean Harlow-like gangster's moll, its George Raft-like hood, as well as its host of ethnic stereotypes. Filmed for a low budget with Karen Morley and a few other contract actors in lead roles, *Our Daily Bread* follows the path of John and Mary from the poverty that inevitably awaits them in the city to the land, whose gifts of plenty are ripe for the taking if only someone is willing to work it.

However, both newly-weds are city people and it is only a fortuitous flat tire which strands Chris, a Swedish farmer from Minnesota, outside their unplowed fields that saves the couple from ruin. With Chris's help, farming begins, providing John with an idea – others with needed skills may be on the road too. He erects signs along the highway, in imitation of the old Burma Shave signs, advertising free housing, and soon the place is full. The usual Hollywood assortment of characters includes plumbers, carpenters, stone masons, plus, for comic relief, two other ethnic types – a Jewish tailor and a Hungarian first violinist – and a shady loner rounds out the assortment of regular folks. Work proceeds as each skilled worker barters his labor in exchange for help from his neighbors – the violinist gives music lessons, the tailor gets to say thanks to his wife, who goes into labor. A form of socialist government, under the one big boss, John, is instituted and harmony prevails.

Trouble arrives in the form of a blonde driving her dead man's roadster – with him still in it! She quickly installs herself and her radio in John's house and makes a play for him. As if the sexual tensions weren't enough, the crops begin to wither and die for lack of rainfall. When the sheriff arrives to foreclose on the farm, however, the group rallies, using a ploy that Iowa farmers had devised to buy back equipment and land at auction for a few pennies. But supplies run low and there is much discontent. The gangster, Louie, turns himself in for the $500 reward on his head to feed the collective, but John decides to run off with Sally. His conscience gets the better of him just as they drive by the pump house, when he realizes that the men could work together and build an irrigation ditch from the reservoir to the land securing water for the fields. John returns, organizes the massive ditch-digging procession, and the film ends with the communards dancing wildly in the mud as the fields fill up and the corn tassels sway in the breeze.

Vidor cleverly shifts registers over and over in the film from domestic melodrama to political exposition. By using the tropes of Hollywood *and* of documentary together, he links the popular romances, gangster films, and even musical comedies to the images that were already becoming Depression icons of the overloaded cars migrating West, the endless lines of men looking for work, the blown-out land, dry and dusty from drought. His use of non-actors contributed to the documentary feel of the film. Much of the film is shot in dark interiors or at night, and the high contrasts and flat spaces lend a sense of claustrophobia to the film. It is only when the people are working in the fields or digging the ditch that the screen opens up, light enters, and physical movement occurs (Figure 11). Here collective labor saves not only the farm but the family. When the corn first sprouts Mary calls John to join her before the new life. He declares that he feels just like a mother at the sight of his shoots. She beams with Hollywood key lighting – a device that often signified pregnancy during Hays Code censorship. (From then on she is always seen knitting, another signifier of maternal bliss.) But her rival, the vampish blonde who smokes, drinks, plays jazz, and intends to open a beauty parlor on the farm, disrupts the couple and the community. Sally's overt sexuality has no place in this collective endeavor, which has lured a colony of families. Both single people – Louie and Sally – must leave the farm; their shady pasts cannot be reformed by the hard labor of the land. Everyone else can become part of the process because they are already collectivized within the nuclear family.

As an instructional film, *Our Daily Bread* actually presents a much more conservative and narrow picture of community life than the pure entertainment offered by *Gold Diggers of 1933* in which the chorus girls forge an alliance to survive the hard times. Still, Vidor's film is significant for a number of reasons – his maverick film made during the EPIC (End Poverty in California) campaign (a grassroots movement Upton Sinclair forged within the Democratic Party in his bid for governor of California) defied the Hollywood moguls, who banded together in what was really the first effort by Hollywood to enter the political landscape. Hollywood studios financed a number of fake newsreel films depicting California's borders being flooded by incoming migrants escaping drought and poverty in the East and Midwest. Their scare tactics, coupled with Roosevelt's refusal to support Sinclair and Sinclair's refusal to make alliances with the left-wing candidates,

ensured that conservative, nativist Republicans would remain in control of the state – the legacy for the succeeding generations being
Richard Nixon and Ronald Reagan. Vidor's film provides a very
different picture of the migrants, suggesting that they represent the
best of American know-how and that given the resources they would
become self-sufficient contributors to the new social order. This same
assembly of different types pulling together would reconvene in the
many Second World War bomber crews of 1940s war films.

How They Brought the Great News from the King of Kings

If Hollywood responded to the headlines with fake newsreels or
sensational dramas, the actual newsreels produced by Movietone and
other companies avoided any references to topical issues. Charles
Peden, a newsreel reporter, recounts the rules governing the stories
covered. 'The Newsreel Public,' he writes, wants

> spectacular accidents; catastrophes such as fires and earthquakes; persona-
> lity shots; racing of all kinds (horses, especially in steeplechase, are more
> interesting than motor cars, because the danger of spills is greater);
> battleships; children (babies preferred); sex – for example, bathing-beauty
> contests, fashion shows, night-club shows, and the like; events with a
> morbid interest, such as murderers' confessions; football, aviation, and
> skiing; animals, particularly polar bears and monkeys . . .[30]

The 'people' hailed by the Left and the 'public' catered to by Movietone appear to have little in common; yet as each sought to capture
'that mythical thing called the public,' a popular and populist culture
developed into a nationalist project.[31] The Movietone vision was one
we now recognize as 'orientalist'; it sought out the exotic in precisely
the way that *National Geographic* packaged difference into cosy proxim-
ity. Peden's chapter headings – 'Shooting the Foreign Legion,' 'Hunting Whales off Kamchatka,' 'The Fire Walkers of Fiji,' the list goes
on – survey others sensationalized and brought home. Most of Peden's
stories were originally published in *Adventure Magazine*; they represent
the standard fare of boys' magazines, including photographs with
captions like 'a close-up of death' showing a frame-by-frame spin-out
of a racing car; a 'tragedy' in the 'twisted, seared mass of metal' after a
dirigible crashes; an 'earthquake' near Naples and an 'accident' depicting a locomotive demolishing a Model A Ford under the heading 'all in
a day's grind.' The glamor of newsreel work contrasts the dangerous
situations the reporters and cameramen find themselves in with the
daily grind of all other professions. These men globetrot in

search of the images designed to stimulate the public with their luridness. Left-wing critics were quick to point out the ideological work of newsreels: Robert Stebbins and Peter Ellis [Irving Lerner] asked 'Are Newsreels News?' Radical film-makers responded with a resounding 'no' and offered instead a few labor-oriented newsreels for public distribution.[32]

The newsreel man both serves the public and remains totally apart from it. He bridges the gap between commercial cinema and documentary, between the news and fiction, by representing already established narratives as 'facts' to be seen, sandwiched between double features, cartoons and serials in the local movie theater. The newsreel man delights in bringing ordinary, middle-class, white people into close contact with exotic others – 'negro men, be they savage or civilized, are quite at ease when being filmed' (p. 24), or lofty persons. Peden gives a thumbnail sketch of various personalities: Coolidge is a born newsreel subject as is John D. Rockefeller, who manages to use his appearance to hawk his wares – 'God Bless Standard Oil,' he chirps into the microphone; Gandhi is a 'tough old bird,' and everyone hates Lindberg (pp. 12–15). (This description comes back to haunt Peden – or rather doesn't, but should – because the book concludes with Peden stationed, like other reporters, outside the Lindberg mansion in New Jersey awaiting news eight days after Lindberg's baby has been kidnapped.) By 1935, the Luce empire had begun *The March of Time* newsreels under the direction of Louis de Rochemont, who extended the Movietone newsreel format to include interviews, talking heads with charts and maps, as well as location shots in what would become a standard news broadcast formula – present a problem, offer a solution – also typical of *Life* magazine's uplifting messages.

When Rexford Tugwell called on Pare Lorentz to direct a number of films for the Resettlement Administration (which eventually was subsumed within the Farm Security Administration), he was calling on a seasoned critic with no experience as a film-maker. Lorentz did possess a keen critical eye about the nature of cinema and sharp dislike for the kinds of movie Hollywood was churning out. He had edited a collection of photographs of FDR which he originally intended as a newsreel. But perhaps more importantly, he was an ardent New Dealer and brother-in-law of John LeCron, an assistant to Secretary of Agriculture Henry Wallace who presided over the Resettlement Administration. Before making *The Plow That Broke the Plains*, Lorentz had met Archibald MacLeish in 1935, shortly after MacLeish had written a long article for *Fortune* about the effects of the drought on a 200,000 acre ranch. According to Lorentz, however, his film would not focus on the individual lives ruined by the Dust Bowl; instead, he told Richard

MacCann: 'We had a special lens made to get the largest possible spread. The motion in our motion picture was going to be *architectural*, the ominous changes in the land itself.'[33]

Lorentz's depersonalized view of history as natural history, in which people figure merely as props, might be seen as a direct refusal of the folksy style that had come to dominate commercial documentary in the form of Movietone Newsreels. In the titillations that the newsreel public seeks we can begin to guess at Lorentz's unease about the depiction of the people. Lorentz clearly wanted to separate his film from both newsreel and Hollywood production values. In their censorship and crass commercialism, both had conflated people's wants and public needs with popularity. His refusal to present people in his films was a declaration of cinema's ability to document larger effects – the natural and unnatural history of a whole continent. For Lorentz, the grasses and the rivers have stories to tell; and film as visual and aural medium can do that without the personalism which he sees as theatrical and literary. Yet at least one reviewer implicitly connected Lorentz's style and message to that of Hollywood: 'Voice, music, and pictures made the rape of 400,000,000 acres more moving than the downfall of any Hollywood blonde.'[34]

Lorentz had been a film critic since the 1920s; in 1930 he had co-authored a book with civil liberties lawyer Morris Ernst on Hollywood censorship which had scathingly attacked the Hays Office and state and local movie review boards.[35] By the end of the decade, he had included political censorship in his list of Hollywood's many sins: 'In one of the most troubled decades the world has known – troubles that make for extraordinary drama – we have been shown on the screen either the tense situation Does She Love Him or have been asked to consider the glories of our great West back in granddad's day.'[36] His criticism went further than most movie reviews of the time, which usually repeated the studio's publicity material: Lorentz claimed many reviewers never even saw the films they wrote up. At least twice during the 1930s, Lorentz also criticized the commercialism of newsreels. His first column in *Judge* explained that 'newsreels have so little news in them' because 'Will Hays won't let them.' Lorentz found that despite the rash of sensational criminal trials and gangland slayings filling the headlines, newsreels persisted in showing everything from 'the wedding of the Aga Khan . . . [to] Horace Liveright judging a contest of intellect between girls from Hunter College and chorus girls. The Hunter girls won.'[37] A few years later he was to chide newsreels for their endless display of battleships 'from bow to stern, port to starboard,' declaring he was 'bored' with the newsreel shots and not quite sure why the country needed a navy except to make profits for

Bethlehem Steel Company.[38] So it is not surprising that six years later, Hays blocked Lorentz's purchase of stock footage of First World War battle scenes for *Plow*, forcing Lorentz to rely on his friend King Vidor to get him into various editing rooms and walk off with their outtakes.[39]

Lorentz's sense of film as a subversive art, one which could undermine the complacency of Hollywood's censorship and corporate bombast, worked its way into his script for *Plow*. He hired radical filmmakers to shoot his sketchy outline of a nation's destruction at the hands of corporate greed, war profiteering, and over-production. Still, according to William Alexander, Leo Hurwitz, Paul Strand, and Ralph Steiner were dissatisfied with the timidity of the film's politics. Lorentz had claimed that 'if the public was too well informed, it might start something, and the idea of a nation in action is always unpleasant to the Hayses of our land who much prefer to leave the problems of humanity in the hands of God and a committee.'[40] But according to Irving Lerner's account, the cameramen felt Lorentz was trading their script with 'epic implications: capitalism's anarchic rape of the land, and – by extension – the impoverishment of all the natural resources of America: mines, forests, men' for a 'wild and private fantasy.'[41] According to a 1939 interview, Lorentz's cameramen 'wanted it to be all about human greed, and how lousy our social system was. And he couldn't see what this had to do with dust storms.'[42] Richard Dyer MacCann points out the constraints under which Lorentz was working by noting that individual Resettlement Administration field officers, who were the intended audience for the film, refused to screen it in their locales. The Texas regional office detailed its complaints in a letter to Rexford Tugwell, head of the Washington office, berating the film's depiction of Texas as a 'dry and windswept area.' Texas congressmen protested against the film, major newspapers attacked it as a libel on the Southwest; MacCann noted 'the hostility of real estate men' as well.[43] Clearly, no government agency could produce a radical indictment of capitalism; it was difficult enough to make a case for liberal New Dealism.

Good Art is Good Propaganda

In an essay on Dorothea Lange, Lorentz praised her portraits of migrants for being

> deeply interested in them as people, rather than as photographic subjects
> . . . . You do not find in her portrait gallery the bindle-stiffs, the drifters, the
> tramps, the unfortunate, aimless dregs of a country. Her people stand

straight and look you in the eye . . . group after group of wretched human beings, starkly asking for so little and wondering what they will get.

But he himself 'was more concerned about Texas and the end of the grasslands than . . . about people.'[44] Lorentz was widely criticized for his abstract, impersonal style, especially by the left-wing film-makers Hurwitz and Strand, whom he hired to shoot his first film made for the Resettlement Authority.[45] It was his insistence on making the grasslands the protagonist of the film, rather than focusing on the people, that infuriated them. As Lorentz himself described the film in *McCall's*: 'Our heroine is the grass, our villain the sun and the wind, our players the actual farmers living in the Plains country. It is a melodrama of nature.'[46] In an essay that appeared in *New Theater* in 1932, Hurwitz and Steiner explained that before the Depression they had focused on 'OBJECTS, THINGS . . . film had been depersonalized, inhuman; the THING, technique, and formal problems were supreme. Even people were considered externally, as objects rather than as human beings.' But with the economic crisis growing, in the place of cinematic formalism they wanted documentary 'theatricalization' and 'dramatization,' which 'must embody the conflict of underlying forces, causes . . . through the invention of circumstances and activities which transform concepts, relationships, and feelings into three-dimensional happenings.'[47] This could only be achieved through personal drama; Lorentz's script remained too abstract. Paul Rotha also criticized both Lorentz's films for having 'no human contact . . . lack of human beings, "difficult" music, over-complex editing,' implying that the films could not successfully sway audiences, especially since the propaganda was tacked on to the end,[48] precisely as the 'Forgotten Man' number had been tacked on to the end of *Gold Diggers of 1933*.

The film opens with majestic vistas of grass, cattle grazing in the distance, wild skies fill the horizon as the narrator intones the natural history of the land. The entire film then presents history in the form of a competing series of left-to-right right-to-left screen confrontations between men and land, tractors and tanks, wind and grass, which knits together social and economic and ecological history. The cumulative effects of poor land use are poor people found in the amazing shots of the farm family 'blown out, burned out.' A man gazes into the distance at dust swirls, a woman vainly sweeps her porch steps (dressed carefully in clean pinafore and heels), a baby plays by an abandoned plow, the sand building a hill around him (Figure 12). Lorentz had told his cameramen to 'Take your cameras into the country and show us what it looks like,' and got back 'some of the most beautiful pictures made for any production.'[49] This devastation, presented through a series of intercuts, shows the links between land abuse and economic and political influences – a series of montages establishes a conflict between the onrushing tractors tearing through the plains moving across the screen and an onslaught of tanks traversing the screen from the opposite direction. But while the tanks and tractors appear to be at odds, the ultimate victim is the land. This classic battle montage – established by Griffith in *Birth of a Nation* and used to heighten tensions in Eisenstein's *Battleship Potemkin* – sets up a curious rhythm in which war enhances production as wheat fields are enlisted in war, but the wreckage occurs in loss of topsoil as much as loss of lives. The culmination of the war production frenzy is the dazzling shot of ticker-tape flying out of control intercut with a jazz combo madly playing until the machine finally crashes, the glass shatters, the music stops. Get the picture? Six years of drought follow on the heels of the 1929 Crash, leaving hungry and homeless families who are forced West. A century of destruction results in mass exodus from the land.

Yet the film ends with a bizarre vision of wholesome middle-class suburbia – the so-called greenbelt communities supported by the FSA – which sport timberframe houses with picket fences built by those who live there with the help of government planning. For a number of reasons, this ending was cut for national distribution – it was aesthetically inconsistent with the rest of the film, and politically suspect, viewed as too propagandist, especially dangerous in its advocacy of resettlement and planned communities, a bit too communistic and a bit too inconsistent with the vision of massive destruction just presented.

Beauty, good art that is, was a tool. Lorentz had argued that film was a visual and aural medium and that few directors understood that image and sound could work together to create complex meanings. To this end, he asked Virgil Thomson to write the score and Thomas Chalmers to read his poetic scripts (his script for *The River* prompted James Joyce to proclaim it 'the most beautiful [prose] I have heard in ten years'[50]). Interestingly, his wildest critical praise was reserved for a film that opened almost simultaneously with *The River*, Walt Disney's *Snow White*, the first feature-length cartoon from that studio. Lorentz points to 'the drawings, the colors, the narration, the sound effects, and the music [that] have all been put together with consummate skill and intensity.'[51] It would seem an unlikely team – Seven Dwarfs and the Mississippi; however, to Lorentz's way of thinking each film explored the capacities of the medium. Disney conveyed 'the very mood and charm and fey emotion of a fairy tale' (p. 149). (Moreover, *Snow White* was a typical 1930s musical in that the central numbers –

'Whistle While You Work' and 'Hi Ho, Hi Ho' – were about collective – one could argue Taylorized – workplaces, and not unlike the production methods operating at Disney's own studio.[52] A gendered division of labor determines that princesses still possess the skills of scullery maids and with the help of the feminized forest animals – cute squirrels, birds, deer, and so forth – can divide up the tasks of housework making the running of the house as smooth as that of a Ford plant; meanwhile the dwarfs toil merrily in a mine virtually free of dirt or danger and bursting with precious jewels.) Lorentz combined 'imagery with personalities, landscapes, words, music and sound . . . the rules of the dramatic hold just as true for a man who is making a picture about unemployment as they do for a man who is directing.'[53] Lorentz refused the category 'documentary';[54] a film was a film, cartoon versions of fairy tales or on-location depictions of floods – the same 'dramatic logic' was at work. In fact, *The River* had its premiere along with Disney's newest cartoon character, Pluto, in New Orleans on 29 October 1937. Lorentz claimed it was because Disney had also suffered lockouts at the hands of the big studios' chain theater companies; the feature turned out to be Hitchcock's *Thirty-nine Steps*, which was having problems getting released by the Hays Office.[55]

'Again,' reiterates Lorentz, 'good art is good propaganda. If a man in Kansas City, profoundly uninterested in European politics, paid money to see some of the pictures I mentioned, he probably was bored – and rightfully so. Because he saw aimless direction, heard a meaningless score, and viewed some third-rate photography.' (Lorentz actually mentions no pictures; instead he chastises: 'extreme left-wingers in movies have taken the attitude that because a movie is liberal it therefore is "good"' (p. 192).) He was extremely bitter about his encounter with Hurwitz, Steiner, and Strand during the filming of *Plow*, taking any chance he could to denounce 'the left-wing, self-conscious, social irony that so often defeats the purpose of creative workmen with a point of view.'[56] Willard Van Dyke, Lorentz's cinematographer for *The River*, also disavowed their politics; he too was impatient with politically motivated images.[57] In an early analysis of Dorothea Lange's San Francisco street photographs of 1933–34, he praised her refusal of 'a personal interpretation of the individual or situation. Neither does she encompass her work within the bounds of a political or economic thesis.'[58] Lorentz's invocation of the people embodied by the common man from Kansas City profoundly uninterested in politics – he writes this in July 1940 when it might be possible to find someone not interested in the wars in Europe and China – suggests he actually shares much with newsreel producers; still, his point is that film audiences are highly sophisticated viewers whose tolerance for bad movies about good subjects is the result of well-refined tastes, developed in part by newsreels and Hollywood.

As a formalist, Lorentz is careful to detach subject-matter from style. In his review of Joris Ivens's *The 400,000,000* and Herbert Kline's *Crisis*, two films about the wars in China and Czechoslovakia, respectively, he notes of Ivens's work: 'here was a movie about something, a story of a great and tragic war in our time . . . . But,' he goes on, the film was dull despite great cinematography, fine script, original score.[59] In both cases, Lorentz finds the films 'ill-contrived,' blaming poor editing for a lack of coherence and pacing that could pull the images, narration, and score together. The dictatorial director – Lorentz was known as a difficult man, 'an artist' – is essential for the affective unity of film. Lorentz praises few directors – Murnau, Vidor, Chaplin, Disney – each meticulous and dictatorial in their control of the film process. Despite regaling film's collective practice, Lorentz was bent on forging a unified whole; each film required a tensile integrity that could be achieved only by subordinating the parts – sound, narration, visuals – to the whole. A critic noted that Lorentz's films were 'made in the cutting room'; Lorentz himself confessed to Van Dyke that he had not written the script for *The River*.[60] Moreover, Van Dyke revealed that he had informed Lorentz 'that a lot of his ideas were literary, not translatable into visual terms' after his assistant Stacy Woodard complained about 'motifs, song of the river, symphony of cotton.'[61] Woodard was bored shooting thousands of feet of film on a sequence that could have been done in five hundred. Van Dyke estimates that Lorentz had one hundred thousand feet of film for a film that would eventually run three thousand feet (p. 47).

In the middle of filming this saga of water, the floods actually began. Lorentz sent his crew through Louisiana, Arkansas, Texas, and Tennessee to follow the rising waters. Van Dyke was elated: 'Maybe it will add the human thing that this film needs,' he wrote his wife (p. 49). But their efforts were thwarted 'by the nature of the catastrophe – as soon as an area is flooded it becomes inaccessible; before it is flooded it isn't "photogenique."' (p. 50). The 'human thing' remained elusive in this saga of another of nature's 'catastrophes,' so Van Dyke wanted to 'hire a family to stage some stuff,' but his assistant Floyd Crosby 'assumed the psychology of a newsreel man. It must be documentary' (p. 50).

This and Lorentz's method of working in the editing room creates an aesthetic of the film strangely akin to Busby Berkeley's rendering of the chorus line and its elaborate choreography for the camera; the endlessly matched chorines assemble another unity – giant neon-lighted violins or enormous pianos, etc. Busby Berkeley, who learned his craft directing military marching bands during the First World

War, also believed in control. His choreography was not musical, however; he choreographed for the camera, producing a mechanical symmetry of movement that defied the logic of proscenium vision and brought the spectator new visual perspectives of the body in motion – perspectives that ironically resembled the precision of scientific imaging techniques designed to graph life.[62] His unnatural images present a highly stylized vision uniting natural and mechanical movement. Precisely the work of the camera. Lorentz's relentless litany of river names and river towns repeats itself throughout *The River* and unites the nation as well. Two-thirds of the nation is embraced by the Mississippi and its tributaries, thus no one can ignore the effects of flood waters (Figure 13). Moreover, as Van Dyke discloses, many of the scenes were staged in exactly the way Vidor had choreographed the irrigation ditch-digging sequence in *Our Daily Bread* as 'music. There is nothing factual about it beside the fact that the men use picks and shovels . . . . I wouldn't even approach a documentary film on a factual basis. Facts need to be interpreted . . . . Acting is not factual, but life interpreted.'[63] Van Dyke was more explicit: '*It has to be controlled.* There is no other way to do documentary stuff and have it mean anything,' he wrote to his wife.[64]

Despite Charles Peden's insistence that 'negro men are quite at ease when being filmed,' Van Dyke found that he needed to ply the 'ten big Negroes' he hired with whisky and cigars to get them to 'loosen up' during the levée-building scene. Then he asked them to sing 'if I brought another bottle of whisky and gave them another day's work. . . . They loosened up, came by the camera with that "certain thing" in their faces, singing a hymn for all they were worth . . . they were fine to work with and took direction like seasoned actors.' Like Vidor's ditch-digging scene, the sequence of 'men and mules/mules and men' required direction. As Vidor noted, had he hired a professional ditch-digger to direct the scene it would not continue thrilling audiences; the men work at a pace unimagined by actual workmen. In the levée sequence, the men re-enact another era's method of working;[65] Van Dyke 'had to hedge a little bit' to get them to appear strained. In so doing, he made sure that they understood the racialized power dynamics of film-making: 'Tomorrow,' one of the men says to Van Dyke, 'we *really* gone make a pitcher fo' you, white Cap'n.'[66] Van Dyke was deeply disturbed by the racism he encountered while working in the South, insisting that a black assistant be paid the same as a white one despite prevailing customs; yet his method of working in this scene fit the norms exactly.[67] By the time *The River* was finished, Van Dyke felt that he had lost control of the film and his work. He wrote: 'I don't like to do news stuff . . . I keep thinking of the drama of this situation, but I think of it in *personal* terms, in terms of kids and women, and men, and the heroic things they are doing. I can't think of water over cities and have it evoke any response' (p. 52) (Figure 14).

I showed *The River* to my classes – one about the 1930s, the other on documentary – at the University of Minnesota in Minneapolis during the spring and summer rains of 1993. Daily, the sky filled with clouds and the rain poured down – downtown St Paul was under water; we followed the path of the swelling river on the news, hearing the names of towns repeated in 1993 from Lorentz's 1937 film. What had looked corny and camp, with its outmoded voice-of-God narration, the self-conscious poetry of the narrative, the score treacly with American folk strains, the melodramatic shots of trees falling, water streaming, smoke billowing, took on a different feel for my students and me. When the narrator drones out the dates of floods – 1903 and 1907, 1913 and 1922, 1927, 1936, 1937! – we silently filled in 1993. When he lists the towns filling with water, we added our own. What had seemed a closed, archival document suddenly was remarkably open and imme-diate. Still, seeing the nation's heartland ravaged, spread out for perusal from above, presented a markedly different vision from that of Lorentz's film which stays close to the river's banks; but our connection to a past history was tangible, precisely Lorentz's desired effect.[68]

The 'most beautiful prose [Joyce had] heard in ten years,' claimed W.L. White, consisted of a long list of the names of the streams, rivulets, brooks, creeks, rivers, and the towns standing along them that run down 'two-thirds the continent.' Again, Lorentz had assembled a melodrama, this time of water, with the music of Thomson and Chalmers's soothing American voice, a tightly edited half-hour film culled from more than fifteen hours of footage. But it is his narrative that afforded the film top prize for documentary in the 1938 Venice International Film Festival.

Down the Yellowstone, the Milk, the White and Cheyenne;
The Cannonball, the Musselshell, the James and the Sioux;
Down the Judith, the Grand, the Osage, and the Platte,
The Skunk, the Salt, the Black and Minnesota;
Down the Rock, the Illinois, and the Kanakee
The Allegheny, the Monogahela, Kanawha, and Muskingum;
Down the Miami, the Wabash, the Licking and the Green
The Cumberland, the Kentucky, and the Tennessee;
Down the Ouachita, the Wichita, the Red, the Yazoo.

Down the Missouri three thousand miles from the Rockies;
Down the Ohio a thousand miles from the Alleghenies;

Down the Arkansas fifteen hundred miles from the Great Divide;
Down the Red, a thousand miles from Texas;
Down the great Valley, twenty-five hundred miles from Minnesota,
Carrying every rivulet and brook, creek and rill,
Carrying all the rivers that run down two-thirds the continent –
The Mississippi runs to the Gulf.[69]

The lyrical invocation of place names links Lorentz to the Whitma-nesque tradition resurrected in the 1920s by Hart Crane and William Carlos Williams. America was an act of imagination for most of the (middle-class) spectators of the film. The great migrations of the 1920s and 1930s were undertaken by the poor – blacks north and southern whites west. Yet in a typical Popular Front equation, Earl Browder, Secretary General of the CPUSA, coined the phrase 'Communism is Twentieth-Century Americanism' for his 1936 presidential bid, link-ing the national heritage to radical change, connecting the poetic imagination of America with the economic dislocations felt by the poor. Lorentz's narration brings together the course of the rivers with the course of American history, tracking the thousand miles of levées from New Orleans to Cairo built by 'men and mules, mules and mud,' which enabled the cotton trade, lumber trade, coal and steel manufac-turing, and the relentless destruction of land and resources for profit, for expansion, for exploitation. He does this by carefully choreo-graphing flowing images of water and land, the labor of men and animals, with staccato images of steamships being loaded, tall trees being felled, smoke pouring from chimneys as the river is transformed from a gentle cascade to seethe with frenzied violence. Again, a horrific picture not easily controlled, even with the magnificent slopes of concrete damming the furious water.

Lorentz had succeeded, like Whitman, Crane, and Williams, in imagining the nation as landscape and language. In so doing, he asks why you need to represent people working to convey public works. Unlike *Plow*, *The River* was hugely successful, even popular, with government agencies and commercial audiences alike. It played for weeks in New York and other major cities, and reaped rave reviews. Its tacked-on ending depicting the TVA project perhaps seemed suffi-ciently monumental to hold the flood waters. A public work that actually seemed to work for people, TVA projects were extremely popular; they created jobs and electricity – incontrovertible goods. Only later, again under the satirical eye of Preston Sturges, did these massive public works projects come in for derision in *The Great McGinty*: 'You think a dam is to hold water,' bellows Akim Tamiroff the corrupt political boss, 'a dam is to hold concrete. And you know what happens to concrete? It cracks.'

By the end of the decade, Hollywood was spoofing the practice of social realism and documentary rhetoric in films like Sturges's *Sullivan's Travels*, a film that makes it clear you can never get out of Hollywood, never leave the land of image for that of truth. And the FSA had given way to the Office of War Information, replacing its lines of down-and-out migrants and farmers with wholesome small-town America abundant with children and foodstuffs. But for a time – and Lange and Lorentz perhaps best embody this – the practice of socially engaged image-making, 'art' as 'propaganda,' as political discourse, as historical fact, even historical agent implied seeking out privation, imaging need, and hoping those representations would produce actions. For the implicit meaning of documentary is not only to record but to change the world – to evince material effects through representation – and to do so through highly personal interventions into public life. In this, the work of committed artists, of documentarians, seems to me a fundamentally postmodern one, one that collapses the divide between action and representation, between image and deed, in much the same way that Barthes claims photography in general collapses the divide between public and private.

This may seem far-fetched in that the dominant emotion of the 1930s documentary was sincerity; slipping as William Stott notes into sentimentality, sometimes to the point of maudlin melodrama. Its declaration of presence – I saw this – requires (or provokes) a belief – If she saw this, it must be true. Never mind that the subjects are posed, their objects rearranged, their actions staged. Still, as Brecht and Benjamin noted in their discussion of photography, without a caption, often an ironic one (and Lange was the master of the understatement) an image is open, too open, to any appropriation. (Witness the prosecution's use of the George Holliday tape of Rodney King's beating at the hands of the Los Angeles Police Department to which I will turn in Chapter 9.) Their call for the caption, for a linguistic interface between image and its reception, was a refusal of the transparency of the image – they paved the way for the contemporary questioning of photographic truth. But, I would argue, so did someone like Lange and to a lesser extent Lorentz. Lange understood and manipulated, perhaps even fashioned, the semiotics of visual and textual interactions for a broad audience.

Hollywood studios had collaborated to produce false newsreels of the hordes of migrants streaming into California in order to defeat Upton Sinclair's EPIC bid for governor of California. Then they provided stock footage to Lorentz for both his pictures, and finally celebrated the newly arrived migrants in *The Grapes of Wrath*. The images of migrant camps came from Lange's work among the pea-pickers in Nipomo in 1936; but they also came from Lorentz's appropriation of themes from Vidor's independently produced political allegory *Our Daily Bread*. What I am suggesting is the slippage among popular culture and people's culture and public culture, between extreme fantasy and harsh reality, between Busby Berkeley musicals and FSA photographs, between Pare Lorentz, 'FDR's Moviemaker,' and Charles Peden, 'Newsreel Man,' in carving out and shaping the icons of depression America with which we live today.[70] The mobility caused by economic and ecological disaster had differing effects and produced differing affects for the men and women who tracked the migrants. Dorothea Lange recalled her encounter with Migrant Mother Florence Thompson as an exchange: she claimed they both understood that each woman could do something for the other.[71] This exchange was hardly an equal one: Lange received material and career benefits from the portrait of Thompson and her children; perhaps she and her children eventually benefited from the migrant camps which the government set up after the plight of these hungry families became a national outrage, spurred in part by the wide circulation of Lange's photographs.[72] Still, unequal economic exchanges and the accompanying social and physical mobility were at the core of Busby Berkeley's surreal visions of the chorus line and Pare Lorentz's ominous portrayal of nature's destruction. Sullivan understands his place in the economy when he views the effects of a moment's pleasure gleaned from a silly cartoon in the lives of those 'less fortunate' than himself. These exchanges across classes, regions, and races hardly threatened dominant culture; in fact, they helped create a national public culture. Yet they did suggest that the nation was compromised by the extremes of poverty and waste devastating vast numbers of people, vast acres of land.

As the recent PBS documentary produced by Blacksides, Inc. on the Depression shows, we still have not yet come to grips with the various images, memories, and conflicts of the 1930s. *Nation* critic Lewis Cole has argued that the seven-part series failed to convey the politics of the era by trying to keep to conventional regional narratives which evacuated the importance of left-wing organizing in the lives and actions of many of the nation's workers and poor. Given what I have been arguing in this chapter, this is hardly surprising. Documentary forms strive to tell the people's story in a way palatable to the public. America's entry into the Second World War solidified the ideological process begun in the 1930s, establishing an unprecedented national consensus around the war effort. The ease with which the nation mobilized for war, and the legacy through the 1950s of a consensus polity, ironically had its origins in an era of domestic turmoil. The ambivalence characterizing the creation of a national public culture that crossed the borders of the popular with the people had been mitigated by such unlikely (female) icons as Snow White, the Mississippi River, the Migrant Mother, and Fay Fortune singing 'We're in the Money' in Pig Latin. The nation – an act of imagination which Benedict Anderson claims is an outgrowth of print culture – wore a new face when visualized by mass circulation films and magazines. And, for the most part, it kept this visage wrinkle-free until the movements for social change – civil rights, anti-war, women's and gay liberation – emerging into full force in the 1960s, altered the national imagination.

PART II

Zones of Privacy

5

Writing the Wrong: The Politics and Poetics

of Women's Vietnam War Reportage

Witnessing War

> He: You saw nothing in Hiroshima. Nothing.
> She: I saw *everything*. *Everything*.[1]

Immediately after the breathtaking opening shots of two bodies making love under a gentle rain of ash, Alain Resnais's and Marguerite Duras's 'false documentary,' *Hiroshima Mon Amour*, follows with newsreel footage and Emmanuelle Riva's incantatory recitation of the 'sites' she has visited in the city – the hospital, the museum, the streets. The photographs, the bodies, the newsreels that fill them, all remnants of historical fact of the atom bomb's devastation encased in archives, buildings, beds, are the standard locations of disaster and remembrance. The same places to which visitors of war-torn Vietnam are taken on their tours of Hanoi and Saigon; the official housings of historical pain. After seeing, the actress, like all sightseers, feels she's learned something: 'I know everything,' she says. In the notes to her screenplay, Duras emphasizes that the predominant 'story' in the film is the 'personal' one about 'love' because traditional, objective documentary will never get at the 'lesson' of Hiroshima.[2] Neither will simple observation; seeing everything means for the French actress knowing everything – the facts – although her Japanese lover insists otherwise. His negation refutes the logic linking vision and knowledge at the heart of documentary efforts.

Despite the documentary and newsreel footage from Hiroshima shot or collected by Resnais and the script's inclusion of passages from John Hersey's report on Hiroshima, Duras insists on the banal love story as the cover for Hiroshima's truth. The invention of the individual witness whose personal story serves as a template for history has been crucial to twentieth-century Western accounts of atrocity and war. The device of the person organizes the accounts of Vietnam which concern this chapter, accounts by non-combatants, many of them women, who like Riva insist that seeing is knowing, that telling is action.[3] Riva's character is in Hiroshima to make a film about peace, but her encounter with the effects of war throws her into a crisis of identity; peace work leaves the self in pieces. When Americans traveled to North Vietnam (as the guests of the Peace Committee) it was to promote peace. Their writings became acts of peace-making. Yet this act precipitates enormous conflicts for those whose primary identification are as writers. What happens when war's effects are filtered through personal stories? How does truth-telling recast social and political agency? What are the connections between witness and historical memory in an age of information? In short, is writing an act? This chapter asks what it is that politically engaged American intellectuals do.[4] The scene of combat is an overwhelmingly masculine spectacle – of boredom and action, life and death – of paralyzing fear and blazing energy. War's theater precludes intellectual contemplation as it excludes female bodies; nevertheless, female intellectuals documented their views of the war in Vietnam, engendering the work of witness.[5]

In his anatomy of the place intellectuals occupy in the United States, *New Radicalism in America*, Christopher Lasch contends that no effective radical change is possible because intellectuals hopelessly mistake cultural radicalism for political activism, substituting what we now call discourse for action. Lasch blames intellectuals, but it seems more pertinent to consider what this implies about the culture and politics of twentieth-century America. Susan Sontag reasons that

> revolution in the Western capitalist countries seems, more often than not, to be an activity expressly designed never to succeed. For many people, it is an *a*social activity, a form of action designed for the assertion of individuality against the body politic. It is the ritual activity of outsiders, rather than of people united by a passionate bond to their country.[6]

To be an intellectual in America is to be alienated from the national culture, even though as I argue in the last chapter, (radical) intellectuals were profoundly responsible for forging it. Ours is a culture of incorporation, as Antonio Gramsci noted in his 1920s essay on Fordism; dissident voices simply get drawn into the cacophony of modern media. Ours is also a politics in which government opponents are given space to dissent, their very acts of dissidence serving to bolster state power. Mary McCarthy remarks on this very paradox in her memoir, 'How It Went,' which serves as introduction for the collection of her writings on Vietnam, *The Seventeenth Degree*. Given this, one might counter Lasch, arguing that for American radicals, the sites for political struggle are pre-eminently cultural ones.

Testifying against atrocities committed in one's name, as the writers and artists who traveled to Vietnam felt compelled to do, perhaps serves as the cardinal political act in the twentieth century.[7] To a large degree Claude Lanzmann makes this point in *Shoah*, as Shoshana Felman so eloquently explains in her theory of testimony. In a mass-mediated age, which depends on the overabundance of image and of rhetoric to capture audience attention, simply declaring: 'I was there. I saw this. That happened,' holds enormous persuasive power. 'We went because it seemed unendurable to stand by and do nothing,' proclaim Tom Hayden and Staughton Lynd, the first American citizens to visit North Vietnam during the bombing and write about their trip.[8] McCarthy was 'longing for an *action*,' even if going to Vietnam really only meant a 'displacement in space.'[9] Like Josephine Herbst a generation before, who 'didn't even want to go Spain. I had to. Because,'[10] these intellectuals went because they felt impelled by the urgency of history intruding into their private lives, their consciences, their dreams. It was a zone teeming with reporters. As Oriana Fallaci notes in her diary of her Vietnam 'tour': 'There was the war in Vietnam, and, if you were a journalist, you were bound to go there. Either because they sent you, or because you asked to go.'[11]

These reports from the front embrace aspects of a number of well-established genres: war correspondence, travel writing, testimonial, personal narrative, autobiography. As such, they are poised at the confluence of a number of literary traditions each with profound gender, racial, and class meanings and histories.[12] Americans, for the most part white, go to Asia to visit and meet 'slant-eyed' people;[13] they are not experts, they are more like tourists – McCarthy notes that she only reads up on a place after she has visited there, preferring to keep her impressions fresh – appearing as oddities on the streets of the North, while the South is literally overrun with the US presence: 'They don't try to hide it!' McCarthy repeatedly says of the 'overpowering . . . display of naked power and muscle' (p. 64). Saigon is little more than Los Angeles' warehouse, the next site for real estate developers.

If this pose as tourist resembles women's travel writings from an earlier (colonial) period, it is tempered by the different agenda informing the trips to Vietnam.[14] These writers go as outspoken critics of America's war; their narratives function differently from the kinds of travel writing which were the result of 'imperial eyes,' in Mary Louise Pratt's terms, looking across the borders of colonial conquest.[15] The complicity of travel narratives and ethnographies with eighteenth- and nineteenth-century colonialism is cause for much of the current self-inspection among anthropologists and feminists; a supreme irony in the case of Vietnam is precisely the ways in which the CIA and the military put the social sciences – anthropology, political science, and sociology – to work in the service of Cold War ideology and very hot forms of battle. McCarthy is scathing in her indictment of the 'human sciences'' culpability in the genocidal 'pacification,' 'hearts and minds,' and 'reconstruction' programs, all of which originated in the research of academics. '[W]e're in a new kind of war,' quotes Martha Gellhorn from the American military indoctrination manual for GIs. 'And the name of this new game is much, much more than just "Kill VC" (Vietcong). We've got to kill VC all right; but there's a lot more to it . . . we must . . . win the hearts and minds of the *people* of South Vietnam.'[16] As the first American woman to report on the bombing of the South, she found a war different from all others she had witnessed, a war not for territory, but for bodies – 'open arms,' 'hearts and minds' – with a hysterical focus on numbers – 'kill ratios,' 'body counts';[17] a war of unspeakable destruction – free-fire zones, napalm, phosphorus, cluster bombs, and massive tonnage – a war of words which only Orwell could comprehend. The horror of the war multiplied by the fury over the lies told.

But the writers do more than travel to a foreign location, they also enter combat zones; their 'tour' is fraught with danger; they are going over to 'the other side,' going 'behind the lines' (the titles of Hayden and Lynd's and Harrison Salisbury's books, respectively), and so partake of the history of war writing. Dating back to Thucydides at least, the horror of battle recounted by eyewitnesses has served as a compelling narrative form. (Within Vietnam, General Giap's writings serve to link the contemporary war of national liberation to others from Vietnam's past. McCarthy finds North Vietnamese students studying the battle strategies from tenth-century resistance to Chinese invaders for their lessons in guerrilla warfare and is appalled at the utilitarianism operating. In her education, war narratives fostered a sense of adventure, or a moral tale, but not a useful purpose.) Since Goya, war's devastation provides a visceral picture for mass consumption; one that is clearly gendered masculine. Combat photographers and correspondents seem as brave as the men in battle, armed only with camera and pen; they are a 'special type of war profiteer' as Gellhorn calls herself,[18] and their identification with the mechanisms of war is usually quite complete. Some of these very reporters and photographers, however, first exposed the outrageous American conduct of the war, declaring like David Douglas Duncan, after photographing the battle for Khe Sanh during the Tet Offensive: '*I Protest!* the tactics. I protest the destruction. And I protest the war rhetoric.'[19] If women travel with averted gaze on the political and economic exploitation of colonialism, war chronicles detail gore and heroism on a grand scale. Both these stances are refashioned in the crucible of this 'new kind of war.' There is nothing like it, not because it is so different – as Gellhorn comments in *The Face of War* – 'starving wounded children, refugees, hunger, homelessness, fear, pain and death' form 'a single plot' – the same wherever – but because it is the United States that is perpetrating this horror.[20]

The few female war correspondents, like Fallaci, confronted conflicting effects of combat. Putting on fatigues and heavy boots to enter Dak To, escorted through the battlefield by a captain who

> hasn't seen a woman for months . . . that's why he took the trouble of bringing me up here, and why he stares into my eyes, and holds out a hand with infinite gentleness each time there is something in my way, his fingers lingering on my elbow for a few moments longer than necessary, while we're wandering about on this hill, clambering over empty shells, bits of twisted metal, trampling over bloodstained bandages and bullets,

Fallaci's cross-dressing converts this pastoral – he 'leads her through the corpses as he would lead her through a field of daisies' – into a vision of hell: underfoot a dead Viet Cong soldier 'lies twisted . . . [a] lizard runs over him, comes wriggling out his neck, stops on one of his eyes and puts his paws right on the pupil.' Fallaci's diary, which like many female travellers she keeps for a relative who remains back home (her niece in Tuscany) foregrounds the gender dislocations that accompanied this 'disgusting war' in which according to her captain 'no one takes prisoners.'[21]

The works I am discussing – Michael Herr's *Dispatches*, Susan Sontag's *Trip to Hanoi*, Martha Gellhorn's *Vietnam – A New Kind of War*, and most thoroughly, Mary McCarthy's *Seventeenth Degree*, each a book-length collection of reports on South and/or North Vietnam, written for newspapers or magazines between 1965 and 1971 – are self-consciously intended to criticize (neo)colonialism and armed conquest, and as such resist the ideological traps of consolidating witness into 'personal experience.'[22] Yet such is 'the power of genre' and its 'law,' that the historical resonances of complicity with, even celebration of, naked power are inescapable.[23] They do not facilitate the process of the war's terrible destruction; quite the contrary, they seek to interrupt it. Yet the forms themselves are overdetermined by their long histories of reducing foreign places to open landscapes – if not necessarily ripe for the taking, then at least spaces of individual self-discovery.[24] Toward the beginning and end of Peter Davis's anti-war documentary, *Hearts and Minds*, the film-makers are confronted by their images. Early on, as two Vietnamese men notice the crew filming after a bombing, they comment (and Davis lets us hear): 'Look, they're focusing on us now. First they bomb us, then they film.' In a parallel moment during the closing shot while the credits roll, a pro-war demonstration breaks into a shoving match with protesters, someone asks the camera: 'What the hell is this? We were over there. We got shot at. You were there too with your damn cameras.' It is not clear whether this man is angry with the demonstrators, the protesters, or the police wielding clubs, but his is the last word.[25] Our vision is our complicity.

Still, these are protest writings, participating in yet another genre with a long history. Perhaps Zola's *J'accuse* best presents the idea of citizens claiming responsibility for their government's actions or perhaps one could look to such American classics as 'Civil Disobedience' or 'Common Sense.' Clearly a post-Enlightenment, liberal sentiment that links private consciousness to public policy (prior to that moment the issue was science versus religious heresy – Bruno, Spinoza, Galileo, etc.), it is premised on individual rights and responsibilities which took on new meanings in the wake of the Nuremberg war crimes tribunals. This version of citizen protest requires a personal stake in the political practice of one's nation. In many ways it enforces the invention of the personal and the individual and so may undercut the possibilities for 'genuine revolutionary change [which] is the shared experience of revolutionary *feelings*,' in Susan Sontag's words (p. 78). However, by giving voice to other less articulate outsiders through self-disclosure, it produces 'imagined communities' of dissenters.[26] Yet what surprises these travellers is the extent to which they find themselves to be thoroughly American when faced with the differences of Vietnamese society.

Far from Vietnam

Talk about impersonating an identity, about locking into a role, about irony: I went to cover the war and the war covered me . . . I went there behind the crude but serious belief that you had to be able to look at anything, serious because I acted on it and went, crude because I didn't know, it took the war to teach it, that you were as responsible for everything you saw as you were for everything you did.[27]

In Jean-Luc Godard's segment of the collectively made film *Far From Vietnam*, we watch a stationary camera rotate 360 degrees while the film-maker describes his efforts to make this film. At one point he remarks that we must bring Vietnam inside ourselves, a sentiment repeated by American anti-war activists in the call to 'bring the war home.' Godard had been denied a visa to travel to North Vietnam to film his part of the 1968 anti-war documentary, so he speaks of the dilemma facing most Western critics of the war: the terrible gap – half a world away – between the daily infusion of Vietnam into one's living room (Mary McCarthy speaks of the war infesting her dreams; Susan Sontag writes of its incursion into her consciousness) and the vast physical and psychic distance separating Americans' (or in this case French) comfortable lives far from Vietnamese peasants living under the hail of antipersonnel bombs.[28]

These internal Vietnams, testimonials of witness, begin in polemic. Neither McCarthy nor Sontag (is this a peculiarly female thing?) claims authority as a journalist (unlike Harrison Salisbury whose reports first appear in *The New York Times*), an Asia expert (this in part is what distinguishes their books from Frances FitzGerald's majestic *Fire in the Lake*), a war correspondent (which Gellhorn was and Herr becomes), or even a political activist (as were Hayden and Lynd), though each sees her work as serving these ends. McCarthy and Sontag are well-known authors with reputations for independence and honesty, who had access to important publications. Both women know that the North invited them for this reason.

Despite being given reams of information on the war's effects and on the North's resilience in combatting the ceaseless bombing of the countryside, the substance of McCarthy's and Sontag's reports are their 'experiences' in this 'foreign' country. Foreignness serves as the ruling metaphor in all writings by Americans about Vietnam. The multiple levels of difference and otherness felt by each displaces these writers who feel in possession of a core self. Their reports differ from other accounts of the North because they give little space to the voices of the North Vietnamese with whom they meet daily. Hayden and Lynd, like Filipina journalist Gemma Cruz Araneta who published her *Vietnam Diary* in 1968, give over their narratives to long passages, quoted verbatim, of awkward denunciations of American aggression and stilted celebrations of Vietnamese resistance. In this, their personal accounts serve as precursors of *testimonios*, a highly mediated form in which the 'as told to' tale involves the transcultural exchange of subaltern culture (in life story) to the metropolis through translation – one language to another, oral history to written narrative – from teller to writer.[29] McCarthy sketches the outlines of the issues, pausing over a hospital bed or a classroom. She tells us what she sees and feels about what she has been told about it; her story resembles the travel narratives arising as the late eighteenth-century companions to the novel, which place the 'experiential unhero,' as Pratt calls him, at the center of an alien 'contact zone.' Its literary antecedent can be found in Aphra Behn's *Oronooko*, which situates a woman as domesticated witness to social and political upheaval in the colonies.[30] In fact, after reading enough of these reports, the eyes glaze over at the monotonous rhetoric, the cast and locations already too familiar. To avoid the sin of repetition, to 'make it new' as McCarthy observes, sends her (and Sontag's even more so) observations inward.

The sense of 'displacement through space' is especially acute for McCarthy and Lynd and Hayden when they meet American POWs, whose status as prisoners elicits one kind of sympathy, whose nationality provokes another, only to be contradicted by their occupations, interests, and politics. McCarthy's 'action,' her attempt to reconcile public and private beliefs and behaviors, testifies to her sense of the unity of the subject. In Vietnam, however, fragmentation – like the anti-personnel weapons used by the Americans – destroys bodily (and psychic) integrity. Herr begins *Dispatches* with the outdated map gracing the walls of his Saigon hotel room, the country itself having been partitioned and repartitioned, named and renamed, to suit the whims of external powers for centuries still struggles to maintain its cultural integrity. So, too, do its foreign observers. But these external observers are broken apart by the war as well – by the visual horrors of the bombings (and of combat). They have travelled literally across the globe only to be confronted with themselves in pieces.

Of course it is not difficult to find direct references to truth and to telling scattered throughout McCarthy's writings. She could hardly stop telling truths.[31] An urge to 'live as witnesses' propelled her on her two journeys to Vietnam (p. 46). She finds herself unable to perform as journalist, unable to ask the probing questions which would force her to 'watch them lie', her 'vicarious shame' at their dissimulation more than she could bear (p. 23). The contradictory role of the 'truthful' in the American mission in Vietnam was paramount for all reporters entering Vietnam's borders – the United States needed to sustain its 'image' of freedom, because it said it was in support of a 'free' South Vietnam that we were there in the first place. Yet this access to the zones of combat, intelligence, and pacification were largely responsible for revealing the faults and falseness of the mission itself. (And the military learned its lesson thereafter, severely restricting journalists' access to the interventions in Grenada, Panama, and the Persian Gulf.) Thus truth itself became a contested if not actually contaminated term – journalists were inundated with reports and briefings and tours of successful campaigns to win 'hearts and minds,' only to have them radically undone by their own eyes. Few could stomach the lies.[32]

This gap in the value of objective truth is heightened for everyone reporting on Vietnam by the corruption of language daily perpetrated by the military and state department personnel. For McCarthy, this is precisely the value of her mission or 'calling' as she refers to it, to go to see Vietnam; the differential between 'objective reporting and political science' and the 'novelist's impressions' puts her readers' 'trust' in her account (p. 27). *The Seventeenth Degree* is framed by meditations about and declarations of truth-telling, a protracted swearing in of the idiosyncratic, the eccentric, point of view she brings to the field – her 'truth-seeking apparatus' as she calls it (p. 28). McCarthy concludes her introduction by way of memoir about 'how it went' with a story of another of her schemes to enlist groups of prominent citizens in protest – this time by organizing a delegation of middle-class, middle-of-the-road Americans to live in Hanoi during the Christmas bombing as witnesses, 'not in the legal but in the Biblical sense,' to the attacks. She imagines David Rockefeller among them, but produces a facsimile of the list of names she had drafted – Ron Dellums, Coretta King, Norman Mailer, etc., who were a far cry from her fantasy of bankers and stockbrokers defying Nixon's bombs – and closes with a caption acknowledging her 'censorship' of five or so telephone numbers from the page. The costs of truth-telling include censorship – self-censorship at any rate – when one discloses the privacy of one's public performance.

'Anyway, the truth I was after in Vietnam would not be found on the battlefront, which would be no different from battlefronts in any other war, but among the people, theirs and ours, in hamlets, hospitals, and refugee camps, on the one hand, in offices and field units, on the other' (pp. 20–21). Of course, as Herr's reports and countless hours of televised news coverage detail, McCarthy was terribly wrong about this, because the war itself represented a different kind of combat.[33] Something McCarthy comes to acknowledge after observing the discrepancies between Marine commanders, who were perfectly willing to acknowledge that saturation bombing created the refugees or that aid was not getting through to secured hamlets, and the Information officers, civilians whose manner resembled used car salesmen who understood that in this war 'The truth cannot be told' (p. 114). And in thus denying the truth – fostering an image – 'are unaware of how they look. The truth they are revealing has become invisible to them' (p. 115).

McCarthy's belief that being 'among the people' would get at the 'truth' of Vietnam, a truth utterly defined by the war's battles yet somehow exceeding it, has a curiously nostalgic ring to it.[34] McCarthy boldly asserts that she went 'to Vietnam looking for material damaging to the American interest' and had no trouble finding it: 'the Americans do not dissemble what they are up to' (p. 63). The vulgar boosterism – overshadowed and exaggerated by the euphemisms surrounding every event and program: defoliants as weed-killers, Operation Cedar Falls for clearing hamlets, New Life Hamlet program and Hearts and Minds project for concentration camps – is so crass and so at odds with visual evidence that new terms – the credibility gap, the 'crisis of credulity' Sontag calls it (p. 70) – followed on the heels of this new racist, genocidal and above all social scientific war of attrition whose true purpose was to destroy Vietnam's rural population; what McCarthy called, explaining the Search and Destroy missions that eventually led to My Lai, a 'demographic solution,' that is, forced urbanization (p. 408).

Truth-telling, the act of witness of self and others, is a work of language with social meanings; for the Western individual, it is about alienation, especially for the dissident, about saying, like Cassandra, what others refuse to believe. But for the Vietnamese intellectuals for whom language is an 'instrumentality,' according to Sontag, another connection to history and self is posited – one that is fundamentally relational – one always refers to oneself as someone's niece, brother, etc. The substances of Vietnam's difference from the West are the basis of FitzGerald's *Fire in the Lake*, which uses ethnographic, cultural, and psychoanalytical theories to elaborate Vietnamese history and show why the American mission can never succeed. The dissonances between the two modes shatters all but the most gung-ho CIA operatives in Vietnam. Yet most journalists, sitting in the briefing rooms of Saigon, cannot hear it either. Herr discovers stories where other journalists find none; the grunts, according to others are barely articulate – hence the name – but Herr hears a horrible poetry of truth in their brute explanations of the mission: 'We're here to kill gooks. Period.' And he is 'there to watch.'[35]

For each the crisis of identity implied in Vietnam's 'otherness' (Sontag uses this term not in its current postmodern but in its very existentialist sense) precipitates a confession of 'Americanness.' At first each author becomes more American in her refusal to hear the language of morality and collectivity constitutive of Vietnamese society. Slowly, each finds herself seduced by what is clearly a wholly different mode of living – a revolutionary society, optimistic even in the face of devastation. This suspension of their usual alienation from their own culture, however temporary (Sontag describes returning to Vientiane as a culture shock as powerful as entering Hanoi) disappears quickly. Her disgust at American cultural imperialism matches McCarthy's sense of Saigon as the garbage dump of America. Though Sontag sees the North Vietnamese having put it all to good 'uses,' making sandals from downed bomber tires, turning bomb craters into fish ponds, fashioning combs and the souvenir rings out of the aluminum bodies of jets, she still feels that North Vietnam presents a 'revolution betrayed by its language' (p. 77). The trinkets and rhetoric disturb McCarthy as well. She finds she cannot mouth the slogans of the revolution, nor can she put the ring on her finger; each gesture compromises her. McCarthy's caveat at the conclusion of her Hanoi account complicates the insider/outsider confusion. At first deeply critical of the United States, then deeply skeptical about Vietnam, then deeply moved by it, then quite cut off from it. These shifts plot a narrative of ambivalence, a narrative fundamentally about *individual* responsibility as a cultural construct.[36] Being against American policy and practice in Vietnam does not necessarily mean being for the Vietnamese; but in the Cold War era of 'America: Love it or Leave it' there is little room for subtlety. Sontag wants to reclaim patriotism and love of country from the 'yahoos.' McCarthy finds she has most in common with the French-educated doctor she meets; her discomfort at meeting captured pilots – they were so ignorant and so uninterested, wanting to know how the Cubs were doing, clearly a world apart from Eastern, monied, intellectual McCarthy – pointed up the class dimensions of the war in 1968: the middle and professional classes can oppose it while the working class fights. Bonds and allegiances are constantly shifting for these visitors; the ground is shaky and not only because of the bombers roaring overhead.

In short, going to Vietnam as a sympathetic American disturbs these writers' self-consciousness. And it is the disturbance that becomes the gripping focus of their reports. Where McCarthy and Sontag try to analyze this discrepancy between beliefs and experiences, as a fundamental difference in culture and history and psychology between Western senses of meaning and Asian ones, between bourgeois notions of individuality and revolutionary ideas of responsibility, between image and reality, Herr embroiders these discordances in his language. His is the hip, pumped-up diction of counter-cultural new journalism, macho and self-indulgent, yet keenly attuned to the 'stories' of the grunts he meets throughout the South. His confrontation with self is forced on him by the soldiers who ask continually why he is there and not carrying a weapon. If the mission is to kill gooks, what is he doing? For whom?

Travel literature has always been fraught with tensions over identity and difference, observation and experience, received knowledge and fresh insights, with the problem of translation – from vision to language, from one language and to another – and of domination – after all it was in part colonialism that initiated travel narratives and national resistance that inspired social commentary.[37] Both Herr and Sontag contrast war photographs and films etched in memory with the visceral facts they can see. Yet in Agnes Varda's segment of *Far From Vietnam*, a group of traveling actors performs an allegorical parody of the war featuring the ever-present bumbling and blustery 'Johnsons,' as the North Vietnamese called the bombers, filling the sky. In the middle of the skit, an air raid siren blasts and everyone – actors, film-makers, spectators, and passers-by – calmly ducks into the cement cylinders lining the avenues of Hanoi to await the all clear. When it sounds, everyone reconvenes and the play continues; whatever damage the bombs have caused remains out of sight. All Hanoi's visitors are struck by its air of normality. Peter Davis opens *Hearts and Minds* with a beautiful scene of village life somewhere in the northwest: children smile and play, girls carry huge buckets of water balanced on their shoulders, women work the fields of this lush landscape.

These discrepancies remain the backdrop of this 'new kind of war' writing: the moral imperatives of witness and testimony in the twentieth century. 'The point of these articles,' writes Gellhorn to introduce an earlier collection of her war reportage, 'is that they are true; they tell what I saw. Perhaps they will remind others, as they remind me, of the face of war . . . memory and imagination, not nuclear weapons, are the great deterrent,' she concludes.[38] The place of writers as witnesses to atrocity assumes new urgency with the advent of mass destruction. The scale of horror, beginning with Spain, calls forth a moral stance that undoes the objective pose of the observer. Describing *The Spanish Earth*, his documentary film about the civil war, Joris Ivens called it 'propaganda on a high level – it is more a *témoignage* or what you call . . . testimony, testimony of a man, where you know how he stands – I don't hide myself.'[39] Writers too must do something for 'la Causa' if they happen to be in Spain and dare back the Republic, someone tells Gellhorn. So she files a story about daily life in Madrid under siege, hoping to gain support for the fight against fascism being staged there. She's a writer but not a war writer, but this is not an ordinary war – it permeates everyday life, and as a novelist she knows all about that. Thirty years later, McCarthy's friends cautioned her against going to Vietnam because she was not a journalist; Sontag feels odd about this lack as well. Yet again, it is precisely their distance from the objective pose of reporting that fires their accounts.

The new kind of war writing is indebted to 1930s reportage (although my guess is that neither McCarthy, Sontag, nor Herr would care to acknowledge this debt): the form that sweeps away ideas of disinterest and demands to know 'Which side are you on?' Reportage – the literary equivalent of participant-observation in ethnography – sways readers through emotional engagement with concrete detail. Moreover, writers themselves were asked again and again to take stands on Spain; neutrality – the pose of Western objectivity and the position of the Western democracies – was unacceptable. This sense of commitment as writers and intellectuals to 'speak up' fuels the Vietnam critiques.[40] The parallels with Spain appeared everywhere: for instance, the title of a 1937 book *Authors Take Sides on the Spanish War* modeled another generation's compilation of the results of a question-naire in *Authors Take Sides on Vietnam.*[41]

If Spain was the 'proving ground' for the Second World War, surely Vietnam is prelude to the Third. Over and over again, writers assert the connections. Bertrand Russell concludes his denunciation of American imperialism by declaring the 'torment of Vietnam, like that of Spain in the 1930s, is a barbarous rehearsal' (p. 183); he is joined by Anita Desai, who uses the language of the American mission to make a similar claim: 'No war since the Spanish Civil War has so stirred the hearts and minds of people all over the word' (p. 172); their analysis is echoed by Susan Sontag who quotes Russell: ' "Vietnam is an acid test for this generation of Western intellectuals" ' (p. 46). This volume designs to draw intellectuals into the fray and effect a change in policy; its limitations, as one writer noted, came from an assumption that the military and policy-makers cared what writers thought. Moreover, the questions were of the 'When did you stop beating your wife?' ilk. Irwin Shaw reminds the editors of the ominous precedent set by the previous volume: many writers denounced Franco, but he prevailed. So what if writers appear more moral than politicians? Can personal testimony elicit political effects? If so, does the divide between private and public erode? During the Vietnam War, dreams, even of those thousands of miles away, were invaded nightly by US bombers. The fact that the North Vietnamese maintained an admiration for the American people throughout the war meant that citizens opposed to the war had to act against it; it was a matter of personal trust. If those being bombed distinguished America from Americans, then it was incumbent on us to reclaim the nation for ourselves and for them.

If Vietnam pushed intellectuals to speak up, the central metaphor of action – of putting one's body on the line – propelled the writers who travelled to North and South Vietnam during the 1960s. Their actions consisted of at least two precise moves – looking, seeing the evidence of massive destruction with one's own eyes, thus rectifying reality with image, looking close up, first hand, experiencing it – 'Have You Ever Been Experienced?' asks Herr of his readers, quoting Jimi Hendrix – provokes a new kind of knowledge unavailable to those who have not gone there. Step two, of course entails writing about what was seen, making sense of it for a larger audience (or in Herr's case, following the absurdist scenarios imagined by Ferlinghetti, Mailer, Ginsburg, Burroughs, making nonsense of it, encoding the surreality of war).[42] The details marking McCarthy's and Herr's reports (different as their writing is) are as much tell-tale signs of themselves as they are of the war. Sontag lifts pages directly out of her diary for *Trip to Hanoi*, presumably the immediacy of experience resists editing. This new kind of war writing wires self-inspection to the observation and exposure of others.

Speech Impediment

> In our society, talk is perhaps the most intricately developed expression of private individuality. Conducted at the high pitch of development, talking becomes a double-edged activity: both an aggressive act and an attempted embrace.[43]

'I think looking closely at things is something that has to be learned,' says Riva to her lover in *Hiroshima Mon Amour*.[44] Surely the reports on Vietnam detail a long process of learning to look. After visiting a 'model' refugee camp, McCarthy travels to Hue with a group of German Catholic relief workers to a 'typical' refugee camp. She fears she cannot convey the

> misery and squalor. My eyes in fact had avoided looking too closely at it, as though out of respect for the privacy of those who were enduring such disgrace. The women stood massed in their doorways to watch us pass; some approached the doctor and asked for medicine. But mostly they just watched, defying us, I felt to watch *them*. (p. 106)

Still, compared to the repeated testimony of Medina and his superiors at his trial that he saw nothing, McCarthy manages not to avert her gaze and, like Gellhorn and Fallaci, details the painful losses borne by the Vietnamese.

If McCarthy has no real stomach for looking, though she details many sites – the garbage filling up the land, the smoke and craters, the filthy leper colony, in the South; the underground schools and factories, the clean hospitals, the floating bamboo bridges, the traffic, in the North – she has an excellent ear. She knows how to listen. Her most recent novel, *The Group*, a tour de force of overheard, reported speech, shifts from one register, accent, mode of talk to another. In many ways, her 'truth-seeking apparatus,' as he calls it, resembles the radio more than the camera. Her antennae are most acute when tracking the 'language' of 'intellectuals' both American and Vietnamese involved in constructing the (dis)course of the war.[45] In a series written for that pre-eminently intellectual journal, the *New York Review of Books*, McCarthy's concern with the complicity of intellectuals in mounting a new kind of war – the political science of genocide – is a pointed reminder to her compatriots that intellectuals must act intelligently, not as intelligence. Her pieces might be read as a direct response to Noam Chomsky's analysis of the 'Responsibility of Intellectuals,' which appeared in *NYRB* only a few months before McCarthy's first 'Report on Vietnam.' Because her class is crucial to the duplicity and atrocity of this war, she needs to salvage some sectors of it.

Even before the Tet offensive, after which one American officer said of Ben Tre, 'We had to destroy it in order to save it,' Vietnam turned into 'a war of ideas,' 'a war of words,' a zone of 'semantic confusion,' as destructive and corrosive as the napalm.[46] With generals reading Mao, ethnographers as military strategists, and the most massive air power unleashing more tonnage daily than were detonated by the Hiroshima atomic bomb, South Vietnam is a vision of hell – a visceral, but also a linguistic, nightmare. In the midst of this Herr finds poets, visionaries, and madmen among the soldiers where other reporters have found illiterates and brutes. Through them he can denounce the idiocy of the war and its spokesmen; he represents their counter-culture, set apart from the tradition of engaged, yet 'patrician' 'intellectuals' that McCarthy as a 1930s sort personifies.[47] Gender and generational differences separate these two reports, yet each confronts – as everyone in Vietnam does – the discordances in language.

For instance, the two leaders of the CIA-sponsored Revolutionary Development program (which restaged the Vietcong cadre training process), Major Nguyen Be and Colonel Tran Ngoc Chau, like the American 'scientists' whose diction and disciplines have invaded and produced South Vietnam, mouth slogans about 'social revolution' denouncing both Vietnamese and American 'corruption.'[48] Armed with a PhD in English literature on Virginia Woolf, Colonel Chau is precisely the kind of intellectual who appeals to CIA operatives according to McCarthy. Like Wesley Fishel of Michigan State University, these scholars view the war as a training ground for theories devised in university classrooms and posh think tanks. They seek to know the enemy's brain – political science becomes science fiction – through 'semantics' generating a 'new political vocabulary,' as in Fishel's oxymoronic essay for the *New Leader* on Diem entitled, 'Vietnam's Democratic One-Man Rule' (p. 122). After reading enough of these reports, one gets to know the names of the guides and commanders as intimates – same tours for visitors, same litany of 'successes,' same programs touted for refugees, same lies about casualties, villages, and crops destroyed. The American information officers trot out their diagrams and talk endlessly of 'the problems of success'; the reporters nod and jot down another set of numbers.

It is not only South Vietnam that presents a vision of verbal disintegration; McCarthy and Sontag find language in North Vietnam troubling as well. McCarthy undergoes 'a sort of speech impediment. Though we talked of the same things, we did not always use the same language' (p. 262). The canned phrases – 'people's liberation army,' 'war of destruction,' 'neo-colonialists' – stick in her throat, their association with the tainted diction of Stalinism disturbs her. So too does the matter of who 'we' were: American bombs were destroying Vietnamese land as the North Vietnamese hosted the American people. McCarthy intuits (and FitzGerald explicates) how the presence of history in Vietnamese culture and language and the potted rhetoric of Marxist revolution were uncannily compatible. The modern Western imperative for writers to 'make it new,' to vary diction and syntax so that no word is ever repeated, is a wholly alien construct to a culture in which the continuity of the past with the present is fundamental – the almost mythic incantatory way that history repeats itself in and through family structure: 'we have a 4,000 year history of struggling against outside invaders who have always failed to overcome the Vietnamese people.' But it is the relative Westernness of the phrases that unsettles McCarthy: 'the vocabulary repelled me precisely because it was so familiar' (p. 272).

Rather than asking about the casualties of the bombing, which would mean using all the locutions she so fervently needs to avoid, McCarthy finds herself asking about the flora and fauna of the countryside through which she passes.[49] In this avoidance she 'was trying to hold onto [her] identity – a matter of loyalty, refusing to betray oneself' (p. 272), yet she could not deny that the terms the North Vietnamese used were 'true.' America was an imperialist aggressor destroying North and South Vietnam. Sontag also describes her 'ambiguities of identity' precipitated by the disjunctures between the ethics and aesthetics of language she hears in Hanoi (p. 35), a gap between what FitzGerald calls, speaking of official United States rhetoric, 'bureaucratic and poetic language' (p. 505). Moreover, reasons McCarthy, 'what the United States calls propaganda is in fact reiteration' (p. 273); the North Vietnamese simply repeat that all hostilities must cease before peace talks can begin. The Americans read this as recalcitrance. Again, the curious alignment of military and policy men with Western forms of intellection – give us something 'new.' In their endless search for a new set of demands, a new story, the entire apparatus of propaganda had passed over into the hands of liberals.[50] Or, as both Senator Fulbright and Daniel Ellsberg assert to Peter Davis, they lied – Ellsberg's litany: Truman lied, Eisenhower lied, Kennedy lied, Johnson lied, Nixon lied – Cold War rhetoric masked imperial designs.

McCarthy connects Vietnamese reiteration to the process of conversion – the sense the North Vietnamese have that everyone is reformable – what Sontag felt to be the 'baby talk' quality of mind she encountered in Hanoi (p. 12). Psychoanalytical theory, so firmly entrenched in the mindset of twentieth-century Westerners that even its critics like McCarthy miss it when it has gone, has no place in this 'historical,' 'ethical' culture. The simple acts of forgiveness and rehabilitation the North Vietnamese employ with their 'enemies' appear to lack sophistication. In McCarthy's account the North Vietnamese accept change axiomatically – that is what revolution is – but not difference, which somehow assumes permanence and at best tolerance. FitzGerald details the process by which the NLF, following the Viet Minh a generation earlier, cultivated hatred – an emotion banished from the Vietnamese social psyche – to mobilize the peasantry politically. Yet this country at war is remarkably civil; the hatred is not directed at the American 'guests.' Hanoi appears peaceful with its tree-lined avenues, lakes, and, paradoxically, its traffic.

McCarthy, Sontag, and Filipina reporter and film-maker Gemma Cruz Araneta all remark on the ways in which 'Hanoi looked so awfully unwarlike . . . . It was most disconcerting to see everyone live such normal lives.'[51] For instance, in two documentary films made in North Vietnam for American distribution – *A Day of Plane Hunting* and *The Women of Telecommunications Station #6* – the camera tracks a group of lovely young women performing their daily chores – tending children, rice paddies, and stoves – only to be occasionally interrupted by the US air force. The women matter of factly shift roles, manning radar and anti-aircraft guns, to track the incoming planes. Their mission accomplished – planes tracked and brought down – they return to women's work, barely perspiring. These films are careful to report, however, on the changing position of Vietnamese women on the 'feminine front' – once you have shot down a bomber, it's hard to take abuse from a man

– a point reiterated by the Women's Association members to Araneta (p. 25).

It seems that virtually everyone goes to the movies while in Hanoi, seeing the same saga of intergenerational revolution: a young girl cuts down the pine trees planted by her father to aid the war effort. Araneta found it 'propaganda . . . gripping, sentimental and full of human interest' (p. 106), but McCarthy noted that she was the only member of the audience to cringe at the mawkish melodrama. Araneta's diary, unlike Sontag's, is given over to the voices of the Vietnamese; so many of the passages she quotes are exactly the same as those Hayden and Lynd record; she is in Hanoi to make a film and finds enormous rage against the imperialists among the same Vietnamese who appear so cool-headed to the Americans. (Perhaps as an Asian Marxist she was privy to a different, truer, affect; they also charged her and her companion for their stay and equipment while the American guests of North Vietnam were not allowed to pay for anything – not even telegrams to their children in the States. Or perhaps it is the power of the camera. Davis films the anger and despair of bombing survivors: a North Vietnamese man whose 'sweet' eight-year-old daughter died in a raid because she was in the yard tending the pigs (the pigs survived, she didn't) picks up her 'beautiful shirt' and hurls it screaming, 'Give this to Nixon, tell him about my daughter.')

This gap between the imagined arena of war, its actual reality – the devastation of the countryside by the incessant bombing – and mundane daily life of the cities lived under the bombs provides a leitmotif for many of the other observations of Vietnam's visitors. McCarthy finds it somewhat obscene that Saigon is so prosperous – where is the privation accompanying war? Gellhorn chastises the American propaganda machine for making things seem worse than they were, as if Vietcong lurked behind every tree in the jungle and grenades exploded on every corner of the cities. Herr comments on the bizarre, but relatively secure atmosphere of the foreign correspondents' hotel in Vietnam to accentuate the sheer terror of 'action.' Davis returns again and again to a Saigon coffin-maker mournfully profiting from the war, having already buried seven of his children. The city is not as bad as the countryside, he declares, where there is no more wood for a proper funeral casket. Fallaci goes to Vietnam in search of the war and finds 'a chaos almost gay in Saigon':

> rickshaws plunging into traffic and swiftly peddling on . . . water sellers scurrying about, their merchandise swinging from a bamboo stick across their shoulders . . . minute women in long dresses, their loose hair waving behind their shoulders like black veils . . . shoeshine boys with brushes and

tins of shoe polish . . . bicycles . . . motorcycles . . . filthy, reckless taxicabs. (p. 3)

Hanoi's foreign visitors dream of action too; the city seems so well-mannered. They all have stories to tell of air raids and the 'thrill' of real danger, knowing they have become acclimatized when they no longer hurry into the hotel bomb shelter because they recognize a false alarm. During McCarthy's interview with Pham Van Dong, an air raid pre-alert is signaled:

> 'If you don't mind,' the Prime Minister said, 'we will stay here in my office.' I did not mind at all; indeed I felt honored to be included in a contempt for danger so strong and evident that it made me feel safe. To this fastidious man, I thought, bombs were a low-grade intrusion into the political scene, which he conceived, like the ancients, as a vast proscenium. (p. 305)

The stage stretched outside the gates of the cities: Operation Rolling Thunder – the saturation bombing of South Vietnam – left visible scars everywhere in the countryside: 'a short trip by helicopter from Saigon in almost any direction permits a ringside view of American bombing,' quips McCarthy in her ironic appropriation of Travel Section writing – red flames, blue-black smoke, purplish-brown traces – a veritable garden of destruction awaits the eye (p. 91). This guise gives McCarthy's outrage full range. Unlike Herr, who indulges in the pastimes of war – even at one point picking up a machine gun and firing for hours during a siege – smoking, talking, flying, walking with the GIs, McCarthy maintains a 'patrician' distance, describing her extensive luggage, relishing her piercing observations and her biting sarcasm.[52] Despite all the efforts of the US information officers to 'showcase' Phu Cuong, the model 'refugee' camp designed to cover over the effects of carpet bombing, McCarthy rightly calls it a 'concentration camp': the war is an abomination and the United States must withdraw immediately, she declares. Paradoxically, Herr's connection to the grunts and his cynicism leave him unable to condemn the war outright.

Early on, McCarthy discusses whether to accompany a pilot on a bombing mission. Bernard Fall urges her to go, saying it teaches restraint because it is so thrilling, but she prefers to keep her passion and so refuses. (Shortly after their conversation, Bernard Fall was killed by a mine; the headlines reaching James West, McCarthy's husband,announced 'American Writer Killed in Vietnam' panicked him.) McCarthy was under strict orders from her husband not to enter combat zones. It proved useful, this demure guise of playing the little lady for the US military brass, but those serving had no such options

– or rather, played them differently. Maxine Hong Kingston describes 'The Brother in Vietnam' as carefully assessing his guilt and responsibility for the war at each turn from the moment of his draft notice through enlisting in the Navy, refusing to train as a translator and finally riding along on a bombing mission. At each point, he refigures the calculus of knowledge/action/complicity to achieve a clear goal – survive Vietnam: 'he had not been killed, he had not killed anyone.'[53]

In a sense both Kingston's brother and McCarthy come to the same conclusion: whether one pushes the button or not, as Americans we are responsible for the destruction of Vietnam. And the destruction in Vietnam is responsible for the horrific dreams invading us nightly. This position is in marked contrast to that of the military. The two pilots featured in *Hearts and Minds*, returning POW Lt George Coker and former Capt Randy Floyd, both describe their work as 'technicians.' Coker says he was 'strictly professional,' although he does admit that a successful bombing is 'deeply thrilling.' He has already declared that he would go back to Vietnam; he believes in the mission. But even the repentant Floyd describes the same gap: 'I never saw people; it's very clean; I was doing a job.' Guiltily, he too details the exhilaration: 'technical expertise – like singing an aria.' On the 'question of intention' – accidental versus premeditated acts – McCarthy finds no Americans perform atrocities – saturation bombing is not intended to kill civilians, the planes warn villages before an attack, only Vietcong – but every act by VC is in accordance with theory therefore is an act of terrorism (pp. 145–6). These two attitudes Gellhorn dubs 'the cheer syndrome, which optimistically falsifies the conditions of Vietnamese civil life' and 'the fear syndrome, which magnifies the Vietcong's lethal threat to everyone in Vietnam' (p. 30).

In her report for the *New Yorker* on the Medina trial, which comprises the penultimate chapter of *The Seventeenth Degree*, McCarthy struggles to listen to the testimony and hear the story behind the jumbled words of each witness, the altered depositions, the changed testimony, the cloudy memory. 'An inadequacy with words, shown by nearly everybody connected with the proceedings, came to seem intrinsic to the mentality behind My Lai' (p. 397). The imprecision of officialese characterizing everyone's speech was symptomatic of the dissociations wrought by Vietnam, in which Americans appear as the affronted innocents when they encounter enemy fire in the field, and in which virtually everybody in South Vietnam is seen as the enemy; in which Johnson portrays himself as tragic figure and Ky as populist reformer. The gap between 'the real war and the war of words,' as Gellhorn noted, produced a crisis in language presaged by Orwell: truth and power felt at Medina's trial only as boredom. Nevertheless, My Lai was the logical outcome of the Search and Destroy missions aimed at wiping out whole villages – including populations, crops, homes, livestock and burial mounds – aimed at the forced urbanization of the entire South Vietnamese peasantry to starve out the NLF.

This sense of inevitability – once the course was set there was no turning back – becomes the lament of the liberal consensus that there were no 'solutions' to Vietnam's 'quagmire.'[54] McCarthy's scathing review of Halberstam's *Best and the Brightest* points to the agonistic portrait Johnson and others painted of themselves, as captives of fate (inscribed through what she calls 'the Future Past tense, the older man would remember'), rather than as powerful and culpable agents of history. Instead, it is as an historical subject, as a responsible citizen who must do something, that McCarthy goes to Saigon, Hanoi, Fort McPherson to witness and to write about what she sees. Writing is also an act of intervention, consciously pursued; but for the Defense and State Department coteries and Johnson himself – those actually commanding the armed intervention into Vietnam – no hint of action appears. Theirs are thoroughly disembodied, schizoid personalities. In her response to *Authors Take Sides on Vietnam*, Jessica Mitford describes the results of sending a telegram to the White House calling for immediate withdrawal only to receive a letter back thanking her for her support: 'this curious little incident served to heighten, for me, the nightmarish feeling that we are governed by deranged Dr Strangeloves with whom communication is fast becoming impossible' (p. 39). Compared to this 'deranged' culture, the paradoxical sanity of the North Vietnamese unsettles its visitors.

Peace (of Mind)

> We are never completely the contemporaries of our own times. History advances in disguise . . . . This is not the fault of history, but the fault of our range of vision, which is cluttered with images and sounds. We hear and see the past superimposed on the present, even though the present is the revolution.[55]

McCarthy writes of 'trying to hold onto my identity' (p. 272), Sontag of her 'ambiguities of identity' (p. 35) while in North Vietnam. The size of their bodies, the color of their skin, their wardrobes – all make them aliens; Gellhorn comments on the awkwardness she felt as an 'overweight, unlovely giant' among the Vietnamese (p. 14): 'We big overfed white people will never know what they feel' (p. 4). The lack of empathy unravels a self-conceit of Americanness: 'we are not maniacs and monsters; but our planes range the sky all day and all night and

our artillery is lavish and we have much more deadly stuff to kill with'
(p. 7). Sontag declares in *Authors Take Sides*: 'America's war on
Vietnam makes me, for the first time in my life, ashamed of being an
American' the nation become 'a criminal, sinister, country – swollen
. . . numbed . . . monstrous' (p. 46). The very qualities of fairness
which for McCarthy represent 'Americanness, a permanent outsider
and hence fitted to judge and bear witness,' an America she associates
with Henry James, was gone forever. Americans were 'backward,
primitive, pitiably undeveloped' (pp. 311, 310). 'The illusion of being
effective' because of her 'objectivity,' because of her status as a successful and therefore 'free' writer, was falling away in North Vietnam.
McCarthy had become a sample of American society – 'the embodiment, the living proof' of one of the 'great' things about it: 'freedom
and the material evidences of it' (p. 316). This burden strips her of her
'subjectivity' even as stubbornly an ' "I" ' keeps asserting itself distinct
from this identity – American. Her 'patriotism,' her sense that she
could not live with herself, which entailed being American, if she did
not do something to stop the nation from 'disfigur[ing] itself' was tied
to a recognition 'that I went chiefly for my own peace of mind' (p. 317).
Self and nation, individual and national identity are thus intimately
linked through travel, witness, and writing. This merger is akin to the
'absence of the sharp distinction between public and private spheres' in
Vietnam 'that must seem exotic to us. It is open to the Vietnamese
to love their country passionately,' notes Sontag, who refuses
these gestures of patriotism as incompatible with American radicalism (p. 79).

For these women, reporting on the effects of America's war on the
people of Vietnam slides into an account of the Vietnamese people's
effects on them: there is outrage at the horror of the war, admiration
for the resilience of the people, and the jarring sense of otherness.
FitzGerald is able to keep her own self-memoir at bay; her story
surfaces briefly, but hers is an epic tale, focused almost entirely on the
men – Vietnamese and American – in Vietnam, as if the women,
herself included, were somehow not a part of the ethnographic and
cultural history of Vietnam. Gellhorn expresses disgust for American
arrogance, lies and destruction in her brief pamphlet but sees her
work (she wrote these for the Manchester *Guardian*) as a war correspondent; the women from Women Strike for Peace and other New
Left groups found political inspiration in the women they met in
Vietnam; but for Sontag and McCarthy the changes in self-perception
shape the story of what was seen. Obviously with over five hundred
journalists in Vietnam by 1966 and with nightly news broadcasts of the
war's ravages (though no images from the North) to have any effect,

their witnessing also must be made 'new.' Revolution really does mean change, but the process unsettles these two women, because its expression occurs in the crude 'baby talk' of slogans and 'instrumentality' whose history reeks to them of Stalinism (p. 79).

The 'interior journey' each takes into the Vietnam 'inside ourselves,' in Godard's terms, highlights for Sontag the 'dilemmas of being an American, an unaffiliated radical American, an American writer' (pp. 86–7); and I might add of an American radical *woman* writer.[56] Unaffiliated, non-Communist American leftism (as McCarthy notes), without a mass movement behind it, is little more than a political 'taste,' precisely because it is so infused with individualism, elitism, and a quirky, almost girlish, pleasure in one's slanted relation to culture.

They went to Hanoi as anti-war *writers*, not as activists, not as members of a movement, but as observers – novelists who 'command' (McCarthy's term) an audience, whose 'usefulness' (Sontag's word) were their commitments to truth, which meant 'aesthetics, irony, ambiguity, indiscretion.' The ethical, historical, two-dimensional, stylized language of revolution, the love of country, the utilitarianism they found in North Vietnam left each unsettled. Yet each comes away quite moved by the exchanges with her guides and hosts. They know they are witnessing something wholly new. This new kind of war engendered new kinds of deeds (bonzes [Buddhist monks] and Americans self-immolate), new kinds of writings (reporters protest), new kinds of intellectuals (professors invent counter-insurgency), new kinds of politics (teach-ins, terrorism). Still, Mary McCarthy's 'epilogue' to *Hanoi* is telling. The ambiguities surrounding the deaths of Dr and Mrs Krainick, German relief aides found buried in a mass grave with another German doctor after the Hue battles during Tet, cloud the picture of North Vietnamese honor and heroism. Their deaths could not simply be blamed on the American bombers. Atrocities happen in war no matter how ethical the culture; this is war. The tale leaves a bad taste in her and our mouths. The costs of telling the truth of war was peace of mind. Long after returning from Vietnam, Kingston's brother still dreams, still cannot taste food. As McCarthy notes, 'Vietnam seized us, altered the pattern of our lives' (p. 42). No one went back to normal life when it was over. Indeed, it never ended. The incursions into private life that accompanied the practice of this war set the stage for the increasingly political nature of privacy in the United States.

6

History in Your Own Home: *Cinéma Vérité*,

Docudrama, and America's Families

An American Family in *Paris Is Burning*

In 1991, *Paris Is Burning*, Jennie Livingston's documentary about the Harlem drag balls, exploded on the screen, vividly portraying the alternative 'community' poor, gay, Latino, and African-American men had forged through their drag balls. The film entered a cultural conversation about the 'disintegration' of the American family already saturated with a narrative about the end of 'traditional values,' as one politician after another mourned the demise of the white, middle-class, heterosexual, male-breadwinning family, and found in its place an array of households – singles, single parents, gay couples, collectives, multi-generational families, two-wage-earning couples – whose configurations were both a cause and effect of changing social and economic conditions since the 1960s. Moreover, with AIDS devastating young urban gay men, the film's exuberance loudly proclaimed the survival of a community under siege.

This chapter tracks the emblem of the American family as it was produced within popular culture during the 1970s. My focus is on two highly acclaimed and extremely popular television series – PBS's *cinéma vérité* portrait, *An American Family* (1973), and ABC's blockbuster docudrama, *Roots* (1977). In this chapter, I look at *cinéma vérité* and docudrama as two sides of the same representational coin: each depicts history and subjectivity through vignettes of intimate life. I am beginning with Livingston's revelation of a culture seemingly at a far remove from the American families television was promoting in the aftermath of the 1960s, because the 'mothers' and 'children' living in 'houses' formed, in the words of one ball legend, 'a looking glass world,' much as the occupants of 35 Wood Dale Lane, Santa Barbara, California or the descendants of Kunta Kinte had.

Livingston's entry into the houses constituting the ball community owed as much to Craig Gilbert's seven-month stay with the Louds as it did to Alex Haley's search for his ancestors. The desire to document family life in cinéma vérité 'style' (seen not only in An American Family but in the Maysles's Grey Gardens (1974), Walter Parkes and Keith Gritchlow's California Reich (1975), the Group W production, Six American Families (1977), and continuing with Joe Berlinger and Bruce Sinofsky's Brother's Keeper (1992)) was a logical extension of the ideology of living cinema as it has been practiced in the United States since 1960.[1] What had begun as the private exposure of public events and figures had inverted into the public display of private, even secret, lives. Livingston's documentary about a subculture hidden among the cracks of gay, Latino, African-American cultures mapped this subaltern space for outsiders, just as Roots's collapse of history and fiction had made a white audience 'comfortable' with African-American history.[2] Like Madonna, another white woman captivated by the balls who capitalized on her transgressive knowledge of them by marketing voguing, Livingston came under attack for her invasion and expropriation of her informants' lives. In this, her situation also mimicked that of Gilbert a generation earlier. Moreover, as critic bell hooks charged, Livingston had made a spectacle of black men for white consumption and pleasure, much as Roots had in 1977.[3]

Paris Is Burning begins with a hushed male voice recounting his father's warning: 'You're black, poor, and gay. That's three strikes against you'; but the film works to unseat this declaration. Its celebration of a triply despised subculture whose own culture values the most crassly commercial aspects of dominant American culture confounds the categories of resistance and hegemony. In so doing, it also dislodges assumptions about political documentary, especially cinéma vérité, as surely as the experimental techniques of recent documentary films by Chick Strand, Trinh T. Minh-ha, and Jill Godmilow I take up in the next two chapters. The complex identities performed at the balls appear more unsettling than the by now conventionalized mechanisms of baring the cinematic devices of truth and realism. 'Realness' exposes realism and even reality as yet another guise dependent upon simulation and consent.

Livingston's film raises questions about both cinéma vérité and political avant-gardist positions in film-making: which is more likely to undo and re-form restrictive identities and ideologies – formal subversion or subversive content? And what if the content itself already questions the conventions supporting reality? Paris Is Burning was among the most widely screened documentaries ever and unleashed cries of outrage when it failed to receive an Oscar nomination. Yet it is not an original film; it breaks no ground formally because it relies on the two most conventional techniques for securing truth claims – talking heads and direct cinema. But who is speaking? During the extended testimony by Dorian Carey, we watch as he applies make-up and transforms himself into a woman. By giving visible and audible space to transvestites, the film challenges assumptions about gender, but also about American culture. 'So this is New York City and this is what the gay life is about, right?' declare two teenage boys Livingston interviews on the street.

Moreover, Livingston's film is hardly seamless; she breaks both the composed interviews and the spontaneous *vérité* shots of the balls and the streets with inter-titles highlighting ball vernacular – walking, reading, shading, voguing, mopping – and with the names of the houses and their legendary mothers; she even occasionally makes us aware of her presence behind the camera. Furthermore, the film is fun – the music is for dancing, the clothes gorgeous, the balls exhilarating – and its pleasure is discomforting. bell hooks expresses rage and disappointment at the pleasure and entertainment (white) audiences derive from the film. She chastises Livingston for invading the privacy of the houses without showing the ball walkers at 'home' in a 'world of family and community beyond the drag ball' and thus 'making a spectacle of black rituals and pageantry.'[4] When *Paris Is Burning* was first shown, it sparked intense reactions from within the (white) gay community because this world of black and Latino gay men was so thoroughly submerged even with an already hidden subculture. The sheer energy of the balls seemed to counter the dismal record of neglect and death from AIDS, gay-bashing, and homophobia. This Paris is located off most maps. In finding it, did Livingston further limit the already minimal spaces where outlaws can congregate? Who benefits from this film? We are left wondering with Dorian Carey about the future of the balls, and its mothers, children, and their houses.

Living (Room) Cinema

Forces changing the meanings and functions of both the family and documentary led to their convergence in the Loud's household. The 1965 *Griswold* v. *Connecticut* case, in which the Supreme Court affirmed the 'right of privacy' to married couples, opened the way for contraceptive use in the wake of the birth control pill as well as legalized abortion several years later. The decision declared privacy and the married home a separate zone, free from government intervention; ironically it was through government intervention, however, in the form of a court decision, that the family could mark itself off from the state and maintain its 'zone of privacy.' At the same time, television news coverage opened the practices of warfare to nightly inspection; writers such as McCarthy and Sontag, who reported on Vietnam, explained their need to visit the combat zones of Vietnam by the deeply personal ways they experienced the war's effects. Furthermore, feminist critiques of gender and sexuality located the nuclear family as the site of women's oppression. In short, the zone of privacy that was family and personal life had become deeply politicized in the late 1960s. Moreover, economic and social factors affecting the middle-class family exploded its 1950s 'father knows best' image: rising divorce rates, the demise of the family wage, increasing female labor force participation, open explorations of sexuality. These explosive issues of late twentieth-century American family life have become the substance of talk shows, pop psychology, disease of the week TV, and so forth. Sociologist Arlene Skolnick argues that the changes in white, middle-class family life felt in post-war America were the result of instability wrought by the Second World War and the Depression which made the 1950s nuclear family (an aberration in the history of Western family practices) seem incontestably normal and natural.[5]

The explosion of *cinéma vérité* in the United States was both a product of and contributor to the cultural politics of the 1960s. Its reality, authenticity, spontaneity, unmediated truth, and direct access to emotion signaled a break with both Hollywood and the overt theatricality of 1930s documentary forms. The American form of *cinéma vérité*, often called direct cinema or living cinema, strayed from its French parentage in its emphasis on action and movement rather than intimate talk captured by Jean Rouch and Edgar Morin in *Chronique d'un Eté*.[6] Critic Steven Mamber and others have tracked the technological advances, ideological mechanisms, and aesthetic concerns that helped *cinéma vérité* emerge as the post-war American documentary form.[7] Equipment such as Nagra tape recorders, portable sync-sound 16 mm cameras, and cheap film stock enabled as few as one or two people to go on location and directly record sound and image simultaneously. Diane Arbus's move away from fashion photography to funky shots of Americana and Robert Frank's street photographs foregrounded a snapshot aesthetic of daily life by featuring submerged aspects of American life. The immediacy of television news brought catastrophic events into the home, making the living room a site of political debate which centered on images rather than words (as radio had).

The 1973 PBS series *An American Family* marked the culmination (and in a sense the death knell) of the direct cinema movement in the

United States. While Richard Leacock, Al and Dave Maysles, D.A. Pennebaker and Frederick Wiseman continued to make films within the boundaries of the form, Craig Gilbert's decision to move into the home, positioning living cinema in the living room of middle-class suburbia, suggested that the erasure of the divide between public and private, a dream of *cinéma vérité*, had been achieved. If the Drew Associates tracked the private moments of public figures such as John F. Kennedy and Hubert Humphrey as they pumped the hands and pounded the pavements of Wisconsin in *Primary*, Craig Gilbert's crew reversed the logic, making public the very private rituals of family life, including the mundane activities leading to such cataclysmic events as divorce and coming out. The family was thus acknowledged to be a public institution, like schools and courts, of political and social control – one of Louis Althusser's Ideological State Apparatuses – through which subjects were interpellated as individuals.[8]

After the 1960s Black Power movement inspired what we now call identity politics among women, gays, and other racial minorities,[9] a corollary and far less progressive analogue bedevilled US politics in the form of 'the rise of the white ethnics.' With people sporting 'Polish Power' buttons and 'Kiss me, I'm Italian' bumper stickers, everyone claimed an ethnicity, everyone, that is, except upper-middle-class whites.[10] It was precisely this lack of ethnic identity, despite their Catholic upbringing, that made Bill and Pat Loud's family so appealing: they were a blank slate (Figure 15). But their beautiful ranch house, good looks, and financial security did not ease the contradictions superintending the family and sexuality in the post-1960s era. In the Louds, Gilbert found a family defined, because of their cultural, economic, and political centrality, as being without definition – raceless and classless. Yet the very process of using the camera to bare their personal lives endowed them with a race (white), a class (middle), and an identity (Californian). By turning their insides out, making their private home public, however, their normality was undermined. Even within the norm, disturbances occur. The center still holds, but just barely: a marriage on the verge of break-up, a son in drag, a daughter having sex – cracks in the structure. What was so remarkable, then, about the Louds was the way their disintegration before the camera foreshadowed other kinds of houses, like those of Pepper La Beija and Willie Ninja in *Paris Is Burning*.

Invading public institutions, *cinéma vérité* specialized in exposing the cracks fracturing their structures, letting everyday events unravel until even the most rigid institutions – prisons, mental hospitals, high schools – appeared chaotic, haphazard, and at the mercy of the quirky individuals within. These films gave us new insights about the fragility and instability of those bastions of order; the wardens, inmates, administrators, patients, students, teachers, principals were all revealed to be a strange assortment of people. These institutions were extreme cases of hierarchical bureaucracies where power resides with those at the top; yet the subtext of virtually all direct cinema exposés was the complicity, vulnerability, and pathos of even those enforcing order most viciously. They were just people after all, low-level employees of the state whose livelihoods depended on keeping things running smoothly. This extreme humanism led direct cinema to focus on private life; yet the exposure of the Louds revealed that even the most private and free space – the suburban home – was but another institution. Like Bridgewater State, where the patients and warders act together in *Titicut Follies*, the family is structured around interdependent clusters of inmates – parents and children, males and females.[11] Escape means not only breaking away from the institution, but breaking it apart. In the case of institutions codified within physical structures, this is a formidable task rarely accomplished. Hence the grim vision, despite moments of humor, of Wiseman's films. However, the structures of the suburban household are more easily rearranged than those determined by brick walls; yet legal binders holding inmates, patients, students, and workers also keep marriage partners and children together. Still, these can be ruptured once the norms – gendered, generational and sexual – have been questioned. When that happens in public, on television, the effect is deeply disturbing.

Television, the private/public medium par excellence, accomplishes this blurring by reducing history to bedroom farce (almost as Marx predicted), and the nuclear family in late capitalist America is its perfect subject. In some respects, television and the family are indistinguishable factors of post-war, middle-class experience.[12] In her memoir of a 1950s girlhood, Charlotte Nekola recalls running back and forth between *Ozzie and Harriet* on the living room television and her kitchen where her mother stood momentarily paralyzed before the pot roast on the counter and the open landscape outside her window.[13] By the 1970s, after feminism and Stonewall, the chinks in the armor of family life were no longer just private matters glimpsed fleetingly by a perceptive daughter. Thus it was through fiction that nostalgic claims about family/history could be maintained. Because feminists and gay activists had begun their political analysis of gender and sexuality with an examination of the family and its role in the production, suppression, and exploitation of women and homosexuals, the family was opened to an institutional inspection. Once the organization of personal life became a legitimate focus of political activism, it also became a significant site for the *vérité* camera as well.

The living room was as likely as the boardroom – more so actually if you believed women's liberation calls to make the personal political – to reveal the contradictions of American capitalism. History unfolded in the crevices of the home as much as it did on the streets or in the courts, statehouses, corporations, and factory floors. *An American Family* decisively displayed for mass consumption what Barthes claimed occurred after photography's invention: 'the publicity of the private' reassembled culture in fundamental ways, making it impossible to distinguish one social sphere from another. Television relayed the Louds' most private moments into other living rooms across the nation invading and reworking the relationships there. Documentary *vérité* seeks the spontaneous outburst that reveals the private person behind its public face – as Drew Associates had done with Kennedy in *Primary*. This humanistic view assumes both a private life at odds with the public persona (which is precisely what Madonna subverts in her *vérité* portrait *Truth or Dare?*) and a public realm wholly inhabited by unique individuals. If emotions are real – more real than the structural formations in which they occur – then film-makers must 'move in' with their subjects, must see them every day at home to know them. According to Mary Ann Watson, this is precisely what Robert Drew suggested to President-elect Kennedy after the success of *Primary*. Drew wanted to move in 'two film teams. One with him on the business side and one with his wife on the home side.' To which Jackie Kennedy apparently replied, 'Nobody is going to move into the White House with me.'[14] Ten years later, by which time direct cinema had become a popular cultural genre, the Louds, Pat looking like a long-haired Jackie, would open their home to a film team for instructional purposes.[15]

A few years later, the Maysles brothers brought their cameras into the estate of Edie and Edie Beale – cousins of the very private Jacqueline Bouvier Kennedy Onassis – after their Long Island mansion was discovered to be infested with rats while the two women – mother and daughter – lived in ramshackle decay. *Grey Gardens* lovingly exposed these two grown women as spiteful children, ill-equipped to function in the world; yet still very much concerned with it. The two Edies opened their bedrooms and baths to the cameras as they bickered about chores, yearned for love, and defiantly refused to maintain their property. The images of *Grey Gardens* are of a fading, but wild, luxury – an elderly woman sunbathes nude, a middle-aged woman dresses like a teenager, garbage coexists with antiques – an oxymoron of two hermits deeply associated with the workings of state and national Democratic politics.

At the other end of the social, political, and economic spectrum, the makers of *California Reich* boast they spent eight months hanging around with the lower-middle-class members of the Nazi movement in southern California before finally shooting any footage of the daily lives and political activities of these families. Is this heroic? *California Reich* focuses on the utter normality of family life among neo-Nazis. They work, have children who, when asked what they would like to do when they grow up, answer 'kill niggers and Jews,' and watch television. The recently aired PBS *American Playhouse* documentary, *Brother's Keeper*, dedicated in memory of David Maysles, follows the story of the Ward brothers, 'Northern hillbillies' accused of murdering their brother, William.[16] Again, the film-makers 'moved in' with the Wards and became part of the community, which rallied to support them. Their cameras, much like Walker Evans's, lingered over the objects, clothing, and beds cluttering their decrepit house in upstate New York. American family life accommodates so much variation because it all looks the same – homes, neat or messy, filled with people.

An American Family was unique only as a non-fictional account of the family on television. Since its earliest days, commercial TV had serialized family dramas and comedies. In the late 1970s, however, a new form – docudrama – reimaged the relationship of family and ethnicity in popular culture, blurring the divide between fiction and history. The Louds represented a singularity, *an* American family, but *Roots* (and later *Holocaust*) brought the world-historical devastation of whole peoples into America's living rooms only to reveal that history served as a backdrop for the daily life of a family, much like those sitting before their television sets. Alex Haley had subtitled his 'faction,' 'The Saga of *An* American Family,' his story yet another instance in the vast mosaic of America.[17] Fictionalizing history inverts the truth-claims direct cinema seeks, but does so within its humanist terms: all structures boil down to individuals. Dave Maysles claimed direct cinema to be 'the most emotionally involving [kind of film]. We wish to show people living their own lives and speaking their own thoughts . . .'[18] Television docudramas picture history through vivid characters who live in families. These television shows lodge truth and history within the psychologies of individuals and their fictional narratives.

Roots was made in an effort to enlist African-American audiences after years of their exclusion and ridicule on television. Its formula was one that, in producer David Wolper's words, could 'make oppression palatable' by placing the family and its tale of generations struggling for land into a classic story of immigrant acculturation. *Roots* would tell a 'positive' story that would be 'comfortable' for an overwhelmingly white audience in the throes of a national backlash against civil rights legislation in communities such as South Boston where violent resistance to busing persisted for years after court orders deemed its public school system racially segregated.[19] If the saga of a slave family could be made to look like the story of white ethnics' entry into America, then the historical meaning of slavery, its stain on American history, could be washed away. Thus both masters and slaves have families, both suffer losses and experience personal joys, although in unequal doses.[20] (Likewise the other major docudrama to follow *Roots*, *Holocaust*, paired a Jewish family with that of an SS officer. We are privileged to intimate moments between the SS officer and his wife talking over the day in bed together; his wife sympathizing with his difficult duties in the same way as the Jewish wife worries over the impending crisis with her husband.) Television (de)humanizes through the inventions and device of the family, it being impossible to represent any other emotional commitment than family attachment. In docudrama, the family is not constructed as *an* institution, as it is in *vérité*, but rather as *the* institution; all others – legal, political, military – fall away. In this, docudrama takes seriously the premisses offered by living cinema – that the living room is a site of political crisis. Yet *cinéma vérité* revels in the wonderful and horrible idiosyncrasies locked within each unit. Docudrama works to prove the absolute sameness throughout time, across cultures, classes, and races of this fictionalized formation. So it avoids confronting more troubling needs for a political and economic redistribution of wealth and power. As Michael Katz observed, in the 1970s, sociological critiques of poverty 'slipped easily, unreflectively, into a language of family, race and culture rather than inequality, power, and exploitation.'[21] Docudrama served up a history of the present dressed in the costumes of the past and it looked just like home.

Neither Average, Nor Typical

The saga of the Louds, 'not *the* American family, but *an* American family,' in the introductory words of producer Craig Gilbert, presents in microscopic detail the ways post-war prosperity was lived among America's white middle class. Beginning with only the sketchiest background about the family prior to the moment of filming, the show, like all living cinema, features present-time experience shorn of sociological or historical context. The opening credits focus the series: first the house appears, then, in succession, Bill, Pat, and each of the children frozen in the middle of doing some typical activity; their portraits surround the house which dominates the frame. If Bridgewater State Penal Hospital contained *Titicut Follies*, 35 Wood Dale Lane contains *An American Family*; yet as in Wiseman's film, the residents of the building are what give it meaning. According to historian Stephanie Coontz, 'by the beginning of the 1970s, for the first time, more Americans lived in suburbs than in any other location.'[22] The Louds' luxurious and spotless home had become a norm (although theirs represented the high-end version) for American family life. Their five children, however, made up a significantly larger family, despite the rise in fertility among the middle class in the early 1950s.

Incredibly successful, Bill has built his own business forging replacement parts for heavy-mining equipment – teeth, pins, and struts for shovels and drag lines. He markets his products world-wide and thus participates in the global economic shifts taking place – profiting from opening markets in Indonesia, on the one hand; suffering through longshoremen strikes in Italy and California, on the other. With a relaxed manner, mutton-chop sideburns, and a raucous volubility, Bill Loud is an alcoholic version of Timothy Leary – entrepreneurial, self-absorbed, Californian. His money makes possible the expansive home in Santa Barbara with a pool and ocean view, the four or five cars including a Jaguar, the lavish jewelry his wife wears, and the comfortable lives of his children, who pursue their interests with the secure knowledge that he will foot the bill for dancing lessons, apartments in Greenwich Village, musical instruments, a horse and stable.

Yet, for all his economic centrality, Bill is not the center of the home as it is represented through the eyes of the film crew, Alan and Susan Raymond, who lived with, filmed, and taped the family for seven months. Pat, his wife and mother of his five children, controls the footage and the family. In her early forties, she is stunningly beautiful – always perfectly made-up, hair neatly done, wearing matching outfits and strands of gold around her neck and wrists. A Catholic marriage in 1950 netted the Louds a child a year, but Pat still has a flat stomach – eat your heart out middle America. Once we see her shopping for groceries, pushing a loaded cart with one hand and pulling another along behind her to stock up for her teenagers; otherwise she spends many hours poolside or talking on the phone, cigarette in one hand, scotch and soda in the other, rarely serving meals, helping her children prepare for school or recitals. She also travels. During the first episode, which includes the first day of filming, Pat is up at 6:30 poaching eggs and pouring mugs of coffee for her family; thereafter, neither Pat nor anyone else is shown doing much housework. This is a mother with plenty of leisure time. Watching it recently – my house littered with newspapers, dirty dishes, legos, books, dirty clothes – I marveled at the ways in which this film occluded the labor of housekeeping. A tidy house: the kitchen tiles sparkle, nobody complains about not having any clean underwear. Where were the invisible hands maintaining this sprawling family? No doubt one or two Chicana domestics took care of this family's physical needs (quite late in the series we glimpse a gardener working in the background). But the physical work of domestic labor within the suburban home is not the point of this project.

The substance of the film is the emotional labor Pat expends caring for her children. Pat's voice and words are stiff and formal. She seems always aware of the camera, performing before it quite self-consciously, even when seen at her most relaxed, smoking in bed with the evening paper. Only after she has kicked Bill out of the house, in the final moments of the ninth episode, does she seem fully at ease, sitting with her three youngest children, listening to her third son Grant sing a Beatles song as evening closes in around them. Her taut guard loosens and we are left wondering whether the tension she exudes was the result of living with a man she no longer loved or respected rather than living with the film crew. This scene follows her trip to her brother and sister-in-law to explain why she wants to divorce Bill. He broke her trust years ago by having affairs with other women; but only now, with the children grown and while she is still young enough, does she have the strength to find someone else. Grilled by her previously divorced sister-in-law, she confesses that despite the twenty years of marriage and the ease with which she and Bill talk, they have never said one word to each other about their feelings. Her desires have drifted away from the lavish style of upper-middle-class southern California. (Unimpressed by Bill's story about a friend giving his wife a Cadillac, she nevertheless asks her son Kevin, touring the Pacific Rim on business for his father, to buy her a jade and gold bracelet.) She prefers to spend the summer at an art colony in Taos, where we see her at a life-drawing class.

With the exception of the flamboyant Lance, her oldest son who has escaped southern California for New York, who dyed his hair silver at fourteen in emulation of Andy Warhol, who gets his mother a room in the Hotel Chelsea and takes her to see *Vain Victory*, a transvestite revue at La Mama, on her first visit to New York, and who shamelessly uses the camera to push his own film career, the Loud children appear to be a dull lot.[23] They are teenagers, barely articulate; they mumble about Michelle's horse, Delilah's tap dance, Grant's band, Kevin's movies, Lance's acting career. Each dreams of fame and indulges interests enabled by Bill's hard work and shrewd business acumen. Still, the children are remarkably caring; they look out for one another, show real affection, fool around but don't fight. Seven months with a film crew following them around exposing their limitations is worth the air time they will receive in kind. Performing themselves may lead somewhere. In fact, both Lance and Pat launched careers from the series – Pat got her own talk show; Lance became a minor celebrity at Warhol's factory.

In any case, southern California life is already lived on display – outside, barely clothed, bodies open to inspection. The closet was wide open revealing not only that Lance owned over a thousand Hawaiian shirts, but more tellingly that the suburban enclosure of the family was bursting. So it is hardly surprising when Pat tells Bill she is seeking divorce in the course of a drunken party at a restaurant during the Santa Barbara fiesta surrounded by friends, the roar of a mariachi band in the background, and the Nagra by her side. Does she hate him that much, we wonder? Only a few hints have leaked that this was a troubled marriage – a fight over whether Bill should refrigerate the cheese he brought back with him from a trip, which Delilah painfully recounts later to her boyfriend, the stiffness in Pat's face, her snide comments and cool voice, the absence of any physical intimacy between them, too much drinking.

Despite this being 1971, the concerns of this American family are utterly domesticated. But for the hair and clothing styles, which tell us this is still the 1960s, one would hardly know there was also strife elsewhere – 1971, the year of Attica, Bangladesh, Vietnam. Pat mentions that there have been bombings in Eugene, Oregon, their hometown, protesting the war; Lance jokingly asks Michelle, after the house almost burns from Santa Ana wind fires, whether a 'blank [sic] panther' had attacked the house; Pat says she's 'too old' for women's lib when she tells her brother why she needs to find another man now. Of course, Lance's world of gay men and drag queens parading the streets of New York and Paris is testament to a new politics and counterculture; he and Pat sit by Bethesda Fountain in Central Park watching hippies hang off the statue tossing frisbees, kissing, and smoking pot. Except for the tacit recognition of gay liberation in the many euphemistic remarks that Lance has finally 'found himself' at the Chelsea, the social upheavals of the 1960s have barely entered the conversations of this household. No one reads books, sees movies, watches the news – rock and roll the only cultural currency circulating through the rooms. Yet everywhere signs of rupture appear: Pat and Bill probably would not divorce but for the changes in the American family brought on by post-war economic boom and educational opportunities for women (Pat is a Stanford graduate); the boys' long hair and dreams of performing in bands, making documentary films, hitchhiking through Europe with theater troupes are emblems of counter-cultural values; the endless drinking and smoking hint of a pervasive drug culture in California; the openness of the family home – a spectacle for the rest of the consumer culture to envy the stuff of prosperity.[24] Unconsciously, the 1960s intrude into the Louds' home, in part because they willingly entered America's living room.

The close monitoring that goes on in the Louds' home – virtually everyone checks in with the others about their day's activities, Lance calls long distance frequently, parents discuss this or that problem of this or that child – typifies the emotional intensity of middle-class family dynamics following the Second World War. In fact Bill Loud, in a letter written to Lance which Bill reads as Lance cycles up Santa Barbara's hills to visit Bill's office, attributes his divorce to 'the famous American social custom, marriage [that] requires a [sic] hundred percent attention and devotion to duty. A living style of all or nothing at all; we must be together in all things.'[25] Pat's and Bill's continual pleas to Lance and the others 'to take care of yourself, get some rest, don't worry' protects the children in a soothing cocoon of love and care. During the first episode, as the camera follows Lance unpacking after he has moved into the Chelsea, he describes his siblings: Kevin is 'humane, the only one to buy presents for the others' birthdays'; Delilah 'lives a very Tammy existence, like Trisha Nixon with spice'; Michelle is selfish and snotty 'made in the image of me'; and Grant is 'talented but arrogant.' Lance sums up what will become clear during the next twelve weeks. Lance's astute eye comes from his training in gauging the emotional timbre of the home in which he was raised. Moreover, the community he finds at the Chelsea and continues to make in Copenhagen and Paris becomes yet another form of this social world of intimacy – he and his roommate Soren and the others on their floor gather nightly to gossip about clothes, friends, stars; they share money, clothing, job possibilities, and escort Pat around the East Village like devoted sons. The burgeoning gay male and transvestite culture of lower Manhattan seemingly so much an anathema to middle-class suburbia nevertheless owes much to its values and habits.

The family saga on television – of which the Louds' exposure is surely the most extreme example – codified a new political grammar. Lance's dissection of his family for the film crew plots both the ways in which the camera's presence created performative gestures within the 'characters' and coached us to understand his break from (and connection to) 35 Wood Dale Lane – traveling across the continent, then further, across the Atlantic to escape what he calls the 'stupidity' of Californians. This 'language of love,' as Coontz calls the discourse of privacy and personal intimacies, governs family life in America (p. 114). Furthermore, this language of intimacy has increasingly encompassed the political vocabulary over the past two decades. The feminist call to make the personal political – an extension of New Left and civil rights calls for prefigurative politics and beloved community – is itself a variation of the values given to emotional well-being within the 1950s middle-class nuclear family.[26] 'The legendary family of the 1950s . . . was the first wholehearted effort to create a home that would fulfill virtually all its members' personal needs through an energized and expressive personal life,' asserts historian Elaine Tyler May. She goes on to conclude that the 'quest for meaning through intimacy' which was at the heart of the 1950s 'containment ethos' continued in the 1960s political and cultural radicalism, extending into Hillary Rodham Clinton's recent invocation of *Tikkun* editor Michael Lerner's 1990s call for a 'politics of meaning.'[27]

The *Roots* of Docudrama

In January 1977, when, according to a recent *People* retrospective on *Roots*, over eighty million televisions were tuned into the epic, I was living on a farm in the northeast interior of Brazil – no electricity, much less TV. Even so, I too had become engrossed in the riveting series as one friend or family member after another wrote to me of their transfixed relationship to their television sets during the eight days it was aired. After more than a decade of nightly images of brutal and dehumanizing violence waged by the American government against the people of Vietnam and of America's cities, perhaps the networks were ready to deal with an earlier manifestation of sanctioned brutality – the peculiar institution of slavery.

The new form of the mini-series inherited from British television was well suited to historical drama, incorporating aspects of both nightly news broadcasts and weekly dramatic series.[28] Alex Haley's 1976 bestseller provided the perfect device for televised history. Essentially a story of the search for origins, *Roots* fit the growing interest in ethnicity and genealogy sweeping 'white' America in the wake of the movements for 'panethnicity' that had radicalized African Americans, Asian Americans, Latinos, and Native Americans during the 1960s and 1970s.[29] With the legitimation of oral history within the academic discipline and its popularization by Studs Terkel, high school and college instructors were sending their students to interview grandparents, bosses, anyone from another generation, about their life stories. Haley's story of searching for his ancestry, and the ways in which that story encoded the history of Africans in the New World as an immigrant population, fit the standards of network television. Parts of the novel had first appeared in the *Reader's Digest*, that other popular purveyor of middle-brow sensibilities. Richard Schickel's negative review in *Time* had bemoaned: '*Roots*, alas, is rooted in the paperback mentality. It is "Mandingo" for middlebrows.'[30] Responding to this critique, Wolper embraced 'Middle Brow' because 'it spoke to all people in a form that they could understand and appreciate.'[31]

The story of the seven generations of Kunta Kinte's progeny living in America presents the African-American family as deeply rooted in American history; Kunta Kinte literally arrives a slave in America with the birth of the nation. Moreover, the triumphal reunion of the family on its own land transformed the story of captivity into one of immigration, a quintessential saga of the American dream culminating in property ownership. '*Roots* is the story of an American family that freely mixes documented fact and fiction based on fact. It is a chronicle of America as told by the losers . . . . It is also a narrative of success.'[32] A significant part of its success, as the commentators in Marlon Riggs's film, *Color Adjustment*, have noted, is the utter familiarity of the scene: the plotting of family mishaps and the stereotypes of black performances. As Madge Sinclair, the actress who played Bell, notes:

> Whatever guise you put it under, people want to see the things that they are familiar with. The fact that Alex Haley's book approaches slavery from a historical, documentary viewpoint does not excuse the fact that we are dressed in these slave costumes and still saying, 'Yassuh, Massuh' and 'nigger' and that little white girl is calling me, 'Mammy Bell, Mammy Bell'.[33]

With over $6,000,000 invested in the mini-series, ABC Television executives explicitly stated their marketing goals. According to Brandon Stoddard, Vice-President of ABC for movies and mini-series: 'We've never been concerned about reaching a black audience. They'll watch it no matter what happens. The question is, will we reach a white audience . . . we did not buy *Roots* as a project that would deal with black history. It is primarily a story that deals with a *family, a very human story. It's brothers and sisters, greed and lust and fear*, and all the things that make *real* drama.'[34] At the same time, Alex Haley was promoting his book *Roots* through frequent speaking engagements and interviews. Invariably, he would include the saga of the twelve years of poverty endured to bring forth the book, culminating in his last voyage back from Africa on a freighter called the *African Star*. Every night he would go down into the hold where 'I had located a big, broad piece of timber in there. I took off my clothes to my underwear, and I would lie on this timber through the night, terribly uncomfortable, extremely cold, trying to imagine I was Kunta.'[35] The horror that he could never do justice to the memory of Kunta Kinta led Haley to consider suicide, he says, but the voices of his ancestors calling to him to finish gave him the strength to continue. This story of the burden of memory and of family responsibility is part of the mystique of *Roots* – it helped turn his story into American history by making history a 'human story.' Because *Roots* was true, 'not just a story. It's historically documented fact,' claimed actor Jitu Cumbuka of the slave ship scenes, realism became part of the marketing strategy. Producer Stan Margulies explains: 'Our ultimate purpose is to be as faithful as possible to Alex's story. One of the things that intrigued ABC is that we didn't invent this, any more than Buchenwald was invented.'[36]

Alex Haley's novel *Roots* uses archival material to develop an imaginary narrative of the unspoken history of Africans in America. Haley's talents as a writer, demonstrated in the magnificent *Autobiography of Malcolm X*, were in creating intense narrative drive to the dispersed facts of a life: giving shape and supple prose to retrieval through oral history of his life in Malcolm's case; in Kunta Kinte's, digging through archives. Personalized and novelized, history becomes a good story in Haley's chronicles. Historians and genealogists have disputed the data and records Haley said he used to reconstruct the names of the key linkage between Kunta Kinte and the slave, Toby.[37] Haley was sued for plagiarism by Margaret Walker, who claimed he had lifted sections of her 1965 novel *Jubilee*, and Harold Courlander, author of the 1967 novel *The African*. (The court dismissed charges in the Walker case and Haley settled out of court with Courlander.) Haley's story mythologized the hidden history of the Middle Passage, weaving folklore, archival material, memories, and fictional devices to fill in 'the unspeakable things unspoken' as Toni Morrison has called them.[38] The translation of the almost 600-page novel into twelve hours of television necessitated even more cuts, elisions, and dramatizations. *Roots*, shot 'on location' in Savannah, Georgia (during the Africa, slave ship, and auction segments) and in ABC's studios, could hardly be seen as authentic history; yet its power for viewers came in part from its references not only to real events but real people with a connection to the living figure of Alex Haley. Looked at now, *Roots* is a period piece; the hairstyles, long sideburns and Afros, speak of a time past – the 1970s not the nineteenth century. The references to present-day America were highly effective.[39] The illusion of reality, despite everyone's performances, is what made *An American Family* such compelling TV; Haley's presence and his real family captivated viewers as well.

But if real people were really being filmed, who owned their stories, their images? The question of property is tied up with issues of propriety for television. Who owns the air waves? The Louds signed releases relinquishing their rights to the series, thus there was nothing they could do when PBS decided to broadcast it again on New Year's Eve 1990.[40] This American family belonged to the public, the Louds no longer possessors of their memories which were part of television history. According to Catherine Egan, Pat Loud found it necessary to go on talk shows and write a book to 'set the record straight' about the unflattering portrait Craig Gilbert's crew had conveyed of her and her family. The very mechanisms that gave An American Family its verisimilitude – the free range of the cameras and tape recorders to follow family members almost anywhere – was seen as a questionable practice by 1977 when Group W produced Six American Families for PBS. Each of these independently made, hour-long films about a range of American families concludes with an interview of the family members in which they comment on the film they have just seen of themselves. As Catherine Egan notes: 'In recording the families' reactions to the original filming, host-reporter-associate producer Paul Wilkes ensured feedback and, consequently, a filmmaker-subject dialogue which is new to the social documentary.'[41] Wilkes himself claimed that this was 'a more honest approach to filmmaking because you show the product to the person.' In the complex and varying ways that honesty, truth, and authenticity are claimed and produced in and through television, both cinema vérité style and docudrama form are open to charges of manipulation. As Wilkes says, 'I can film the "peachy cream family" of the century and make them look horrible just by the editing.'[42] Conversely, even slavery looked pretty good once it was dressed up in the enduring family whose members include Cecily Tyson, Leslie Uggams, Lou Gossett, Jr, Ben Vereen, and LeVar Burton. Television authenticity is an oxymoron at best. Perhaps the scene of the family (and its TV set) is what needs authenticating.

While the commitment to viewing the PBS series, An American Family was large, its weekly hour-long format followed the standard practices of established television viewing habits, cultivating an audience for a particular time slot and training it to look in on schedule.[43] Roots, airing eight consecutive nights for a total of twelve hours, asked television viewers to refashion their viewing habits and etch out the weeknights from 23 January 1977 solely to watch two hundred years of history unfold. By the final episode, an estimated 80,000,000 viewers were tuned in, the largest audience in television history – surpassing even the Superbowl.[44] What accounts for this extraordinary phenomenon? Michael Steward Blayney argues that Roots's popularity springs from its clever revision of the Noble Savage mythology that romanticizes the 'vanished' Indians of the past only after the possibility of actual Native American resistance has been undermined. In producer David Wolper's words, the return to Africa made the story one of 'a strong, powerful family image of a black family held together in love, honor, and courage . . . ,' thus appealing to both black and white audiences.[45] In this he echoes one of the show's critics. Eric Foner argued in *Seven Days* that 'the narrow focus on the family inevitably precludes any attempt to portray the outside world and its institutions. To include these institutions would undermine the central theme of *Roots* – the ability of a family, through unity, self-reliance, and moral fortitude, to face and overcome adversity. Here lies one reason for the enormous success of *Roots* among whites as well as blacks.'[46] *Roots's* powerful family further assured white viewers that they would not be subject to condemnation for the horrors of slavery nor held responsible for the endemic racism still gripping the nation.

This talk about the strong family was part of a discourse circulating within the new social history that challenged the image of the 'tangle of pathology,' as Daniel Patrick Moynihan had described the black family in 1964.[47] Sociologist Carol Stack suggested that the kinship networks among urban black families were a strategy of survival not a symptom of pathology. Her theories were buttressed by the historical analyses of the black family offered by Herbert Gutman and Eugene Genovese.[48] Lest we find television contributing to this progressive revisionism, it is important to remember that in making the black family into 'an American family' – and one safely from the past at that – ABC offered a 'powerful family' that was almost wholly male-dominated.

The invention of the strong family with a past helped produce an enormous audience (as *Dallas's* Ewings would a decade later). However, critic Stuart Byron was appalled at the sexist and homophobic implications of *Roots's* phallocentrism. Byron accuses Haley of implicitly claiming that only through a male genealogy can the African-American family be maintained and sustained, because his search for 'the African' is really a search for the African man. Haley's saga of fathers and sons presents an antidote to the complaints of Moynihan and others about 'the black matriarchy,' but it also makes the African-American family securely patriarchal; thus, says Byron, Haley avoids 'the more disturbing implications of William Styron's *The Confessions of Nat Turner* – that it was only when blacks were allowed to separate themselves from the family unit that revolt became possible.'[49] Byron's questionable choice of an exemplary case notwithstanding (certainly Frederick Douglass makes precisely this point in his narrative when he claims that family ties keep many slaves from running away), his point is that the heirs of Kunta Kinte look strangely like more vital cousins of Ozzie and Harriet.[50] If Haley's family represented the best outcome of

147

the hardships families endured in America, the Louds embodied the nightmarish side of the American Dream – affluence spawning divorced parents, dissolute children, a family centered around a selfish and vain mother, and gender-bending teenagers: a right-wing fantasy of women's and gay liberation gone suburban.

Sociologists posit two models to explain ethnic identity: primordialist connections forged through family to nation or religion, and as such practically eternal; or instrumentalist reactions to economic and political marginality, a collective strategy that fades away with embourgeoisement.[51] The two shows I have been discussing make claims that identity is forged through the family and in the household. In *Roots*, the strength of the black family can be traced through its direct connections to Africa, its ability to maintain linguistic and narrative links to a distant and almost wholly erased past. This primordialist fantasy on television, I suspect, is both an answer to and result of the instrumentalist portrait of the Louds, a family virtually shorn of ancestry.[52] These Americans are already Westerners – come to California like so many before them to remake themselves yet again. In a bit of genealogy offered when Pat visits Eugene, she narrates the life stories of her family and her husband's, her voice-over complementing the home movie footage and snapshots she has gathered. She tells us that the home she grew up in has been demolished and is now a parking lot. An apt metaphor for her marriage, which counters the nostalgic tug of origins undergirding family stories, especially as they came to be portrayed in docudrama. Yet the Louds themselves would not have become a subject for television had not the calls for self-determination and national identity begun by African Americans and picked up by other racial minorities and women and gays led to journeys of self-inspection among all Americans for their 'roots.' Haley must go 'home' to Juffure, Gambia to hear the *griot* tell of his ancestors; Lance finally arrives 'home' at the Chelsea having found his true family at the Factory.

Burning Down the House

Finding the right house is the aim of the two gay Latino boys director Jennie Livingston meets on the street toward the end of *Paris Is Burning*. Livingston's appropriation of direct cinema as a style undoes the 'straight mind,' as Monique Wittig calls it, by featuring poor, African-American, and Latino gay men's performances of 'realness' at the drag balls of Harlem. Yet it does so as a fairly 'straight' *cinéma vérité*, hours spent following various of the legends and would-be legends of the balls; it is they who queer the form. As a white lesbian, Livingston has to cross a number of thresholds to enter these uptown houses; but we get no clue about how she negotiated this from the film; she never questions her voyeurism. Black and Latino male gay culture is welcoming: 'I came, I saw, I conquered . . . . That's a Ball,' remarks Pepper La Beija, legendary mother of the House of La Beija. The balls are open to all; but at the same time, quite closed. Kim Pendarvis explains that only 'faggots' will be able to succeed in realness, because they are 'stunts in themselves' whose daily existence teaches survival as self-surveillance. While girls have a bit of this talent, straight boys are utterly hopeless: 'Stupid,' spits Kim. The degree to which one is denied power and made invisible in culture renders an inverse awareness of the mechanisms of power and how it is displayed on the body. One mother, Willie Ninja, before making it big, taught modeling classes at the Fashion Institute of Technology, training girls how to walk like women.

Livingston's subjects defy simple plottings. Like Madonna, who appropriated the voguers' style for her Blond Ambition and then wreaked havoc with *vérité* convention in *Truth or Dare?*, the ball walkers deconstruct the visual cues of truth and reality, in effect undoing the logic of direct cinema. Thus 'executive realness,' one of the 'categories' in the balls, perfectly enacts the dress codes, facial expressions, deportment of young bankers. A profession wholly closed off to poor gay men because of racist and heterosexist social relations is pried open by them through a careful reading of effects. Balls test reading comprehension: realness of the performer, judged by the audience and judges, then projected on the streets. The ultimate success of 'femme realness queens,' notes one seasoned ball legend, is not only winning the category but making it home safely on the subway that night still in drag. The extensive categories open to voguing offer visions of fame and fortune, but some might be viewed as natural and everyday, daily encountered in neighborhoods, like school girl or bangee girl. These walks 'read' daily life as being as thoroughly saturated with complex codes open to insult and interpretation as that of the yachting set.

Within ball culture, that is, within the houses that structure the balls, possibilities open up – here 'men gather together under one roof and decide to compete,' says Pepper. The house is 'a gay street gang' and the ball a 'street fight – the house streetfights at the ball . . . by walking in a category.' The houses, asserts virtually every mother interviewed by Livingston, provide 'families – groups of human beings in a mutual bond' that often replace the original family after the young gay child has been rejected by father and mother. The two teenage boys explain that 'they want to be with their kind . . . just like a community . . . like belonging to a religious community wants to pray together. . . this gay community, they want to be together.' In what Judith Butler calls a 'rearticulation of kinship,' a sense of history invoked by interviews of former legends, upcoming walkers, and those who have not yet walked, Livingston outlines a genealogy for these families/houses/ communities, sketching the ways in which gay subculture has changed over time.[53] Years ago, the balls were drag-queen shows where Las Vegas-style costumes were featured and those who walked made their own outfits. 'Now,' says one surviving legend Dorian Carey, 'it's all about acquisition' – with categories in designer labels necessitating the specialized skills of 'mopping,' that is, shoplifting, to get what one needs – 'polyester is out.'

Realness plays on passing, 'to be able to blend – that's what realness is.' So, 'the idea of realness is to look as much like your straight counterpart – not a take-off or satire. It is actually being able to be.' Thus when Octavia Saint Laurant shows up at the annual supermodel contest along with thousands of other girls, she is 'no different' from any of the girls who have auditioned over the years, says one of the officials. Her dream of being a famous model in *Vogue* – unlike that of Venus Xtravanganza whose dream is to be a spoiled, rich, white girl – appears attainable. Octavia has mastered the realness of modeling designer apparel, the realness of being a famous and photographed woman. Mastering femaleness is simple, even for a preoperative transsexual, but becoming white – crossing the racial apartheid in America – provokes another story. Venus may have fair skin, blond hair, and green eyes, she may be tiny and appealing to the men who pick her up, but she still has a penis and, more damning, a Puerto Rican accent; she can never be a spoiled, rich, white girl.[54] Tragically, she is murdered.

In foregrounding whiteness as a mask, the ball queens endow it with ethnic and racial markings as overdetermined as those already deter- mining their lives. Whiteness and femaleness are categories that slide into each other, as bell hooks notes, contributing to the erasure of African-American and Latina womanhood. This slippage is due to the racism that, in the past, as Dorian Carey sadly comments, meant no one wanted to be Lena Horne; only the white stars were real enough to be imitated. Pepper and Willie, mothers of their respective houses, understanding the market have no use for sex changes. (Does this make them the embodiment of the phallic mother?) In their refusal to materialize (sex) changes on the body, they implicitly reject the racial codings associated with that female figure as well. Pepper says that women are oppressed, so why would one want to become one? It's money that would be nice to have. Willie wants to bring voguing to Japan. He works the runways of high fashion so deftly that by the epilogue of the film, he is an international star – been to Paris not only *Paris Is Burning*. They introduce the third term in Venus's chain of desires – wealth.

The ball walkers and voguers Livingston interviews express a 'politics of envy' in Carolyn Steedman's terms; a class resentment at the status of African Americans and Latinos who lack access to wealth and comfort available to white, middle-class Americans, as much as anger at the privileges of heterosexuality.[55] In this story of gay subcultural life, desire is coded through material effects. In the final scene when many of the 'stars' of the film reveal their fantasies about the future, conventional notions of success for white, middle-class, heterosexual women in 1950s America predominate. Each legend is filmed stretched out on her bed relaxed and seductive in the pose of a 1950s movie star: like Pat Loud at twenty, Venus wants a husband and a house and a white wedding dress; but Octavia wants to be a great model and have her sex change operation. Their bodies and lives give new dimensions to these yearnings in the 1990s. Two years later, Venus is murdered by a client, found strangled under the bed in a seedy hotel room – the poverty that forced her into prostitution makes her transvestism even more dangerous. Early in the film, Pepper bemoans how poor his children are. When Livingston tries to find out what kind of work these 'working girls' do, she is told that for the most part they hustle, or maybe they work in a club as a dancer. Class differences separate the ball walkers from their categories, and from the film-maker and her audience. While passing as a straight man or woman is key to walking, shifting class (and ethnic) positions secures the category. Executive realness, prep school realness, yachting, high fashion – all require a level of very expensive tailoring. As one legend remarks: 'All my life I felt cheated,' wanting things impossible to possess – the 1950s ideals of whiteness embodied by Marilyn Monroe, the invisibility of straight love, the power and prestige of wealth.

In giving voice to the mothers' and children's contradictory feelings of class resentment experienced in the mundane arenas of clothes, food, and leisure, Livingston's film opens up the interconnections between family identity and commodity fetishism. Steedman's moving memoir of her and her mother's lives offers a feminist recasting of Freud's family romance.[56] According to Freud's theory, the male child's fantasy that he is a foundling or the illegitimate son of an aristocrat restructures feelings of dissatisfaction with his parents, particularly with his father. The child imagines another house into which he might have been born; a wealthy, high-status father could offer the child much more than the real-life parent can. In the houses 'ruled with a soft glove' (as Pepper La Bieja says), children find the communities and protection that their biological families often cannot provide. Within the balls, they find a 'looking glass world' in which the effects of racism, homophobia, and poverty are masked, even erased. At a ball, everyone can walk.

In formulating a political analysis of envy, Steedman pushes past the literary and philosophical treatments of *ressentiment* to unpack a class dimension to desire.[57] When bell hooks chides the ball walkers (and Livingston) for celebrating a 'brutal imperialist ruling-class capitalist patriarchal whiteness,' she implies that the desire for material objects comes from false consciousness, commodity fetishism, reification, and as such is a purely mechanical reaction to American life.[58] In effect, she moralizes about the classed and raced and sexed voyeurism of the film-maker and her audience, but also about what are the proper or improper possessions, desires, and behaviors of the ball walkers. For Steedman's mother, envy drove a wedge between her and others of her class; excluded from the middle class, she felt no allegiances to any social groupings, voted Tory, followed Food Reform, saved for a New Look coat, and seethed with inexpressible anger. The children, however, become incorporated within a network of houses whose expression of identity at the balls assures a sense of location and community, a place perhaps of honor and memory if one becomes a legend. In different ways, Steedman's mother's story and those of the mothers and children Livingston tracks suggests that organizing around, not necessarily against, a politics of envy may be an essential part of combatting poverty's ideological effects.

Livingston's film bestowed material benefits on some of her subjects. On the one hand, Willie Ninja and Pepper La Beija gained fame and notoriety and work as dancers, choreographers, consultants for designers and singers; Octavia modeled before a camera. (Pepper sued Livingston over the film's revenues claiming a share of the film's take.) On the other hand, Livingston could do nothing for Venus, and most of the children still depend on prostitution to make a living. Moreover, the dissemination of voguing via Madonna and Livingston co-opted and mainstreamed it. Could the balls still provide the looking glass world they once had for their impoverished children? Many of the older legends testified that the balls had had a long history, evolving as styles and politics changed. Surely subcultures reinvent themselves constantly as the meaning and practice of dominant culture shifts; and just as surely the sexual, class, and racial dynamics superintending the lives of the children of ball houses remain as asymmetrical as ever.

152

Does making visible the invisible, subaltern, or hidden doom its culture? Or, as James Clifford argues, is the narrative of doomed cultures part of the ethnographic conceit of discovery and revelation?[59] The ethnographer constantly needs to search out a dying culture, and in so doing, ensures its death and secures his or her lament over it. Livingston's ethnography asks none of these questions. In this, hooks is correct, it seems a terribly retrograde film, one that declares with Pepper La Beija, 'I came. I saw. I conquered.' His invocation of imperialism is ironic and self-parodic; the ball walkers' power does not extend past the hall. But what of Livingston? Was she acting like the walkers or like Caesar when she walked in on the balls with her camera? Like Pepper appropriating Caesar's speech, Livingston takes another's space for her own use. Is this sort of filmmaking the same as imperialism? Are the balls? Certainly not, balls appropriate, not expropriate. Spectacle, visual display, is what the balls are about; you cannot walk unless someone else is there to compete and others there to watch and be seen. Livingston is exposing, not exploiting. But the line between the two is a fine one. After decades of cinematic and theoretical critiques of documentary and ethnographic invasions, naiveté is hardly credible. Something disturbs. Maybe it is the pleasure provoked by the film, maybe it's a coyness we sense thirty years after *cinéma vérité* 'moved in' with the first family and fifteen years after ABC found its *Roots*. When Livingston entered the House of La Beija, she was revisiting the history of direct cinema and of popular cultural productions of family history, rooting around for another American family.

The direct cinema movement had made intimate the spaces of public performance, further confounding the social divisions separating privacy from the public sphere; power governed at home as it did at work, at school, in government offices, and between nations. But living cinema could expose the insides of institutions only by effacing the histories of these structures. They simply are, without referents elsewhere. Direct cinema's 'read' of reality is also a kind of 'realness.' A read in ball culture is an insult; living cinema puts down institutions by miming them precisely and thus showing that they are highly unstable, filled with private zones of pain, humiliation, anguish, joy, pleasure, and mockery. They work on those subject to them through everyday encounters with authority. They are shameful places because they are so shameless in their guilelessness, their arrogance. In an excruciating scene from *Titicut Follies*, Dr Ross forcefeeds a resisting patient and keeps up a running commentary about what a good boy this patient is. We watch as the doctor's cigarette ash grows impossibly long, horrified, praying it won't fall into the funnel filling with the liquid which is poured through the patient's nose into his stomach. The sheer casualness of the scene, the regularity with which this must have happened, is clear from the relaxed banter; nothing out of the ordinary here. Nor was anything extraordinary about the routines at 35 Wood Dale Lane; in fact, it was their triviality that was so gripping. Through the style of *vérité*, this matter-of-fact effect also works in *Paris Is Burning*. Nothing is strange in this place, either; like Haley's 'saga,' another American family survives.

PART III

Maps of Aggression

7

Ethnographies of Women: *Soft Fiction* and

Feminist Theory

If the ethnographic documentary project of bringing an American family to view in each of America's homes marked the limit of *cinéma vérité*, it also presaged the beginnings of the feminist restructurings of gender at home, at work, and in the curricula of colleges and high schools. Ethnography had 'moved in' to its own backyard, fieldwork being as much about self-inspection as travel into other cultures. Thus Margaret Mead, America's pre-eminent anthropologist of gender and longtime advocate of using documentary films within anthropology, proclaimed *An American Family* 'a new kind of art form . . . as new and as significant as the invention of drama or the novel – a new way in which people can learn to look at life.'[1] But even if the lens were focused on 'us' not 'them,' the invasion of personal space and the power of the camera's unrelenting gaze, the tape recorders' ever-open microphones, and, most significantly, the editor's scissors, still left this form of ethnographic film-making firmly lodged within its imperialist legacy. Feminist anthropologists were searching for new methods as well as new practices to unpack the differing constructions of the 'sex-gender system,' as Gayle Rubin had called it, at home and elsewhere. The by now tired 'freedom' of direct cinema, which Pat Loud noted resulted in 'the treatment of us as objects and things instead of people,' could not provide feminist ethnographic film-makers with a form that would not strip its subjects 'of such honor and dignity as [they] owned.'[2] Other strategies were necessary.

In 1979 I saw Chick Strand's most recent film, *Soft Fiction*. I have not stopped thinking about it since and have often wondered why, apart from one very fine review by Marsha Kinder in *Film Quarterly*, virtually nothing has been written on the film.[3] I want to do three things in this chapter: talk about the film, talk about why practically nobody else has talked about it, and, in so doing, propose some alternative models for feminist film theory. As I see it, Strand's film, which re-presents many of the crucial aspects of 1970s feminism in North America, disappears somewhere within the tapestry of differing strands of feminist discourse. One thread was the emergence of cultural feminism with its separatist politics that drew upon its dual focus on pornography as the cause of women's victimization by male sexual aggression and on de-eroticizing lesbianism.[4] Another was the rise of psychoanalytical feminism and its installation within the Academy by feminist cultural theorists which often meant that only films responding to Oedipal narratives received attention.[5] Strand's film engages elements important to all these configurations, but it twists each of them just enough to make her film politically incorrect to cultural feminist theorists and theoretically unsophisticated to feminist cultural theorists. Incorrect *and* unsophisticated – no wonder it disappeared from feminist memory. This chapter is an attempt at retrieval: but it is also an examination of the forces producing feminist political correctness and theoretical sophistication and the potential both these criteria have to narrow the range of feminism's practices. Finally, as I perform my role as feminist film critic, I want to suggest that this process is itself a form of documentary, that is, it is both a spectacle and speculative. The idea of critique as cultural performance, one that relies on a subject of agency, can perhaps point a way out of the political impasses that both identity politics and psychoanalytic theory construct for feminism.

The mid- to late 1970s represent a crucial moment in the brief history of the second wave of US feminism. A number of mutually sustaining, though at times antagonistic, developments put much feminist politics, culture, and theory on courses we are still tracking. Alice Echols has argued that by 1975 the feminist movement in the United States had come to be dominated by what she calls cultural feminism – a tendency to replace radical political critiques of gender with counter-cultural celebrations of woman's culture. Echols has traced the decline of a radical interrogation of gender. I would like to focus on the developing feminist film culture of this period to examine some of the ways that cultural forms scripted (as well as were scripted by) this transformation.

At least since Vertov and Eisenstein set out to represent the everyday transformations in the streets, homes, and workplaces of post-revolutionary Russia, film culture has had a special relationship with radical political movements.[6] The appropriation of classic film languages to, in the words of Mao Ze-dung, 'expose' dominant ideology

and the development of counter-cinematic techniques to 'extol' subcultural struggle against hegemony figure directly in the construction
of revolutionary masses.[7] Moreover, as Walter Benjamin asserts, as a
popular form – anyone can be in a film and everyone can be an expert
on film – film itself helps produce a mass subject.[8] (How many times
did we watch *The Battle of Algiers* before demonstrations during the
1960s?) Film's mass appeal coalesces the disparate strands of a culture
and re-presents them to themselves. Thus even in its oppositional
forms, it also participates in the process of consolidation of hegemonic
power by incorporating, coopting and realigning radical challenges:
the women's liberation movement, like many radical movements
before it, immediately grasped the importance of cinema as an arguing
tool – the women in the New York Newsreel collective brought their
cameras to film the 1968 Miss America Pageant where members of the
women's liberation movement staged a counter-pageant on the Atlantic City Boardwalk, including a garbage bin for disposing various items
of female torture – bras, girdles, high heels; this was the event during
which women first allegedly burned bras.

By 1979, the women's liberation movement had crumbled into a
variety of tendencies – radical, cultural, socialist, liberal – over a series
of issues – racism, homophobia, institutionalization, pornography. I
shall focus on the latter two. The debate over pornography had
developed from a number of sources. With the establishment of rape
crisis centers and battered women's shelters during the mid-1970s,
many feminists became appalled at the extent to which violence against
women permeated our culture. In addition to establishing these
alternative institutions to counter the further violences of patriarchal
bureaucracies of the state, the law, and the family, feminist theory
focused attention on the power of ideology, especially as it was dissemi-
nated by popular culture, to 'manufacture femininity,' by exposing
advertisements, popular women's magazines, the Miss America contest as sites that were doing more than, in the words of one song,
'killing us softly.'[9] It appeared that one did not have to frequent a porn
shop to find images of women bound, gagged, and ready for anything.

These images appeared directly linked to the rise in rapes and
assaults, and while it seemed impossible to do anything about the latter
– police seemed unwilling or unable to prosecute wife batterers – the
process of bringing a rapist to trial seemed almost as brutal as the rape
itself – the images themselves, certainly reflective and perhaps even a
cause of the sexualization of violence, could be challenged directly
through zap actions, through Take Back the Night! marches, and
increasingly through efforts to control their dissemination by fighting
against 'pornography' with legal challenges asserting that it violated

women's civil rights as a form of sex discrimination. This process culminated in the Meese Commission hearings in which prominent feminists testified along with members of fundamentalist churches and law enforcement agents for the necessity of outlawing pornography.[10] As pornography increasingly came to be seen as the enemy, as the cause and effect of women's victimization, cultural feminist theorists, such as Kathleen Barry in *Female Sexual Slavery* (1978) and Andrea Dworkin in *Intercourse* (1984) painted vivid pictures of female bondage to a rapacious male sexuality. In their views, women's so-called natural sensuality was destroyed by men's fundamental need to dominate, control, and even 'murder' women through sex.[11]

The anti-pornography position was not the only feminist analysis of women's sexuality at the time; Angela Carter's *Sadeian Woman* 'put pornography in the service of women' by exploring women's relationship to classic sexual allegories of domination and submission as productive and potentially liberating.[12] The infamous 1982 Barnard Conference on the Woman and the Scholar explicitly sought to address the ways 'women get sexual pleasure in patriarchy' by 'acknowledging that sexuality is simultaneously a domain of restriction, repression and danger as well as a domain of exploration, pleasure and agency.'[13] Anti-porn feminist assumptions about the directly causal relationship between images of women as victims and the actual victimization of women through sexual violence presumed the sociologically based understandings of the image that marked the earliest forms of feminist film criticism.[14] However, by 1975, feminist semiotic and psychoanalytic theories influenced by Lacanian re-readings of Freud had reshaped feminist film theories about representation and its power to reflect social meanings. These theories asked: Was the 'Black and Blue' woman in the Rolling Stones ad 'real,' or did she signify something about women's ambiguous position within the masculinist ideology celebrated by the Stones which nevertheless was mediated by the ironic incorporation of biker and S/M subcultures into popular culture? Clearly, the regime of the visual itself was fully implicated in the production of androcentric ideologies about female sexuality, but it was naive to read that relationship as a directly causal one. The unconscious – that politically incorrect formation – not to mention the mechanisms of narrative structure, audio envelopment, and visual spectacle harbor (and produce) an array of desires that exceed the bounds of the rationalist positivism that underpinned the sexual theories of anti-porn feminists. Pleasure, argue the radical pro-sex feminists, cannot be legislated. Still, the images, both hard-core porn and soft-core Madison Avenue, demanded (and produced) a feminist response.

Within film cultures, the 1970s mark a decisive moment in the production of feminist codes. The brief film history I am about to outline provides a catalog of the differing forms of responses to the debates within feminism about sexuality and gender. Hollywood was busily responding to liberal feminism's growing acceptance among the middle class with female buddy pictures like *The Turning Point* (Ross, 1977) and *Julia* (Zinneman, 1977). In 1974, film critic Molly Haskell had denounced the trend away from 'woman's pictures' with the argument that the male buddy films popular during the 1960s and 1970s, exemplified by *Butch Cassidy and the Sundance Kid* (Hill, 1969), reduced the place of women within cinema to an insignificant object as it traced the romance between two male outlaws. Hollywood female buddies attempted to recapture a female movie-going audience. These films looked back to the melodramas of the 1940s, unlike *Thelma & Louise*, Hollywood's most recent female buddy film which has regendered the image of the liberated outlaw, eliciting hysteria among many male (and some female) critics.

In addition, independent, feature-length films, like Claudia Weill's *Girlfriends* (1978), were attempting cross-overs between dominant and alternative cinemas for a largely female audience. This film in particular reconstituted one trend of overtly feminist independent cinema – the establishment of a realist aesthetic based on *cinéma vérité* techniques – to authenticate women's lives on screen.[15] Employing female talking heads, hand-held cameras, and multiple protagonists to let women speak their lives, films like *Janie's Janie* (Ashur et al., 1971) and *Rape* (Elam, 1975) became organizing tools teaching women how to set up consciousness-raising groups, women's health clinics, rape crisis centers, and so on. These films, along with revisionist historical films like *With Babies and Banners* (Goldfarb, 1977) and *Union Maids* (Reichert and Klein, 1977) or *The Woman's Film* (San Francisco Newsreel, 1970) challenged the absence of black and white working-class women's voices and lives from American (film) history as they constructed a collective form of solidarity, a feminist 'we,' amid their audiences.[16]

Still other independent film-makers were experimenting with structural and theoretical subversions of the cinematic image and its narrative to undercut the 'technologies of gender' inscribed in the apparatus itself. This feminist-theoretical approach expanded after the pathbreaking – even seminal – publication in 1975 of 'Visual Pleasure and Narrative Cinema' by film-maker/critic Laura Mulvey.[17] Her Lacanian-tinged appropriation of Freudian concepts of the split subject allowed her to shift focus, if you will, from the screen to the spectator. Rather than viewing the screen image as a direct (or at best mediated)

161

rendering of reality – à la Molly Haskell – Mulvey sought to locate the differing positions assumed by male and female spectators when they encountered the curiously disjointed, though apparently seamless, phenomenon of classic Hollywood cinema: its tension between the narrative thrust of the male characters and the visual spectacle of the female body. This elicited contradictory responses in masculine and feminine viewers because the narrative produced an identification with the male character while the visuals interrupted this process as they demanded an equally powerful fetishization of the female body. She argued that the process requires us to look with the gaze of the male at the spectacle of feminine lack no matter what our sex. Further, she claimed that only a radical break with the regime of vision constructed by classic narrative cinema could force us to turn away from the identification/objectification process (with its positioning of the spectator as masculine). This could be accomplished by an avant-gardist cinema which defers the pleasures of voyeurism attendant on the display of female bodies. Of course, the history of the avant-garde is full of women's bodies deployed to interrupt conventional narrative (for instance, the sliced eyeball in *Un Chien Andalou*: Buñuel, Dali, 1922), or to foreground the materials of cinema (e.g. the winking 'China doll' in George Landow's *Film in which There Appear Sprocket Holes, Edge Lettering and Dust Particles*, 1966), but Mulvey was arguing for an explicitly feminist avant-garde, one which, if you followed the logic of her argument into her films, would give voice to the mother, would require us to listen carefully to the 'riddle of the sphinx.'

Mulvey's theory – like those of Claire Johnston and other cinesemiotic feminists – locates the significance of cinema in its spectacle. It is the spectacle that deploys the spectator's gaze. This model, while opening up the possibility for textual analyses of how filmic meaning (and gendered subjectivity) is produced, argues that cinema constructs itself through the highly static categories of sexual difference. Much as cultural feminists saw male objectification of women as a totalizing, unidirectional process, cinema was understood to enclose objects and subjects within distinct boundaries. Men look; women are to be looked at. Later revisions of this model – including Mulvey's own 'after-thoughts' or Mary Ann Doane's 'masquerade' – still presumed that the spectacle as a relation of subject to object was epiphenomenal to the cinematic/psychoanalytic apparatus. Women's position was less securely anchored in both scenes – the cinematic and the psychoanalytic – but it was still locked into the total apparatus of the desiring machine.[18] This model, with its 'scientific' methodology gleaned from Christian Metz's '*la grande syntagmatique*,' was perfectly suited to counter academic critics of both film studies and women's studies: the subsequent feminist film theory became rigorous with a vengeance. Yet what I think was missing was a sense of the dynamic intersubjectivity of the performance of cinema – both of the bodies on screen enacting conscious performances and of the bodies in the audience taking up and remaking these performances (un)consciously and collectively.[19] Something different happens in a movie theater from what occurs in a dream or fantasy. Other people surround you – coughing, laughing, eating, kissing – who have also traveled to the theater, paid money, and expect affective results. In short, the performance of cinema – on screen and in the audience – is fundamentally social. And while this was certainly obvious to Mulvey, the uses to which her analysis has been put often forget this crucial aspect of cinema.

By crossing generic borders to rewrite the same old story and reshoot the same old scene differently from the Hollywood process of sublating feminism into its own generic category – the woman's film the feminist counter-cinema Mulvey and others sought, grounded in the traditions of avant-gardist cinema, could speak the female voice to challenge conventions about narrative and pleasure. Some films – such as Sally Potter's *Thriller* (1979), a theoretically grounded, anti-theory feminist investigation of Mimi's death in Puccini's opera *La Bohème* as murder, Michele Citron's *Daughter Rite* (1979), a fake 'documentary' exploring two sisters' relationship to their dead mother, or Weinstock et al.'s, *Sigmund Freud's Dora*, (1979) a film that, among other things, retells Freud's case history from his patient's point of view – sought to undo a variety of conventions inherited from the narrative traditions of both European art cinema and Hollywood. Often using grainy film stock, optically printed footage, still photographs, unsynched sound, they estrange the audience through 'alienation effects' like direct address to the camera, blurred images, garish colors, discontinuous narratives, etc.

Because these films encoded many of the desired traits Mulvey had articulated, they became the focus of critical attention – appearing in festivals and courses and on the pages of increasingly respectable film journals. In *Allegories of Cinema*, David James argues:

> Like previous avant-garde cinemas, feminist theory both contested the cinema of the hegemonic social formation and consolidated alternative communities . . . [T]his feminist practice of film theory was also a determinate option within the historical situation of feminism; it made it possible for a dispersed, highly educated, bourgeois community, without ready access to production, to engage in cinema, even as it made cinema the means by which that community could produce and organize itself . . . . Critical writing acquired a new importance in disseminating avant-gardist projects to women at large, and it often had to stand in for the films themselves; but

theory also commandeered film production . . . the most interesting films were being made in virtual illustration of theoretical issues developed in feminist scholarly articles.[20]

Quickly, a feminist canon was established.[21] But what of other films by women that also challenge the regimes of Hollywood and the art house? What of Marie Mencken or Maya Deren, both foremothers of the American avant-garde cinema whose lyrical and formalist films explore the private spaces of women? Their films made in the 1940s and 1950s pushed the boundaries of American cinema to include celebrations of male homosexual desire (Broughton, Kuchar, Anger), altered states of consciousness (Kubelka, Brakhage), and the medium itself (Landow, Snow, Warhol). Even before women's liberation had named itself and its enemy, Gunvor Nelson's and Dorothy Wiley's dissection of women's social position through relentless images of pregnant women vomiting, menstruating women disposing of blood-ied tampons, and mothers changing soiled diapers, *Schmeerguntz* (1966) challenged the underground to acknowledge female oppres-sion. Ann Severson's *Near the Big Chakra* (1972), whose 'unhurried view of 37 human female vaginas ranging in age from 3 months to 56 years' exploded both structural film's contentless content as well as the pornographic project to make (the female) sex visible.[22] It caused a near riot at its premiere at the Ann Arbor Film Festival. Taken together, these films and others mark the beginning of the second wave of feminist (film) practices. Nelson and Wiley's montage might be thought of as an answer to Stan Brakhage's scratch marks covering over his wife Jane's pregnancies and labors, while Severson's insistent content transgressed the 'pure politics of perception' governing structuralist-materialist films.[23] Paradoxically, these films imply a uni-versal woman's culture which should have been compatible with cultural feminism; they all interrogate narrative and cinematic prac-tices that have fetishized the female image and thus should have been of interest to theoretical feminists. Yet they rarely figure in discussions of feminist film by either cultural or psychoanalytic feminists. Why? To answer this question, as well as begin outlining an approach to femi-nism and film that avoids the static positionings of masculinity and femininity constructed (albeit differently) by both cultural and psy-choanalytic feminisms, let me turn to the work of Chick Strand.

Chick Strand's *Soft Fiction* recirculates many of the clichéd narratives and images about women's erotic and sexual fantasies within its visual and sound tracks. Bringing to focus questions about the range of female sexuality and fantasy, the modes of female address, the genre(s) of women's stories, the form of the female body as visual spectacle and narrative subject, *Soft Fiction* dwells between the borders of ethnography, documentary, avant-garde, and feminist counter-cinema.[24] Its title locates it at the interstices of soft-core porn, documentary, and narrative films. Strand herself describes her beautifully shot, black-and-white film as an 'ethnography of women.'[25] In doing so, she places it directly within the realm of anthropological film-making, where she began her career. Strand invokes yet resists the idea of the 'exotic' cultural Other that forms the subject of much ethnography.

One of Strand's earliest films, *Mosori Monika* (1971), investigates the impact of a Spanish mission on the Warao Indians of central Venezuela through the differing narratives of a young Spanish nun and an elderly Warao woman. This film exposes the missionary project as an essentially imperialist one that teaches the Indians 'how to live a human life . . . . The life of a man,' while demonstrating that the Warao cagily employ a form of resistance to the colonial presence of the mission despite their apparent willingness to be clothed, fed, and fêted by the nuns. Strand's narrow focus – on the stories of these two women – and her evocative close-ups of the bodies of men and women working, resting, eating, playing, break many of the conventions of the anthropological documentary by refusing to present the 'whole' picture of the culture (Figure 16). In her justification of that film, 'Notes on Ethnographic Film by a Film Artist,' she challenges the conventions of 'wholeness' which Karl Heider had established as the mark of well-wrought ethnographic cinema.[26] Arguing for the use of extreme close-ups, fragmented movements, and the 'small talk' of daily life, she seeks to 'get a microscopic view of one of the threads that make up the tapestry of the whole culture.' Locating the partial and the conditional, her films 'evolve in the field' into 'works of art' rather than scientific 'textbooks.'[27]

Since the mid-1960s Strand has been filming the life story of her friend Anselmo, an Indian from northern Mexico, who makes his living as a street musician. Because each film involves a level of 'performance' that is self-consciously rendered to alter the 'purity' of ethnographic forms, she describes the films variously as 'experimental documentary,' 'expressive documentary,' or 'intimate documentary.' Her first film, *Anselmo* (1967), is a 'symbolic reenactment of a real event,' in which Strand tried to fulfill Anselmo's wish for a 'double E-flat tuba.' She failed to find one, but managed to locate a brass wrap-around tuba which she smuggled into Mexico and presented to him. Later, they reproduced the transaction for the camera. In *Cosas de mi Vida* (1976), Strand traces ten years in Anselmo's life as he struggles to endure poverty. The film is narrated by Anselmo in English, although he does not speak the language. Strand translated the Spanish narration Anselmo provided and then taught him how to say it for the film. Again, Anselmo 'performs' himself as a subject for these (unauthentic) ethnographies. Her most celebrated film, *Mujere de Milfuegos* (1976), presents a 'fake' ethnography about the 'women who wear black from the age of 15 and spend their entire lives giving birth, preparing food and tending to household and farm responsibilities,' by depicting 'their daily repetitive tasks as a form of obsessive ritual.'[28]

The idea of transforming the ethnographic film from an observational tool, one which records daily life and/or ritual as data, into an expressive, intimate, experimental documentary requires a sense of cinematic address as performative. It also presumes that cultural identities and ideas of the individual subject are constructed as performances – for the self, for others, for the camera – within various cultural arenas. Performing everyday activities as rituals for the camera undermines the concept of ritual as well as the concept of cinema. It suggests that the images on the screen respond to the capacities of the 'actors' to take up one position, leave it, and take up another in a stylized fashion. Perhaps this same sense of mobility – of moving in and out of a performance – occurs for the spectator too, who, rather than being locked into a unified, or even split gaze, is always calling up various performative aspects of identity which echo, refuse, confront, or merge with the screen performances. To give another example, toward the end of Trinh T. Minh-ha's film about Senegalese women, *Reassemblage* (1982), the film-maker remarks:

> I come with the idea that I would seize the unusual by catching the person unawares. There are better ways to steal. With the other's consent. After seeing me laboring with the camera, women invite me to their place and ask me to film them . . . . What I see is life looking at me/I am looking through a circle in a circle of looks/115° Fahrenheit. I put on a hat while laughter bursts behind me. I haven't seen any woman wearing a hat . . .

The film-maker takes up her position among the women she has been filming and responds to their responses to her. They are happy to be filmed but the filming must be by invitation. The village women engage the film-making process as an exchange of looks, as a gesture and recognition of differences, and so perform their daily lives for Trinh, who herself becomes a spectacle for her subjects (Figure 17).

Recent feminist and gay studies theories of performance stress the constructedness and historically contingent nature of gender and sexual identities. Judith Butler, for instance, argues that 'gender is an identity tenuously constituted in time, instituted on exterior space through a *stylized repetition of acts*.'[29] Denise Riley suggests that the condition of 'women' is as contested and historically indeterminate as the mythical category of 'woman.' Neither term – women, woman – she declares, can sufficiently pin down the multivalent claims and strategies (as Butler calls them) entailed in constituting a subject. I believe feminist politics must take its cue from gay and lesbian political activists and become self-conscious of its contingent aspect – of itself as a performance responding to its own cultural space and historical period.

Likewise, I would argue that feminist film theory needs to embrace its performative quality, both as it speaks of an object productive of and produced by performances, and as it becomes another form of cinematic performance. The overvaluation of the psychoanalytical model, which reads the effects of the cinematic apparatus through the subject's unconscious responses to the imaginary, forgets just how constructed and how performative even that primal scene is. After all, the 'scene' to which cinematic voyeurism supposedly refers is rarely seen – it is an imaginative reconstruction, a symbolic performance, of desire.[30] For all its critique of narrative realism as oppressive and of critical reflectionism as vulgar, feminist psychosemiotic film theory has perhaps unconsciously reinstated a reflectionist aesthetics by declaring the cinematic apparatus to be a map of the unconscious. Rather than describe film's contents as reflective of sociological formations (like gender roles), cinesemiotics represents cinematic form as a mirror of imaginary constructions (like sexual difference). By prying film away from its historical references – to performers, film-makers, critics, and audiences – psychoanalytical feminist film theorists veer close to the analyses of cultural feminists.

Strand's manufacture of 'ritual' performances, her reconstructions of real events, her rephrased translations, indicate to me that the ethnographic scene, as much as the psychoanalytical, is also a performance that depends on the film-maker's desire for the encounter and the informant's willingness to act it out for an audience.[31] Films like hers and Trinh's depict the historicity of cinematic engagement by calling attention to the performances of documentary film's subjects and objects. Strand describes another recent film, *Artificial Paradise* (1986), as an 'Aztec romance and the dream of love. The anthropologist's most human desire, the ultimate contact with the informant.' A romance *and* a dream: a cultural construction and a psychic re-enactment. Thus, as an 'ethnography of women,' which is just a group of Strand's friends who visit her home in Tujunga Canyon between 1976 and 1979 to tell their stories, Strand's film challenges the notions of the 'exotic' and the 'whole' and of the 'informant' and the 'scientist,' but also insists on social relations in cinematic address. 'The erotic content and style' of *Soft Fiction* suggests the malleability and the pornographic (i.e. mythic, in Angela Carter's sense) quality of all fictions, including ethnographies, and the fictionality of all oral and visual testimonies, especially those of feminine desire.[32]

The film begins with a sequence of train sounds and horizontally moving patterns of light and dark. It takes a few minutes to orient oneself to the sound and image which finally resolve into a close-up of a woman's face against a window. She departs the train and like Maya Deren in *Meshes of the Afternoon* (1943), to which *Soft Fiction* pays homage, walks in the late afternoon southern California sun through some greenery to a locked house. She remains outside, but the camera enters the room and surveys it voyeuristically: checking the kitchen, bathroom, bedroom – recreating the dizzying descent of the staircase in *Meshes* – grazing the shadow of the film-maker herself to discover a woman sitting in an armchair near a window calmly smoking as a woman's voice-over exhorts us to 'move, first one way then the other – gathering, lifting, squeezing, releasing, just so it feels good.' This reference to counter-cultural California sensuality also nods to a female avant-garde film history.[33]

Beginning with Germaine Dulac's *La Souriante Mme Beudet* (1922) and continuing through Deren's *Meshes* and Menken's *Glimpses in a Garden*, much of women's avant-garde cinema develops as an exploration and exposure of interiors. Deren's and Strand's cameras scrutinize the empty houses they enter, but these houses are their own, turning the voyeuristic gaze into an exhibitionist display of its objects. However, where Deren multiplied her own body to display the terrors and desires of the female subject, Strand includes the voices of many women to demonstrate the multiplicity and resistance of women's fantasies. Like Carmelita, the Warao woman, whose incorporation into the mission can be read as victimization but whose own rendering of it challenges us to read resistance in her very acceptance of the nuns' offerings, the women tell stories of incest, addiction, and Nazis which are potent tropes for women's victimization. Yet the women's voices, the images they construct to accompany their tales and the sequencing of these images counter preconceptions of female powerlessness by substituting in its place the power of acting.

As the seated woman begins her story, initiated by rubbing the curving bannister of the Pasadena Art Museum, her desire to 'become this railing – become this piece' invites us to question the very terms of representation that objectify women's bodies. That the play on the word 'piece' is deliberate, we hear in her slow, precise language; we see her lips, nose, and eyes peering directly into the camera: cinematic convention tells us she is revealing truth. The camera leaves her as she asks, 'Haven't you ever wanted to live within black fur?' The tactile transvestism of this woman's desire – to inhabit curved alloyed metals, black fur, to turn her body into an object of touch – destroys the sensation of inside/outside for us as it extends the body into new spaces, new desires. It also transgresses both cultural feminism's and psychoanalytical feminism's rigid resistance to (yet ironic insistence on) woman's objectification. The speaking subject of this sequence desires objecthood.

Another woman reads a letter to Strand recounting the story of a photographer whose escapade at a rodeo she had gone to shoot ends with her giving a series of blow jobs to anonymous cowboys in a dark dormitory room. The incidents seem 'inevitable' to the letter writer; her loss of control at the rodeo becomes visible to the letter reader in her handwriting – she fails to capitalize her I's. Already mediated on several levels (the woman's story appears as a letter written to Chick but read by a giggling woman to the camera) her story is deeply ambivalent. Has she been coerced? Is this a case of gang rape? Or is it a staging of a fantasy which oscillates between her power as voyeur, as photographer, and theirs as exhibitionists, as sexual cowboys? After she and her camera escape unharmed from this encounter, she picks up yet another cowboy to photograph. He takes her to a stable where she photographs him naked except for his belt, hat, and boots – the regalia typical of S/M scenes – and where again she gives him a blow job while his buddies watch. Her fear is countered by her excitement, which is mediated further by his final remarks of comfort: 'It will make a good story to tell your grandchildren.' In a bizarre reordering of the female oral tradition, sexual pleasure exists for the man in his fellated orgasm, but for the woman, who never quite gets off herself, it is deferred, available only in the verbal recreation of desire through memory, narrative, and performance.[34]

In this story, Strand and her informant manipulate one of the privileged scenes of hard-core porn, the blow job, evoking visceral reactions from audience members about the woman's status as a 'victim.'[35] Linda Williams has argued that the growing popularity during the 1970s of feature-length porn films like *Deep Throat, The Devil in Miss Jones* (Damiano, 1972) and *Behind the Green Door* (Mitchell, 1972) signaled that there was an audience for the visible evidence of desire as a fetishized commodity and that mass media could produce it. These films invoked women's demands for more and better sex through fantasies that fulfilled male desire, thus resisting the threat of feminism by constructing women's desire as sexually exciting for men. Like radical feminist Anne Koedt, *Deep Throat* rejects 'the myth of the vaginal orgasm,' but, as it orchestrates its 'sexual numbers' around the ejaculation of fellated penises into Linda Lovelace's ecstatic face, its ultimate audience is male.[36] Still, the narrative appeal to a broader audience (one that presumably included heterosexual women) refracted the messages of soft-core melodramas, like *Looking for Mr Goodbar* (Brooks, 1977), which also assumed women's independent desires for sexual adventure, but provided cautionary tales about the dangers of arousing male sexual aggression for their largely female audiences.[37] The soft-core films looked back to the 1940s woman's film genre, and to the popular woman's romances found in *True Confessions*, where transgressive sexuality in a woman always resulted in shame and punishment.[38]

But in *Soft Fiction*, the photographer returns to her pleasure and her power. In her ironic reply to us, not to her handsome cowboy, she asserts, 'Well, photography is a power to be reckoned with,' revealing that after she prints his photo she discovers his name on his belt, tracks him down, obsessively follows him home, and declares: 'I know where he lives now.' As Strand says of all her 'informants,' they take 'responsibility for having had the experience. It's not that they take responsibility for the experience happening but for "having had" it.'[39] The claim of 'responsibility' challenges women's victimization in/by narrative by asserting that their stories are conscious re-enactments. The process occurs as a translation – a refashioning of the experience into a narrative and visual sequence. This recurs at various times throughout the film, which continues to switch codes between the expressionistic frame of the woman's quest (for pleasure?) and the concrete documentary-like stories women tell about the real and fantasized causes and effects of these quests – stories of pain, violation, and desire.

The next shot reveals a sun-drenched kitchen. We watch a woman enter naked, her body strong; she is unselfconscious of it as she switches on the radio before she starts preparing a hearty breakfast of juice, coffee, eggs, and buttered toast. The show, *Grand Central Station*, begins with the sounds of a train over which the narrator intones 'This is a love story,' reminding us that 'The door to the great white way is usually through the back alley.' At this point, we hear a voice-over as a woman describes a sensuous memory of swimming in a pond as a child – diving 'in and up and down' – until, tired, she ran to her grandfather who was waiting with a towel. She describes walking back to their cabin, watching the drops of water splashing in the dust. Then, matter of factly, states, 'I was young, only seven. We would make love on the couch, the red couch, I trusted grampa – even fell into enjoying it.' She describes how he kissed her and undressed her, noting that only once did she see his penis, 'like a snake, a pink velvet snake . . . he used it on my clitoris . . . he wanted to teach me how to make love . . . how to be

170

sensual.' By this time, she is eating. The camera no longer displays her whole body, but again is extremely close-up. Cutting into the egg yolk with the side of her spoon and smearing it over the whites, she remembers how 'It scared me – it was too close and too strong . . . I just wouldn't allow myself to be alone with him – jump out of bed, feign sleep, all the typical tactics of female avoidance – I learned them young – now I'm a master. Pursued and captured, really captured cause there's no way out . . .' she declares, as she exhales her after-breakfast cigarette.

Again, ambivalence is crucial to the performance of this scene. Hers is the only body we see whole, performing a whole act, her story distanced by the off-screen narrator. Her voice is strong, ironical, yet vulnerable. She is angry, but the circumstances she has constructed to disclose her secret imply that she has power over them. Hers is certainly 'Not a Love Story' and the 'responsibility' is certainly not hers, yet her image and her story – its disembodied narration running over her real-time act – unpack the cinematic baggage this story of female powerlessness holds for us and perhaps her.

The film now cuts to a clichéd image of feminine eroticism as a nude woman dances to Sidney Bechet's rendition of 'Petit Fleur,' and we see the play of light and dark as her body and hair break the sun's rays. This diversion momentarily breaks the tension of captivity encoded in the woman in the kitchen story and in the previous use of the extreme close-up in the woman at the museum and rodeo stories. But the next woman tells about being 'really hooked.' Again, lips, eyes, brow are prominent in extreme close-up, as the woman chain smokes, drinks wine, and describes her 'plan,' her 'program,' to become hooked first on a man, then on the pain he caused, then on heroin to escape the pain. Ultimately, she kicks, despite wondering why: 'It was so good, so clear, so real, so spacious. But I did it – that was the plan and I exorcised him.' The exorcism extends into the film-making process. Strand claims that 'the most incredible part of making the film was my relationship to the women when they were talking and being on camera, and doing it knowing the result, knowing that they would be on this big screen and a lot of people, strangers, would see them . . . them telling it on camera acted as an exorcism . . .'[40] In other words, the informants became self-styled performers for an audience that was both distant from yet intimate with the 'connections' in these stories.

The complicity among storyteller, film-maker, and audience in the production of a voyeuristic fantasy continues as we watch a dog setting itself into a comfortable position on an armchair. The soundtrack is of loud voices – a train station perhaps, no, an audience at a performance who break into applause when the dog stands revealing that it has only three legs. Then a white face and white hands emerge from the blackness, the woman begins singing Schubert's 'Death and the Maiden,' whose lyrics evoke the longing for 'dreams,' for 'sleep.' In calling forth the romantic vision of desire as death, the conventional reading of women's masochism is reinserted as a commentary on the women's stories so far. Yet, by doing so through a soprano's rendition of the *Lied*, the female body as a performative tool is reasserted. Although each story has been painful – we see the women's faces contort, hear their voices crack as they speak – they have all been humorous as well. Each woman has restaged her 'tragedy' into a story of power and pleasure by the styles of their telling and the compositions of their images. Still, these tropes of captivity are the stuff of female masochism, their 'true confessions,' the stories of surrender and desire that fueled my politically incorrect pre-adolescence. As if to confirm our secret complicity with the mechanisms of pornographic surrender, after the *Lied*, we find the traveling woman again. Watching her leave the house, her suitcase opens exposing yards of cloth and a sequined teddy.

The final segment frames a tight, nervous face, 'OK,' she says, 'this is going to be a little bit difficult.' Her story is set during the war in the Poland of her childhood, when she says 'it was demanded of me that I stay quiet . . . people were after you.' It is not clear whether her family was hiding Jews or were themselves Jews in hiding, but after a neighbor informs on them, the Gestapo visit her home. She 'remember[s] being put on a Gestapo officer's lap to divert his attention – I understood that – what my job was . . . I remember flirting with him.' Her faltering voice continues with a memory of being awakened by her mother when she was 3½ and walking at night for miles:

> It was necessary for me to be very brave. I remember that I liked that and I remember that I like that now – that I was brave then. And I remember a hill with fire and explosions of all sorts. I remember how frightened everyone was and my father carrying the bird cage with the kittens. And I remember feeling proud that I didn't want to be carried. And I remember that hill and there was something very bad going on on the other side, and then there's a blank.

Unlike the preceding stories of sexual adventure and surrender, which emerge as coherent, well-plotted narratives – the stuff of conventional melodrama – these memories of historical necessity are fractured, disrupted, and lack clarity. Yet, even here, the sensation is of control, of the power this young girl experienced despite, or rather because of, knowing she was an object of exchange in a larger transaction.

172

The last images of the film return to more classic images from soft-core porn – a woman's abandon as a shower of clear water washes over her, a woman walking barefoot along the shore, two naked women frolicking on horseback (Figure 18). These also are the staples of California independent film-making of the 1960s – the sensuous display of the body at play in nature. Like the Schubert *Lied*, the train journey, or the solo dance, they recontain the stories of female transgression and pleasure in the face of masculine power within the limits of conventionalized depictions of female desire. Yet the stories undercut this containment, violating boundaries, just as the excesses of the extreme close-ups explode the documentary conventions of the talking head by overvaluing the partial elements of the face – lips, brows, nostrils – and body – hands, legs, feet. These fragmented, cut-up icons of femininity which appear commodified in advertisements have been recharged by the speakers. By allowing movement in and out of frame, the stationary camera enables the speakers to take control of and produce their images.

The stories in *Soft Fiction* flow out of each other, the way one might reveal secrets to a stranger on a train, or whisper late at night to girlfriends. They are intensely private and personal, yet by orchestrating them within the compositions of avant-garde cinematography, documentary address, ethnographic film-making, and soft-core porn, Strand wants us to begin questioning how female pleasures are experienced and represented in patriarchal culture. The film's ethnographic inquiry seems to ask: what are the narrative and visual components of white middle-class women's (hetero)sexualities? How are they represented and performed in bourgeois culture? The stories acquire their meanings through a complex interplay of image, sequence, and sound. The tight framing of faces restricts women's bodies as cinematic spectacle, yet we also participate in a voyeuristic invasion of private space and conventionalized modes of displaying female desire as well as listen in on some juicy secrets. The stories seem private, yet their performances enter public spaces. In the process, the tropes of the victim are recast through the process of storytelling into a grand panorama leading from narcissistic joy to genocidal horror. As they invoke a history of genres – melodrama, case study, gossip, romance – all too familiar in their containments of women's desires and their commodifications of women's pleasure and pain, these stories ask us to step outside conventional narratives and images put forth by hard- and soft-core porn, and by their anti-porn feminist critics, to allow for the possibility that the 'story is a sexual fantasy lived out.'[41] In its development of women's powers of performance –

powers depending on cultural contradictions that recognize both the Oedipal narrative's power over, but also its ancillary status for, women – this film also challenges the psychoanalytical model of spectatorship. In so doing, the verbal and visual performances of desire present what Adena Rosmarin calls 'the power of genre' as a put-on, because here the genre's power is put on and displayed through its clichés.[42]

Strand's limited ethnography provides a partial view of the culture of heterosexual practices which are both oppressive and pleasurable to women. Her picture of white, middle-class women's culture owes much to the boy-crazy girls' gossip sessions I remember from junior high school slumber parties in which secrets, fantasies, and homoerotic desires merged with popular cultural renderings of woman's surrender. However, this fantasy depends on and fuels the racism and class division that produces the fantasy of women's culture in the first place (for instance, the only black woman on screen is seen dancing nude to Bechet – jazz and the black woman's body being icons for white dreams of sexual escape). In short, the film becomes retrograde in its obsessive explorations of white, middle-class heterosexuality. Thus, to a certain extent, *Soft Fiction* participates in the anti-porn feminist hysteria that elides women's victimization by male sexuality with genocidal practices of fascism as it moves from the private fantasy experienced outside political contexts to the intrusion of military force into the domestic space.[43] The straightforward presentation of women's voices, coupled with the ecstatic images of female sensuality, appear to be 'unsophisticated' representations of desire.[44] These distortions reveal the fault lines of, because they stem from, Strand's investment in a universalized vision of women's culture.

Moreover, Strand is caught in a serious dilemma when she embraces (albeit critically) ethnographic cinema. On the one hand, ethnography as a historical practice in which white people look at and (through cinema) display people of color maintains imperialist relations of domination. On the other hand, by turning the lens on her own culture – that of white, middle-class film artists – Strand's ethnography of women would seem to rectify the colonial relationship of ethnographer to informant; the women who speak tell their own stories to their friend in her home, actually deciding how they want to be framed as much as what they want to say – they perform themselves. Yet by removing her lens to her own backyard, is *Soft Fiction* merely narcissism masquerading as ethnography? In either case, as sympathetic, yet still colonizing, spectator of the other, or as empathetic exhibitor of the self, Strand's films, by invoking ethnography, despite problematizing subject and object, inevitably graph their own tensions.

Nevertheless, her films depend on the performances of their informants' memories appearing simultaneously authentic and constructed. As restagings, the artifice involved in the deliberate diction and the claustrophobic framing of *Soft Fiction* constructs speaking subjects who eventually call into question the possibility of a 'culture' of women about whom one could make an ethnography. The stories indicate the ways in which culture is performative – a function of competing collective strategies of storytelling and acting we carry out in all their contradictory forms every day.

I am not seeking to rehabilitate *Soft Fiction* by inserting it into an existing canon of films. I would hope that my discussion of the film has pointed up some of the polarized positions within feminisms – anti-porn/pro-sex, cultural/psychoanalytical – that verge in their drive toward purity and truth on the aestheticization of politics which Walter Benjamin called fascism. I believe we need to rethink the categories governing our political and cultural theorizing in order to begin the revolutionary process of (re)politicizing art. Feminism in the United States has relied on cultural performances – from the Miss America pageant demonstration through the Women's Pentagon Action to the Guerilla Girls' recent billboards and the Lesbian Avengers' sidewalk fire-eating – to present its politics.[45] Theory also might best be considered as a performance – a collective playing out of cultural codes in public spaces which are socially and historically constructed and reconstructed in response to political challenges. Strand's film and the many others that step out of bounds demand that we constantly inspect the ways, in the name of political correctness or theoretical sophistication, we police the borders of feminism.

8

National Bodies: Gender, Sexuality, and

Terror in Feminist Counter-documentaries

Tour Guide

At one point in experimental playwright Richard Foreman's 1970s epic phantasmagoria, *Rhoda in Potatoland*, someone declares that only a tourist ever really knows a city. After all, who else would wander empty boulevards at three in the morning after the streetcars stop running? Except for the homeless who have no choice, no resident of any of the world's cities would take the liberties afforded those whose daily life is lived elsewhere. Simone de Beauvoir and Jean-Paul Sartre made it a habit to stay up all night at least once in any new city they visited, roaming through vacant quarters full of the rhythmic breathing of sleep, she tells us in her memoir of their early years together. The pose of outsider highlights cultural differences, brings them to the fore, as wealthy, leisured visitors travel from one country to another in search of new experiences. But it also can ease differences; in the global migrations and circulations of bodies and capital that mark the final decades of this century of world wars, evil empires, and transnational economies, dislocation and alienation are increasingly normal experiences for anyone.

Three films by women directors made between the late 1970s and late 1980s – *Journeys from Berlin/1971*, *Far From Poland*, and *Surname Viet, Given Name Nam* – focus this chapter's discussion of gender, exile, and the national unconscious. In these counter-documentaries, a place away from home and the possibilities and terrors dislocation/relocation offer women are seen as part of a longer, ambivalent history of figuring national identities through gender. Chapter 5 looked at reportage by women who traveled to North and South Vietnam as a form of travel writing, and the preceding two chapters examined the incursion of ethnography into the American home and family; these three films might be considered postmodern antidotes to the travel films and slide-shows tourists bring home from their trips abroad.

A turn away from ethnographies of others toward local explorations of home and its secrets marked Chick Strand's rupture of the ethnographic form, one aspect of women's subversion of a conventional genre – the anthropological film. Another route some women have taken is to unravel the travelog. Whether the women travel to war zones to report on their findings, as the critics of the Vietnam War did, or merely set up their cameras in their living room, as did Jill Godmilow, these documents of other places, other lives, participate in, yet break down, the traditional voyeurism that accompanies travelogs. These tourists sense their complicity in a network of terror which implicates them as privileged artists in coercive state violence; yet, as women and outsiders, their observations refocus the visual spectacle of nationalism and its violences with an intimacy born of exile. As outsiders set apart, they work to hear what is barely whispered. In so doing, they establish a visual poetics of gender and nation which foregrounds the embodied voice comprising each formation.[1]

Neither *Surname Viet, Given Name Nam* nor *Journeys from Berlin/1971* is strictly speaking a documentary; each uses codes derived from documentary to frame a highly personal rendering of melodrama as a response to a major political crisis – terrorism and war. *Far From Poland* is not a straight documentary either. Godmilow tracks her frustrations at not being able to make her documentary through re-enactment, restaging, and domestic melodrama. For each film-maker, questions of gender, national identity, violence, and community are central to the figuring of bodies on screen and through language. In effect the slippage of genres mirrors the convergence within feminist theorizing of the public/private split. Feminist anthropologists such as Sherry Ortner, historians such as Denise Riley and Lynn Hunt, political theorists such as Nancy Hartsock, and literary theorists such as Rita Felski have demonstrated the varied ways in which the domestic sphere is a construction of the state, even as political culture depends on private institutions.[2] Felski argues that feminism itself creates the conditions for a new reckoning of the processes of politics through what she calls 'the feminist counter-public sphere,' in which the slogan 'the personal is political' refigures the divisions governing proper and improper politics.

With the undoing of genres and the gendered conventions differentiating domesticity from politics each frames, the authority of the film-maker is also destabilized, and along with it, the legitimacy of her national identity. The nation here becomes more than an imaginary projection of the state; it functions also to mark off any collective entity in which the subject forms a self-knowledge – gender, sexuality, political affiliation – as much as regional location. Each film explores the meaning of crossing borders – national boundaries separating peoples by language and history. Like the tourist who senses cultural flows in the currents of the air – lacking intimate access to the argot of the locale – these film-makers rely on their sensations to chart dangers and opportunities. Dorothy knew something was up when she and her house landed in Oz: 'Toto, I have a feeling we're not in Kansas anymore.' Like Alice, who alternately shrinks and expands after falling down the rabbit hole, the body of the tourist is steeped in violence; its entry into a foreign place a secondary result of imperialism. These films, like the tourist safely ensconced in a luxury hotel suite, meditate on terror from a distance; yet each foregrounds the bodily harm and psychic damage of state-sanctioned violence. The body is plastic, adapting to new situations, even as it stubbornly retains its origins and can never quite fit in. The making of these films disturbed each film-maker; so, too, the experiences of viewing them leave their viewers' bodies riddled with tensions.

Lately, questions about the relationship between feminism and nationalism are being raised everywhere.[3] Women's groups are organizing in Bosnia, in the West Bank, in South Africa, in India to confront the dual failures of nationalist and feminist politics as they have thus far been practiced.[4] American feminism has been remarkably ethnocentric, continuing the long-standing leftist tendency to view the United States as 'exceptional'; yet the films I discuss in this chapter indicate that American feminist film-makers have been working to understand their positions in global political culture. Yvonne Rainer's film parallels her years in Germany during the 1970s, when left-wing urban guerrillas were locked in a struggle with the growing state police apparatus. Jill Godmilow's film addresses the romance American leftists have with other people's political uprisings – specifically the striking shipbuilders in Gdansk organizing Solidarity – in the face of decreasing efficacy at home. Trinh's film unravels the after-effects of America's war on Vietnamese women. These films, like Chick Strand's, circulate among the genres of avant-garde, documentary, narrative, and personal film-making. They rely on the use of autobiography and biographical narratives to tell their stories and unpack the history surrounding them; yet each questions the authentications of the tale and the teller. However, it is through interrogating national identities and cultures that these films find a space for women's stories. In this they echo Strand's earliest film, *Mosori Monika*, by looking at the intersecting and conflicting visions women have of their positions within a history of violence in national/religious/political cultures.

These films in one sense continue the prevailing solipsism of American feminism, but at the same time they push it outward to consider other locations, bodies, stories, and histories. They stretch feminist autobiography into feminist autocritique by stepping beyond the borders of the United States. Appropriations and double appropriations may actually be substitutes for politics, in the usual sense of resistance against, but these films prefigure a productive politics of subversion.[5]

Is The National Body Female?
The Woman Question/The National Question

In Lynn Hunt's provocative analysis of the symbolic discourses enabling and encoding *The Family Romance of the French Revolution*, the image of the polluting woman is coupled to that of the Republican mother. Linda Kerber has noted that the figure of Republican motherhood in the early American colonies also served to temper the potential disruptions of the family offered by the newly enacted social and sexual contracts forged through bourgeois revolutions. The Republican mother forestalled the power of women by reconfining their role to that of mother. Hunt suggests that this is not merely instrumentalist but indicates the ways in which the social psyche of a culture figures itself through family melodramas. Following Freud's highly symbolic account of civilization in *Totem and Taboo*, she suggests it is no accident that domestic melodrama emerges in revolutionary France. This form of exaggerated theater represented a simultaneous gender and generational struggle which mapped conflicts about the new social/sexual arrangements made possible by the Republic. Doris Sommers has also pointed to the interconnections between romance and nation-building, suggesting that in Latin America cross-cultural intermarriages in fictional form served to bridge conflicts over land, identity, and power in the emerging states.[6] If the nation is so deeply implicated in the gender figurings of romance and melodrama, then films attempting to describe national identities and women's positions within them seem especially precarious projects. Film is the inheritor and mass disseminator of these romances and melodramas of national culture. These films I consider here decompose the gender/nation nexus to find a space for a national identity of woman. The place names in the titles of the three films hint at location as an identity.[7]

Perhaps national locations and historic acts need a fictional form to be documented effectively. Thomas Waugh details how much Joris Ivens's 1930s documentary film *The Spanish Earth* made in the midst of

179

the Civil War depended on the lyrical script written by Archibald MacLeish, John Dos Passos, and Ernest Hemingway and the narrative editing Helen Van Dongen learned while apprenticing in Hollywood.[8] Ivens's decision to 'personalize' the war through the 'story' of one village and one family was part of the discussions arising during the Popular Front about 'the people' and their interests. I have already argued that the conditions that helped forge a national public culture in the United States and elsewhere were a direct result of the collusion of popular and populist cultures, such that *The Spanish Earth* has much in common with *The River*, despite the differing political affiliations and purposes of their directors. Its aesthetic achievement was judged as much by the eighteen ambulances bought with the proceeds of its US screenings as by its cinematic beauty. The use-value of cultural objects can be found in their material effects, which extend far beyond their box office receipts or their aesthetic appeal. As ideological and affective forms, their use-value can be felt, for example, in a consolidation of longings into a collective identity.[9]

The women's 'documentaries' I am discussing in this chapter form but a small part of the film work by women undertaken during the remarkable decade of the 1980s. The bulk of women's film work, as I have already noted, can be found in the many historical documentaries, emerging avant-garde films, as well as new women's narrative cinema coming out of independent productions in the United States and abroad and, perhaps most significantly (for these films at least), in the explosion of feminist theories of performance, spectatorship, representation, and apparatus accompanying the rise of women's studies and film studies disciplines. These three films typify the questioning of realism among feminist semioticians. Each enacts the subjects of its political and personal commitments and thus scrutinizes its own complicity with desire for others through fictionalized treatments of history. In essence, all function as homologies of the theoretical and political conditions prevailing during the grim years of Reaganism.

Let me turn briefly to a series of scenes from a film by someone who is neither an American nor a woman which presents many of the issues crucial to understanding the romance of nation and women's place within it. I must have seen Gillo Pontecorvo's *Battle of Algiers* a dozen times during my first year at Berkeley in the late 1960s. Hardly a night passed when some political group was not showing it as a fundraiser or as an inspiration for the demonstrations the following day. We came back over and over to hear the crowds of veiled women ululating in the streets, their high-pitched, unearthly sound disrupting the flow of traffic in downtown Algiers; we came to watch one of the young women transform herself from a veiled Muslim into a mini-skirted beach bunny to cross the French army checkpoints ringing the Casbah into the French quarter and plant the bombs that would terrorize the Europeans dancing and drinking each night, seemingly oblivious to the war surrounding them. These were images of women's subversiveness, in each case using tools we knew had kept them oppressed – the veil, the mini – in new and creative ways. Gesturing without words – ululating *en masse* or singly batting long eyelashes at the guards – these audacious women showed us that our very exclusion from history and politics would become a handy weapon in the coming struggle. These were weapons already at our disposal and the lesson of the Algerian War reminded us not to surrender them. The armed women in Algiers whose long caftans shrouded artillery and ammunition – even the nasty French colonials could not imagine patting down these black-clad, kohl-eyed specters – enabled the urban guerrilla warfare that eventually sent the French home in defeat. But no sooner had national liberation been proclaimed than these same women were expected to retreat within the walls of their Casbah homes.

The scenes were so powerful that despite not having seen the film in twenty-five years, I can both hear and see these women as if I had watched them yesterday. The double revolution that feminist anti-imperialists saw ourselves fighting was played out for us in the film. When we gathered in women's affinity groups and marched as women, we mimicked those Algerian women as best we could, ululating in solidarity with the women of North Vietnam and Oakland. This was a romance of Third World imagination we American women sought to make our own; an unthinking cultural appropriation. My foray into nostalgia tells you more about me than about the film; but it is meant to shed some background light on the thinking that went into this chapter. What seems crucial here, at least for me and my memory, are the ways in which the codes of documentary were enlisted for such dramatic, even melodramatic, ends; or perhaps the ways in which conventions of melodrama – the disguises, the crowds, the lone woman unprotected – became codes for representing revolutionary acts. The trappings of documentary adorning them provided enough mask of truth to make one think this had really happened and the camera had really been there to see it: this woman really had cut her hair and permed it and bleached her eyebrows to pass from one quarter to another, from one nationality to another, on a deadly mission. Of course, she was an actress, but the force of left-wing documentary then exploding in the United States by the Newsreel Collectives in New York and San Francisco was such that her performance seemed authentic, not staged. History was unfolding before our eyes; one could believe because the street locations, the army uniforms, the NLF radio pronouncements were neither sets, nor costumes, nor sound-tracks: they were real. In fact, the entire film is a fictionalized account of the war, a romance of national identity no less compromised than John Ford's vision of the American West in *Stagecoach*.

Like the films I discuss in this chapter, *The Battle of Algiers* masks its genre. Coded as a documentary – black-and-white footage, hand-held camerawork, newsreel-like sequences and titles – *The Battle of Algiers* is a fictional film made up of re-enactments to look the part of a documentary. Its pointed intervention into both political history and documentary aesthetics and its complex depiction of the status of women within the Algerian NLF were early indications that political film-making could move in different directions from those offered by documentary. Can films that use actors and foreground performance be considered documentaries in the post-direct cinema era? How far can the boundaries of documentary be pushed? Is Grierson's famous definition – 'the creative interpretation of actuality' – open to infinite expansion? Who is the subject of agency being mobilized by the documentary in films with jarringly avant-gardist poetics? What shape does the audience for these films take? How do the films find their audiences? To whom, about whom, and for whom do they speak? Bill Nichols has argued that 'voice' is a key effect of documentary rhe-toric.[10] But what is being said is at least as important as who is saying it.

Berlin

During the early years of the second wave of feminism, it was not uncommon to think of patriarchy as a transhistorical, cross-cultural phenomenon linking all women across time and borders into what Susan Sontag, picking up on the rhetoric of feminist and anti-imperial-ist politics, called 'The Fourth World of Women.'[11] Whether residing in the First, Second, or Third Worlds, women stood united outside the boundaries of geopolitical history by virtue of our biology and its effects. But if ideally women comprise another world all our own, in reality women's identities are fractured by the racial, class, regional, ethnic, and religious affiliations animating political subjectivities.

After the flurry of woman-oriented documentaries from the late 1960s through to the end of the 1970s many directors, for reasons of politics, finance, history, found themselves crossing borders to reframe questions about film-making and women's subjectivity through interrogations of national identity as gendered political practice. Living in Berlin on a DAAD (German Academic Exchange) fellowship during the turbulent era of the Baader–Meinhof Gang (known later as the Red Army Faction), and the subsequent institution of state terrorism in response, Yvonne Rainer found herself rethinking her own life as the daughter of anarchist parents alongside her position as an American artist/dissident abroad. *Journeys from Berlin/ 1971* takes the chaos of West Germany as a point of departure for a series of 'journeys,' inquiring into an adolescent girl's past (through her journal entries), a middle-aged woman's attempted suicide (during her sessions in psychoanalysis), and the history of political violence (through a discussion between a woman and man about art and politics). These journeys are meditations about the place and efficacy of art and sexuality in historical memory. They point out specifically gendered meanings in the history of political activism and sexual desire for women. The memoirs of the 'Russian Amazons' whose anarchist *attentats* helped bring down the Czars, the letters of Ulrike Meinhof and other incarcerated women, the diary entries of a young girl coming of age amidst political activists in a complacent era of American history – all exceed the conventional narratives about women and political action. Rainer's film explores, untangles, and refits the words of women's political and sexual desires. Strictly speaking, this film is not a documentary. Far from the discourses of truth, objectivity, and authenticity, it echoes radical documentaries' expanded notions of American politics and cinema. These differences are national as much as gendered and sexual, and it is through looking at the extreme case – Rainer's *Berlin* – that I hope to unravel some dilemmas posed by documentary portrayals of other places.

Journeys from Berlin/1971 (1979) comments on and enacts many of the same formal and thematic elements as Chick Strand's film. In this personal meditation on political violence, however, Rainer enters a more explicitly political terrain than the fantasy zone of *Soft Fiction*. But as a 'formalist citation of political issues,' she too depends on the cinematic as performance.[12] Like *Soft Fiction, Journeys* presents a series of discontinuous narratives and images; yet Rainer's aesthetic choices disconnect sound from sight. Rainer has explained that 'the soundtrack is *extremely* important in this film. It's very detailed. The intention was to create an environment that you could visualize from the sounds alone . . . the images are almost incidental.'[13] David James argues that Rainer's modernist impulses stem from her connections to structural film-making's manipulations of the medium and to art cinema elaborations of narrative. As a 'structuralist meta-text her film can propose nothing about sexuality,' according to James; because one sees through the content to the medium, or vice versa, nothing can be said about either. All is registered as a mediation, as a performance, rather than as a truth or a position or an instrumentality. But perhaps this is the point.

Four discourses dominate the verbal portion of the film: a middle-aged white woman (played by avant-garde film critic Annette Michelson) speaks to her psychoanalyst about her suicide attempt. A man and woman (played by *Village Voice* film critic and film-maker Amy Taubin and conceptual/performance artist Vito Acconci) discuss the history of political violence, particularly citing and reading from the writings of the Russian anarchists of the 1870s Vera Figner, Vera Zasulich, and Angelica Balabanoff, twentieth-century American immigrant anarchists Emma Goldman and Alexander Berkman, and Ulrike Meinhof (leader of the Red Army Faction in Germany), as they cook, eat, and wash up after dinner together. (These first two discourses are interrupted periodically by a 'breather' who invokes names from political and movie history.) A young girl reads from her diaries written during the early 1950s; and rolling titles document the growth of the repressive post-war German state police apparatus.

The visuals primarily consist of two aerial tracking shots – one of Stonehenge and the other of the Berlin Wall – a horizontal pan of a mantelpiece filled with the objects mentioned in the soundtrack, including photographs of Goldman, Figner, Meinhof, Rosalind Russell, a revolver, steaming spaghetti, a marble column capital, a boat, etc.;[14] views outside the windows of moving cars and trains from three different apartments in New York, London, and Berlin; a man and a woman walking in front of an ornate Gothic church; and a long shot into an apartment where a woman is giving a recorder lesson to another woman (Figures 19–20). Only in the case of the psychoanalysis scene is the soundtrack lip-synched, and even here jumps and silences interrupt the speech. None of the other speakers appears on screen. Voice is more significant than the embodied speaker or cinematic image. Rainer has commented that within the first twenty minutes of the film virtually every visual image has already been seen; the rest are repetitions which take on new meanings after the stories and conversations are heard.[15]

Like Strand, Rainer crosses a number of generic boundaries, those demarking documentary (especially as it has come to be associated with leftist politics), narrative (especially as it is deployed in the domestic melodrama of the woman's film), and the avant-garde (especially in its exposure of the personal and the disclosure of subcultural insider 'jokes'). Speaking of *Film About a Woman Who . . .* (1974), Rainer might

also have been describing *Journeys* when she notes that the constructions of various film languages were at work through 'the *acting* of
the narrative film, the *inter-titles* of the silent movie, the *subtitles* and
dubbing of the foreign language film, the *voice-over* of the documentary
and the flash back, and the *face-front-to-camera delivery* of Godard.'[16] It
helps to know Rainer's personal history as a choreographer and
performer and daughter of anarchists, her past films and dances, as
well as her place within feminist theory to understand the 'cultural
fetishes' of the film.[17]

This film is the one least favored by feminist film critics, perhaps
because it moves outside the purely melodramatic and psychoanalytical. At the same time, it comes under fire from leftist film critics as
'pseudo-politics' because it refuses to intervene into cinematic or social
organizations of power. In *Journeys*, the discourse and performance of
public history are enacted and encoded by the woman question to
produce, in the quoted words of Ulrike Meinhof, 'psychiatrification, as
a device of psychological warfare [which] aims to persuade the destroyed fighter of the pointlessness of revolutionary politics. . . .'
Political economy further enters into the domestic space of the avant-
garde artist's loft as Taubin and Acconci debate the relative merits of
Meinhof's (and the New Left's) adventurism and the anarchists' *attentats*, while acknowledging their own political ineffectualness. Moreover, when Michelson declares 'My cunt is *not* a castrated cock. If
anything, it's a heartless *asshole!*' Rainer seems to be criticizing the
Lacanian-influenced feminist criticism that has been responsible for
cultivating an audience, even producing the discourses, for her films.
The private musings of a young girl were written by someone who
claims: 'When I was fifteen, Emma Goldman's autobiography was one
of the great books in my life.'[18] Where's the personal, where's the
political?

Rainer's films display the cinematic textualization of feminist psychoanalytic and semiotic film theory of the late 1970s and as such have
entered into the arena of critical cinema and its study. As films of,
about, and by performers, they are rooted in an aesthetics of modernist allegory which privileges the artist's alienation from the forms of
her culture. As such, her films seem embedded in an individualist
response to social and cultural violence. But the patent falseness of the
acting, the multiple levels of mediation as speech and reading merge
into one another, and the ridiculous comings and goings of the
performers behind the (psychoanalytic) scenes, question these
assumptions. The cultural history of anarchism as a movement and an
ideology, as well as a catalyst for political demonology and hysteria,
grounds what otherwise appears as introspection. Despite Michelson,
the patient, achieving some understanding of her suicide attempt and

appearing 'cured' by all her inane talk, and Taubin, the artist, resolving 'to stop trying to become a better person . . . so I might attend to what has to be done now,' and the young girl vowing 'to learn to love myself, then I will love humanity' – despite all this, one hardly feels comforted by this chorus of self-proclaimed actualization and insight. The state retains its power. Rainer describes the effect as follows:

> It is only when the patient stops believing in the absoluteness of her powerlessness in relation to others – men and women – that she can confront her suicide attempt . . . . The patient takes responsibility for her own destructiveness – and stops struggling with the shrink. She assumes responsibility for her own life. This is truly the sphere of psychoanalysis – and the personal . . . . Although the differences between personal autonomy in a prison and in the streets of the democracy are substantive, an analogy can be made. The patient's situation in *Journeys from Berlin/1971* can be seen as analogous to Meinhof's. The former, in her limited sphere, has taken her first faltering steps out of the imaginary dimension of her powerlessness. Meinhof, on the other hand, has died a victim, never having figured out where her powerlessness ended or real power began. Both ended at the hands of the police, or 'state apparatus.' . . . The personal and the political are not synonymous. They overlap and intertwine. And one must struggle constantly to assess one's power, or lack of it, in every sphere of one's life.[19]

But Rainer does not leave the film there. Instead, she ends on the sober note of Taubin reading Meinhof's letter to Hanna Crabbe about the power of the state to 'psychiatricize' political prisoners. Since the late nineteenth century, popular images of the crazed anarchist woman have served to elide dangerous politics and sexuality in a single body. The anarchist woman comes to stand for the radical upheaval of both domestic and public affairs through the double threat of 'free love' and 'dynamite.' With neither state nor family to rein in excessive female bodies, anarchism unhinges authority. While anarchism is often dismissed by both the Right and Left, the figure of the anarchist woman is the nodal point of extreme hysteria.[20] Meinhof's disturbing letter – full of powerful insights about the state's use of psychiatry, yet strangely lacking in insight about herself – is intercut with Rainer's own voice and image in a videotaped letter to her mother recounting the experience of watching *Morgen Beginnt das Leben* (Werner Hochbaum, 1933). She sentimentally describes the audience's gasps of recognition at a city that no longer exists. Germany's past stubbornly remains despite denials. The final title quotes H. Herold, head of the German Federal Criminal Investigation Bureau, and states: 'The aim of all enemies of the State is the deliberate creation of an opposing power over and against this State, or the denial of *the State's monopoly of force.*'

All these quotations and meditations and performances, including the deadpan acting of Michelson, dislocate and destabilize the film as a source either of truth or entertainment about both the political and the personal. The *Lives of Performers* are always also lies of performers. When the credits roll, ending with a list of funders

> The British Film Institute
> Deutscher Akademischer Austauschdienst
> New York State Council on the Arts
> Center for Advanced Visual Studies, MIT
> Christopher di Menil
> Beard's Fund, Inc.
> The Rockefeller Foundation

we are reminded that personal expression is always at the convenience of the state and corporate capital. The list of financiers ironically reminds us of the contradictions of late capitalist nations, at once putting the squeeze on dissidents and marginal communities and opening spaces for challenges to their hegemony by dissidents and marginal communities. How do we proceed? To whom do we speak?

Rainer talks about the responsibilities privileged women – middle-class, white citizens of democratic nations – have to acknowledge their own power and complicity in the systems of desire and repression operating around and within us. Furthermore, Rainer reminds us of the powers of the bourgeois state to recuperate transgressive art. Perhaps no language can accommodate the young Yvonne's growing sexual desire and alienation from her parents because the usual paths of adolescent rebellion are closed off when her parents encourage her nonconformity. Similarly, the language of psychoanalysis, which is designed to express, in fact produce, sexual desire as discourse, is limited by its failure to account for the historical specificity of any one woman's experience, much less to acknowledge the political meanings of cultural identity and social involvements. The German police deemed female terrorists crazy; even going so far as to claim that Meinhof's activities resulted from surgery to remove a brain tumor she underwent shortly before springing Andreas Baader from prison.[21] Languages this bereft are dead languages, but they are all we have, suggests Rainer.

Rainer's aesthetic alienation as the bourgeois artist replicates the position of many feminist film critics – myself among them – who find ourselves materially and discursively insulated from the daily grind of women's lives in most of the world. Like her film critic actors who perform themselves performing others, we sometimes read the words and images all around us with an equally eerie detachment from their sources and effects. This film, like the others I discuss in this chapter, reflects, if it does not directly participate in, the crisis of the Left during the Reagan–Thatcher era.[22] Dissatisfied with traditional socialist politics, because of cogent critiques by feminists, gays and lesbians, and people of color about oppressive formations that are not strictly economic – political film-makers intensely scrutinize documentary forms associated with past politics. The journeys that Rainer's characters take in and out of history, politics, popular culture, landscape, and sexuality are those of American avant-garde cinema and feminist theory during the 1970s. They restage the interruptions of political practice by psychoanalytical theory and vice versa, as spectacles of women's frustrated desire, intellectual curiosity, and cultural exclusion from dominant cinematic practice. The comical, self-parodic style reminds us to question our roles as agents of culture.

Poland

The title of Jill Godmilow's 1984 film pays homage to the great French, collectively made documentary protest against the war, *Far From Vietnam*. Like Jean-Luc Godard, whose sequence tracks his inability to obtain a travel visa to North Vietnam, Godmilow's effort to go to Poland to film the emergence of Solidarity is frustrated. Her application for a visa is denied, so her film must be made from afar. The gap between documentary desires and political activities becomes the substance of Godmilow's extended meditation on the complex ways in which Solidarity had 'broken through a wall of fear,' demonstrating that you 'create your own social reality' when 'you act'; this is the central meaning of all revolutionary political projects. Like Rainer's cinematic anatomy of political violence, Godmilow's film tracks its political questions through an ironic melodrama involving herself and her male lover Mark, a younger video artist whose 'only connection to Marx is of the Groucho, Harpo, Chico and Zeppo kind.' Mark acts as her aesthetic conscience. Warning her against the 'terror of the mediocre,' he mocks her attempt to tell the Poles' story by suggesting that she is 'using them' as a balm to her guilty liberal conscience. Her film is yet another gallant attempt to rescue what for him is a failed politics romancing other people's collective action.

The affair between Jill and Mark – between documentary film-maker and video performance artist – also maps the distance between American and Polish interpretations of what Solidarity means. The scenes between Jill and Mark – directed by Ruth Maleczech, who plays the Gdansk shipyard crane operator and strike leader Anna Walenty-nowicz in the film – are awkward and stagey. Ending either in irreconcilable conflict and tension, or in the more conventional conciliatory kiss, these scenes ironically keep the film honest. Their very constructedness and falsity – their reliance on generic, rather than spontaneous codes – shows just how coded the spontaneous is as well. American attitudes appear polarized through the different interpretations offered by Ronald Reagan and Michael Harrington, each of whom appears on Godmilow's video monitor describing what Solidarity is – an anti-communist and a socialist movement, respectively. Poles both in America and in Poland believe variously as well, as do those in Solidarity and those in the Polish government or Communist Party who experience the 1980 movement differently depending on class, generation, region, etc. Of necessity, the film highlights its lacks – the film's gaps, its failures – which presage Solidarity's difficulties and foreground the impossibility of covering everything – whether by political organization, documentary film-making, or heterosexual romance.

Far from Poland begins with the film-maker standing before a screen describing how she had been in Poland when the strike at the Gdansk shipyard began. She had flown back to New York, raised money and a film crew, bought airline tickets, but was denied a visa. 'I was determined to tell the real story,' she says, after reading from notes made during her 1980 stay in Poland. The notes contain the conventional enthusiasms for revolutionary élan: 'overnight ten million people were reinventing language, politics, a nation. . . .' Godmilow's enthusiasm is immediately undercut by the appearance of a young riveter who removes his 1940s-style helmet and begins, 'Hi, I'd like to tell you a story . . . a story of a woman steeped in the documentary tradition of the Left' who sets out to make a film on the 'miracle' of Polish social rebirth.

During the 1960s and 1970s, many radicals were looking back at the history of American left-wing and especially labor movements searching for radical precedents; at the same time, film-makers, disillusioned with the limitations of *cinéma vérité*, sought alternatives to its lack of context and ahistorical fetishizing of the present and spontaneous. For instance, Julia Reichert, Miles Mogulescu, and Jim Klein's 1977 film *Union Maids* used archival footage and contemporary interviews of three black and white, working-class women from the Chicago area to detail their experiences organizing during the 1930s. Each of the union maids – Sylvia Woods, Kate Hyndman, and Stella Nowicki – had been CIO organizers whose accounts of their experiences were collected in Staughton and Alice Lynd's oral history, *Rank and File*. The shifts between black-and-white grainy images of mass demonstrations and the composed discussions with the older women gives a sense of the authenticity and authority of experience. Yet these films often cloaked the truth of history by repressing certain key information: the women interviewed had been active CPUSA members. Instead, their involvement in the strikes appears personally motivated; they are heroic individuals rising to the occasion. Moreover, as historian Linda Gordon pointed out, the films paint a rosy picture of racial and gender relations within CIO unions.[23] We don't come to understand that heroism is often a result of solidarity – of knowing that a movement is behind one so that actions are not individualistic and spontaneous, but orchestrated and collective. Films like this worked to inspire their audiences using a formula typical of Hollywood narratives, what Noel King called 'the historicist-humanistic.'[24]

Filmed in the midst of struggle, *Harlan County USA*, Barbara Kopple's 1976 magisterial vision of striking coal miners, salvages *cinéma vérité* to convey the emotion of solidarity among Kentucky coal miners powerful enough to counter a corrupt international leadership – leading to United Mine Workers President Tony Boyle's downfall and eventual imprisonment for ordering the murder of reform candidate Jock Yablonski and his family – and the coal mining companies, each subsidiaries of major oil companies, that have kept the region in near-feudal conditions for over a century. The film showcases people with long memories stretching back to the 1930s, the era of Bloody Harlan, when the struggle to organize the United Mine Workers carried on by John L. Lewis ushered in one of the most violent episodes in the history of American labor. Kopple hauled her equipment, crew, and credit cards from New York to Kentucky and moved in with miners' families; she got up every morning for the 'sunrise revival' to discourage scabs from entering the mines (we see her and crew members walking the line) and followed the ten-month strike to its end – settled only after Lawrence Jones, a young miner, was shot and killed by company thugs. However, the film departs from *cinéma vérité* by providing background and context with archival footage from the 1920s and 1930s, testimonies from elderly miners, and interviews with doctors at the black lung center in West Virginia, with UMWA organizers, with miners and their wives. In addition, titles fill in information about the local, the international, and the coal industry. Finally, the soul-wrenching voice of Hazel Dickens haunts the film, her ballads continue the tradition of musical documentary begun in the 1930s by Florence Reece (who sings 'Which Side Are You On?' in the movie) to remember former strikes, black lung, hunger, and poverty.[25] All this works to secure and structure the nobility of the striker as well as the heroic pose of the film-maker, who is threatened at gun point and beaten along with the strikers. Kopple's film won an Academy Award as well as praise among progressives, but it was denounced by radical film-makers and theorists as ideologically suspect because hopelessly illusionistic, relying on the semantics of realist cinema to draw an emotional catharsis from its audience.[26] In Solidarity, it appeared, Godmilow had found another Harlan County.

While the riveter continues to mock Jill's attempts to recreate the enthusiasm over Solidarity that had greeted Kopple's vision of Harlan County, Godmilow's voice-over tells us that this is Mark, who has left this mocking tape in her deck. She smokes as she watches him on TV; the camera tracks away to reveal him standing in the kitchen doorway watching her watching the tape of him. They argue over the meaning of Solidarity for art and politics, the place of humor and propaganda in the work of political artists – a battle against intellectual mediocrity. Jill appears to win this round. But her position is immediately undercut in the next scene. Here we watch as two hands carefully pack a suitcase with boxes of Carolina rice, Maxwell House instant coffee, and other brand-name foodstuffs. Jill's voice recounts a conversation with a Polish friend who counsels against going to make the film. It will be used, she argues, as propaganda for or against Solidarity by the Americans or the Poles, and the result will be further to endanger people whose lives are already in turmoil. Jill insists she is making 'art, not propaganda,' but the voice of her friend warns ominously: 'Jill, artists can rationalize anything. Take the film money and buy food with it; this is the only moral thing to do.' The scene ends as the hands place the last of the groceries – a tin of Polish ham – into the case and close it. With all these warnings, caveats, and interruptions, with all the prevarications, arguments, and distanciations, it becomes anticlimactic to learn that when Godmilow's visa is denied, she determines to go ahead with the film, cobbling it together from American news reports (here is Lech Walesa riding the waves of shoulders through jubilant crowds of strikers) re-enactments, and footage obtained from Solidarity's film agency. Because Godmilow cannot take us to Poland, the 'film refuses to assume the role of information dispenser or armchair tour guide.'[27]

The rest of the 'first act' consists of intercut scenes of Ruth Maleczech and Elspieta Komorowska re-enacting a long interview by Polish journalist Hanna Kral of Anna Walentynowicz about how her early experiences led her to become a leader of Solidarity. This interview takes place across a table in an empty loft decorated with hand-painted Solidarity banners. Periodically, a man's voice supplies background details about Anna, at one point reminding us that this interview is a re-enactment of an interview that took place secretly in January 1981. His revelation that this scene is fake becomes important later, as the stability and authenticity of the film unravels. Anna's interview is staged much as Annette Michelson's analysis in Rainer's *Journeys*: a woman talks of her life to another whom we only glimpse from behind. Anna's story begins when she is orphaned by the war and wanders the countryside finding work as a farm laborer. Eventually, she runs away from what is essentially servitude to the shipyards, where she enrolls in a training course to become a welder. Central to Anna's life story, and to Godmilow's story of Solidarity, is Anna's increasing defiance of the bureaucracy governing the working lives of the Gdansk shipbuilders leading to her efforts to take control of her work time and her union (and by extension Godmilow's tribulations of making documentary films).[28] Interviewed, translated, restaged, acted, and interpolated by voice-over, Anna Walentynowicz barely exists in the flesh: we catch her in a black-and-white television news flash after her triumphant reinstatement at the shipyards. Yet so moving is the story and its delivery that at the end of the interview, Elspieta Komorowska remarks, 'Ruth, you're crying.' Embodying the strike through Anna rather than through Lech, the national leader of Solidarity, recasts the movement significantly. Godmilow, like Kopple, Rainer, and Trinh, is interested in displaying how revolution develops in and through a woman's life, how her story produces and reframes history: the woman, a question that interrupts its narrative.

This extended disclosure is intercut with the saga of Jill's attempt to acquire footage of Solidarity's meetings, actions, and factory organizations. She enlists the aid of a friend whose cousin is head of the Solidarity film agency. As they await the telephone connection to Warsaw, Irene Gross, her husband, Jill, and two friends discuss Solidarity: What can one make of a mass movement of ten million, a movement thankfully without ideology, remarks Irene at one point, relishing in the disputatiousness of democratic politics? Her husband describes how Poland's 'structures that generated mediocrity' finally tumbled at the hands of the disenfranchised, talented people banding together in Solidarity. We watch these conversations, occasionally interrupted by calls to and from the operator, on a monitor in Jill's studio. Again, despite the spontaneous quality of the conversation, though set questions are asked periodically, the effect is of premeditation, hesitancy, and distancing: a film of a tape playing seen first on one then on another monitor fails to come to a conclusion, literally resisting stability by shifting from one screen to another. Later, these monitors rebroadcast television news tapes: Barbara Garson describes why she is attending a pro-Solidarity rally in New York: 'It's their faces,' she enthuses, 'that's why I'm a Socialist.'[29] Then Ronald Reagan and Michael Harrington and Dan Rather and CNN appear. As in *Berlin*, in *Poland*, the spoken word drowns out image. There was simply no access to the direct unmediated scene of revolution, the events (re)occur through language. This emphasis on the spoken word in the postmodern documentary differs from both the earlier 1930s attempts thoroughly to integrate voice, image, and music à la Lorentz or the *cinéma vérité* effect of spontaneous synchronous sound and physical movement. Here the action is relayed in words that of necessity take precedence over images.[30]

Act I of *Far From Poland* ends triumphantly as Anna recounts how she was brought back to the shipyards and climbed onto a steam shovel amidst a huge crowd chanting the slogan on the banner encircling her: WE DEMAND REHIRE WALENTYNOWICZ. A stirring piano *étude* plays: Chopin updated for 1980 Poland. This vision of workers' solidarity and power is already certain to be undercut; we already know the history of the events: that the Polish government instigated a military crackdown on the union, ultimately declaring martial law. But even if the audience were unaware of the unfolding events, the seeds of disarray have been planted by Mark's cynicism, and by the tentativeness of Jill's enthusiasm. Without actually being there to experience and see for herself the social transformations Poland was undergoing, Godmilow must rely on secondhand accounts as the rest of us must. The documentarian holds no special knowledge, a fact she further demonstrates through her manipulations of the medium: re-enactments, filmed video replays, staged readings, false documents, domestic melodrama, and television news.

Act II parallels the first act of the film; it also features re-enactments of interviews published in Solidarity organs. The first interview is not, however, about the making of a revolutionary but tracks the unmaking of a former state censor, identified by his official code name, K62. The interview takes place in two locations: inside a car driving through the rain or while walking along a path through an isolated field (Figure 21). Before K62 begins his story about how he came to be a censor and what he did at his job, Godmilow, commenting about the news reports from Poland, declares that 'language itself is changing as the people become intoxicated with telling the truth.' Polish worker-poet Boleslaw Fac calls Poland before the Gdansk strike the 'National Front of Mutes' resulting from years of lies, repression, drivel, and silence.[31] After conversations with Szczecin shipyard workers, journalist Ryszard Kapuscinski claimed:

A battle was fought on the coast for language, for our Polish language, for its purity and clarity, for restoring an unequivocal sense to words, for cleaning out phraseology and idiocies, for liberating it from the plague of understatements . . . . They protest against everything that smacks of falsehood, of untruth, of kidding, of diluting, of dodging . . . . During those August days words suddenly revived.[32]

Godmilow's emphasis on the spoken word, an effect of her inability to gather visual footage, also highlights the struggle to liberate language accompanying the 1980 strikes. Polish director Andrzej Wadja explains that his film, *Man of Iron*, a fictional account of the Gdansk strike, 'transgresses against the art of film, because the emphasis is on words . . . what Walesa actually says is more important than his visual appearance.'[33] In short, the profound transformations wrought by Solidarity may not be spectacular, in that they do not fit the scopic economy of the cinema, the revolution in Poland occurs at the level of language – retrieving the spoken and written word becomes a powerful force for Poles. Godmilow's decision to re-enact interviews resonates with Claude Lanzmann's direct interviews in *Shoah*. Each suggests that the rhetoric of postmodern documentary has shifted the film form away from visuals: they produce a cinema of the word as much as of the look.

Truth-telling, the work of documentary itself, has already come under intense scrutiny in the film. Without recourse to the usual signs of authenticity – actual bodies speaking their own words, immediate and unrehearsed actions, archival footage – we have had nothing but falsity: staged melodrama between Mark and Jill, re-enacted conversations, faked letters, television news or footage acquired from Solidarity's film agency are all sources tainted by bias. How can the documentary film-maker remain simultaneously independent and authoritative when others provide her images? How does one tell the truth? Is it possible in a society corrupted by decades of state censorship even to imagine telling the truth, much less practice it?

As K62 describes his decision to become a censor (he wanted to be a journalist and thought the job would 'train my mind for that kind of work'), a laugh track comments on his remarks. His details about the process of censorship, the ways it works into the fiber of daily life, suggest that the intoxication with truth is itself an already doomed binge. This extended interview is cut up and interrupted by a series of differently registered stories: black-and-white half-inch video footage taken by a German film crew of interviews with actual workers in their plants; then blackouts during which a piano solo plays as Jill recounts three dreams about Fidel Castro phoning her to argue about

Solidarity, political art, and the role of history, interrupted by Jill watching the news accounts of the army take-over of the university on 2 December 1981. From this point on, Solidarity is under attack, and the international political crisis precipitates increasing tensions within the domestic melodrama between the heroine and her lover. As Jill watches a monitor showing Michael Harrington arguing that Solidarity is a democratic socialist movement, Mark points out the limited and self-aggrandizing functions of left-wing discourse, including documentary film-making; once again, however, they kiss and make up over pancakes.

In yet another 'interview,' 'miner' Adam Zaruski describes how Lech Walesa has come to Silesia to ask that the miners give up their basic demand to have Saturdays free. In essence he asks that they work for Solidarity on Saturday in order to avoid economic collapse. This time the announcer discloses that this is a fictional portrait gleaned from a composite of actual people to dramatize events among the coal miners of Silesia, a crucial sector of Solidarity's support because coal is the basis of all Polish industry; the realistic setting of an actual mineshaft where the interviews take place is undercut by the unauthentic Polish accent delivered by actor Mark Margolis. Jill receives more footage from Solidarity, young intellectuals editing an English-language newspaper about the national congress called to determine whether the union should move to challenge the state's political power. It is this challenge that will, of course, bring down the full force of the state on Solidarity, sending most of its leaders to prison.

Mark enters the loft ('Hi honey, I'm home') to find Jill watching Reagan's speech about how the Poles 'were betrayed by their own allies,' making political hay for his campaign against the Evil Empire on the backs of workers' suffering, even as he was moving to crush labor unions in the United States. Jill has to come up with an ending. The usual one – that Mark declares comes complete with the 'documentary insurance policy' against failed revolutionary movements: 'this film is not responsible for historical forces beyond its control' – won't work. 'Get yourself another movement,' Mark tells an outraged Jill. 'I'm joking,' he laughs before they kiss again and drink a champagne toast. It's Christmas after all. As in the classic melodrama of family rupture, usually at the hands of a woman who defies gender norms where only two possible endings are available, the woman dies or marries, both situations removing her threat to heterosexual institutions, Jill seems to have come around to Mark's position and love triumphs over a failed politics. But the film does not end here. An epilogue dated 1988, four years in the future, tells how Godmilow received a lucky break. The great Polish film director Andrzej Wadja had provided her with the outtakes of his film in progress, 'Dear Mr Premier,' about Wojciech Jaruzelski's political exile and rehabilitation. It consists of a series of letters written to his daughter Magda and read as he prepares to leave the mountain where he has been under house arrest for five years. Jill tells us that the part of the general is played by a Polish actor but the soundtrack has been added by her. The melancholy story of Jaruzelski ending in the dustbin of history grows as he describes the gardening that yields him a job as town gardener of Kosno. 'Your generation is obsessed with historical detail,' he complains to her, noting the various journalists, historians, and archivists who have come to visit him over the years. His final letter describes a moment of terror as he is pursued on a lonely road, only to be asked about his current life by an interested man who has recognized him.

But still the film is not yet over. In the final frames, Jill appears in front of her monitor and mentions two letters she received from Polish friends; she tells two stories, each spoken in Polish accents: Wanda concludes, 'the nation's back is broken – the intellectuals are to blame'; Richard declares, 'those sixteen months were the most important time in thirty-five years of Polish history.' Godmilow then catalogs her failures as a film-maker, listing what the film is not about and thereby casting further suspicions about documentary. Finally, she remembers 'one more thing': the part of Jaruzelski was played by American actor John Perkins, 'Okay, I'm done.' This ultimate appropriation – and a parody at that, the scenes from Poland are themselves staged – undercuts virtually all the rest of the film. When the credits roll we discover that the 'Letters of Wojciech Jaruzelski' were written by Jill Godmilow and Mark Magill. Credits play an important ideological role in documentary film, legitimating its truths, like the footnote in a scholarly essay through reference to authorities, detailing the political economy of independent film-making through its list of funders. In much the same way that the credits serve to unhinge and destabilize the documentary codes in Michelle Citron's 1979 film *Daughter Rite*, alerting the audience to the fact that the characters who appear as sisters in the film are actresses (and eliciting rage in most audience members for being manipulated), *Far From Poland* 'lacks manners, violating film etiquette,' as critic Pat Aufderheide put it, and so disturbs documentary expectations.[34]

Godmilow's deconstruction of the documentary form leaves little space for action; essentially she poses a philosophical question, much like that posed by Solidarity: what happens when people take charge of their work, when people claim authority to define the terms of their lives, and so reinvent a language through which to do this? What happens when a documentary film-maker is denied access to the subject she desires? What happens when the competing definitions of that subject offer no single story about it? What exactly is the function of the documentary film? Is instruction in correct thought or revolutionary uplift enough, or is a new rhetoric necessary to interrogate outmoded political and aesthetic practices? Surely the women investigating these questions – Strand, Rainer, Trinh, Godmilow – were not alone. For example, Bill Brand's *Home Less Home* and Jean-Pierre Gorin's *Poto and Cabenga* both take apart conventions of documentary address as they investigate the lack of housing in urban America, on the one hand, the curious family life and linguistic patterns of identical twins in San Diego's sprawling lower-middle-class suburbs, on the other. Yet, as I have been arguing throughout this book, the questions of documentary – questions about representation and agency – implicate gender and sexual differences as metaphors and templates for the relations between historical actors and their historiographers.

In the era of feminist critique, women's investigations into areas that are not gender-specific (like Poland's Solidarity movement) still resonate with a feminist agenda to interrogate modes of representation and to produce another kind of historical agent from the one found in standard accounts of politics. Moreover, as these films reveal, gender and its representation emerge as central issues in nationalist political formations. The 'female' genre of melodrama has a long association with working-class audiences and themes.[35] In the simplistic dichotomy of good workers and evil bosses, it was easy to know 'Which Side You Were On.' But as Godmilow demonstrates those 'sides' appropriated by others for their own uses are far from clear cut. Godmilow provides a cautionary tale; but what is she warning us about – truth, art, love, money, politics?

Progressive politics in the United States in the 1980s was marked by the emergence of a number of solidarity and anti-intervention movements working in consort with radical and revolutionary movements in El Salvador, Nicaragua, South Africa, Palestinians on the West Bank and Gaza, etc.[36] Direct action organizations, according to Barbara Epstein, are part of 'two distinct arenas within the movement for social change . . . the nonviolent direct action movement . . . [and] an issue-oriented movement.' She goes on to discuss the ways in which these new political formations, concerned with building a prefigurative community based on mutually arrived at decisions, attended carefully to process. For Epstein, a veteran of both the New Left and the Old, this was both marvelous and frustrating as strategy, tactics, and sometimes even political analysis took a back seat to what seemed to be merely personal concerns.[37] These international solidarity movements, however, were often not internationalist in focus; it seems that the specificity of each political situation precluded any theorizing or organizing on a global scale, and the mode of organizing – direct action, witness, sanctuary – was of necessity local and small-scale.[38] The energy to challenge dying regimes, be they fascist or communist, multinational or state capitalist, was expressed elsewhere; our job was merely to voice solidarity. Effecting change in the United States seemed an impossible task – tens of thousands descended on Washington in huge demonstrations against military support of the right-wing regime in El Salvador, but the killing continued. Massive demonstrations to reaffirm the hard-won 'right' to abortion sent state legislatures (often dominated by anti-abortion representatives) with the aid of the Supreme Court chipping away at women's reproductive freedom. The largest demonstrations in support of gays and lesbians occurred in the midst of the AIDS epidemic and homophobia and the celebration of family values. Even if Jesse Jackson won primaries in some states, alliances among progressives were being sundered by racial tensions, the erosion of working-class solidarity was accelerating even as the middle class was being impoverished; homelessness became another neighborhood.

The relentless successes of the New Right during the period when the films I am discussing were made provides a partial explanation of why feminists looked at various national bodies outside the United States. Others seemed capable of challenging law, power, and convention even in the face of extreme oppression. Others 'broke through a wall of fear' which was still enclosing the American political landscape. What I'm trying to suggest is not that there is a direct, mechanical linkage between counter-cinema and the splintered reactions by the Left to Reaganism; rather that in their focus on other (failed) revolutionary movements and their concern with refashioning the gendered conventions of documentary and narrative, these films mapped struggles in the Academy and within the Left about the contours of progressive politics. The internationalism practiced by solidarity movements is of a different kind from that provided to the international brigades in support of the Spanish Loyalists in 1936, or that engaged in by American citizens critical of their government's war in Vietnam during the 1960s. The years since Nixon had been forced out of office – a day for dancing in the streets and banging pots in my working-class neighborhood in Massachusetts – had culminated, not in renewed democratic socialist politics, but in a fragmented Left and a unified highly conservative Right whisking into office Ronald Reagan, staunch anti-communist president of the Screen Actors Guild, law-and-order governor, spokesman for corporate America, with a mandate that included, in his mind, breaking any law inconveniencing his quest to undermine the Evil Empire. The internationalism expressed in these films is of a piece with a splintered Left, each revealing a romantic longing (tempered with a healthy dose of skepticism) for others elsewhere, who seem to have created the conditions for collective identity and political solidarity lacking among American progressives.

Vietnam

Trinh T. Minh-ha takes the title of her 1989 film from a 'socialist courting ritual.' According to Trinh, in 'recent socialist tradition . . . when a man encounters a woman, feels drawn to her, and wants to flirt with her, he teasingly asks, "Young woman, are you married yet?" If the answer is negative, instead of saying no, she will reciprocate, "Yes, his surname is Viet and his given name is Nam." '[39] In this neat equation of gender and national identity, the marital status of a woman is never in question. Women are tied to husband and nation through traditions, especially the four virtues, *cong, dung, ngon, hanh* (be skillful in her work, modest in her behavior, soft-spoken in her language, faultless in her principles), and the three submissions: 'Daughter, she obeys her father/Wife, she obeys her husband/Widow, she obeys her son.'[40] In a series of beautifully composed and lit scenes, Trinh's film explores post-revolutionary Vietnamese culture through the memories of five Vietnamese immigrants to the US. *Surname Viet* also relies on a number of translated and re-enacted interviews. These interviews, first conducted in Vietnamese by a French woman and translated into French, were then translated into English to be played by American women born in Vietnam. Like the other films discussed in this chapter, the work of translation, transliteration, and re-enactment becomes the form by which postmodern documentary decodes itself; thus meanings embedded in language take on great significance, almost eclipsing that of the image. Still, by interpolating archival materials (footage from the war, photographs of the 'informants') with footage Trinh shot in Vietnam and San José, the stark images constructed for the 'interviews' reverberate with the indelible visuals of war's devastation. We know this country and how it looks; the pictures already implanted take on new dimensions through the words.

The horrific personal experiences of war – bombings, migrations, internments, imprisonments, assassinations – double back and recirculate among larger populations. Through traditional songs and dances and in the archival footage, other dimensions of historical truths are layered over the voices of women. The Vietnamese women now living in California contend with new forms of American imperialism and aggression – beauty contests and English classes, for instance. At one point in the film a voice comments: 'Always recurring in the prisoner's mind is the fear of a time when the witnesses themselves die without witnesses, when History consists of tiny explosions of life, and of deaths without relays' (p. 67). But witness without word is not enough, the voice and its many languages – song, story, poetry – center the film. Its locus is the face: in profile, segmented, written over with text, falling out of the screen. Like all of Trinh's films, the visuals are carefully composed and excruciatingly beautiful; color, light, framing, *mise en scène* evoke a sense of time that is outside and beyond time, exceeding history and ordered by ritual, and space, 'an empty subject,' as Trinh says of the Senegalese village life in her first film, *Reassemblage*. Vietnamese culture, four thousand years in the making, is marked by both tremendous stability and continuity and enormous rupture and fragmentation. A nation under constant invasion, colonized first by one then another imperial power, still maintains its integrity; yet integrity is based on reinvention. Toward the end of the film the various names for Vietnam are catalogued: Van-Lang, Nam-Viet, Hoang Viet, Dai-Viet, An-Man (Bac Ky-Le Tonkin; Trung Ky-An Nam; Nam Ky-La Cochinchine), French Indochina (Viet-Nam, 'Nam).[41] These multiplying identities paradoxically locate a national unity extending across the Pacific Ocean into exile. The women who have appeared as the 'interviewed' Vietnamese 'play' themselves at home in their San José immigrant community, and the images of flux – a nation, women, a film – return in the dance of the boat people drifting across the screen. Women's lives figure both the continuities and ruptures of Vietnamese culture, their experiences at once tragic and heroic, mythic and mundane, awkward and graceful, true and false.

The pun on national naming and romantic affiliation decenters the documentary film, especially its use of the interview as authentic voice (a voice is heard defining 'interview' as 'an outmoded tool of documentary') as much as it interpellates subjectivity through nationality. Trinh argues that 'the risk incurred in this form of feminine-nationalist in/directness is, for me, the same risk taken in the simultaneous filmic construction and deconstruction of the first person interview in documentary practice' (p. 192). Claiming a position from which to speak one's memories undermines collective history, much as the story of national unity extinguishes differences. Trinh's film clarifies how submerged women's claims are within those of national and ethnic identity. Can there be women within a nation? Can there be a nation within women? *Surname Viet* asks, as did Godmilow's gallows humor about Solidarity, in what space within movements for national liberation can women's voices be heard?

Trinh's films and writings cross generic and stylistic categories. She tries to 'theorize *with* film' rather than about film, just as in her writings she theorizes through poetic discourse. Theory is sensuous for Trinh, giving full play to the eye, the ear, and the unconscious as much as to philosophical methods. Both Trinh and Rainer have been prolific critics as well as film-makers; each began work in the performing arts, Rainer as a dancer/choreographer, Trinh as a musician/musicologist. The versatility with which each moves among discursive practices from one form to another, one language to another, reclaims virtuosity for film-making. In this, they paradoxically recall the great 1930s documentarians like Pare Lorentz, whose works incorporated literature, music, and still photography to forge a national cultural identity. However, these women's films break down borders, exploring exile, expatriation, immigration, and tourism by questioning genres, ethnicities, genders, ideologies; yet the mammoth effort to combine so many diverse forms into their films suggests an antidote to or perhaps another form of nationalist incorporation as they try to represent its antithesis. If the nation is an imagined community, as Benedict Anderson argues, calling itself forth through the devices of mass media – print, film, radio – can it be subverted through the private and local such as traditional song, formalist imagery, personal testimonial, invented memory? The imagined communities called up in *Berlin, Poland, Viet/Nam* push against national boundaries; they are not nationalist but rather internationalist, depicting the myriad ways women migrate, expatriate, flee, and fantasize from one nation to another.

The 1980s became one of the great eras of mass migration. We can celebrate the dissemination of cultures across borders while condemning its brutal cause: the internationalizing of capital. The corrosion of national-popular cultures that this entails paves the way for hybrid visions of alter(n)ity. While feminist documentaries stress women's experience of difference within culture, none is willing to universalize women's cultural experience. The stories these films tell are of precise national, historical differences linked to diverse political economies; yet each suggests that women's experiences of the nation have varied alignments. To some extent, socialist politics and revolutionary change are embedded in the circumstances and crises defining each film; each interrogates the status of the state and daily life after the economic transformations resulting from post-war capitalism and revolutionary activism. When the German government advocates state terrorism and censorship to combat political dissent, the grim history of Germany's past echoes clearly; Polish nationalism resonates with its history of anti-Semitic authoritarian regimes like the Catholic Church, even as Solidarity defies Soviet control and the local Stalinist party apparatus; the liberation of Saigon did not automatically free Vietnamese society from centuries of women's oppression: the land and people were in ruin, the government and economy in chaos, but women were still expected to follow the four virtues. The films cannot present inspirational images of revolution as did *The Battle of Algiers*. Those images are too tainted with the history of revolutionary failures, failures especially poignant for women as in Pontecorvo's neglect of Muslim oppression of women, yet revolutions, as Hunt and Kerber argue, make possible women's historical agency.

Moreover, the story of revolution makes thrilling cinema; perhaps this is precisely why it is so troubling for the women directors; the cinematic fervor needs to be tempered unless these films become fodder for a discredited (inter)nationalist project. Trinh says as much when she paraphrases Baudrillard late in the film:

> War as a succession of special effects: the war became film before it was shot. Cinema has remained a vast machine of special effects. If the war is the continuation of politics by other means, then media images are the continuation of war by other means: immersed in the machinery, part of the special effect, no critical distance. Nothing separates the Vietnam war and the superfilms that were made and continue to be made about it. It is said that if Americans lost the other, they have certainly won this one. (p. 88)

Perhaps feminist counter-documentarians take their cues from the telephone breather whose calls keep interrupting the psychoanalytical sessions starring film critic Annette Michelson in Yvonne Rainer's film, *Journeys from Berlin/1971* and look to

> those movie women Katy Hepburn facing the dawn in her posh pad with stiff upper chin. Merle Oberon facing the Nazi night with hair billowing in the electric breeze. Roz Russell sockin' the words 'n' the whiskey to the best of them. Rita Hayworth getting shot in the mirror and getting her man. Jane Wyman smiling through tears.

As the voguing stars of *Paris Is Burning* know so well, those movie women have more screen reality than any of the putatively real women telling their stories of personal pain and triumph in any number of women's documentaries, feminist narratives or disease of the week television movies. Getting away from both the Hollywood and left-wing documentary convention of tough womanhood triumphing over personal disaster, the deconstructive feminist documentary supplants real women with actors by letting them speak the words of actual women. In a radically different but comparable manner, the women's stories we hear resemble the 'talking heads' Julia LeSage has suggested is the hallmark of the feminist consciousness-raising documentary aesthetic, but they turn the lens slightly, enough to challenge the genre itself. The 'tasks of these translators' are to represent the differences between stories as they move from one language to another, from one location to another, from one voice to another. In the process, 'the original undergoes a change,' says Walter Benjamin, and provides a way to come to terms with 'the foreignness of languages.'[42] But is this enough? What does deconstructing the documentary leave us with? Whether deconstructive or instructive, the category of documentary remains. Why do we want to keep using it?

To some extent, each film investigates the failures of traditional revolutionary movements, including varieties of tactics like terrorism, guerrilla warfare, national liberation, militant labor unions. Each strategy proves inadequate for some segment of the populace, incapable of overcoming state power, even becoming trapped within the logic of state power. For example, Vietnam's successful elimination of the enemy aggressor left the women of Vietnam Trinh surveys with lives still troubled by restrictions that long preceded those of one government or another. These films detail how tenacious are the contradictions and complexities of staging revolutions in which women's needs are to be taken into account more fully than as emblems of national identity. The films represent a sort of cultural embellishment of the problematic situation of left politics in the 1980s, when solidarity groups, direct action movements, and identity-based politics emerged as the splintered inheritors of the broad-based radicalism of earlier moments, each exhibiting a curious combination of liberalism, guilty attempts by those benefiting from US imperialism to temper its effects, and revolutionary romance with other national liberations.

In addition, they are travelogs through the precarious grounds of contemporary feminism as it seeks to understand itself within global political and economic systems. In the face of a consolidated multinational capitalism promoted by a rabidly militaristic US foreign and domestic policy, deconstruction – fragmentation, splintering, tearing down, and exposing the contradictions in New Right agenda – occupied much of the political energies of progressives: we were fighting for our lives and for the meager rights and freedoms we gained so recently. Theories about new social movements rethink the foundational beliefs of left-wing politics by shifting the focus away from material relations, i.e. away from a strictly class analysis (in the face of labor's retreat) toward social and political subjectivities. They search to explain the powerful consensual hegemony of postmodern late capitalism. Beginning with the Black Power calls of the late 1960s, spreading to women's and gay liberations, new social movements stress the emergence of ethnic, sexual, and racial identities as the sites of conflicting and radical critiques of American hegemony. By foregrounding differences within national languages and histories through women's voices, these films participate in the aggregation of new social arrangements within political economies and through aesthetic forms.[43] Yet, as Barbara Epstein notes in her critique of the nonviolent direct action movements, excessive attention to process can obstruct strategic analysis. To a certain extent, in responding to the contradictory history of gendered representations in documentary through excessively formalistic manipulations, the films block their effectivity. Just as endlessly worrying over an organization's process can result in a movement so purified of contradictions it cannot function, constantly monitoring a documentary's form can become an end in itself. The cinematic choices these visionary directors made have an eerie parallel in the diminished political possibilities available in the Reagan era. As such the films serve as guides to the place of women in the nation, the place of language in identity, the place of documentary in politics.

9

Video *Vérité*: Rodney King in the City of

Angels of History

The previous chapter looked in depth at women's cinematic responses to state terror. The counter-documentary forms Yvonne Rainer, Jill Godmilow, and Trinh T. Minh-ha devised were designed in part to acknowledge how women's voices tell of their experiences in the production of culture (such as in psychoanalysis) while at the same time suffer their occlusion from the arenas of politics. The film-makers chose to foreground formal innovations in order to call attention to the deficiencies in recent political documentaries, espe-cially in the reliance on talking heads and archival footage to shore up historical authenticity, two strategies developed to correct the histor-ical gaps in *cinéma vérité*. However, with the easy availability of cam-corders and VCRs, a new era of video *vérité* is upon us, as America makes its own home videos. This chapter explores the most famous 81 seconds of home-recording: George Holliday's brief tape of Rodney King's beating at the hands of four officers from the Los Angeles Police Department. It serves as a coda to the book's examination of the politics and rhetoric of documentary forms.

When Gil Scott-Heron proclaimed that the revolution will not be televised, the age of CNN and electronic warfare had not yet come to pass. But with increasingly popular primetime shows like *Rescue 911* and *I Witness Video*, with the new mode of advertising *vérité* seen in the 1992 presidential campaign commercials for George Bush or in the series of EPT (Early Pregnancy Test) ads featuring couples learning whether the woman is pregnant, and with local news stations exhorting concerned citizens to phone in news as it happens from their cellular phones or send in their videotapes for immediate rebroadcasting, what we do have is the counter-revolution, if you will, being televised.

With the omnipresence of surveillance cameras observing us cash checks, buy jeans, enter elevators, and stroll through office building lobbies, the videography of daily life is normalized. I cite Patty Hearst's image as Tanya, bank-robber soldier in the Symbionese Liberation Army, as the first 'home video *vérité*' in the sense that her blurry figure penetrated the daily lives of millions of television viewers, becoming an emblem of what Barthes calls 'the publicity of the private.' But surveillance technology is double-edged; they watch us, but we also can watch them. It is this ambivalence I want to chart. Or as Aretha put it, 'Who's zooming who?'

More than sixty years ago, writing on the occasion of the ninetieth anniversary of the invention of photography, Walter Benjamin concluded his 'short history' with the following observations and questions:

> The camera is getting smaller and smaller, ever readier to capture fleeting and secret moments whose images paralyse the associative mechanisms of the beholder . . . . Not for nothing have Atget's photographs been likened to those of the scene of a crime. But is not every square inch of our cities the scene of a crime? Every passer-by a culprit? Is it not the task of the photographer – descendant of augurs and haruspices – to reveal guilt and to point out the guilty in his pictures?[1]

Still at the heart of urban representations of racial and class conflicts today, Benjamin's queries might have been posed about the various events circulating around Rodney King.

A Configuration Pregnant with Tension

The Angel of History, Benjamin's representative of materialist historiography, stands arrested, 'face turned towards the past,' eyes focused on its wreckage piling up and scattering underfoot as the winds of time blow her blindly forward. For Benjamin, the moment when 'homogeneous, empty time' blasts open the 'continuum of history' gives us a glimpse of the past exploding into the present and with it of 'the revolutionary chance in the fight for the oppressed past.' George Holliday's 81-second home video of four police officers brutalizing Rodney King provides us with one such 'monad,' 'where thinking stops in a configuration pregnant with tensions and gives that configuration a shock.'[2] Here before us is the visual evidence of the continuous present of the past. The City of Angels itself explodes and it is all on tape for us to see. What remains, however, (*pace* Marx) is to *interpret* it.

For anyone with just a passing acquaintance with the LAPD, it comes as no surprise that they beat, even kill, poor, African-American and

Latino Angelenos. There is a direct link from Watts (1965) through Ronald Reagan to South Central. The recent report on the 'cause' of the Los Angeles 'riot' indicates all one needed to do was read the findings of the McCone Commission's report on the Watts uprising to understand the 1992 rebellion. The cops have functioned as an occupying army containing the unruly populations since the 1920s.[3] As ex-police chief Daryl Gates proudly claims in his autobiography, 'Assault is not a dirty word . . . . We stop thousands of people each year in a pro-active effort to deal with crime.'[4] The majority of those stopped are male African-American and Latino youths whose presence is likened to 'the enemy within' formerly characterizing the Red scare. The ubiquitous sound of choppers circling South Central in John Singleton's *Boyz 'n the 'Hood* powerfully indicates just how much the LAPD's operations depend on methods derived from counterinsurgency warfare in Vietnam. In fact SWAT, inaugurated by returning Green Berets, was based on guerrilla warfare. The chief of the District Attorney's Hardcore Drug Unit insists 'this is Vietnam here,' and Mayor Bradley calls black gangs 'the Vietcong abroad in our society.'[5] With this staged warfare, police and community members are pitted in battle. Police brutality charges are legion in Los Angeles, the city and county have paid out a small fortune in wrongful death and assault claims to victims.[6] But until Rodney King's beating, this had remained mostly an 'internal affair,' the violence confined to poor communities of color which remain invisible and contained by the Department's internal affairs office.

The Apparatus of Real Events

In 1970, the Raindance Corporation began publishing *Radical Software*, a journal for 'the alternate television movement.' In its inaugural issue, the editors sought 'to design and implement alternate information structures which transcend and reconfigure the existing ones.' Imagining a revolutionary utopia in which 'VTR systems and video cassettes will make alternate networks a reality,' the editors hoped to provide people 'making their own television . . . a means of social change and exchange.'[7] Portapaks, VTRs, cassettes, and CATV would remake the relations of vision demanded by commercial television viewing. By bringing an interactive camera directly into the streets, the public would achieve a new kind of radical relationship to itself; the immediacy of video could be an organizing tool for building a collective citizenship and the medium itself could be expanded to induce new forms of consciousness. Various video collectives detailed their projects in the journal, which served as a distributor of tapes as well as a handbook on hardware and software technologies. In this early moment, the emphasis on building up a network and library for alternative uses of the medium and for alternative politics occurred simultaneously with the increasing use of video as surveillance. For instance, *The Black Panther* published a photograph of video cameras mounted on telephone poles on Blue Hill Avenue in the heart of Boston's black community and described how the Black Panther Party was using video cameras to document police brutality.[8]

The dream that portable technologies could open up the public sphere to participatory democracy prompted Bertolt Brecht's call in 1927 to program directors of German radio stations to 'bring the apparatus to the real events and not limit yourself to reproduction or reporting . . . to approach important meetings of the Reichstag and above all also go to important trials.'[9] His early call for C-SPAN and Court-TV actually had more in common with the ultimate goal of Antfarm and Videofreex and other video guerrillas: power to the people through information about the workings of power. Like radio, what was so promising about video was its immediacy. Just as Brecht had anticipated television's entrance into the Senate and the court-room through another medium, the vision of on-the-street video was curiously a replay of the earliest days of cinema. In the 1890s, the Lumière brothers sent teams of camera operators equipped with film processors and projectors across the continents to document and display their inventions by filming the daily lives and environments of common people and then projecting the raw footage. Thus the fathers of newsreel and documentary cinema also pioneered interactive viewing, attempting almost simultaneous shooting and viewing, which, like most subsequent documentary images, relied heavily on the presence of bodies.[10] Because, according to Bill Nichols, 'the body stands at risk,' it makes for compelling viewing.[11] Daryl Gates put it this way in his autobiography: 'any visual depiction of force can appear worse than it is.'[12] As 'star,' the presence of the body, especially the body in pain, signifies truth and reality with an immediacy that needs no contextualization.[13]

Theorists of the ethnographic film have long insisted on 'wholeness,' in the words of Karl Heider – 'whole bodies and whole peoples in whole acts' – to provide the necessary context for the information coded in the anthropological film.[14] Yet film-makers as diverse as Trinh T. Minh-ha and Chick Strand challenge this equation of whole-ness with reality as an ideological construct that accords with neither actual perception nor cinematic representation. Neither the eye nor the camera can take in wholeness; wholeness, like Georg Lukács's totality, is a dream. Partiality is the province of the lens, whether in the eye or the camera. Wholly visible bodies are often those furthest removed from lived experience. The bodies we see as bodies, with the exception of our children or our lovers, are those of performers, athletes, stars, or victims – spectacles.

Film-makers working in and around documentary quite consciously fragment whole bodies and whole acts through a variety of cinematic techniques of framing and editing. When they do feature them, as does Chantal Akermann in her fictional anatomy of real-time melo-drama, *Jeanne Dielman, 23 Quai du Commerce, 1080 Bruxelles,* the effect of realism is undone through exaggeration. The impossible duration of actually watching someone button a bathrobe or make a meatloaf defies cinematic conventions of the Real. Eighty-one seconds of 'whole bodies' performing 'whole acts' – four white police officers beating a black man writhing on the ground – is not cinematic; it is excruciating to watch, because it unfolds in real time.

Video's promise is of an immediate visual experience. Because of its cheapness and its portability, the subject/object distinction blurred. What you see is what you get with video. Video cameras don't just record; they also project. This simultaneity seems to return control to the objects of its gaze. An army of freelance roving video guerrillas could track the news, shooting footage omitted by the networks to reveal the underside of American culture and give voice and visage to the dispossessed as they organized to take control of their lives.[15] The revolution may not be televised, but television could be revolutionary. These various agendas, for both alternative and commercial television and film, serve as a backdrop for the night of 3 March 1991, when George Holliday, fooling around with his newly acquired video camera, ran onto his balcony and blasted Rodney King, one of the hundreds of black men roughed up by the LAPD, into history.

The Most Objective Piece of Evidence

George Holliday's tape unquestioningly presented visual proof of what was already common knowledge: the LAPD battered black men and got away with it. Here was the means to bring justice to Rodney King *and* to expose the racism and violence of the force. Despite Daryl Gates's claim that this was an 'aberration,' NBC and CNN made sure that the nation watched segments of the 81-second sequence over and over. (As such the images acquired a mantra-like, mesmerizing status held only by the Zapruder film and perhaps the Patty Hearst bank robbery tape.) So prosecutor Terry White would repeatedly urge the jurors to 'believe' the 'most objective piece of evidence' available to 'your own eyes.'[16] However, the force of this direct evidence had already been diluted in the 'flow' of television.[17] Ironically, it was this flow that the defense sought to break up in an attempt to reroute the vision of the jury from the videotape as a whole (Prosecutor White challenged the defense to play the tape in real time) onto the fractional segments, the 'frames,' and overcome the 'evidence' of sight with the power of the word. Essentially *California v. Powell, Wind, Briseno, and Koons* staged a semiotic battle between two complementary but antagonistic codes of meaning: the visual and the linguistic.

Briefly, where the prosecution relied on the 'facts' of the visual text solely – what could be seen on the tape – without acknowledging the context of the tape, i.e. rampant police brutality and racism in Los Angeles (after all, this is the same Prosecutor's Office that works closely with the police), the defense sought to recontextualize the tape by using a purely textual method. In effect, the defense team acted as newscasters providing a voice-over narration of the events on tape. A medium already associated with the news – videotape – of a current event caught 'as it happens' which then became part of the news as it was daily rebroadcast during the news, the Holliday tape was ideally suited to the defense attorney's strategies of reinterpreting its images. Like *cinéma vérité*, television news relies on about a 20:1 ratio, but the selection process is designed to highlight the announcer's and journalist's story, not reveal the drama of the subjects' lives. However, unlike cinema, in which images usually produce the narrative and visual logic of a film, during the news, a reporter steers the images. Because this is how news is presented, how it happens for us as a genre, it made sense in an illogical way to give credence to the voice over the image during the trial. For, as one cameraman declares, 'Television news is little more than an illustrated lecture,' which is precisely 'what the jury saw.'[18] Through various means of mechanical reproduction, the defense used the tape as evidence against itself.

The defense repeatedly broke down the tape into 'frames.'[19] In this, Kimberle Crenshaw and Gary Peller argue it was following an already established legal precedent, which Justice Thurgood Marshall dissenting in *Richmond v. Croson*, named 'disaggregation.'[20] Ironically, by stopping each 'frame' and explaining what was happening before and after, or rather speculating about what might have occurred before or after each image, the defense produced a series of new narratives starkly in contrast to the narrative supplied by the whole 81-second tape. Its most powerful testimony came when its star witness, 'use of force expert' Sgt Charles Duke, stopping each frame, explained how Rodney King was in control of the action and how the officers were merely responding appropriately to King's escalating show of force. At no time, according to Duke, does an officer beat King, rather Mr King 'rises' (this action taking place in a stopped image) and challenges the officers. Virtually 'everything Mr King did is aggressive.' At various points, the witness shows how Mr King's 'leg is cocked' or his 'arm is triggered' provoking the officers to respond with 'strokes.' (Note the passive voice indicating how Rodney King is separate from his body which has been transformed into a weapon.)

Moreover, because the first few seconds of the tape are blurry, the testimony of California Highway Patrol officers that Michael Powell severely beat King around the face and head cannot be visually corroborated by the tape. By exhorting the jurors to *look* at the 'entire video,' Prosecutor White ultimately undercut his case because these crucial seconds could not be seen clearly. Finally, despite the prosecutor's insistence that Rodney King be referred to as Mr King, and reminders that he is a human being, the defendants continually described him as 'a duster,' 'an animal,' 'bear-like,' 'buffed out,' thus 'an ex-con,' 'a monster with a one-track mind,' 'super-strong,' and so forth. Of course, his body was nowhere in the courtroom; instead, his presence was graphed through the tape onto the monitor, a visual image open to interpretation. Furthermore, by emphasizing the taped visuals, Rodney King can only be seen as body; he lacks a voice.[21] On the other hand, the defense team had hired feminist psychologist and eye-witness testimony expert, Elizabeth Loftis, as a consultant. Her job was to 'humanize' the officers by attending to their attire, their posture, the placement of their family members in the audience, and their modes of speech during their testimonies.

Anticipating my argument in 1930, Bertolt Brecht, after seeing a series of elegantly shot art and advertising photographs, cautioned

> that less than ever does the mere reflexion of reality reveal anything about reality. A photograph of the Krupp works or the A.E.G. tells us next to nothing about these institutions. Actual reality has slipped into the functional. The reification of human relations – the factory, say – means that they are no longer explicit. So something must in fact be *built up*, something artificial, posed.[22]

Incapable of detailing the exploitation of the workers inside the walls of the plant, or the mass destruction of the armaments made, the photographed images, imposing sheets of concrete, appear abstractly beautiful. Thus Benjamin, in quoting Brecht, calls for the 'caption,' the insistence of historical memory.

Interestingly, at various times in his autobiography, the copyright of which indicates its publication date as July 1992 (thus pointing out how it appeared after the LA rebellion), Gates relies on both captioning and semiotic analyses. For instance, in his discussion of the Eulia Love incident in which two LAPD officers gunned down an emotionally unstable widow in front of her home, he states: 'Frame by frame, as if analyzing a film, I reviewed the facts . . .'[23] Moreover, in his account of the King incident, he focuses on the digital and audio tapes transmitted from Powell's squad car back to police headquarters. First, he displays his knowledge of information systems – one gained through his invention of 'policing based on the formation of military-type units' (p. 114) – by insulting those who fail to understand the differences between these two processes, then he acknowledges Benjamin's point that context is all when he points out how officers are using 'jargon' and 'slang' to speak to each other, pointing out that these irruptions of the officers' unconscious may not be racist (pp. 348–9).

The Holliday tape acted as a videographic trope, a synecdoche for the many other unrecorded beatings of African Americans and Latinos by the LAPD. Its context was the racist nation in which we live. Needing no caption, it spoke for itself: black man beaten fifty-two times by four white cops. But as Martha Rosler reminds us, 'Photography (and, clearly, videotape) is dumb.'[24] The prosecutors and the rest of us, having seen the tape, knew it spoke for itself. But it seems the defense had read Brecht and Benjamin and stood them on their heads. That was not an aesthetic object, but a monument of exploitation; this was not a racist police assault, but a model of enlightened restraint in the face of an aggressor 'out of control.' Thus the defense 'built up,' in their terms, 'buffed out,' Rodney King, that is, they 'captioned' him.[25]

We need to be clear about the racial divisions operating in this case and in the readings it gave rise to. Simi(otic) Valley, the seamy and idiotic site of the Ronald Reagan Library and home to about one quarter of the LAPD,[26] is purposely far removed from South Central, but perhaps not so far from Weimar Germany.[27] The defense understood that the jury already knew how to interpret the gestures of the black man's body as violent from the countless nightly news broadcasts detailing the 'gangsta wars' in LA. The momentary disruption of this knowledge by Holliday's tape paradoxically had been smoothed over by the defense's use of frame-by-frame textual analysis; all that was needed was a parallel image to realign the racial asymmetry underpinning American culture. Thus when the 'riots' broke out, we were given another image to caption Holliday's tape: that captured by the news cameraman circling South Central in a helicopter of white truck driver

Reginald Denny being dragged and beaten on the corner of Florence and Normandie by four black men.[28] This doubling effect served to cancel the impact of the Holliday tape, realigning racial norms for the television audience, justifying the jury's verdict, and providing a grim lesson in 'the fairness doctrine' and 'the equal time rule.'[29]

Close Readings Can Incur Misreadings

One immediate outcome of the uprising, lost to many observers not keyed into film studies, was the statement issued by the Society for Cinema Studies immediately following the verdict. The resolution enacted declared:

> 1. The verdict to acquit four white Los Angeles Police Department officers contradicts powerful visual evidence – video evidence of excessive police brutality seen globally.
> 2. The reaction in the streets of Los Angeles and other cities is fueled by the jury's deliberate refusal to 'see' this visual evidence the way that most of us – regardless of color – saw these images.
> 3. But how did they 'see' this video? They saw it repeatedly, repeatedly desensitized to its power and effect. They saw it in slow motion, analytically – as the defense supplied a 'reading' of the appropriateness of each officer's reaction. This demonstrates how close readings can incur misreading. Our outrage is that, even with visual evidence, Blacks' experiences of police brutality does not count.
> 4. As media educators, we must voice our outrage at this verdict and endorse all efforts to indict the LAPD officers for civil rights violations.[30]

Benjamin insisted that in the age of mechanical reproduction, the 'aura' of originality and truth was simultaneously undermined and democratized. Holliday's tape, however, had achieved a kind of aura, the most objective piece of evidence, which left it open to mechanically reproductive effects that could realign its origins and truth.[31] Paradoxically, in the age of mechanical reproduction, which for Benjamin was primarily a visual age, words attain inordinate power; they become a necessary antidote to the fetishized image. Alarmed that its techniques of close reading have been wrongly appropriated, the SCS protests misreadings derived from the very practices its members championed. But is this enough? As this trial and the subsequent images and events attest, the battle over a contextualizing narrative, over a 'caption,' over representation has important material effects on the street and in the courtroom as well as in the lecture hall. Like direct cinema, textual analysis – semiosis – is extremely open – to all. We cannot control interpretation or the modes of its reproduction. Still, like George Holliday, we can intervene into the apparatus of real events, disturbing the flow of history. So, like the Angel of History, our work needs to 'bring about a real state of emergency,' to 'seize hold of a memory as it flashes up at a moment of danger' and challenge business as usual. Perhaps Spike Lee's recent recontextualizing of George Holliday's tape – a montage intercut with the American flag as back-drop to the opening credits of *Malcolm X* where Malcolm's voice exhorts us to remember that the black man can never be an American – presents a counter-frame to the defense's use of Rodney King's image at the trial.

Sometimes, in our postmodernist jubilation about writerly texts, we seem to forget that the very openness we celebrate is there for anyone's taking. Public access to cablecasting has allowed Tom Metzger to syndicate his 'Race and Reason' program, even as it gives time to Paper Tiger television. The controversy about the Holliday tape and the LAPD officers' trial sends us back to debates raging throughout the 1960s and 1970s over the ability of *cinéma vérité* and alternative video to liberate vision and to those of the 1930s about realism's significance to the working class. In a so-called pluralistic democracy we need to be aware of how important representation and historic referencing are to each other and to relations of power and knowledge. Simply celebrating the possibility of producing meaning is not enough.

History

To close, I offer the following story: in September 1992, *The New York Times* reported on a mural painted in Dorchester, Massachusetts by members of the Boston Youth Clean-Up Corps during the summer with federal money provided in the wake of the LA uprising. The mural depicts the Rodney King events in a series of images beginning with the beating and culminating in the rebellion. To emphasize the 'cinematic' element of the mural, each panel is tracked by a series of symbolic objects – a bottle, fifty-two billy clubs, a camcorder, fifty-eight bodies – which form the sprocket holes of each frame.[32] The Boston Police Department objected to the mural and to the public funding it received, seeing it as an assault on them, an incitement to violence. However, the teenage artists from this multiracial community simply replied (as the title of the mural insists): but this is 'history.' This really happened, we all saw it on TV.

The power of the framed image to document events is tremendous. But as the controversy over the Boston mural indicates, it is the reconstruction and reproduction of the image that holds the possibility for interpreting *and* changing history. The image itself, like the 81-second videotape, is subject to being broken down and built up by anyone. So when neighborhood youth provide another context for viewing the racial and class tensions in urban areas like Dorchester in the 1990s, the complications and contradictions of the violence endemic to poverty and racism get other captions than those provided by the cops, the news, or the two political parties. The police wanted to paint over the murals. (In this they were taking their cue from the LAPD, who regularly painted over the graffiti of the Crips with the insignia of the Bloods and vice versa). This act of aggression against a representation of violence (like the defense strategy in *California v. Powell et al.*) would clearly provoke further tensions between the community and the police. However, a compromise was worked out: the mural remains intact, but the kids have agreed to paint one last frame depicting the improved relations among citizens and police in Dorchester. As coda and caption, this panel points toward a reconciliation between interpretation and experience, between power and representation. If Rodney King's story (as object of violence, spectacle and its commodification) is this nation's most perfect thesis, perhaps this mural (as representation of pain, memory, and community) stands as its antithesis, compelling all of us to work toward synthesis.

I wrote this chapter before the Federal trial against the four LAPD officers took place, which resulted in the convictions of two officers, Michael Powell and Stacy Koons. As was clear from the aggressive prosecution, the government attorneys had learned something about semiotics from the state trial. Rodney King's body and voice presented a visual and aural counter to the videotaped 'frame.' However, many police departments, anxious to avoid charges of brutality, have installed video cameras in squad cars to document arrest procedures, recreating the video *vérité* effects of seeing themselves every Saturday night on *Cops*. The appeal of the camera as the authority for truth continues.

EPILOGUE

One More Thing

Every Saturday morning for the past fifteen years I spend an hour on the telephone long distance with one of my girlfriends. Our chats range from griping about work and husbands, wondering about children and poetry, analyzing sex, politics, and culture – the usual gossip of contemporary, overeducated, middle-class women facing middle age in the United States. It takes us a long time to hang up. Inevitably, there is always 'one more thing' to say and it can't wait a week. 'One more thing' is the plea my children sing out to me every day: one more TV show; one more cookie; one more story before bed. It seems that their desires for filling in, filling up, are the origin of our needs to tell (and wreak havoc with) the truth.

At the conclusion of Jill Godmilow's counter-documentary about Solidarity, *Far From Poland*, the film-maker recounts three stories about Solidarity's impact on Polish society. Each voice, replicated by Godmilow, provides another version of the aftermath of martial law, adding to the already densely layered narrative of the film. Godmilow's last word off-handedly adds 'one more thing': in the 'outtakes' of Andrzej Wadja's 'new' film she has 'acquired' the part of General Jaruzelski was played by an American actor. With this final clue, we come to understand that nothing we have heard or seen in this film is trustworthy. There will always be one more thing. Just as there is no Wadja film, the missing evidence that can confirm the truth of a document can always be added to: one more thing leads to another and then another still.

So here it is: one more thing.

During the summer of 1974, I worked as a teacher in a Head Start program in east Cambridge, Massachusetts. In addition to serving preschoolers, we also ran a day camp for school-age kids. Because we were in a school building with a large industrial kitchen, one of the activities the camp offered was cooking, my specialty. East Cambridge is a desolate urban landscape filled with housing projects, MIT, the NECCO candy company, and Polaroid. We were hopelessly underfunded; there are only so many different things you can cook with government surplus flour, cheese, and lard; we'd run the gamut of pretzels, pancakes, and pizzas by the second week. I supplemented the foodstuffs, but on fifty dollars a week I had little extra cash. We spent a lot of time singing and dancing on the enormous steel tables – the basement kitchen was cool and had a radio. The kids asked questions: Did I have a mother? Where did God go at night? Why was my nose so big? The usual philosophical inquiries of children. But this was camp and we needed something to do.

So we decided to approach the neighborhood corporations for help. NECCO arranged a tour of the factory. Each kid brought home a Sky Bar (my favorite candy bar as a kid) and a roll of pastel-colored sugar discs wrapped in translucent paper. Polaroid unloaded about ten of their new line of 'Swinger' cameras (cheap plastic cameras designed for children) and some film. I took the kids, aged four to eight, into our neighborhood to shoot pictures. The immediacy of the Polaroids was exhilarating but so was the ambition of the kids' projects. They began experimenting with overshooting, jamming the camera so the film would double expose, scratching and marking over the images as they congealed, and collage, cutting them up with other pictures. The work was extraordinary; but, as with the limited menu, we had no money to buy more film once the original stock was gone. The cameras were junk too; they barely lasted the summer. One of the pictures was taken by an eight-year-old boy of his brother, a sweet-faced kid, emerging out of the bars surrounding the concrete schoolyard. It is a poignant depiction of dreams and freedom and of the prison-like quality of this institution of learning. He gave it to me to keep and remember him by. I thought I'd never forget, so I never wrote his name down. Of course I forgot. But I have the picture. It is with this amateur snapshot documenting a boy's summer vacation – his brother, his school and day camp, his neighborhood and his enormous imagination – that I want to conclude this volume (Figure 22).

The pictures these children shot come from the largest group of those who must be represented: children. Children hold no social, economic, or political status in our culture. They are despised, ignored, abused, and condescended to even as they figure among the stock pieties cherished in the popular imagination.[1] As a child I had always felt badly treated, not because I had a brutal childhood – my parents were generous, loving, adventuresome and, as we traveled up through the middle class with America's post-war prosperity, financially secure – but because I was so irrelevant. Now, as the mother of two sons, I bristle at the continual insults they suffer whenever their presence intrudes on the exclusive world of adults in shops, restaurants, theaters, sidewalks. Children are expected to remain in restricted zones – schools, playgrounds – fenced in and under supervision.

Ever a poignant subject for photographers as diverse as Lewis Carroll and Jacqueline Livingston (not to mention the countless mothers, fathers, aunts, and uncles at birthdays and beaches), children rarely represent their views with the technologies of still or moving or video cameras. A number of artists have given children a chance to shoot back at the world. Most notably, Jim Hubbard has traveled the country holding workshops for poor children. Their photographs have been collected and displayed in exhibits and coffee table catalogues, occasionally appearing on the op-ed page of *The New York Times*. When avant-garde film-maker James Benning bought his daughter, Sadie, a Fisher-Price video camera for her sixteenth birthday, he enabled her to delve into her experiences as a young lesbian growing up in Milwaukee. Locked in the privacy of her room, like so many teenage girls, daily charting her feelings, Benning's video diaries (such as *Jollies*, which has won prizes in numerous festivals) push the limits of this child's toy into a new form of documentary artistry.[2] My own brief venture helping children walk through their world armed with a camera gave me a sense of the power inhering in that tool. A camera is a weapon; it claims authority.

This book has explored a wide variety of attempts by and for those locked out of the house of representatives, those who must be represented – workers, migrants, poor people, women, gays, African Americans, Latinos – to enter the houses of representation. It has shown this to be a complex process involving negotiations across class, racial, gender, and sexual borders as individuals find their private lives invaded by the spectacle of public outrages and then seek to illuminate political problems through personal explorations. I have tried to write a book that would be of interest to film-makers, photographers and journalists, scholars and activists, critics and artists. The cases I have outlined have focused on questions of agency and representation. Who is speaking? For whom? To whom? About what? Those who cannot represent themselves and so must be represented have been historically dispossessed. One can read this admonition – they must – as a declaration of failure: because *they* cannot speak for themselves; *we* must do it for them. Or perhaps it is a plea for recognition: because *they* have not been heard; *we* must listen. It is this doubled and contradictory sense that I have tried to bring out in this book.

I notice as I write this that I have shifted from a language of images to a rhetoric of speech. After having explored the various forms of visualization that have been the core of the documentary project for at least one hundred years, the question of voice now appears central to me, which is why I begin this book with Claude Lanzmann's *Shoah*, a memorial of and to the human voice and conclude with the case of *California* v. *Powell et al.* In reality, those who must be represented have, in so many ways, been overexposed, inspected endlessly.

These essays range across time; each uses the rhetorics of gender and history as tools to unravel the knotty questions of class formation, popular culture, nationalism, race and ethnicity, family structure, sexuality and work in twentieth-century America, questions central to the work of documentary in the age of mass media. I hope the book will be of value to progressives as we struggle to leave behind the terrible legacies of this century. By analyzing the work of documentary in and for movements working for social, political, and economic justice, I have tried to point out how the subjects of historical agency called forth by documentary can become the objects of left-wing intellectuals' desires. As Isaac Julian remarks:

> There's always this tension if one wants to comment on the way documentary films are constructed, but then the way your subject is positioned with that text, is a problem. Then there is the extra, what I would call the burden of representation – making films about subjects that have not been given voice – that you face in relationship to trying to give that subject in some way its own voice without it being the 'authentic' voice.[3]

The limits of documentary form are to be found within this tension, a tension I would argue central to any revolutionary politics: how to critique and deconstruct the present and simultaneously imagine and prefigure a future without doing violence to the past; how to sketch a poetics of politics and a politics of poetry simultaneously. The representation of politics practiced by documentary address is also about the politics of representation, as objects of inspection become subjects of action. Inevitably this book, too, exhibits its own gaps and tensions, but, unlike Jill Godmilow, who at the conclusion of *Far From Poland* lists all the issues her film neglected, I leave them unvoiced. Not just 'one more thing,' but many more things must be said. I listen attentively.

Notes

Introduction

1 See Barbara Foley, *Telling the Truth: The Theory and Practice of Documentary Fiction* (Ithaca, NY: Cornell University Press 1986).

2 Much ink has been spilled on this vexed topic. I suggest people look at Bruce Robbins, *Secular Vocations: Intellectuals, Professionalism, Culture* (London: Verso 1993); Nancy Armstrong and Leonard Tennenhouse, *The Imaginary Puritan* (Berkeley: University of California Press 1992); Alan Wald, *The New York Intellectuals* (Chapel Hill, NC: University North Carolina Press 1985); Andrew Ross, *No Respect: Intellectuals and Popular Culture* (New York: Routledge 1989) for historical and theoretical models I find useful.

3 'The Writings of Dziga Vertov,' *Film Culture Reader*, ed. P. Adams Sitney (New York: Praeger 1970), pp. 370, 362.

4 See Trinh T. Minh-ha, *Reassemblage* (1980) for an ethnographic film that interrogates the process of visual anthropology. Her book *Woman, Native, Other: Writing Postcoloniality and Feminism* (Bloomington: Indiana University Press 1989), expounds a theory of ethnographic work as a conversation by Western men about themselves.

5 Paul Rotha, with Sinclair Road and Richard Griffith, *Documentary Film*, 3rd edition (London: Faber & Faber 1952), p. 199.

Chapter 1

1 Walter Benjamin, 'Theses on the Philosophy of History,' *Illuminations*, ed. and intro. by Hannah Arendt, trans. Harry Zohn (New York: Schocken 1969), p. 257.

2 *Memory of the Camps* (Great Britain, 1985), Executive Producer, Sidney Bernstein; Producer, Sergei Nolbandov; Treatment Adviser, Alfred Hitchcock. For more on this moving film, see Annette Innsdorf, *Indelible Shadows: Film and the Holocaust*, 2nd edition (Cambridge: Cambridge University Press 1989).

3 Martha Rosler, 'in, around, and afterthoughts (on documentary photography),' in *Three Works* (Halifax: Nova Scotia College of Art and Design 1981), p. 82.

4 Benjamin called for writers to pick up the camera in order to instruct photographers on the importance of verbally contextualizing an image. The sequence of images in a film serves to caption the images by linking them temporally and so inevitably sculpting a narrative. See 'A Short History of Photography,' *Germany: The New Photography, 1927–33*, ed. David Mellor (London: Arts Council of Great Britain 1978), pp. 60–76; and 'The Author as Producer,' *Reflections: Essays, Aphorisms, Autobiographical*

Writings, ed. Peter Demetz, trans. Edmund Jephcott (New York: Harcourt, Brace, Jovanovich 1978), pp. 220–38. Susan Sontag echoes Benjamin's discussion in *On Photography* (New York: Farrar, Strauss and Giroux 1977) and anticipates Rosler's pithy remark when she describes 'what no photograph can ever do – speak' (p. 108).

5 John Grierson, unsigned review of *Moana, New York Sun*, 8 February 1926. Reprinted in Lewis Jacobs, *The Documentary Tradition*, 2nd edition (New York: W.W. Norton & Co. 1979), p. 25.

6 'The Writings of Dziga Vertov,' *Film Culture* 25 (1962): 50–60, pp. 60, 52.

7 Dziga Vertov, 'From Kino-Eye to Radio-Eye' and 'Kino-Eye,' in *Kino-Eye: The Writings of Dziga Vertov*, ed. Annette Michelson, trans. Kevin O'Brien (Berkeley: University of California Press 1984), pp. 87–8 and p. 67.

8 This is from an early Lumière program, reproduced in Georges Sadoul, *Histoire Générale du Cinéma*, revised edition, vol. 1 (Paris: Donoël 1973), p. 290, and quoted in Stephen Heath, 'Technology as Historical and Cultural Form,' in *The Cinematic Apparatus*, ed. Teresa de Lauretis and Stephen Heath (New York: St Martin's Press 1980), p. 1.

9 Georges Sadoul, *French Film* (London: The Falcon Press 1958), pp. 2–4.

10 See Lisa Cartwright, *Physiological Modernism: Scientific Cinema and the Technologies of 'Life'* (Minneapolis: University of Minnesota Press forthcoming).

11 For the London sequence in *Bram Stoker's Dracula*, Coppola used a Pathé camera to recreate the visual sensation of an early cinematograph. See Manohla Dargis, 'His Bloody Valentine' (interview with Coppola), *Village Voice*, 24 November 1992, p. 66.

12 Clearly, these early examples rely solely on the image to communicate; however, it would be impossible to consider the didactic functions of the documentary film without understanding the importance of sound technologies to its purpose.

13 Karl G. Heider, *Ethnographic Film* (Austin: University of Texas 1976) is the classic of its field. His injunction to shoot 'whole bodies and whole peoples in whole acts' summed up the prevailing ideas about ethnographic film-making for at least half a century (p. 125).

14 'The documentary film was founded on the Western middle-class need to explore, document, explain, understand, and hence symbolically control the world. It has been what "we" do to "them".' Jay Ruby, 'The Image Mirrored: Reflexivity and the Documentary Film,' in *New Challenges for Documentary*, ed. Alan Rosenthal (Berkeley: University of California Press 1988), p. 71. See also Trinh T. Minh-ha's work: *Reassemblage* (1982); and *Naked Spaces – Living is Round* (1985) as well as *Woman/Native/Other* (Bloomington: Indiana University Press 1989), especially chapter 2, 'The Language of Nativism: Anthropology as a Scientific Conversation of Man with Man,' and 'Outside In Inside Out,' in *Questions of Third Cinema*, ed. Jim Pines and Paul Willemen (London: British Film Institute 1988).

15 These terms are often used interchangeably; however, Eric Barnouw, *Documentary: A History of the Non-Fiction Film* (New York: Oxford 1974) distinguishes between the American objectivist cinema of Drew Associates, Richard Leacock, D.A. Pennebaker, and the Maysles by referring to it as living cinema (Leacock's name) or direct cinema, to distinguish it from the more interventionist film-making of the French director, Jean Rouch. See also Louis Marcorelles, *Living Cinema: New Directions in Contemporary Film-making*, trans. Isabel Quigly, (New York: Praeger Books 1973); and Stephen Mamber, *Cinéma Vérité in America: Studies in Uncontrolled Documentary* (Cambridge, MA: MIT Press 1974). I take up the politics of *cinéma vérité* in chapter 6.

16 For a complete history of the making and censoring of Wiseman's film, see Carolyn Anderson and Thomas W. Benson, *Documentary Dilemmas: Frederick Wiseman's Titicut Follies* (Carbondale, IL: Southern Illinois University Press 1991).

17 In one of television's ever-present self-referential moments, this became a subject of an episode of *Civil Wars*. A team of documentary film-makers traces the proceedings of an 'amicable' divorce, follows the law partners around, exposing their foibles and intrudes into the negotiations until it becomes apparent that each party is furious at the other and Mariel Hemingway stops the film by placing her hand over the lens.

18 For a thorough discussion of the expectations and limitations of direct cinema through a dissection of *Primary*, see Jeanne Hall, 'Realism as a Style in *Cinéma Vérité*: A

Critical Analysis of *Primary*,' *Cinema Journal* 30 (Summer 1991), 24–50. In an interview, co-editor Ellen Hovde describes the two Edie Beales of *Grey Gardens* (1975) as 'very flamboyant, very theatrical, very funny, in the midst of a crisis.' Alan Rosenthal, ed., *The Documentary Conscience: A Casebook in Film Making* (Berkeley: University of California Press 1980), p. 376.

19 Of course, some women were editors also, including Ellen Hovde; see Rosenthal, *Documentary Conscience*, p. 374.

20 ' "The illiteracy of the future," someone has said, "will be ignorance not of reading or writing, but of photography." But must not a photographer who cannot read his own pictures be no less accounted an illiterate? Will not the caption become the most important part of the photograph?' Walter Benjamin, 'A Short History of Photography,' in Mellor, p. 75.

21 Bill Nichols, *Representing Reality* (Bloomington: Indiana University Press 1991), p. 265. Bill Nichols's *Representing Reality*, one of the few book-length theoretical studies of documentary film since Barnouw's classic, begins with a taxonomy, for all genre studies begin here, by examining its 'modes of representation,' i.e. how a film tells its story and makes its argument. To some degree, his four types correspond chronologically to the development of documentary: expository employs the classic voice-of-God narration; observational minimizes the film-maker's presence; interactive presents the film-maker actively engaged with his/her subject; and reflexive draws attention to the construction of the film. Other studies would include: Jack C. Ellis, *The Documentary Idea: A Critical History of English-Language Film and Video* (Englewood Cliffs, NJ: Prentice Hall 1989); and William Guynn, *A Cinema of Nonfiction* (Rutherford, NJ: Associated University Presses 1990). There are dozens of collections and anthologies of essays about documentary; in addition to those already cited, two of the most relevant to this book are Michael Renov, ed., *Theorizing Documentary* (New York: Routledge 1993) and Thomas Waugh, ed., *'Show Us Life': Towards a History and Aesthetic of the Committed Documentary* (Metuchen, NJ: The Scarecrow Press 1984).

22 For instance, see John Marshall's films about the !Kung, particularly, *N!ai: The Story of a !Kung Woman* (1980) as well as the work of Sol Worth and John Adair with Navajo film-makers from the 1966 series *Navajos Film Themselves*, reported in Worth and Adair, *Through Navajo Eyes: An Experiment in Film Communication and Anthropology* (Bloomington: Indiana University Press 1972). In 1968, Canada's National Film Board instituted its Challenges for Change/*Société Nouvelle* project under the direction of Colin Low to disseminate film technologies to indigenous populations throughout the nation.

23 Reprinted in Bill Nichols, ed., *Movies and Methods* (Berkeley: University of California Press 1976), pp. 44–64 and translated into a dozen languages.

24 During the 1960s, in the United States, a movement for politically engaged cinema coalesced in the Newsreel collectives, whose logo was a pixilated image of a movie camera and a machine gun shooting the audience. Begun by a number of New Left film-makers such as Robert Kramer to bring the struggles of oppressed people (African-Americans, Vietnamese) into view to counter the classic 'objective news format,' the internal dynamics of these collectives quickly established a division of labor between experts (usually white men with professional experience) and their assistants – women and minorities. As those at the bottom of the production crews demanded training and access to equipment to film their own struggles, the groups often split and eventually Third World Newsreel emerged to sponsor films by and about self-determination movements and struggles globally. See Bill Nichols, 'Newsreel Film and Revolution,' *Cineaste* 5, no. 4 (1973): 7–13; Michael Renov, 'The Imaging of Analysis: Newsreel's Re-Search for a Radical Film Practice,' *Wide Angle* 6, no. 3 (1984): 76–82; John Hess, 'Notes on U.S. Radical Film, 1967–80,' *Jump Cut* 21 (1979): 31–5; and David E. James, *Allegories of Cinema: American Film in the Sixties* (Princeton, NJ: Princeton University Press 1989).

25 Ana M. Lopez, '*The Battle of Chile*: Documentary, Political Process, and Representation,' in *The Social Documentary in Latin America*, ed. Julianne Burton (Pittsburgh: University of Pittsburgh Press 1990), p. 274.

26 Guzman, quoted in Lopez, p. 274.

27 Compare this with the description D.A. Pennebaker gives of the 'script' of *Don't Look Back* (1967): 'This is not the script from which *Don't Look Back* was made. The film was made without a script. This is simply a transcript of what happened and what was said . . . . This is only a record of what happened.' Pennebaker's introduction to the Ballantine book of his film, quoted in Marcorelles, p. 25.

28 Bill Nichols, *Representing Reality*, p. 142.

29 Fredric Jameson, *The Political Unconscious: Narrative as Socially Symbolic Act* (Ithaca, NY: Cornell University Press 1981), p. 35.

30 The term comes from David Bordwell, Janet Staiger, and Kristin Thompson, *The Classical Hollywood Cinema: Film Style and Mode of Production to 1960* (New York: Columbia University Press 1985). Christian Metz systemized the analysis of narrative cinema. Psychoanalytic semiotics has been crucial to much feminist film theorizing. See Laura Mulvey, Kaja Silverman, Teresa de Lauretis, Mary Ann Doane, Constance Penley among many others, all discussed in chapter 7.

31 For a history of US-sponsored films, see Richard Dyer MacCann, *The People's Films: A Political History of U.S. Government Motion Pictures* (New York: Hastings House 1973). During the 1930s, radical film-makers in America organized film cooperatives to produce and distribute films about working-class solidarity and anti-fascism. See William Alexander, *Film on the Left: American Documentary Film from 1931 to 1942* (Princeton, NJ: Princeton University Press 1981) and Russell Campbell, *Cinema Strikes Back: Radical Filmmaking in the United States, 1930–1942* (Ann Arbor, MI: UMI Research Press 1982). I take this up at length in chapter 4.

32 Ruth McCormick, review of *Union Maids*, in *Cineaste* 8 (1977): 51. I discuss these critiques in chapter 8.

33 Dan Georgakas, 'Malpractice in the Radical American Documentary: The Good, the Careless, and the Misconceived,' *Cineaste* 16 (1987–88): 46–9, p. 49.

34 See, for example, Noel King, 'Recent "Political" Documentary: Notes on *Union Maids* and *Harlan County, USA*,' *Screen* 22 (1981): 7–18.

35 Renee Shafransky, '*Seeing Red*: An Interview with James Klein and Julia Reichert,' and *Seeing Red*, a film review by Dan Georgakas, *Cineaste* 8 (1984): 24–8. See also Jeffrey Youdelman, 'Narration, Invention, History,' in *Cineaste* 7 (1982): 8–15, rpt. in *New Challenges for Documentary*, ed. Alan Rosenthal (Berkeley: University of California Press 1988), pp. 454–64 for an historical overview of didacticism in leftist documentary film-making.

36 Julia LeSage makes this point persuasively when she argues that women's political documentaries used the female talking head for a number of strategic political reasons: to challenge the use of the female body on screen with the female voice; to re-enact the consciousness-raising experience of speaking bitterness; to incorporate the audience into a collective. Julia LeSage, 'The Political Aesthetics of the Feminist Documentary Film,' *Quarterly Review of Film Studies* 3 (Fall 1978): 507–24. See also E. Ann Kaplan, 'Theories and Strategies of the Feminist Documentary,' and Patricia Erens, 'Women's Documentary Filmmaking: The Personal is Political,' in Rosenthal, *New Challenges* for additional defenses of the feminist uses of women as talking heads.

37 Sonya Michel, 'Feminism, Film and Public History,' *Radical History Review* 25 (1981): 47–61.

38 The best account of the theory of testimony as historical witness in *Shoah* appears in Shoshana Felman, 'The Return of the Voice: Claude Lanzmann's *Shoah*,' in Shoshana Felman and Dori Laub, *Testimony: Crises of Witnessing in Literature, Psychoanalysis and History* (New York: Routledge 1992), pp. 204–83.

39 After the publication of Jean-Claude Pressac's book documenting the Auschwitz gas chambers, *The Auschwitz Crematoria: The Machinery of Mass Slaughter*, an enraged Lanzmann challenged the desire for objective documentary proof in the form of archival items (letters, bills of sale, architectural plans) from the holocaust. These calls for proof discount the stories of survivors and in effect 'legitimate the arguments of revisionists, who become the point of reference for future debate. I prefer the tears of the barber from Treblinka in *Shoah* to a Pressac document on gas detectors.' Quoted in Roger

Cohen, 'Book on Nazi Murder Industry Stirs French Storm,' *New York Times*, 28 October 1993, p. A3.

40 Lenny Rubinstein, veteran documentary film-maker, accuses Lanzmann of making a film 'far too long, too visually dull and marked by Lanzmann's singularly unpleasant efforts at being an incisive interviewer.' He feels that Lanzmann indulges in 'guilt-slinging' in his interviews with the Poles and submits the Jews to excessive 'stress.' He finds little new information disclosed by the film for anyone already knowledgeable about the holocaust and doubts that the 'deadening monotony' of the visuals will help educate others. '*Shoah*,' *Cineaste* 14(3) (1986): 39–41. It is not that I disagree with Rubenstein's assessment, but I feel Lanzmann was fully cognisant of these criticisms and precisely wanted to foreground them. His style became a critique of documentary; his film its last word. For a discussion of the effects of the length and of the different venues for showing the film, see Thomas Doherty, 'Representing the Holocaust: Claude Lanzmann's *Shoah*,' *Film and History* 17 (February 1987): 2–8.

41 Claude Lanzmann, *Shoah: An Oral History of the Holocaust* (New York: Pantheon 1985), pp. 141–2. All quotations from the film are from this edition.

42 All quotations are from a public lecture by Claude Lanzmann at the University of Minnesota, Minneapolis, MN, 2 April 1990.

43 Jill Godmilow, 'Far From Finished: Deconstructing the Documentary, An Interview by Brooke Jacobson,' in *Reimagining America: The Arts of Social Change*, ed. Mark O'Brien and Craig Little (Philadelphia: New Society Publishers 1990), p. 181. I discuss Godmilow's film at length in chapter 8.

44 Godmilow, p. 180 (emphasis in original).

45 Walter Benjamin, 'Theses on the Philosophy of History,' p. 255.

46 The focus of *Shoah* is exclusively on the extermination camps designed to fulfill the Final Solution through the words of those who saw what happened to the Jews murdered in the camps located in Poland. Thus the film also looks at the ways in which Poles had aided or evaded the Nazis' project. The overwhelming number of survivors were male; women, especially women with children, were much more likely to be killed immediately on arrival at a death camp, thus women's voices are barely present. Lanzmann's focus on Jewish victims of the Nazis does not suggest that others – gypsies, gays, communists – were not also victims; instead, his focus is on the particular history of European anti-Semitism aimed at eliminating an entire population.

Shoah is, in many ways, a critique of the powerful documentary film by Alain Resnais, *Night and Fog*, which indiscriminately collapses the differences between concentration camps, slave labor camps, and extermination camps as it evokes horror through visuals with a voice-over full of guilt and remorse. At the time it was made, 1955, and even now, Resnais's film set the tone for documentaries about the holocaust.

Chapter 2

1 For more on this, see Carolyn Kay Steedman, *Landscape for a Good Woman: A Story of Two Lives* (New Brunswick, NJ: Rutgers University Press 1987). Her readings of the stories provided by the watercress girl in Henry Mayhew's *London Labour and the London Poor* and of Freud's Dora from 'Fragments of an Analysis' (pp. 128–139) point to the differences and similarities between 'documents' and 'case studies' and what this means for class and gender relations.

2 James Agee and Walker Evans, *Let Us Now Praise Famous Men* (Boston: Houghton Mifflin 1960), p. xiv. All further references to the book will occur in the text.

3 Trinh T. Minh-ha, *Woman, Native, Other: Writing Postcoloniality and Feminism* (Bloomington: Indiana University Press 1989), p. 65.

4 Georg Lukács, *History and Class Consciousness*, trans. Rodney Livingstone (Cambridge, MA: MIT Press 1968), pp. 164–6 (emphasis added). Lukács is referring to Marx's 'Fetishism of Commodities and the Secrets Therein,' in which he indicates the relationship between commodities is shrouded in the 'mist-enveloped region' that

obscures the social relations among men into that of a relationship between things, in a manner wholly unlike that of vision, which entails a connection between the subjective experience of light exciting the optic nerve and the objective properties of the object emitting its light (*Capital* v.1 [Chicago: Charles Kerr & Co. 1906], p. 83).

5 Lukács, pp. 100, 122.

6 Lukács, p. 197.

7 A few years later, the German Workers' Photography Movement launched the first inexpensive mass magazine of photos and text to promote a 'proletarian eye' with which to counter bourgeois control of representation in both 'art' and 'industrial' photography. Their journal 'proclaim[ed] proletarian reality in all its disgusting ugliness, with its indictment of society and its demand for revenge.' Yet, editor Edwin Hoernle acknowledged that few workers could see in any other way than through the lenses of bourgeois perception. Edwin Hoernle, 'The Working Man's Eye,' in *Germany: The New Photography, 1927–33*, ed. David Mellor (London: Arts Council of Great Britain 1978), pp. 48–9.

8 See Steedman, pp. 12–15 for more on Lukács's (and Marx's) failure to register class consciousness as a psychological process that begins in childhood.

9 Martha Rosler, 'in, around and afterthoughts (on documentary photography),' *Three Works* (Halifax: Nova Scotia College of Art and Design 1981), p. 82.

10 Sigmund Freud, *The Standard Edition of the Complete Psychological Works*, trans. and ed. James Strachey, vol. 10 (London: Hogarth Press 1955), p. 160.

11 Freud, *SE* 10: 245.

12 Freud, *SE* 16: 369.

13 We might also think about his discussion of the 'Family Romances,' *SE* 9: 236–41. Here, the desire on the part of the older child to reinstate the exalted parental figures of early childhood takes the form of debasing the parents – particularly the father – and in boys entails imagining a new father of higher economic and political status who was a lover of the mother and thus is the real father.

14 See Rachel Bowlby, *Just Looking: Consumer Culture in Dreiser, Gissing and Zola* (New York: Routledge 1985), chapter 2 for more on this connection.

15 Laura Mulvey's now classic declaration: 'Sadism demands a story' has been revised by Teresa de Lauretis to read 'and a story demands sadism.' Each theory of narrative argues that the desire mobilized in narrative (cinema) is always at the expense of someone. Laura Mulvey, 'Visual Pleasure and Narrative Cinema,' *Screen* 16 (Autumn 1975): 3–16; and Teresa de Lauretis, 'Desire in Narrative,' *Alice Doesn't* (Bloomington: Indiana University Press 1984).

16 Michael Hiley, *Victorian Working Women: Portraits from Life* (Boston: David Godine, Publisher 1979), p. 72.

17 Hiley, pp. 91–2. 17.

18 Trilling, 'Greatness with One Fault in It,' *Kenyon Review* 4:1 (Winter 1942): 99–100.

19 John Roger Puckett, *Five Photo-Textual Documentaries from the Great Depression* (Ann Arbor, MI: UMI Press 1984). The photo-textual form was enabled by technological advances in printing and was indebted to the popularity of *Life* magazine, which following its 1936 inauguration, spawned numerous imitators.

20 F. Jack Hurley, *Portrait of a Decade: Roy Stryker and the Development of Documentary Photography in the Thirties* (Baton Rouge: Louisiana State University Press 1972), p. 70.

21 Walker Evans, handwritten draft memo to Stryker, 1935, in *Walker Evans at Work* (New York: Harper & Row 1982), p. 112.

22 See Maren Stange, *Symbols of Ideal Life: Social Documentary Photography in America, 1890–1950* (Cambridge: Cambridge University Press 1989) especially chapters 3 and 4 for a persuasive analysis of this process.

23 Walter Benjamin, 'A Short History of Photography,' in Mellor, pp. 69–76.

24 See, for instance, Newton Arvin, 'A Letter on Proletarian Literature,' *Partisan Review* 3 (February 1936): 12–14. E.A. Schachner, 'Revolutionary Literature in the United States Today,' *Windsor Quarterly* 2 (Spring 1934): 27–64.

25 Barbara Foley has made this point effectively in a paper presented at the Midwest MLA Convention 1988, entitled 'Marxist Critics of the 1930s and Bourgeois Aesthetic

Theory,' and incorporated into her book *Radical Representations: Politics and Form in US Proletarian Fiction, 1929–1941* (Durham, NC: Duke University Press 1993).

26 Reprinted in Charlotte Nekola and Paula Rabinowitz, eds., *Writing Red: An Anthology of American Women Writers, 1930–1940* (New York: The Feminist Press 1987), pp. 203–14. See Charlotte Nekola, 'Worlds Unseen: Political Women Journalists and the 1930s,' in *Writing Red*, pp. 189–98 for more detail.

27 Georg Lukács, 'Reportage or Portrayal?' (1932), reprinted in *Essays on Realism*, ed. Rodney Livingston, trans. David Fernbach (Cambridge, MA: MIT Press 1981), p. 49.

28 Lukács, p. 49.

29 Walter Benjamin, 'The Author as Producer,' *Reflections*, ed. Peter Demetz (New York: Harcourt, Brace, Jovanovich 1978), pp. 229, 231.

30 Robert Warshow, 'The Legacy of the Thirties,' *The Immediate Experience* (Garden City, NY: Doubleday 1962), p. 38.

31 See Andrew Ross, *No Respect: Intellectuals and Popular Culture* (New York: Routledge 1989) chapter 1 for more on this.

32 See Miles Orvell, *The Real Thing* (Chapel Hill, NC: University of North Carolina Press 1990), especially the last chapter.

33 For an astute explanation of the 'postmodernist realism' of Evans's and Agee's project, see T.V. Reed, 'Unimagined Existence and the Fiction of the Real: Postmodernist Realism in *Let Us Now Praise Famous Men*,' *Representations* 24 (1988): 156–76.

34 William Stott, *Documentary Expression and Thirties America*, 1973 rpt (Chicago: University of Chicago Press 1986), p. 266.

35 For an elaboration on the gendered implications of the dread of mixing genres, see Jacques Derrida, 'The Law of Genre,' *Glyph* 7 (1982): 202–32.

36 Jacqueline Rose, *Sexuality In the Field of Vision* (London: Verso 1986), p. 51.

37 'The fixing of language and the fixing of sexual identity go hand in hand; they rely on each other and share the same forms of instability and risk.' Rose, p. 228.

38 Agee was not unaware of the homoerotic elements both in his life and his text. While completing the manuscript, he and his second wife, Alma Mailman, the working-class Jewish protégée of his ex-father-in-law, conceived a child. Agee instigated a 'romantic liaison' between Alma and Walker Evans, eventually leading to a sexual encounter which Agee insisted on watching, after which he wrote to Evans that he was 'sorry and contemptuous of myself. However much . . . you happen to like each other, good: I am enough of an infant homosexual or postdostoevskian to be glad. However much you don't, that's all right too: I am enough of a "man" not to care to think particularly whether I care or not.' Laurence Bergreen, *James Agee: A Life* (New York: E.P. Dutton 1984), p. 239. It would appear that all the elements Freud discerned in the Rat Man's case – anxiety over his homoerotic desire for his father and for his father's liaison with a woman of lower-class status resulting in the desire to visually penetrate the mystery of sexual difference – were put into play here by Agee. For a theoretical and textual analysis of the homoerotics of male collaboration, see Wayne Koestenbaum, *Double Talk: The Erotics of Male Literary Collaboration* (New York: Routledge 1989).

39 See Susan R. Suleiman, *Authoritarian Fictions* (New York: Columbia University Press 1983) on the dual pulls of 'ideological fiction' which are akin to documentary reportage.

40 Paul Goodman, 'Review,' *Partisan Review* 9 (Jan.–Feb. 1942): 86.

41 Ruth Lechlitner, 'Alabama Tenant Families,' *New York Herald Tribune Books*, 24 August, 1941: 10.

42 Benjamin, 'A Short History of Photography,' pp. 70–71.

43 Benjamin, p. 75.

44 See John Berger and Jean Mohr, *Another Way of Telling* (New York: Pantheon 1982) for a contemporary meditation on the problem of disclosing the lives of peasant communities through images composed by (sympathetic) intellectuals. 'A photograph quotes from appearances, but in quoting simplifies them,' p. 119.

45 For an elaboration of this idea, see Charles Wolfe, 'Direct Address and the Social Documentary Photograph: "Annie Mae Gudger" as Negative Subject,' *Wide Angle* 9 (1987): 59–70.

46 See John Hersey, 'Introduction,' p. vii. See two recent examples: Miles Orvell, *The Real Thing*, which argues that *Let Us Now Praise Famous Men* culminates a modernist search for authenticity; and T.V. Reed, 'Unimagined Existence and the Fiction of the Real,' which argues that Agee and Evans commence a postmodernist search for a political form of narrative.

47 Howell Raines, 'Let Us Now Revisit Famous Folk,' *New York Times Magazine* 25 May 1980: 31–46. Scott Osbourne, 'A Walker Evans Heroine Remembers,' *American Photographer* (September 1979): 70–73, 'Let Us Now Praise Famous Men – Revisited,' *The American Experience 109*, WGBH Educational Foundation, 29 November 1988.

48 Dale Maharidge and Michael Williamson, *And Their Children After Them, The Legacy of Let Us Now Praise Famous Men: James Agee, Walker Evans, and the Rise and Fall of Cotton in the South* (New York: Pantheon 1989).

49 See Martha Rosler, 'in, around, and afterthoughts (on documentary photography),' for an extensive unpacking of the issues involved in exposing documentary to a political critique.

50 This legend is also specious; where Agee discloses the ways he rummaged through the meager possessions of the Gudgers, implying that Evans was somehow purer by simply photographing what was there in view, Agee's descriptions, presumably of what he is seeing, are at odds with Evans's images. James Curtis argues persuasively that while Agee was opening drawers, Evans was rearranging furniture and objects into their classic poses. See James Curtis, *Mind's Eye, Mind's Truth* (Philadelphia: Temple University Press 1989).

Chapter 3

1 See Joan Wallach Scott, 'Gender: A Useful Category of Historical Analysis,' in *Gender and the Politics of History* (New York: Columbia University Press 1988), p. 42: 'gender is a constitutive element of social relationships based on perceived differences between the sexes, and gender is a primary way of signifying relationships of power.' In 'The Technology of Gender,' de Lauretis asserts: 'The construction of gender is both the product and the process of its representation.' Teresa de Lauretis, *Technologies of Gender: Essays on Theory, Film, Fiction* (Bloomington: Indiana University Press 1988), p. 5. However Judith Butler, *Gender Trouble: Feminism and the Subversion of Identity* (New York: Routledge 1990), challenges these perspectives by suggesting that although they see gender as a signifying practice, they still rely on foundationalist assumptions about subjectivity. 'Gender,' she says, 'proves to be performative – that is, constituting the identity it is purported to be. In this sense, gender is always a doing, though not a doing by a subject who might be said to preexist the deed' (p. 25).

2 Karl Marx, *The Eighteenth Brumaire of Louis Bonaparte* (New York: International Publishers 1963), p. 124.

3 Antonio Gramsci, 'The Philosophy of Praxis,' in *Selections from the Prison Notebooks*, trans. Quentin Hoare (New York: International Publishers 1971), p. 324.

4 For a discussion of a contemporary encounter between working-class female poets and a middle-class female critic, see Maria Damon, ' "Tell Them about Us",' *Cultural Critique* 14 (Winter 1989–90): 231–57, in which Damon introduces poetry by three young women living in south Boston during the 1970s busing crisis. Here is how one of the D Street writers describes their situation: 'We're watching ourselves watching you watching us, we look at ourselves *through* you' (p. 253, emphasis in original).

5 Denise Riley, *'Am I That Name?': The Category of 'Women' in History* (Minneapolis: University of Minnesota Press 1988); and Linda Gordon, 'Family Violence, Feminism and Social Control,' in *Women, The State and Welfare* (Madison: University of Wisconsin Press 1990), pp. 178–98 argue that during the nineteenth century in both Britain and the United States the realm of the social was created by and for middle-class women's supervision. Nancy Armstrong, *Desire and Domestic Fiction: A Political History of the Novel*

(New York: Oxford University Press 1987), explains how this supervisory role was encoded and produced through literary forms developed in eighteenth-century Britain.

6 I consider this a companion piece to the previous chapter in which I theorize the implications of cross-gender and cross-class looking. In 'Voyeurism and Class Consciousness,' I look in detail at *Let Us Now Praise Famous Men* for clues to the history of specular relations. These I take to be founded on a classed sexuality which empowers bourgeois men to regard poor women as embodiments of sex/knowledge.

7 Virginia Woolf, *A Room of One's Own* (New York: Harcourt, Brace and Co. 1929), pp. 113, 107.

8 This is Gramsci's term for the intellectuals whose function it is to maintain order and hegemony for the ruling class, in contradistinction to 'organic intellectuals' who rise from within the subaltern classes to forge revolutionary movements. See Antonio Gramsci, 'The Intellectuals,' in *Selections from the Prison Notebooks*, trans. Quentin Hoare (New York: International Publishers 1971), pp. 3–23.

9 Margaret Bourke-White described herself as a foreigner, as did journalist and Smith College graduate, Lauren Gilfillan, whose book-length account of her life among striking coal miners, *I Went to Pit College* (New York: Literary Guild 1934), outlined the limits of middle-class women's ability to enter the lives of the working class. See my discussion of this work in *Labor and Desire* (Chapel Hill, NC: University of North Carolina Press 1991).

10 This scene can be found in Caroline Slade's *Triumph of Willie Pond* (New York: Vanguard Press 1940), and in Ruth McKenney's *Industrial Valley* (New York: Harcourt, Brace and Co. 1939), as well as in Martha Gellhorn's *Trouble I've Seen* (New York: William Morrow 1936). Variations can be found in Marita Bonner's story, 'The Whipping,' of how a young black mother is jailed for murdering her son after relief fails to help her feed him; and Meridel LeSueur's story, 'Sequel to Love,' which reveals how the state invades the reproductive bodies of young women, in Charlotte Nekola and Paula Rabinowitz, eds., *Writing Red: An Anthology of American Women Writers, 1930–1940* (New York: The Feminist Press 1987). Slade was a prominent social worker whose novels often criticized the welfare institutions for which she worked. *Willie Pond* damns the logic of ADC (Aid to Dependent Children, the precursor to AFDC), the result of which is that an unemployed father is more valuable to a family dead than alive. McKenney's account of Akron, Ohio during the Depression contrasts ineffectual social services with militant Unemployed Councils and industrial unions.

11 Fielding Burke [Olive Tilford Dargan], *Call Home the Heart*, 1932, rpt. (New York: The Feminist Press 1983), p. 383.

12 For a moving tale of the politics of refusal and envy animating one working-class woman (and as such defying the cultural criticism surrounding working-class identity), see Carolyn Steedman, *Landscape for a Good Woman: A Story of Two Lives* (New Brunswick, NJ: Rutgers University Press 1986).

13 Ramona Lowe, 'The Woman in the Window,' in Nekola and Rabinowitz, eds., *Writing Red*, p. 83 (emphasis in original).

14 Steedman, *Landscape for a Good Woman*, pp. 1–2.

15 Sandra Cisneros, *The House on Mango Street* (Houston: Arte Publico Press 1984), pp. 8–9 (emphasis in original).

16 Meridel LeSueur, 'I Was Marching,' in *Salute to Spring* (New York: International Publishers 1940), pp. 159–60. For more on the skewering LeSueur received from then CPUSA-heavy Whittaker Chambers, see my *Labor and Desire*.

17 In effect, this is Susan Suleiman's point in her marvelous study of French *romans-à-thèse*, *Authoritarian Fictions: The Ideological Novel as Genre* (New York: Columbia University Press 1983).

18 James Agee and Walker Evans, *Let Us Now Praise Famous Men*, 1941 rpt. (Boston: Houghton Mifflin 1980), p. 454.

19 Margaret Bourke-White, *Portrait of Myself* (New York: Simon & Schuster 1963), p. 147.

20 Margaret Bourke-White and Erskine Caldwell, *You Have Seen Their Faces*, 1937 rpt. (New York: Arno Press 1975), frontispiece.

21 Agee and Evans were extremely critical of Bourke-White's photographic style – their book was a self-conscious refusal of the choices Bourke-White and Caldwell made – nevertheless they also ranged through the minds and possessions of their subjects, albeit in secret. Even a purist like Dorothea Lange, whose phototextual book with text by her husband, Paul Schuster Taylor, is another correction to the overdramatized words and images in *You Have Seen Their Faces*, also shot from odd angles and quoted her informants out of context, altering the meaning of their words. At least Bourke-White and Caldwell were open about their arrogance.

22 Bourke-White, *Portrait*, p. 142.

23 Editor's Note, *Life* 1:1 (November 1936): 3.

24 Bourke-White, *Portrait*, pp. 126–7.

25 Notice how this title foregrounds the difference between 'you' and 'their faces' and does so by emphasizing voyeurism – seeing. Contrast this with the D Street writer's exhortation to Damon to 'tell' 'Them' about 'Us.' The girls demand action from Damon as they claim their subjectivity – 'us' writers – over and against 'them,' academic critics.

26 William Stott, *Documentary Expression and Thirties America*, 1973 rpt. (Chicago: University of Chicago Press 1986), pp. 222–3.

27 Walker Evans, quoted in Stott, pp. 222–3.

28 I should note that I wrote this chapter during the 'Nannygate' disclosures involving the nominations for Attorney General, first of Zoë Baird, who had hired illegal immigrants and failed to pay their social security taxes, and then of Kimba Wood, who had neglected to pay taxes for her legal housekeeper; the parallels were inescapable: when a woman makes a lot of money, it's scandalous. Glaring class differences among women ignite tremendous public fury, even as Baird struggled to play down her class privilege. She spoke at her confirmation hearings about her plight in terms of gender (she was acting as a mother) and ethnicity (she was concerned as a Jew about how babysitters would respond to her household), but failed to register the plight of her exploited employees.

29 Stott quotes a review of *You Have Seen Their Faces* by Norman Cousins which dares to assert that Bourke-White's photographs will do as much to ameliorate the plight of tenant farmers as Stowe's novel did to arouse anti-slavery sentiments (p. 220).

30 Walker Evans, *Walker Evans at Work* (New York: Harper & Row 1982), p. 136.

31 Stott, pp. 267–8.

32 Vivian Dahl, ' "Them Women Sure Are Scrappers",' in Nekola and Rabinowitz, p. 252.

33 Henry Mayhew, *London Labor and London Poor*, vol. 1 (London: George Woodfall 1851), p. 151.

34 Milan Women's Bookstore Collective, *Sexual Difference: A Theory of Social-Symbolic Practice*, trans. Teresa de Lauretis and Patricia Cicogna (Bloomington: Indiana University Press 1990), p. 123. The Collective details a history of the genealogy of women's freedom in the entrustment of one woman to another. Their theory is radically anti-Enlightenment, rejecting a rights-based analysis of liberation. However, its focus on disparity and the retrieval of the symbolic mother leaves it open to the critiques which Teresa de Lauretis launches in her introductory essay to the collection.

35 I am indebted to Asha Varadharajan's useful distinction between failed resistance and no resistance, which she offered in conversation with me.

Chapter 4

1 In response to the question of audience, Agee replies: 'Some of the time you are writing for all men who are your equals and your superiors, and some of the time for all the deceived and captured, and some of the time for nobody.' James Agee and Walker Evans, *Let Us Now Praise Famous Men* 1941 rpt. (Boston: Houghton Mifflin 1980), p. 322.

2 Bruce Robbins, *Secular Vocations: Intellectuals, Professionalism, Culture* (London: Verso 1993), p. 149.

3 Robbins seems to know this unconsciously too if I read his footnote as an after-thought in which he links Agee's position to fellow *Time* writer Whittaker Chambers's accusations about Hiss, which are in turn linked to Williams's association with Anthony Blunt in Cambridge. For Robbins, the meaning of work as a location which undoes inside/outside, institutional/oppositional practices is crucial. Many of his insights inform my discussion of the breakdown of barriers formally and economically between Holly-wood and government, between fantasy and documentary, between work and leisure, within the context of the Depression.

4 For retrospective histories and analyses of Popular Front film culture in the United States, see William Alexander, *Film on the Left: American Documentary Film from 1931 to 1942* (Princeton, NJ: Princeton University Press 1981); Russell Campbell, *Cinema Strikes Back: Radical Filmmaking in the United States, 1930–1942* (Ann Arbor, MI: UMI Research Press 1982); Thomas Waugh, 'Joris Ivens' *The Spanish Earth*: Committed Documentary and the Popular Front,' in *'Show Us Life': Toward a History and Aesthetics of the Committed Documentary* (Metuchen, NJ: Scarecrow Press 1984); about British Popular Front docu-mentaries, see Bert Hogencamp, *Deadly Parallels: Film and the Left in Britain, 1929–1939* (London: Lawrence & Wishart 1986); and Rachel Low, *The History of the British Film, 1929–1939: Films of Comment and Persuasion of the 1930s* (London: George Allen & Unwin 1979). Hogencamp also writes about 'Workers' Newsreels in Germany, the Netherlands, and Japan During the Twenties and Thirties,' in Waugh, *'Show Us Life.'* The Popular Front as a US literary formation – institutionally through the Writers' Congresses and aesthetically through revivals of Whitman and other American authors – has been a subject explored in depth by many scholars of the 1930s. See Barbara Foley, *Radical Representations: Politics and Form in US Proletarian Fiction, 1929–1941* (Durham, NC: Duke University Press 1993) and my *Labor and Desire: Women's Revolutionary Fiction in Depression America* (Chapel Hill, NC: University of North Carolina Press 1991) for the most recent discussions of the political/formal effects of Popular Front on left-wing authors. The standard texts are Walter Rideout, *The Radical Novel in the United States, 1900–1954: Some Interrelations of Literature and Society* (Cambridge, MA: Harvard Univer-sity Press 1956); and Daniel Aaron, *Writers on the Left: Episodes in American Literary Communism* (New York: Harcourt, Brace, and World 1961); both books were recently reprinted by Columbia University Press.

My focus here is on the dominant and official cultural practices, clearly influenced by the Left and especially the Popular Front, of imaging the poor and imagining the nation. This was hardly seamless; there was a struggle between left-wing and conservative mem-bers of Hollywood and of the New Deal about the direction of each organization; never-theless, those on the Left in effect shaped the debates about culture from the 1930s on. New works by Michael Denning, *People's Theater: Orson Welles and the Mercury Theater* (London: Verso forthcoming) and Alan Wald, *Writing from the Left* (London: Verso 1994) will shed much light on the cultural prominence of left-wing artists in the post-1930s decades. This chapter looks at the more widespread and popular appeals to national cultural identity made through documentary images and their incorporation into the movies.

5 There are so many examples that I am merely picking from three recent articles in *The New York Times* which happened to appear the week I was completing this chapter. First, Neil Gabler tracks the conflation of celebrity persona with real persona; then Steven Spielberg's new film about the holocaust is likened to *Shoah* and *The Sorrow and the Pity* (See *Arts and Leisure*, 12 December 1993). On Monday, 13 December, we are informed that D.A. Pennebaker's documentary, *The War Room*, has become one of the most popular films in Washington because of its 'dramatic' intensity; like *Dave*, a Hollywood flop, its appeal lies in its quality as 'home movie,' with cameos by leading Washington 'pols.' On Tuesday, 14 December, we find Michael Moore of *Roger and Me* filming a fictional documentary about Canadian–US foreign relations. I could go on – and will in chapter 6.

6 See Rita Felski, *Beyond Feminist Aesthetics: Feminist Literature and Social Change* (Cambridge, MA: Harvard University Press 1989); and Nancy Fraser, *Unruly Practices: Power, Discourse and Gender in Contemporary Social Theory* (Minneapolis: University of Minnesota Press 1989).

7 For a comprehensive look at contemporary public culture and the interconnections among media, politics, and the Academy, see Bruce Robbins, ed., *The Phantom Public Sphere* (Minneapolis: University of Minnesota Press 1992).

8 See, for example, Robert Sklar, *Movie-Made America: A Cultural History of American Movies* (New York: Random House 1975), which argues that the dialogue between politics and Hollywood throughout the twentieth century shaped virtually all aspects of American culture. For a personal response to the movies as historical repository, see Gore Vidal, *Screening History* (Cambridge, MA: Harvard University Press 1992). Vidal describes the effects of watching endless Hollywood films interspersed with 'March of Time' newsreels on his own consciousness as a very personal one: his father and grandfather were often subjects – Luce was 'a master of the art of screening history' (p. 35). Ironically, Vidal notes that 'On our screens, in the thirties, it seemed as if the only country on earth was England and there were no great personages who were not English, or impersonated by English actors . . . our history was thought unsuitable for screening' (p. 39).

9 See Kathryn Reisdorfer, 'Seeing Through the Screen: Women in Soviet and German Films from 1919 to 1939,' PhD diss., University of Minnesota 1993; and the forthcoming dissertation by Jeanne Freiburg on German and Swedish popular films of the 1930s for exhaustive analyses of the rise of fascism, Stalinism, and the welfare state facilitated through depictions of motherhood in these national cinemas. These examples of popular culture as a public policy designed to produce a united people indicate the interconnections between the economy, the state, and culture.

10 See Theodor Adorno, *Prisms*, 1967 rpt. (Cambridge, MA: MIT Press 1981) for essays about the culture industry.

11 Mervyn LeRoy, as told to Dick Kleiner, *Mervyn LeRoy: Take One* (New York: Hawthorn 1974), p. 119.

12 More typical of comic attention to the Depression might be found in another Busby Berkeley movie, *Roman Scandals*, in which Eddie Cantor, after losing his job, faints from hunger and awakens to find himself transported back in time to ancient Rome where he is now employed, albeit as a slave. By the end of the decade, Hollywood had focused on the maternal icons of privation brought to light by Lange's 'Migrant Mother' and the many fictional and documentary accounts of hungry mothers written by left-wing writers in Jane Darwell's heroic Ma Joad in *The Grapes of Wrath*.

13 These and all subsequent quotations from *Gold Diggers of 1933* are taken from the published screenplay, *Gold Diggers of 1933*, edited with an introduction by Arthur Hove (Madison: University of Wisconsin Press 1980), pp. 55–6.

14 Rabinowitz, *Labor and Desire*; Barbara Melosh, *Engendering Culture: Manhood and Womanhood in New Deal Art and Theater* (Washington, DC: Smithsonian Institute Press 1991); and Elizabeth Faue, *Community of Suffering and Struggle* (Chapel Hill, NC: University of North Carolina Press 1991) all look at the iconography depicting the 'crisis of masculinity' ushered in by the war and exacerbated by the Depression. These male failures found their way into novels, cartoons, plays, sculptures, and murals, as did their antidote – the strong proletarian man and his family.

15 See Michael Denning, *Mechanic Accents: Dime Novels and Working-Class Culture* (London: Verso 1985) for a discussion of the political allegories of working-class consciousness embedded in popular fiction, especially crime novels of the nineteenth century.

16 Berkeley described how he chose his dancers: 'Once I had 723 girls show up on a call for one of my Golddiggers pictures. I was all afternoon picking girls out of this large number; and finally I ended up selecting three girls out of the 723. My sixteen regular contract girls were sitting on the side waiting; so after I picked the three girls I put them next to my special sixteen and they matched, just like pearls.' Bob Pike and Dave Martin, *The Genius of Busby Berkeley* (Reseda, CA: Creative Film Society 1973), p. 64.

17 See Meridel LeSueur, 'Women on the Breadlines,' *New Masses* (January 1932): 5–7.

18 Willard Van Dyke, 'Letters from *The River*,' *Film Comment* 3 (Spring 1965): 38–56, p. 40.

19 This information comes from the unpublished manuscript of Davis's autobiography.

20 Richard Dyer, 'Entertainment as Utopia,' in Rick Altman, *Genre: The Musical, A Reader* (London: BFI & Routledge & Kegan Paul 1981).

21 For instance, one minute of a Berkeley production cost about $10,000 for each number which lasted between seven and ten minutes; there were usually three to five numbers per film. The total budget for *42nd Street* was $379,000. Pike and Martin, p. 55.

22 See, for instance, 'A Chorus Girl's Job,' *New Theater* 3 (March 1934); and 'Not Sunny for Girl Slaves in "Sunny" Florida,' *Daily Worker* 4 January 1929, p. 4, which discuss the poor working conditions suffered by female chorus line dancers. Dorothy Arzner's 1940 movie (screenplay by left-wing writer Tess Slesinger), *Dance, Girl, Dance*, exposed the underside of Hollywood and Broadway by showing that most women never made it out of the sleazy bars and burlesque houses which first employed them as 'dancers.' Again, Hollywood followed the lead of the radical press.

23 Dorothea Lange and Paul Schuster Taylor, *American Exodus: A Record of Human Erosion*, 1939 rpt. (New Haven, CT: Yale University Press 1969), p. 48. Subsequent quotations are referenced parenthetically in the text.

24 See William Guynn, *A Cinema of Nonfiction* (Rutherford, NJ: Associated University Presses 1990) for a discussion of the relationships between history, discourse, and narrative in documentary film. This study uses the semiotics devised by Christian Metz to analyze narrative film to segment and typologize the documentary. Documentary films 'belong to the class of social discourses – juridical or historical – that seek to account for actual occurrences in the phenomenal world' (p. 13). Guynn's discussion is an updated version of Paul Rotha's typology in which he distinguishes the documentary film from the newsreel: 'The essence of the documentary method lies in its dramatic dramatization of actual material. The very act of dramatizing causes a film statement to be false to actuality.' He goes on to distinguish types of documentary: 'the descriptive, or journalist' and 'the impressionistic.' As a form of reportage, 'the descriptive film prohibits that dramatization of natural material which is the essence of the impressionist approach.' Paul Rotha, with Sinclair Road and Richard Griffith, *Documentary Film*, 3rd edition, revised (London: Faber & Faber 1942), pp. 117, 176.

25 This story is detailed by Catherine Preston, 'Migrant Mother and the Historical Endurance of Cultural Representations,' Paper presented at the Social Science Historians Convention, Minneapolis, October 1990.

26 This photograph was part of a group taken in Lange's characteristic style – slowly approaching her subject from distance – with long captions. These families touched her profoundly. The image immediately preceding Figure 10 is captioned: Three families camped on the plains along US Highway 99, Kern County, California. They are camped behind a billboard which serves as a partial windbreak. All were in need of work. No water. First family: originally from Oklahoma, been in California twelve years. Two children, California-born. Had small dairy near Merced, cattle became TB-infected. Been on road for two years. Second family: Five children, six to fourteen years. Third family: came from Missouri, three children. Used to be a butcher. Worked nineteen years in one packinghouse, became ruptured.

The image immediately following is captioned: Billboard along US Highway 99, behind which three destitute families of migrants are camped. Kern County, California. 'Something will break loose. That's my hope. People are goin' round day and night. I've had three good starts in my life. Had place paid for, had to mortgage the first (1929) to pay for the second, so I lost both. Was where we wasn't rich, but everybody knew me, and I could get what I wanted to. Now nobody knows me. I can't feed these five children of mine on seventy-five cents cotton, so I'm pullin' out of here, but I don't know where I'm goin'. The only thing I look to for a change is the election – I look to this election for a change.'

27 See James Curtis, *Mind's Eye, Mind's Truth* (Philadelphia: Temple University Press 1990).

28 This discussion about Lange's uses of the family and body as metaphors come from papers presented at the November 1993 American Studies Association convention in

Boston during the session entitled 'Dorothea Lange: Self, Body, Other'; see Sandra S. Phillips, 'Dorothea Lange: A Woman's Work. A Re-evaluation of Lange's Photography in Relation to Her Life,' and Sally Stein, ' "Peculiar Grace": Dorothea Lange and the Testimony of the Body.'

29 Judith Fryer takes up Lange's work for the War Relocation Authority during the 1940s by looking at the photographs made to document Executive Order 9066 in ' "The Color of My Skin, the Shape of My Eyes": The Japanese American Internment, Photographed by Dorothea Lange, Ansel Adams, and Toyo Miyatake,' presented at the ASA Convention, November 1993, Boston. These photos have not had the wide attention given to Lange's FSA photos because they remain housed in the National Archives (as war records) rather than the Library of Congress, and because the government was unhappy with the results. Here again, Lange relied on her conventional iconography of the family uprooted, of community in disarray, of men in distress, to bring home the magnitude of the outrage perpetrated on these Americans. Here though it was not nature or abstract economic forces destroying the fabric of society, but the same government that had set about overcoming those natural and man-made disasters of the 1930s. The same government paying her salary – the images reek with irony. But as Fryer indicates, they also reek of sentiment, invoking the trope of victimization to convey affect. As such they come out of the traditional cultural work of middle-class female reform analyzed by Jane Tompkins and discussed in chapter 3, which always also smacks of imperialism.

30 Charles Peden, *Newsreel Man* (Garden City, NY: Doubleday, Doran and Company, Inc 1932), pp. 22–3. Peden goes on to note that different cultures are more or less amenable to the camera, but may have varying reactions to the subjects depicted. He even takes an incursion into political commentary when he mentions that a theater in Poland was bombed because a German newsreel was shown there.

31 Jean Stovel, organizer of a housewives' flour boycott in Seattle, declared in 1936: 'We are that mythical thing called the public and so we shall demand a hearing.' Quoted in Annelise Orleck, ' "We Are That Mythical Thing Called the Public": Militant Housewives During the Great Depression,' *Feminist Studies* 19 (Spring 1993): 147.

32 *New Theater and New Film* 4 (April 1937): 12–15, 44–5. Peter Ellis [Irving Lerner] had criticized Luce's March of Time newsreels in *The New Masses* (July 1935): 29–30 and (August 1936): 18. For more on Frontier Film's newsreels, see Alexander, *Film on the Left* and Campbell, *Cinema Strikes Back*.

33 Richard Dyer MacCann, *The People's Films: A Political History of US Government Motion Pictures* (New York: Hastings House 1973), p. 63.

34 W.L. White, 'Pare Lorentz,' *Scribner's Magazine* 105 (January 1939): 7–11, 42, p. 10.

35 Again, in this they were echoing criticisms launched in the left-wing press. See, for instance, S[am] B[rody], 'The Movies as a Weapon against the Working Class,' *Daily Worker*, 20 May 1930, p. 4, where he denounces Hollywood movies as 'imbecilic,' designed 'for doping the minds of workers,' then blasts the censorship of newsreels by the Hays Office, noting 'the Sacco-Vanzetti films, movies records of which have been destroyed' and the police power to 'rul[e] out whatever [is] . . . objectionable in a newsreel.'

36 Pare Lorentz, 'Movies with Blinders,' *Lorentz on Film: Movies 1927–1941* (Norman: University of Oklahoma Press 1986), pp. 167–8.

37 Lorentz, 'Newsreels,' *Lorentz on Film*, pp. 37–8.

38 Lorentz, 'Who Puts the Navy in Every Newsreel?' *Lorentz on Film*, p. 82.

39 This comes from MacCann, *The People's Films*, p. 68.

40 Lorentz, 'Newsreels,' *Lorentz on Film*, p. 39.

41 Irving Lerner, '*The Plow That Broke the Plains*,' in Herbert Kline, ed., *New Theatre and Film, 1934 to 1937: An Anthology* (New York: Harcourt Brace Jovanovich 1985), pp. 313–14; Alexander, *Film on the Left*, pp. 98–9.

42 White, p. 9.

43 MacCann, pp. 80–81.

44 Pare Lorentz, 'Dorothea Lange: Camera with a Purpose,' *US Camera* (1941): 93–116, pp. 94–5, 98.

45 See Alexander and MacCann for accounts of this.

46 Lorentz, 'The Plow That Broke the Plains,' Lorentz on Film, p. 136.

47 Ralph Steiner and Leo T. Hurwitz, 'A New Approach to Filmmaking,' in Kline, New Theatre and Film, pp. 302 and 305.

48 Paul Rotha with Sinclair Road and Richard Griffith, Documentary Film, pp. 199–200. Rotha did acknowledge that the films were successful in raising awareness of both the problems of erosion and flooding and the importance of government programs to solve them. More importantly, he notes that Lorentz's efforts galvanized US documentary film-makers because of the government sponsorship.

The critiques of the tacked-on endings were not reserved for Hollywood romances and musicals and government propaganda, left-wing writers were constantly accused of adding 'conversion' endings to their proletarian novels to conform to the correct political line.

49 Lorentz, 'Plow,' p. 135.

50 Quoted in White, p. 9.

51 Lorentz, 'Snow White,' Lorentz on Film, p. 149.

52 See Richard Schickel, The Disney Version: The Life, Times, Art and Commerce of Walt Disney (New York: Simon & Schuster 1968).

53 Lorentz, 'Good Art, Good Propaganda,' in Lorentz on Film, p. 192.

54 In this, he resembles the recent refusals of the generic designation by Claude Lanzmann, Trinh T. Minh-ha, and others. It seems that the term 'documentary' is viewed as an epithet by many film-makers, damning for precisely the reasons this book explores; documentaries are films that mobilize another kind of subjectivity from that called forth by classic narrative cinema, one which foregrounds a personal stake in political practice, a subject of agency who appears perhaps too instrumentalist for either the tastes of the entertainment industry, on the one hand, or the art scene, on the other.

55 See 'The Making of The River,' in Pare Lorentz, FDR's Moviemaker: Memoirs and Scripts (Reno: University of Nevada Press 1992) p. 57.

56 Lorentz, 'Dorothea Lange: Camera with a Purpose,' p. 97.

57 Where there were constant conflicts between director and cinematographers of The Plow, Lorentz and Van Dyke were able to collaborate successfully on The River. It seems this was due as much to Lorentz's anti-Semitism (Van Dyke wrote to his wife that Lorentz had told him he was glad to have 'found a young gentile' to work on his new film) as to their common rejection of ideological art. Van Dyke, 'Letters from The River,' p. 45.

58 Willard Van Dyke, 'The Photographs of Dorothea Lange: A Critical Analysis,' Camera Craft (October 1934): 461–7, p. 461.

59 Lorentz, 'The 400,000,000; Crisis', in Lorentz on Film, p. 164. This review was coupled with one about a new Hollywood romantic comedy, Love Affair, and Lorentz sadly acknowledges that moviegoers are going to get the wrong impression of documentaries. He points out that 'both The 400,000,000 and Crisis put together were made for what it cost for one week's shooting of Love Affair. And no one on the Love Affair set was in any particular personal danger while he worked. Yet neither factual film is as good as it should be' (p. 165).

60 White, p. 9; Van Dyke, 'Letters from The River,' p. 46.

61 Van Dyke, 'Letters,' p. 44. Guynn, A Cinema of Nonfiction calls The River a discursive film; that is, it overtly refers to itself as a 'problem-solving' picture and so distinguishes itself from narrative whose codes often cover over their source of enunciation.

62 See Lisa Cartwright, Physiological Modernity: Scientific Cinema and the Technologies of 'Life' (Minneapolis: University of Minnesota Press forthcoming).

63 King Vidor, King Vidor on Filmmaking (New York: David McKay Co. 1972), pp. 222–3.

64 Van Dyke, 'Letters,' p. 52.

65 In this staging of levée-building from time past with day workers sometimes used to build levées during the 1930s, Van Dyke was recalling the directorial decisions made by Robert Flaherty in Nanook of the North for the whale-hunting scene.

66 Van Dyke, 'Letters,' p. 47.

67 In some ways this scene resembles the scene Agee describes in Let Us Now Praise

Famous Men, 'Early Sunday Morning,' in which the white landlord forces his black tenants to sing for Agee and Evans, who then offer them fifty cents in payment for their performance. See chapter 2.

68 The aerial shots taken from helicopters, many of which are piloted by Vietnam veterans, of flooded fields and whole towns under water relied on a wholly different documentary effect, that of the nightly news update most powerfully referenced in the ubiquitous sounds of the helicopter recalled from Vietnam footage. Yet these too served to link the nation behind this so-called natural disaster.

69 I am using the script found in Pare Lorentz, *FDR's Moviemaker: Memoirs and Scripts,* p. 61.

70 These were the titles each chose for his self-promotional book.

71 Dorothea Lange, 'The Assignment I'll Never Forget,' *Popular Photography* 46 (February 1960).

72 Preston, 'Migrant Mother and the Historical Endurance of Cultural Representations,' details the frequency with which the photograph was shown during the 1930s: in 1936, it appeared in *Survey Graphic, US Camera, Midweek Pictorial;* in 1938, it was exhibited in New York, included in a catalog celebrating the one hundredth anniversary of photography's invention and appeared in Archibald MacLeish's book, *Land of the Free;* in 1939, Edward Steichen again included it in *US Camera;* and on and on. I have chosen to write about other work by Lange because Migrant Mother has been thoroughly analyzed by James Curtis, 'Dorothea Lange, Migrant Mother, and the Culture of the Great Depression,' *Winterthur Portfolio* 21 (Spring 1986): 1–20; rpt. in *Mind's Eye, Mind's Truth,* who explains how Lange's background as a portrait photographer helped pose the shot; he orders the images of the Thompson family. Wendy Kozol, 'Madonnas of the Fields: Photography, Gender, and the 1930s Farm Relief,' *Genders* 2 (Summer 1988): 1–23 looks at the conventional woman-as-mother iconography within many FSA images.

Chapter 5

1 Marguerite Duras, *Hiroshima Mon Amour,* trans. Richard Seaver (New York: Grove Press 1961), p. 15.

2 See Duras's screenplay notes: 'Their personal story, however brief it may be, always dominates Hiroshima. If this premise is not adhered to, this . . . picture would be of no more interest than any fictionalized documentary. If it is adhered to, we'll end up with a sort of false documentary that will probe the lesson of Hiroshima more deeply than any made-to-order documentary' (p. 10). Duras's comments on and within her screenplay focus on the trauma of recounting history. She develops techniques for avoiding cliché by overemphasizing it in a fictional love story – this personal story is precisely what dominates the narratives about Vietnam as well.

3 In his analysis of popular forms of Vietnam 'documentaries,' including the hundreds of self-published 'memoirs,' collections of letters and oral histories, television epics, left-wing documentaries, and Hollywood films, entitled 'Eyewitness: Documentary Styles in the American Representations of Vietnam' (in John Carlos Rowe and Rick Berg, eds., *The Vietnam War and American Culture* (New York: Columbia University Press 1991)), John Carlos Rowe describes the exculpatory effects of substituting 'personal experience for historical and political knowledge . . . that has tended to mythologize the special value of direct experience' (p. 149). He is absolutely correct, as I argue here; however, I tend to think this 'realist' means of persuasion has a much longer history.

4 In no way does this chapter attempt to be exhaustive – the sheer volume of writings on the war is staggering. Sandra Wittman, *Writing About Vietnam: A Bibliography of the Literature of the Vietnam Conflict* (Boston: G.K. Hall 1989) lists over three hundred personal narratives in press – rather, like the rest of this book, I am selectively choosing key works as emblems of more general theoretical issues about personal responsibility and political commitment facing radical documentarians.

236

5 Much has been written on the gendered effects of the Vietnam War; see Susan Jeffords, *The Remasculinization of America: Gender in the Vietnam War* (Bloomington: Indiana University Press 1989).

6 Susan Sontag, *Trip to Hanoi* (New York: Farrar, Strauss, & Giroux 1968), p. 78. Further references will appear in the text.

7 Oral histories of victims of torture or relatives of *disapparacidos*, or illiterate indigenous peasants in Central and South America have served to destabilize political and military régimes as well as literary conventions of authorship, genre, narrative voice. *I, Riguberto Menchú: An Indian Woman in Guatemala*, ed. and intro. Elisabeth Burgos-Debray, trans. Ann Wright (London: Verso 1984) begins with a declaration that her story is the story of her people. See John Beverley's discussion of the politics and poetics of *testimonio* in 'The Margin at the Center: On *Testimonio*,' *Modern Fiction Studies* 35 (Spring 1989) and ' "Through All Things Modern": Second Thoughts on *Testimonio*,' *Boundary 2* 18 (Summer 1991): 1–21; both reprinted in Beverley, *Against Literature* (Minneapolis: University of Minnesota Press 1993).

8 Staughton Lynd and Tom Hayden, *The Other Side* (New York: New American Library 1966), p. 1. Actually, Women Strike for Peace sent the first delegation of Americans (all women) to North Vietnam in Spring 1965 but, like much of women's work in and out of the New Left, this was neglected as no one produced a major report on the journey. See Amy Swerdlow, *Women Strike for Peace: Traditional Motherhood and Radical Politics of the 1960s* (Chicago: University of Chicago Press 1993), p. 132.

9 Mary McCarthy, *The Seventeenth Degree* (New York: Harcourt, Brace, Jovanovich 1974), p. 26. This volume included essays which originally appeared in journals such as *New York Review of Books* and *The New Yorker* but were issued as separate books by HBJ, McCarthy's publisher, as *Vietnam* (1967), *Hanoi* (1968), and *Medina* (1972). All further references appear parenthetically in the text.

10 Josephine Herbst, 'The Starched Blue Sky of Spain,' *Noble Savage* 1 (1966): 76; rpt. in *The Starched Blue Sky of Spain and Other Memoirs* (New York: HarperPerennial 1992).

11 Oriana Fallaci, *Nothing, And So Be It*, trans. Isabel Quigly (Garden City, NY: Doubleday and Co. 1972), p. 2.

12 Hayden and Lynd in 1965, Salisbury in 1966, McCarthy in 1967 in the North; Martha Gellhorn in 1965, Herr in 1966–67, Fitzgerald in 1965–66, McCarthy in 1966 in the South.

13 This is how McCarthy describes the children crowding around a GI, p. 101.

14 For instance, Margaret Fuller writing about participating in the political upheavals in Italy of the 1840s; Mary Wollstonecraft had done the same thing in Paris of the 1790s, as had Aphra Behn in Guinea of the 1680s.

15 See Mary Louise Pratt, *Imperial Eyes: Travel Writing and Transculturation* (London: Routledge 1992) for a description of what she calls the 'anti-conquest' discourse of early ethnographic and travel writing. Sara Mills, *Discourse of Difference: An Analysis of Women's Travel Writing and Colonialism* (London: Routledge 1991) dissects women's contribution to colonial enterprises through discourses of 'personal' accounts, (non-political) descriptions of local custom, etc. See also the forthcoming dissertation by Susan Kollin of the University of Minnesota on 'the first white woman trope' organizing white women's accounts of travel into 'native' areas. McCarthy is not insensible to this; she is acutely aware of how easily one's writing can leak into an imperialist and racist project. See pp. 270–71.

16 Martha Gellhorn, *Vietnam: A New Kind of War* (Manchester: Guardian Booklet 1966), p. 2.

17 See Michael Bibby, 'Hearts and Minds: The Body in American Resistance Poetry of the Vietnam War Era' (PhD dissertation, University of Minnesota 1993) for a discussion of the ways in which the war produced a new poetics of the body in women's, African-Americans', and veterans' writings.

18 Martha Gellhorn, *The Face of War* (New York: Simon & Schuster 1959), p. 3.

19 David Douglas Duncan, *I Protest!* (New York: Signet 1968), n.p.

20 Gellhorn, *Face*, p. 7. But when did the deliberate observation of war by noncombatants begin? My guess is that it is a fairly modern occurrence, which coincides with

the advent of photography and mass circulation presses, resources that already bring the war home. I am thinking of Florence Nightingale in the Crimea, which was the first photographically imaged war; Walt Whitman volunteering in the hospitals and Matthew Brady on the battlefields of the American Civil War, of Gellhorn and Herbst and Weil and countless others in Spain, who worked with film-makers such as Joris Ivens.

21 Fallaci, p. 22. In his recent memoir, Peter Arnett describes the 'Vietnam press corps [as] a male bastion that women entered only at the risk of being humiliated and patronized . . . . The military made few concessions to the special needs for privacy of women reporters and photographers. We reporters tended to disparage the abilities of the women and gossip about them and their relationships . . .' He goes on to describe the Dak To battle where he too was stationed, with the same horrific images as Fallaci but without the ironic distance offered her because she was a woman. Peter Arnett, *Live from the Battlefield: From Vietnam to Baghdad, 35 Years in the World's War Zones* (New York: Simon & Schuster 1994), p. 220.

22 John Carlos Rowe, 'Eyewitness: Documentary Styles in the American Representations of Vietnam,' explains how this mechanism defuses any criticisms of the policies and practices of the US government during the war.

23 Jacques Derrida, 'The Law of Genre,' *Glyph* 7 (1982): 202–32; Adena Rosmarin, *The Power of Genre* (Minneapolis: University of Minnesota Press 1986).

24 In her discussion of two works by 'hyphenated colonials,' Camus and Wright, Pratt argues that even though these writers critically explore the contradictions of post-coloniality as it emerges in Africa during the 1950s, they rely on tropes, such as the 'promontory scene' and the 'experiential unhero,' long operating in the colonialist and anti-conquest narratives (pp. 221–4).

25 For discussions about this and other Vietnam war documentary films, see Linda Dittmar and Gene Michaud, eds., *From Hollywood to Hanoi: The Vietnam War in American Film* (New Brunswick, NJ: Rutgers University Press 1990). David Grosser, ' "We Aren't on the Wrong Side, We Are the Wrong Side": Peter Davis Targets (American) Hearts and Minds,' in this collection discusses the scene of the Vietnamese running and commenting on the filming as part of the strategy of provoking empathy within the viewers for the feelings of the Vietnamese people. Rowe, 'Eyewitness,' sees it as a 'metacinematic commentary' designed to unsettle viewers' respect for documentary images.

26 Benedict Anderson's concept of the nation as an imaginary construct-in-opposition can be a model for understanding other forms of consolidation, such as the communities of dissenters hovering around 'the movement' against the war. *Imagined Communities: Reflections on the Origin and Spread of Nationalism* (London: Verso 1983).

27 Michael Herr, *Dispatches* (New York: Avon 1977), p. 20.

28 The compilation film, edited by Chris Marker, includes segments by Resnais, Godard, Varda, Klein, Ivens, Lelouch.

29 Staughton Lynd and his wife, Alice, later collected oral histories of militant union organizers in *Rank and File*. Each case exemplifies a trust that the power of authentic voices of the people can effect change. I am indebted to Liz Faue for pointing this out to me.

30 See Stephanie Athey, 'Contested Bodies: The Writing of Whiteness and Gender in American Literary History' (PhD diss., University of Minnesota 1993).

31 For only one instance; in the single reference to McCarthy in Howard Fast's memoir, *Being Red* (Boston: Houghton Mifflin 1990), she appears at the Waldorf Conference challenging the organizers to let her speak, 'Because I'll tell the truth' (p. 202).

32 Gellhorn expresses disgust about the US practice of propaganda, noting that its effect is to alienate the South Vietnamese whose experiences directly contradict what is officially said. Duncan says of the pathetic military explanations for the destruction of Hue simply, 'I, personally, resent being thought so naive, even downright idiotic . . . I resent people trying to sell military victories and defeats the same way they pitch 101-millimeter cigarettes, shaving cream, and deodorants' (n.p.).

33 See Gellhorn and Frances FitzGerald, *Fire in the Lake: The Vietnamese and the Americans in Vietnam* (New York: Vintage 1972) on 'the people's war' in the writings of General Giap.

34 As Martha Gellhorn tells it: 'When I was young I believed in the perfectibility of man . . . . "People" were good, by definition . . .' (*Face*, p. 1).

35 Herr, p. 20. Peter Arnett, in retrospect, echoed this dissonance between himself as a reporter and the men in combat: 'I was an interloper, a voyeur on desperate ground,' he says of his assignment to Dak To. 'I had been proud of a certain professional detachment, but now I felt ashamed of my neutrality, useless with my notebooks and cameras and water bottles. I didn't even carry a gun, so I was just one more liability for the surviving defenders' (p. 233). Of course, Herr refuses this 'professional detachment'; still he too is a voyeur and knows it.

36 See Noam Chomsky, 'The Responsibility of Intellectuals,' *New York Review of Books*, 23 February 1967: 16–26.

37 I am thinking of Alexis de Tocqueville on American democracy, Karl Marx on the civil war in France, among others.

38 Gellhorn, *Face*, p. 8. Rowe, 'Eyewitness,' argues that the personal appeal to truth has a unique ideological meaning for Vietnam War reports; but Gellhorn's plea was written in the 1950s, pushing the idea of the personal backward. In fact, as this entire book argues, twentieth-century documentary projects have been fundamentally about personal interventions into public history, and political analyses accomplished through personal portraits.

39 'Joris Ivens Interviewed by Gordon Hitchens, 20 November 1968, American Documentaries,' *Film Culture* (Spring 1972): 211. Thomas Waugh dissects Ivens's choice to focus on a personal experience in this documentary; see 'Joris Ivens' *The Spanish Earth*: Committed Documentary and the Popular Front,' in Thomas Waugh, ed., *'Show Us Life': Toward a History and Aesthetics of the Committed Documentary* (Metuchen, NJ: Scarecrow Press 1984). See William Alexander, *Film on the Left: American Documentary Film from 1931 to 1942* (Princeton, NJ: Princeton University Press 1981), pp. 149–67 for more about radical films about the Spanish Civil War.

40 Nancy Zaroulis and Gerald Sullivan entitled their history of 'American Protest Against the War in Vietnam, 1963–1975,' as it is subtitled, *Who Spoke Up?*, a question taken from an I.F. Stone editorial of 17 October 1966 in *I.F. Stone's Weekly* declaring: 'This is the crime our country is committing. And this is what we must condemn, lest a later generation ask of us, as they ask of the Germans, who spoke up?'

41 Cecil Woolf and John Bagguley, eds., *Authors Take Sides on Vietnam* (London: Peter Owen 1967). All citations appear in the text.

42 See their entries in *Authors Take Sides*.

43 Sontag, p. 78.

44 Duras, p. 28.

45 These are the central chapters of *Vietnam* and *Hanoi* respectively.

46 'War of ideas' is McCarthy's phrase, p. 128; Gellhorn, *Vietnam*, pp. 30, 13 used the phrases 'war of words,' and 'semantic confusion.'

47 In *Intellectual Memoirs: New York, 1936–1938* (New York: HBJ 1992), McCarthy refers to herself a number of times as 'patrician.' See, for instance, p. 63.

48 See FitzGerald, pp. 470–75 for a detailed account of this program.

49 See Pratt, p. 27, on the conjunction of natural history, travel writing, and the imperialist enterprise. McCarthy is certainly aware of this history. She quotes from the eleventh edition of the Britannica the entry on Annam which proceeds from a list of animals and plants to a description of the Annamese: 'his hair is black, coarse, and long . . .' She concludes: 'The old Britannica would not be spared if we white people began our cultural revolution.' Yet resists her conclusion as well: 'But the tea, the cardamon, and the mulberry? Must the mind be forbidden to collect them in its neo-colonialist trunk?' (p. 271).

50 Gellhorn, FitzGerald, and McCarthy are particularly astounded by the zeal with which liberals have taken on the work of official lying once reserved for totalitarian states.

51 Gemma Cruz Araneta, *Hanoi Diary* (Manila: 1968), p. 13. Further citations appear parenthetically in the text.

52 McCarthy, *Intellectual Memoirs*, p. 68.

53 Maxine Hong Kingston, *China Men* (New York: Knopf 1980), p. 298.

54 See the exchange between Diana Trilling and McCarthy included in *Hanoi* over 'solutions.' 'Quagmire' was the term used by David Halberstam in the title of his Vietnam book, *The Making of a Quagmire* (New York: Random House 1964); Duncan refers to Vietnam as a quagmire too. The image of the swamp sucking everything into it might have come from Hitchcock's view of 1960s America, for instance, the final scene in *Psycho* in which Marion Crane's car is dredged from the swamp behind the Bates Motel – even big American machines get sucked into the mud.

55 Second Female Voice, *Vent d'Est* in *Weekend and Wind from the East: Two Films by Jean-Luc Godard* (New York: Simon & Schuster 1972), p. 127.

56 The difficulties they faced coming to terms with their fears and their powers of persuasion seem gender-inflected. Herr is racked with fear often – he purposely puts himself in the line of fire – but he never doubts his authority to write about it and about the lunacy of the war. Likewise, the measured tones of Salisbury's report and the partisan accounts by Lynd and Hayden do not betray this ambivalence – an ambivalence about voice and about observation which is at odds with the very acute powers both women know they possess as writers. See my *Labor and Desire: Women's Revolutionary Fiction in Depression America* (Chapel Hill, NC: University of North Carolina Press 1991) for an analysis of the dynamics of gender and writing animating the work of left-wing women (including McCarthy) writing during the 1930s.

Chapter 6

1 See Jeanne Hall, 'Realism as Style in *Cinéma Vérité*: A Critical Analysis of *Primary*,' *Cinema Journal* 30:4 (1991): 24–50.

2 This is *Roots*'s producer David Wolper's term. See Marlon Riggs's *Color Adjustment* (1991).

3 hooks's scathing attack on *Paris Is Burning* first appeared in *Z* and was included in *Black Looks: Race and Representation* (Boston: South End Press 1992), pp. 145–56; also included is her critique of Madonna, pp. 157–64. Herman Gray has mounted the most cogent critique of *Roots*'s racist fantasies in *Color Adjustment*.

4 hooks, p. 154.

5 See Arlene Skolnick, *Embattled Paradise: The American Family in an Age of Uncertainty* (New York: Basic Books 1991).

6 Almost as soon as *cinéma vérité* arrived in the United States its 'truth' was being questioned. See for example, Henry Brietrose, 'On the Search for the Real Nitty-Gritty: Problems and Possibilities in *Cinéma-Vérité*,' *Film Quarterly* 17 (1963–64): 36–40.

7 See Steven Mamber, *Cinéma Vérité In America: Studies in Uncontrolled Documentary* (Cambridge, MA: MIT Press 1974).

8 Louis Althusser, 'Ideology and Ideological State Apparatuses (Notes Toward an Investigation),' *Lenin and Philosophy and Other Essays*, trans. Ben Brewster (New York: Monthly Review Press 1971).

9 During the 1960s and 1970s, movements for self-determination were not necessarily about identity; however, new identities were forged in organizing around specific oppressions. For an analysis of the rise of 'Asian American panethnicity,' see Yen Le Espiritu, *Asian American Panethnicity: Bridging Institutions and Identities* (Philadelphia: Temple University Press 1992). Her sociological study of rise of a new ethnicity – Asian-American – mirrors Robert Blauner, *Racial Oppression in America* (New York: Harper & Row 1972) which analyzes the invention of African-Americans (or formerly, Negroes) among post-diasporic blacks; and the invention of Native American (Indian) for the diverse tribal peoples inhabiting the Americas; and the various designations of Hispanics/Latinos for Spanish speakers native-born and immigrants in the United States.

10 In 1969, I remember my roommate in Berkeley, a midwestern WASP, bemoaning her (lack of) origins, which clearly put her on the side of oppressors in America; I consoled her, 'Look at the bright side, at least you're a woman.'

11 For a psychoanalytic and Foucauldian reading of *Titicut Follies* as an Oedipal drama of the 'carceral society,' see Dan Armstrong, 'Wiseman's Realm of Transgression: *Titicut Follies*, the Symbolic Father, and the Spectacle of Confinement,' *Cinema Journal* 29 (Fall 1989): 20–35.

12 See George Lipsitz, 'The Meaning of Memory: Family, Class, and Ethnicity in Early Television,' in *Private Screenings: Television and the Female Consumer*, ed. Lynn Spigel and Denise Mann (Minneapolis: University of Minnesota Press 1992), pp. 71–110.

13 Charlotte Nekola, *Dream House: A Memoir* (New York: Norton 1993).

14 Mary Ann Watson, 'Adventures in Reporting: John Kennedy and the *Cinéma Vérité* Television Documentaries of Drew Associates,' *Film and History* 29 (May 1989): 26–43, p. 29.

15 In her letter to The Forum For Contemporary History, Pat Loud explained the decision to let Craig Gilbert into 35 Wood Dale Lane: 'We really believed, so help me, that by letting all of us hang out, we might help to free some pent-up soul out there.' She goes on to ask, 'Why else would educational television, which turns up its nose at the merely sensational and titillating, be interested in us?' Quoted in Ron Goulart, *An American Family* (New York: Warner Paperback Library 1973), p. 235.

16 The Maysles had shot the segment on 'The Burks of Georgia' for *Six American Families* about an impoverished, rural, white family.

17 Alex Haley, *Roots: The Saga of An American Family* (Garden City, NY: Doubleday and Co. 1976), emphasis added. After challenges to the veracity of some of his material, Haley took to calling his work a 'faction.'

18 Maxine Haleff, 'The Maysles Brothers and "Direct Cinema",' *Film Comment* 2 (1964): 19–23, p. 19.

19 These quotations come from Wolper's remarks in *Color Adjustment*.

20 Lauren R. Tucker and Hemant Shah, 'Race and the Transformation of Culture: The Making of the Television Miniseries *Roots*,' *Critical Studies in Mass Communications* (December 1992): 325–36 dissect the ways in which ABC altered Haley's already questionable narrative to make it even more palatable for a white audience. They focus on Ed Asner's character, the slave-ship Captain Slater, whose conscience-stricken pose as a Christian makes him a suffering individual along with his cargo.

21 Michael Katz, *The Undeserving Poor: From the War on Poverty to the War on Welfare* (New York: Pantheon 1989), p. 8.

22 Stephanie Coontz, *The Way We Never Were: American Families and the Nostalgia Trap* (New York: Basic Books 1992), p. 88. Further citations within the text.

23 This was certainly Anne Roiphe's assessment in 'Things Are Keen But Could Be Keener,' a portrait of the Louds she wrote for *The New York Times Magazine* and reprinted in Goulart, pp. 9–27.

24 Arlene Skolnick cites the Louds as exceptions to the '1970s and the Culture of Nostalgia,' still their family is typical of middle-class, white families in post-war America. *Embattled Paradise*, pp. 125–50.

25 Goulart, p. 203.

26 See Wini Breines, *Community and Organization in the New Left, 1962–1968: The Great Refusal* (New York: Praeger; South Hadley, MA: J.F. Bergin 1982); Alice Echols, *Daring to Be Bad: Radical Feminism in America, 1967–1975* (Minneapolis: University of Minnesota Press 1989); and Sara Evans, *Personal Politics: The Roots of Women's Liberation in the Civil Rights Movement and the New Left* (New York: Knopf 1979) for the interconnections among feminists and the New Left.

27 Elaine Tyler May, *Homeward Bound: American Families in the Cold War Era* (New York: Basic Books 1988), pp. 11, 221.

28 For a good overview of the history of television docudrama, tracing its beginnings in 'theater, literature, radio, motion pictures and early television,' see Robert B. Musburger, 'Setting the Stage for the Television Docudrama,' *Journal of Popular Film and Television* 13 (Summer 1985): 92–101, p. 101. David Wolper, executive producer of

Roots, who chaired a symposium on docudrama in 1979, begins by defining it as 'the dramatization of an historical event or lives of real people, using actors or actresses' yet concludes 'that the docu-drama is a creative interpretation of reality.' He lifted John Grierson's definition of documentary, 'the creative interpretation of actuality.' Lee Margulies, 'Academy of Television Arts and Sciences Docu-drama Symposium, 1979,' *Emmy Magazine* (Summer 1979): D1–D40, pp. D–6, D–10.

29 See David Lopez and Yen Espiritu, 'Panethnicity in the United States: A Theoretical Framework,' *Ethnic and Racial Studies* 13 (April 1990): 198–224 for an analysis of 'the bridging organizations and the generalization of solidarity among ethnic subgroups' especially Asian Americans, Native Americans, Indo Americans, and Latinos. Robert Blauner, *Racial Oppression in America* had argued that African Americans became a 'race' in the New World after diverse peoples from many parts of Africa were forced together under slavery.

30 *Time* (24 January 1977); quoted in David Wolper with Quincy Troupe, *The Inside Story of TV's 'Roots'* (New York: Warner Books 1978), p. 259.

31 Wolper and Troupe, p. xiii.

32 Stephen Zito, 'Out of Africa,' *American Film* 2 (October 1976): 8–17, p. 10.

33 Zito, p. 13.

34 Zito, p. 13, emphasis added.

35 Quoted in Jeffrey Elliot, 'Alex Haley Raps,' *Sepia* (November 1977): 23–7, p. 27, but the story appears in virtually every account of the writing of *Roots*.

36 Doris Black, 'Television's Most Ambitious Black Program,' *Sepia* (February 1977): 36–44, p. 39. Given that the next major docudrama to be aired was *Holocaust*, this connection between the American institution of slavery and Nazi concentration camps is telling. Clearly ABC understood that history's losers could be made into television successes if the ethnically marked family could triumph over adversity.

37 See Leslie Fishbein, '*Roots*: Docudrama and the Interpretation of History,' in *American History/American Television: Interpreting the Video Past*, ed. John E. O'Connor (New York: Ungar 1983), pp. 279–305, esp. pp. 294–6.

38 Toni Morrison, 'Unspeakable Things Unspoken: The Afro-American Presence in American Literature,' *Michigan Quarterly Review* 28 (Winter 1989): 1–49. Morrison's novel of slavery, *Beloved* (New York: Knopf 1987) was also based on 'fact,' a newspaper clipping she found about a runaway slave mother who murdered her children rather than see them returned to bondage.

39 Wolper and Troupe, pp. 250–74, includes a sampling of reviews and statements about the series from figures as diverse as David Duke, Grand Wizard of the Ku Klux Klan in Louisiana, to Eric Foner, Professor of History at Princeton, from the *Guardian* to the *National Enquirer*.

40 See Lance Loud, '20 Years Louder,' *American Film* 16 (January 1991): 64.

41 Catherine Egan, '6 American Families, And How They Reacted to their Portrayals,' *Film Library Quarterly* 11: 1&2 (1978): 5–14, p. 5.

42 William J. McClure, 'Finding the 6 Families: An Interview with Paul Wilkes,' *Film Library Quarterly* 11 (1978): 15–18, p. 18.

43 PBS spent over $1,000,000 on *An American Family*, making it the most expensive documentary at the time. The network, like ABC, launched an extensive marketing campaign; the Louds appeared on the cover of *Newsweek* and were featured in a *New York Times Magazine* article. See Loud, p. 64. Both shows generated mass-market paperbacks published by Warner Books, which included scripts, pictures, listings of casts and crews, and samplings of reviews and responses.

44 The numbers range as high as 90,000,000.

45 Wolper and Troupe, p. 174.

46 Wolper and Troupe, pp. 263–4.

47 Moynihan's report was merely the most well known of a long line of studies that had determined that because of slavery the black family was in disarray. Daniel P. Moynihan, *The Negro Family: The Case for National Action* (Washington, DC: US Government Printing Office 1965).

48 Carol Stack, *All Our Kin: Strategies for Survival in a Black Community* (New York: Harper & Row, 1974); Eugene Genovese, *Roll, Jordan, Roll: The World the Slaves Made* (New York: Pantheon 1974); and Herbert Gutman, *The Black Family in Slavery and Freedom, 1750–1925* (New York: Random House 1976). These were among the most significant social historical challenges to the image of African-American family breakdown.

49 Stuart Byron, 'Family Plot,' *Film Comment* 13 (March–April 1977): 31.

50 Herman Gray makes essentially this point when he fits the Huxtables, especially Bill Cosby, within an older sitcom mold, in 'Television, Black America, and the American Dream,' *Critical Studies in Mass Communications* 6 (1989): 376–86.

51 I am lifting this schematic model from Espiritu, pp. 3–7.

52 One of Roiphe's critiques of the Louds is that they have no 'culture'; in fact she finds 'negative culture or culture minus' ruling the home. Goulart, p. 23.

53 Judith Butler, *Bodies That Matter: On the Discursive Limits of 'Sex'* (New York: Routledge 1993), p. 124.

54 See Ira Livingstone and Judith Halberstam, 'Introduction,' *Posthuman Bodies* (Bloomington: University of Indiana Press forthcoming) for a discussion of the slippage among whiteness and straightness and wealth that Venus's desire encodes.

55 Carolyn Kay Steedman, *Landscape for a Good Woman: A Story of Two Lives* (New Brunswick, NJ: Rutgers University Press 1987), esp. 'The Weaver's Daughter,' pp. 27–47.

56 Sigmund Freud, 'Family Romance,' *Standard Edition of the Complete Psychological Works*, vol. 9, trans. and ed. James Strachey (London: Hogarth Press 1955), pp. 236–41.

57 Fredric Jameson, '*Ressentiment* and Literature,' Keniston Lecture, The University of Michigan, 4 February 1994 explains the historical connections between the philosophical and class implications of the terms.

58 bell hooks, 'Is Paris Burning?,' *Black Looks: Race and Representation*, p. 189.

59 James Clifford, *The Predicament of Culture: Twentieth-Century Ethnography, Literature, and Art* (Cambridge, MA: Harvard University Press 1988).

Chapter 7

1 Margaret Mead, 'Background: *An American Family*,' *TV Guide* 21:1 (January 1973): 21–3. 'I do not think *An American Family* should be called a documentary. I think we need a new name for it. . . . *An American Family* may well prove to be more controversial than showing open heart surgery or the birth of a baby on the screen' (p. 23).

2 Patricia Loud, 'Letter to the Forum for Contemporary History,' 23 February 1973, in Ron Goulart, *An American Family* (New York: Warner Books 1973), pp. 237–8.

3 Marsha Kinder, 'Soft Fiction,' *Film Quarterly* 33 (Spring 1980): 50–7.

4 See Alice Echols, *Daring to be Bad: Radical Feminism in America, 1965–72* (Minneapolis: University of Minnesota Press, 1989) for a complete analysis of this trend.

5 For overviews, see Judith Mayne, 'Feminist Film Theory and Criticism,' *Signs* 11 (Spring 1985): 81–105; and Paula Rabinowitz, 'Seeing Through the Gendered I: Feminist Film Theory,' *Feminist Studies* 16 (Spring 1990): 151–69.

6 In the United States, William Alexander, *Film on the Left* (Princeton: Princeton University Press 1981); and Russell Campbell, *Cinema Strikes Back* (Ann Arbor, University of Michigan Press 1981) have detailed the radical cinematic practices of 1930s filmmakers. Julianne Burton's *Cinema and Social Change in Latin America* (Austin: University of Texas Press 1986) has brought the words of radical film-makers in Latin America to North America. For many of them, Cuban cinema has served as a model for radical filmmaking in the Third World – so-called Third Cinema. Sylvia Harvey, *May '68 and Film Culture* (London: British Film Institute 1978) explores the interconnections of revolutionary situations and cinematic practices. See also *Cineaste* and *Jump Cut* for numerous discussions of film as political practice.

7 These two terms are borrowed from Mao Ze-dung's *Yenan Talks* (Beijing: Foreign Language Press 1942).

8 See Walter Benjamin, 'The Work of Art in the Age of Mechanical Reproduction,' for a further explanation of this process. *Illuminations*, ed. Hannah Arendt (New York: Schocken 1969), p. 234.

9 As early as 1939, Marxist-feminist Mary Inman had theorized mass culture under capitalism as productive of/for femininity: see Mary Inman, 'Manufacturing Femininity,' in *Writing Red*, ed. Charlotte Nekola and Paula Rabinowitz (New York: Feminist Press 1987), pp. 304–15; the 1975 film *Killing Us Softly* presented examples from magazine advertisements of women's enslavement to commodities.

10 See, for example, the Minneapolis and Indianapolis ordinances against pornography sponsored by Andrea Dworkin and Catherine MacKinnon, which rely on MacKinnon's theories of sexual harassment as sex discrimination and as an abrogation of women's civil rights. The implications of these legislative attempts to control pornography are spelled out in Lisa Duggan, Nan Hunter, and Carole S. Vance, 'False Promises: Feminist Antipornography Legislation in the U.S.,' *Women Against Censorship*, ed. Varda Burstyn (Vancouver: Douglas and Macintyre 1985), pp. 130–51.

11 See Alice Echols, 'The New Feminism of Yin and Yang,' in Ann Snitow, Christine Stansell, and Sharon Thompson, eds., *Powers of Desire* (New York: Monthly Review Press 1984), pp. 439–59, for a fuller discussion of the implications of these theories of women's and men's sexualities.

12 Angela Carter, *The Sadean Woman and The Ideology of Pornography* (New York: Pantheon 1978), p. 37.

13 Hanna Alderfer et al., eds., *Diary of a Conference on Sexuality* (New York: Faculty Press 1983), pp. 1, 38.

14 See Marjorie Rosen, *Popcorn Venus: Women, Movies and the American Dream* (New York: Coward, McCann and Geoghagan 1973); Joan Mellen, *Women and their Sexuality in the New Film* (New York: Horizon Press 1973); Molly Haskell, *From Reverence to Rape: The Treatment of Women in the Movies* (New York: Holt, Rinehart and Winston 1974); Brandon French, *On the Verge of Revolt: Women in American Films of the Fifties* (New York: Ungar 1978) as mid-1970s examples of early feminist film histories that correlate the representation of women in the movies to their (changing) social positions in American society.

15 See Julia LeSage, 'The Political Aesthetics of Feminist Documentary Films,' *Quarterly Review of Film Studies* 3 (Fall 1978): 507–23; and Annette Kuhn, *Women's Pictures* (London: Routledge & Kegan Paul 1982), pp. 131–55.

16 Amy Farrell, 'History with a Vengeance: Feminist Historical Documentaries of the 1970s,' paper presented at the NWSA conference, Towson, MD, June 1990 offered this insight.

17 Laura Mulvey, 'Visual Pleasure and Narrative Cinema,' *Screen* 16 (Autumn, 1975): 3–16, rpt. in Mulvey, *Visual and Other Pleasures* (Bloomington: Indiana University Press 1989).

18 For another critique of theories of the gaze, see Judith Mayne, 'The Limits of Spectacle,' *Wide Angle* 6 (Autumn 1984): 4–15.

19 I should note that in 'Changes: Thoughts on Myth, Narrative and Historical Experience,' Mulvey reconsiders the spectacle/spectator model, situating it as a polemical intervention made at a precise moment in the political histories of feminism and film. *Visual and Other Pleasures* (Bloomington: Indiana University Press 1989), pp. 159–76.

20 David James, *Allegories of Cinema: American Film in the Sixties* (Princeton, NJ: Princeton University Press 1989), p. 332.

21 See Kuhn, *Women's Pictures* (1982); and E. Ann Kaplan, *Women and Cinema* (New York: Methuen 1984), books that began to codify the feminist film canon.

22 *Canyon Cinema Catalogue*, no. 6, p. 210.

23 See Lucy Fischer, *Shot/Countershot* (Princeton, NJ, Princeton University Press 1989), for an argument that women's cinema is intertextually linked to traditional cinemas of Hollywood, Europe, or even the avant-garde because it revises the terms of their discourses. In 'In the Name of Feminist Film,' B. Ruby Rich pointed out that Severson's

film could never be considered a structuralist film because its content was too highly charged. *Chrysalis* 2 (1982).

24 Patricia Mellencamp describes the strategies of 'heterogeneity' in recent feminist film and video: '(1) the emphasis on enunciation and address to women *as subjects* . . . (2) the telling of "stories" rather than "novels" . . . (3) the inextricable bricolage of personal and theoretical knowledge; (4) the performance of parody or the telling of jokes . . . (5) an implicit or explicit critique and refashioning of theories of subjectivity constructed by vision; and (6) a transgression of boundaries between private and public spaces and experiences . . .' *Indiscretions* (Bloomington, Indiana University Press 1990), pp. 130–31. *Soft Fiction* employs virtually all of these strategies.

25 This was how Strand described *Soft Fiction* in a public lecture before its screening. Ann Arbor, MI, November 1979.

26 Karl Heider, *Ethnographic Film* (Austin: University of Texas Press 1976) states: 'A basic principle of ethnography is holism . . . . From this principle come the related dicta of "whole bodies," "whole people," and "whole acts" ' (p. 7).

27 Strand, 'Notes on Ethnographic Film by a Film Artist,' *Wide Angle* (1978): 45–50. This is precisely the same point Trinh T. Minh-ha has made about her controversial 'documentary' about Senegal, *Reassemblage* (1982): 'I knew very well what I did not want,' she says of making the film, 'but what I wanted came with the process . . . . My approach is one which avoids any sureness of signification . . . the strategies of *Reassemblage* question the anthropological knowledge of the "other." ' Constance Penley and Andrew Ross, 'Interview with Trinh T. Minh-ha,' *Camera Obscura* 13–14 (Spring–Summer 1985), pp. 89, 93; rpt. in Trinh, *Framer Framed* (New York: Routledge 1992).

28 *Canyon Cinema Catalogue* 6, pp. 221–3.

29 Judith Butler, *Gender Trouble: Feminism and the Subversion of Identity* (New York: Routledge 1989), p. 140.

30 For an interesting reading of the 'Wolf Man' case presentation of the primal scene as anal penetration, and as such a fantasy of male homoeroticism, see Lee Edelman, 'Seeing Things: Representation, the Scene of Surveillance, and the Spectacle of Gay Male Sex,' in Diana Fuss, ed., *Inside/Out* (New York: Routledge 1991), pp. 93–116.

31 This goes back to Robert Flaherty's re-enactments of the whale kill in *Nanook of the North* (1925).

32 Kinder, p. 50.

33 They also nod to the genre Deren invented, *film noir*, with its sinister and claustrophobic interiors speaking as loudly as any fast-talking detective; and to the one Strand rejects – *cinéma vérité*.

34 Thanks to Jane Gallop for this pun made in connection with the panel, 'En/Countering Censorship: Feminist Transgressions,' at the 1990 American Studies Association Convention in New Orleans where I presented a version of this chapter.

35 'Chick Strand at the Cinematheque,' *Cinemanews* 3/4/5 (1980), p. 11.

36 See Linda Williams, *Hard Core: Pleasure, Power and the 'Frenzy of the Visible'* (Berkeley: University of California Press 1989) for a full analysis of the genre of feature-length porn films.

37 See Ann Snitow, 'Mass Market Romance: Pornography For Women is Different,' in *Powers of Desire*, pp. 245–63.

38 In addition to Snitow, 'Mass Market Romance,' see Tania Modleski, *Loving with a Vengeance* (New York: Methuen 1986); and Janice Radway, *Reading the Romance* (Chapel Hill, NC: University of North Carolina Press 1987).

39 'Chick Strand at the Cinematheque,' *Cinemanews*, p. 11.

40 *Cinemanews*, p. 1.

41 *Cinemanews*, p. 14.

42 Adena Rosmarin, *The Power of Genre* (Minneapolis: University of Minnesota Press 1987).

43 The most recent example of which is Catherine MacKinnon's exaggeration of the number of rapes suffered by women in Bosnia. The brutality of this form of terrorism does not need inflated figures; it needs accurate testimonials from the survivors.

44 See Kaja Silverman on the 'sophisticated' feminist films of the avant-garde. *Soft Fiction* is not among them. *The Acoustic Mirror* (Bloomington: Indiana University Press 1988), p. 153.

45 For a discussion of the politics and poetics of the Women's Pentagon Action, see T.V. Reed, *Fifteen Jugglers, Five Believers: Literary Politics and the Poetics of American Social Movements* (Berkeley: University of California Press 1992).

Chapter 8

1 Kaja Silverman, *The Acoustic Mirror: The Female Voice in Psychoanalysis and Cinema* (Bloomington: Indiana University Press 1988) is the most extensive analysis of the (psychic) effects of the voice in cinema.

2 See Sherry Ortner, 'Gender Hegemonies,' *Cultural Critique* 13 (Fall 1989): 35–80; Rita Felski, 'Feminism, Postmodernism, and the Critique of Modernity,' *Cultural Critique* 14 (Winter 1989–90): 33–56; and Nancy Hartsock, 'Postmodernism and Political Change: Issues for Feminist Theory,' *Cultural Critique* 14 (Winter 1989–90): 15–34 all in the two special issues on 'The Construction of Gender and Modes of Social Division.' Lynn Hunt, *The Family Romance of the French Revolution* (Berkeley: University Of California Press 1992); and Denise Riley, *'Am I That Name?' The Category of 'Women' in History* (Minneapolis: University of Minnesota Press 1988).

3 To cite only one instance, see the Summer 1993 issue of *Feminist Review* entitled, 'Nationalism and National Identities.'

4 See for instance, *Zene za Mir* [Women for Peace Anthology], published by Women in Black, Women's Lobby, Group for Women Raped in War, Belgrade, 1993. Or for another, more historical example, see the case of 'That Magic Time: Women in the Telangana People's Struggle' in India, detailed by Vasantha Kannabiran and K. Lalitha, in Kumkum Sangari and Sudesh Vaid, eds., *Recasting Women: Essays in Colonial History* (New Delhi: Kali for Women Press 1989), pp. 180–203.

5 For a discussion of the productiveness of 'imagined violence' for gay and lesbian politics, see Judith Halberstam, 'Imagined Violence/Queer Violence: Representation, Rage, and Resistance,' *Social Text* 37 (Winter 1993): 187–201.

6 In addition to Hunt, see Linda Kerber, *Women of the Republic: Intellect and Ideology in Revolutionary America* (Chapel Hill, NC: University of North Carolina Press 1980); and Doris Sommer, 'Irresistible Romance: The Foundational Fictions of Latin America,' in Homi K. Bhabha, ed., *Nation and Narration* (New York: Routledge 1990), pp. 71–98.

7 See Elspeth Probyn, *Sexing the Self: Gendered Positions in Cultural Studies* (New York: Routledge 1993); and Adrienne Rich, *Blood, Bread and Poetry: Selected Prose, 1979–1985* (New York: Norton 1986) on the importance of the politics of location for feminists. Artist Judy Chicago's adoption of her place of birth as her surname is the classic statement by a feminist linking identity to place.

8 Thomas Waugh, 'Joris Ivens's *The Spanish Earth*: Committed Documentary and the Popular Front,' in *'Show Us Life': Towards a History and Aesthetics of the Committed Documentary* (Metuchen, NJ: The Scarecrow Press 1984), pp. 105–32.

9 See Timothy Brennan, 'The National Longing for Form,' in *Nation and Narration*, pp. 44–70 or recent arguments over GATT concerning Hollywood's impact on the national culture industries of Europe.

10 Bill Nichols, 'The Voice of Documentary,' *Film Quarterly* 36 (Fall 1983): 17–30.

11 Susan Sontag, 'The Fourth World of Women,' *Partisan Review* 40: (1973), pp. 180–206.

12 See David James's discussion of Rainer's work in *Allegories of Cinema: American Film in the Sixties* (Princeton, NJ: Princeton University Press 1989), esp. p. 332; and Jonathan Rosenbaum's assessment of *Journeys'* failures in *Film: The Front Line–1983* (Denver: Arden Press 1983), pp. 132–40.

13 Jonathan Rosenbaum, 'The Ambiguities of Yvonne Rainer,' *American Film* (March 1980): 68–9.

14 The objects lining the mantelpiece and the voices casually invoking their names recall the documentary phototextual books of the 1930s where the images of the fireplace-as-altar filled with relics – family portraits, old calendars, figurines, cut-glass bowls, a shoe, and so forth – conveyed an unsettling beauty in privation, a holiness of things possessed, at the same time as they highlighted the shoddiness of poverty. Surveying objects is a stock trope in documentary, as I have already remarked, an attempt to speak through the surface of depth.

15 See Rosenbaum, 'The Ambiguities of Yvonne Rainer,' p. 69.

16 Yvonne Rainer, *Work: 1961–73* (Halifax: Nova Scotia College of Art and Design 1974), p. 278.

17 R.B., Review of *Journeys from Berlin/1971*, in *Revue du Cinéma* (January 1981): 129, my translation.

18 Rosenbaum, 'The Ambiguities,' p. 69.

19 Yvonne Rainer et al., *The Films of Yvonne Rainer* (Bloomington: Indiana University Press 1989), p. 22.

20 In the United States, dime novels such as *Red Ruin* (1881) depicted sexual depravity and political violence as symbiotic elements of anarchist women. See Margaret Marsh, *Anarchist Women: 1870–1920* (Philadelphia: Temple University 1981). The need to explain anarchy through psychological rather than political terms seems to me directly connected to the explosiveness of female sexuality associated with it.

21 See the hysterical account by Anthony M. Burton, *Urban Terrorism: Theory, Practice and Response* (London: Leo Cooper 1975), p. 13, among many others. The literature of terror-hysteria is vast, and female terrorists hold a special allure. Edgar O'Ballance claims: 'The terrorist need not be a man. In fact, many female terrorists are more determined and deadly than their male colleagues.' In addition to the various attributes a terrorist needs according to O'Ballance: political beliefs, bravery, intelligence, education, money, support, and publicity, most significant for explaining the aberrant behavior of female terrorists is their 'killer instinct.' *Language of Violence: The Blood Politics of Terrorists* (San Rafael, CA: Presidio Press 1979), p. 301. For more scholarly descriptions of terrorism, which is always defined in the West as emanating from those not holding state power, see Peter H. Merkl, ed., *Political Violence and Terror: Motifs and Motivations* (Berkeley: University of California Press 1986).

22 This has been an ongoing debate since the demise of broad-based movements during the 1970s. Basically two stories emerge – the pessimistic and the happy one. The former views the decline of the Left resulting from the fragmentation because of feminism, gay liberation, identity politics; the latter sees a more positive outcome – new social movements. See Alice Echols, ' "We Gotta Get Out of This Place": Notes Towards a Remapping of the Sixties,' *Socialist Review* 22 (April–June 1992): 9–33; a recent reprise occurred in *The Nation*, 7 March 1994 in an exchange between Norman Rush, who had declared socialism dead a few weeks earlier, and Barbara Ehrenreich et al.

23 Linda Gordon, 'Union Maids: Working Class Heroines,' *Jump Cut* 14 (March 1977): 34–5.

24 Noel King, 'Recent "Political" Documentary: Notes on *Union Maids* and *Harlan County USA*,' *Screen* 22 (2) 1981: 7–18, p. 12.

25 In 1934, a young Smith College graduate, Harriet Woodbridge, writing as Lauren Gilfillan, traveled to the coalfields of Western Pennsylvania to report on the strike there. She joined the struggle only to be reminded that she was an outsider. Her novel, *I Went to Pit College*, about her tenure in Avelonia, PA, described her position as a sympathetic middle-class woman within the mining community riven by ethnic, religious, and racial divisions, and tensions between rival unions with suspicions about intellectuals. Kopple does nothing like this; with the exception of two remarkable scenes where she films herself confronting the leader of the company thugs, her presence is not recorded. For a detailed discussion of the novel as an ethnography of class and gender differences, see my *Labor and Desire: Women's Revolutionary Novels in Depression America* (Chapel Hill, NC: University of North Carolina Press 1991).

26 Anthony McCall and Andrew Tyndall fault Kopple for maintaining 'the conventional position of the filmmaker as the person with "knowledge" ' in a film where

'social events were portrayed instead of confronted.' 'Sixteen Working Statements,' *Millennium Film Journal* 1 (Spring/Summer 1978), p. 36. Yet Christian Metz, architect of cinesemiotics, said *Harlan County USA* was 'a very good film. . . . It is unfair, in a sense, to call a film into question on terms which are not within the filmmaker's purpose. She intended to support the strike and she did it. It's a marvelous film and I support it.' 'The Cinematic Apparatus as Social Institution – An Interview with Christian Metz,' *Discourse* 1 (Fall 1979), p. 30. E. Ann Kaplan, argues with Metz against purists for different 'levels' of political discourse within cinema. See 'Theory and Practice of the Realist Documentary Form in *Harlan County USA* in *'Show Us Life': Theory and Practice of Committed Documentary*, pp. 212–22.

27 Pat Aufderheide, 'Poland without Dogma,' *In These Times* (3–9 October 1984): 21.

28 In the Canadian documentary film, *Calling the Shots* (d. Janis Cole and Holly Dale, 1988), about women in Hollywood, Godmilow remarks that she tired of working without a screenplay, depending on the spontaneous actions and words of her subjects; so she turned to narrative which afforded her more directorial control, scripting her film about Gertrude Stein and Alice Toklas, *Waiting for the Moon.*

29 During the 1930s Hugo Gellert, a cartoonist for the left-wing journal *New Masses*, illustrated selections from Karl Marx's *Capital* (Figures 4–5). Gellert's drawings of solidly muscled workers were Americanized visions of the new Soviet man, the man of marble, representing the virile worker as proletarian hero. These heroic figments of radical imagination and desire (in an interview in the 1980s Mary McCarthy describes the faces of the men in the Gdansk shipyard resembling those of the workers in this country she watched picket the great industries during her youth in the 1930s) would overcome both the crisis in capitalism and the malaise the lost generation was suffering after the First World War. Gellert envisaged a female masculinity for the working-class woman.

30 Again, Godmilow uses titles effectively as well, interrupting Anna's story at one point to list the twenty-one demands of Solidarity; so too, print figures in cinema – a reminder of silent film.

31 Boleslaw Fac, 'Lech Walesa, The Man Who Spoke Up,' in *The Book of Lech Walesa,* intro. Neal Ascherson (New York: Simon & Schuster 1981), pp. 47–8.

32 Ryszard Kapuscinski, 'Notes from the Seaboard,' in *August 1980: The Strikes in Poland,* ed. William F. Robinson (Munich: Radio Free Europe Research 1980), p. 446 (originally in Polish in the Warsaw journal *Kultura*, 14 September 1980).

33 ' "I Am Indebted for It to This Man with a Moustache": An Interview with Andrzej Wajda,' by Maria Mrozinska, in *The Book of Lech Walesa,* p. 182.

34 Aufderheide, p. 21.

35 For a discussion of early films' appeal to working-class audiences through melodrama, see Steve J. Ross, 'Struggles for the Screen: Workers, Radicals, and the Political Uses of Silent Film,' *American Historical Review* 96 (April 1991): 333–67.

36 For one of the few analyses of 1980s progressive politics see, Mike Davis and Michael Sprinker, eds., *Reshaping the U.S. Left: Popular Struggles in the 1980s* (London: Verso 1988).

37 Barbara Epstein, *Political Protest and Cultural Revolution: Non-Violent Direct Action in the 1970s and 1980s* (Berkeley: University of California Press 1991), pp. 13–24. These process-oriented organizations in their efforts to achieve consensus often exhibited a drive toward purity not unlike certain motives underlining identity politics to purge the straight white man within. I am indebted to Laura Schere for this insight.

38 I am exaggerating, certainly. In Ann Arbor, where I was a graduate student from the late 1970s to the mid-1980s, the same group of students and faculty was active in divestment campaigns, Latin American solidarity, women's issues, gay rights, teaching assistants' union, and a revived black action movement. But even if the same bodies appeared at rallies, actions, sit-ins, etc., each issue was somehow dissociated from the others. My sources are anecdotal but virtually every campus appeared as atomized and politically moribund.

39 This and all quotations from the screenplay and interviews come from Trinh T. Minh-ha, *Framer Framed* (New York: Routledge 1992), p. 142. Further citations in text.

40 Trinh, p. 83.

41 Trinh, p. 89. Homi K. Bhabha describes the time/space of the nation as a pedagogical and performative shifting of boundaries, languages, histories, and cultures, which can never contain the 'imagined community' of a people, in 'DissemiNation: Time, Narrative, and the Margins of the Modern Nation,' *Nation and Narration*, pp. 291–322.

42 Walter Benjamin, 'The Task of the Translator,' *Illuminations*, ed. Hannah Arendt, trans. Harry Zohn (New York: Schocken 1969), pp. 73–5.

43 They do so for a specific audience, one akin to the segment of the Professional-Managerial Class (PMC) first identified by the Ehrenreichs in *Between Labor and Capital* (Boston: South End Press 1982) that Fred Pfeil profiles in 'Making Flippy-Floppy: Postmodernism and the Baby-Boom PMC,' in Mike Davis, Fred Pfeil, and Michael Sprinker, eds., *The Year Left*, vol. 1 (London: Verso 1985), pp. 268–95.

Chapter 9

1 Walter Benjamin, 'Extract from *A Short History of Photography*,' 1931, in *Germany, The New Photography, 1927–33*, ed. David Mellor (London: Arts Council of Great Britain 1978), p. 75.

2 Walter Benjamin, 'Theses on the Philosophy of History,' *Illuminations*, edited and with an introduction by Hannah Arendt, trans. Harry Zohn (New York: Schocken 1968), pp. 253–64.

3 See Mike Davis, *City of Quartz: Excavating the Future in Los Angeles 1990* (New York: Vintage 1992) especially chapters 4 and 5 for a complete history.

4 Daryl F. Gates with Diane K. Shah, *Chief: My Life in the LAPD* (New York: Bantam 1992), pp. 114, 326.

5 Gates, pp. 109–16; Davis, p. 268.

6 In one incident among many during the LAPD's HAMMER operation to eradicate gangs, houses were razed on one block of Dalton Street. The city paid over $3 million in damages. See Davis, *City of Quartz*, p. 277. The recent civil suit brought by Rodney King against Los Angeles has so far resulted in a $3,900,000 judgment in his favor; the second part of the trial has yet to begin.

7 *Radical Software* 1 (1970): 1.

8 *The Black Panther* 24 October 1970, p. 9.

9 Bertolt Brecht, 'Vorschlage für den Intendenten des Rundfunks,' in *Schriften zur Literatur und Kunst*, vol. 1 1920–32 (Berlin: Suhrkamp Verlag 1967), p. 124, trans. Joel Weinsheimer.

10 Georges Sadoul, *French Film* (London: The Falcon Press 1958), pp. 2–4.

11 Bill Nichols, ' "Getting to Know You . . .": Knowledge, Power, and the Body,' in Michael Renov, ed., *Theorizing Documentary* (New York: Routledge 1993), p. 190. For other examples of the ways in which Rodney King's body focused academic discussions of racism, see John Fiske, 'Rodney King: A Body of Evidence,' paper presented at the American Studies Association convention, Boston, November 1993, and the first section of *Reading Rodney King, Reading Urban Uprising*, ed. Robert Gooding-Williams (New York: Routledge 1993), entitled 'Beating Black Bodies,' which includes essays by Judith Butler, Ruth Wilson Gilmore, and Houston Baker.

12 Gates, p. 2.

13 Bill Nichols, *Representing Reality: Issues and Concepts in Documentary* (Bloomington: Indiana University Press 1991), p. 265.

14 Karl Heider, *Ethnographic Film* (Austin: University of Texas 1976), p. 125.

15 The portapak revolution never happened, despite the efforts of a few media collectives such as Metro Sensory Media in Detroit to produce alternative points of view to the news. (George Corsetti recorded the destruction of Poletown, a section of Detroit, to make way for a Chrysler plant, documenting the resistance of the residents to their own exile in stark contrast to official celebrations of Detroit's 'renaissance.' The resulting video, *Poletown Lives!*, was transferred onto film for national distribution.)

16 *The 'Rodney King' Case: What the Jury Saw in California* v. *Powell* (Court TV 1992). All quotations for the trial are taken from this two-hour video documentary of the trial broadcast on TV. The fetishizing of vision, sight, looking is evident here in the title: we see what the jury saw. Moreover, the commodification of the case (as about Rodney King not the cops) is evident; this slickly packaged tape was meant to sell.

17 This is Raymond Williams's description of TV's process, *Television: Technology and Cultural Form* (New York: Schocken 1975), pp. 96–118.

18 See Todd Gitlin, *The Whole World is Watching: Mass Media in the Making and Unmaking of the New Left* (Berkeley: University of California Press 1980), p. 264; and Glasgow University Media Group, *Bad News* (London: Routledge & Kegan Paul 1976), p. 29.

19 For at least twenty-five years, since Penn's *Bonnie and Clyde* and Peckinpah's *Wild Bunch*, slow-motion sequences of graphic brutality have aestheticized violence. The defense relied on this piece of collectively unconscious cinesemiotics to blunt the horrifying impact of the tape in real time. See Patricia Greenfield and Paul Kibbey, 'Picture Imperfect,' *New York Times*, 1 April 1993, p. A15 for a discussion of the legal ramifications for evidence of pictorial manipulations.

20 See Kimberle Crenshaw and Gary Peller, 'Reel Time/Real Justice,' in *Reading Rodney King, Reading Urban Uprising*, pp. 56–70, esp. p. 70, where they quote from Marshall's dissenting opinion: 'The majority . . . takes the disingenuous approach of disaggregating Richmond's local evidence, attacking it piecemeal, and thereby concluding that no single piece of evidence adduced by the city, "standing alone," . . . suffices to prove past discrimination.'

21 Houston Baker discusses the historical context of the 'scene' of King's body stemming from a long process of silencing African-American men, in 'Scene . . . Not Heard,' Gooding-Williams, pp. 38–48.

22 Bertolt Brecht, quoted in Benjamin, 'Short History,' p. 73.

23 Gates, p. 196. Subsequent citations appear in the text.

24 Martha Rosler, 'in, around and afterthoughts (on documentary photography),' *Three Works* (Halifax: Nova Scotia College of Art and Design 1981), p. 82.

25 This is hardly a point that went unnoticed by various commentators: see Charles Hagen, 'The Power of a Video Image Depends on the Caption,' *New York Times*, 10 May 1992, *Arts and Leisure Section*, p. 32 on the defense's strategy of 'captioning'; and Patricia J. Williams, 'The Rules of the Game,' *Village Voice*, 12 May 1992, pp. 32, 41 on the defense's choice of words to describe King. This latter piece is reprinted in Gooding-Williams, pp. 51–5.

26 See Carolyn See, *Making History* (Boston: Houghton Mifflin 1991) for a devastating portrait of seamy, see me, Simi Valley.

27 See Davis, *City of Quartz*, for a detailed picture of the racial and class divisions superintending Los Angeles's history. In addition, see Rhonda M. Williams, 'Accumulation as Evisceration: Urban Rebellion and the New Growth Dynamics,' Melvin L. Oliver, James H. Johnson, Jr, and Walter C. Farrell, Jr, 'Anatomy of a Rebellion: A Political-Economic Analysis'; and Thomas L. Dunn, 'The New Enclosures: Racism in the Normalized Community,' for analyses of the political economy of 1990s Los Angeles, all in Gooding-Williams. See also, Jerry Cohen and William S. Murphy, *Burn, Baby, Burn* (New York, Avon 1966) on the Watts rebellion lest this appear a new phenomenon.

28 As Denny himself pointed out in an interview on *Inside Edition*, the four African-American citizens who left their homes and risked their lives to save him, as well as the black surgeon operating on him, were never pictured. Denny has filed a suit charging civil rights violations against the city; he claims that even as he suffered for lack of police protection, South Central has been discriminated against because the LAPD has routinely failed to provide adequate security for its residents. Reported on *All Things Considered*, NPR, 28 October 1992.

29 Like the contest over the images of racial violence, the contest over naming the 'events' in LA have political meanings important to semioticians. The semantics of naming – riot, anarchy, terror, rebellion, uprising, insurrection – defines the fissure between official codings – police, news media – and populist ones – participants,

radicals. This struggle on the level of language shadows the struggle to frame the images of the King beating on tape.

30 This statement was widely circulated and printed in full in *Jump Cut* 37 (July 1992): 2.

31 In his most recent testimony, during the civil trial to decide the outcome of the suit Rodney King filed against the city of Los Angeles, Officer Briseno, who had previously testified to witnessing King being beaten in the face and head, changed his testimony after viewing a new, 'enhanced' version of the Holliday tape. *New York Times*, 5 April 1994, p. A11.

32 'Teenagers' Mural of Beating Angers Boston Police,' *New York Times*, 8 September 1992, p. A14. A photograph of a section of the mural appears on the cover of *Reading Rodney King, Reading Urban Uprising*.

Epilogue

1 The recently published Carnegie Corporation of New York report, 'Starting Points: Meeting the Needs of Our Youngest Children,' details the miserable conditions under which American children below the age of three live, noting that nearly a quarter of all infants and toddlers in the United States live in poverty, many subject to abuse, suffering from poor medical care, surrounded by violence. See *New York Times*, 12 April, 1994, p. A1. The picture hardly improves as children grow up. For only one instance, in many states, girls under eighteen must obtain parental consent (or a judge's decree) to obtain a legal abortion.

2 Unfortunately, more parents could not provide their children with this resource. Fisher-Price video cameras disappeared from the shelves because the military snapped up most of the stock. Attached to each 'patriot missile,' these cameras offered a cheap way for us to watch all those 'smart bombs' zeroing in on their targets during the Gulf War spectacle. Thanks to Ruth Bradley for this.

3 Quoted in Trinh T. Minh-ha, *Framer Framed* (New York: Routledge 1993), p. 193.

Index